# ANGLO-AMERICAN STRATEGIC RELATIONS
# AND THE FAR EAST
# 1933–1939

Cass Series: Strategy and History
Series Editors: Colin Gray and Williamson Murray
ISSN: 1473-6403

This new series will focus on the theory and practice of strategy. Following Clausewitz, strategy has been understood to mean the use made of force, and the threat of the use of force, for the ends of policy. This series is as interested in ideas as in historical cases of grand strategy and military strategy in action. All historical periods, near and past, and even future, are of interest. In addition to original monographs, the series will from time to time publish edited reprints of neglected classics as well as collections of essays.

1. *Military Logistics and Strategic Performance*, Thomas M. Kane

2. *Strategy for Chaos: RMA Theory and the Evidence of History*, Colin Gray

3. *The Myth of Inevitable US Defeat in Vietnam*, C. Dale Walton

4. *Astropolitik: Classical Geopolitics in the Space Age*, Everett C. Dolman

5. *Anglo-American Strategic Relations and the Far East, 1933–1939: Imperial Crossroads*, Greg Kennedy

# ANGLO-AMERICAN STRATEGIC RELATIONS

## AND THE FAR EAST

### 1933–1939

## Imperial Crossroads

**GREG KENNEDY**

*Joint Services Command and Staff College, UK*

FRANK CASS
LONDON • PORTLAND, OR

*First published in 2002 in Great Britain by*
FRANK CASS PUBLISHERS
Crown House, 47 Chase Side,
Southgate, London N14 5BP

*and in the United States of America by*
FRANK CASS PUBLISHERS
c/o ISBS, 5824 N.E. Hassalo Street,
Portland, Oregon, 97213-3644

*Website*: www.frankcass.com

© 2002 G. Kennedy

British Library Cataloguing in Publication Data

Kennedy, Greg
  Anglo-American strategic relations and the Far East,
  1933–1939: imperial crossroads. – (Cass series. Strategy
  and history; no. 5)
  1. Great Britain – Foreign relations – United States
  2. United States – Foreign relations – Great Britain  3. Great
  Britain – Foreign relations – East Asia  4. East Asia –
  Foreign relations – Great Britain  5. United States – Foreign
  relations – East Asia  6. East Asia – Foreign relations –
  United States  7. East Asia – Strategic aspects  8. Great
  Britain – Foreign relations – 1910–1936  9. United States –
  Foreign relations – 1933–1945
  I. Title
  327.4'1'073'09043

ISBN 0-7146-5188-5
ISSN 1473-6403

Library of Congress Cataloging-in-Publication Data

Kennedy, Gregory C., 1961–
77Anglo-American strategic relations and the Far East, 1933–1939: imperial crossroads /
  Greg Kennedy.
    p. cm. – (Cass series–strategy and history, ISSN 1473-6403; 5)
    Includes bibliographical references (p.  ) and index.
    ISBN 0-7146-5188-5 (cloth)
    1. United States–Foreign relations–Great Britain.  2. Great Britain–Foreign
  relations–United States.  3. United States–Foreign relations–1933–1945.  4. East
  Asia–Foreign relations–United States.  5. United States–Foreign relations–East Asia.  6.
  East Asia–Foreign relations–Great Britain.  7. Great Britain–Foreign relations–East
  Asia.  8. East Asia–Strategic aspects.  9. East Asia–Politics and government–20th
  century.  I. Title.  II. Series.

  E183.8.G7 K46 2002
  327.4105'09'043–dc21
                                                                            2002017529

Typeset in 10½/12 Minion by Vitaset, Paddock Wood, Kent
Printed in Great Britain by Bookcraft (Limited), Midsomer Norton.

# Contents

# Series Editor's Preface

Historians tend to focus on great turning points on which to hang their tales. Thus, the momentous events lying between the beginning of the German offensive in the west on 10 May 1940 and the surprise attack on Pearl Harbor on 7 December 1941 seem to provide the specific context for what Churchill so eloquently termed the 'Grand Alliance'. Indeed, that terrifying descent towards hell provided the impetus to fundamental changes in the relationship between the two nations. What then seemingly saved the world of democratic, liberal capitalism was the willingness of two great men, Winston Churchill and Franklin D. Roosevelt, to place the quarrels of the past in abeyance and look towards the future. It is certainly one of the great stories of the twentieth century, and one of the few that has a positive connotation.

However, in focusing on the turning point alone, historians miss the larger context within which events occur. From our perspective at the beginning of the twenty-first century, the formation of the connection between the United States and the United Kingdom between 1940 and 1942 seems obvious and natural. But from the perspective of the pre-war period, the creation of such an alliance seemed more problematical. At that time, the relationship between the United States and Great Britain appeared far less likely to provide the basis for a lasting alliance or even an alliance that could stand the strain of a great war against Nazi Germany. It was not just the memory of America's great revolutionary war of independence (the myths of which still echo in bad Hollywood movies) that had provided many Americans with an abiding, deep distrust of the British and their Empire, feelings deepened by the mass migration of so many from Ireland in the nineteenth century; many other Americans also viewed themselves and their nation as the natural replacement for Britain as the leading power in the world.

As such, since the start of the twentieth century, the US military had seen Britain as being as natural an enemy as Japan. While there were US military plans for a war against Japan (the so-called 'ORANGE' plan), there were also plans for a conflict with Britain. Thus, the emergence of a relationship in the Pacific between the British and the Americans in response to an increasingly aggressive and dangerous (to the international order) Japanese regime would prove of enormous importance, when, in 1939, the Germans triggered the second great war of the twentieth century. That strategic relationship did not arise out of some deep sense of common civilization or belief in the commonality of 'Anglo-American' interests. Rather, it arose out of old-fashioned concerns for balancing the rising risks to both nations as the Japanese threatened both. In other words, the relationship represented the actual processes of balance of power at work.

This splendid book by Greg Kennedy chronicles the establishment of connections and, above all, a level of trust between those charged with defending the interests of the Anglo-American nations in the Pacific. It begins in the early 1930s, not at the end of the decade. As Kennedy suggests in his Introduction, the strategic policy-making elites of the two nations were able to construct mental maps of each other, on which so much was to be built by Churchill and Roosevelt in their creation of the 'Grand Alliance'. Those mental maps rested on an understanding of the parameters within which each nation was reacting to the emerging strategic environment in the Pacific. And we must not forget that strategic policy-makers, then, as always, cast their work in an atmosphere of enormous uncertainty and ambiguity, an atmosphere made that much more uncertain by the nature of the Japanese polity. As the years passed, the understanding of each other's national positions deepened among those who dealt with the day-to-day problems of policy-making. When the dark events of the late 1930s broke on strategic policy-makers, there already existed a depth of understanding among those who made policy that had not been there at the beginning of the decade. Kennedy has managed in clear, understandable fashion to unravel the actual processes of strategic policy-making at the level of day-to-day, month-to-month relations. In every respect, this book is a major contribution to our understanding of how strategy is made in the real world – in this case, the establishment of trust and perceptions on which the eventual Anglo-American special relationship would be created in the early years of the Second World War.

WILLIAMSON MURRAY
*Series Co-Editor*

# Acknowledgements

In the course of events that surrounds the construction of such a work there are always many debts incurred. I apologize now to any who read this and feel I have slighted them because they have not been mentioned, for it is not my intention to do so.

My first debt of gratitude goes to those people who believed in my work and abilities and offered freely and fully their company on this journey. Professors Keith Neilson, Donald M. Schurman, John Ferris and David French have given more than their fair share of time, patience, knowledge and, most importantly, their friendship, over the years. All were instrumental in anything of worth that is produced here and responsible for none that is wrong or in error. I owe them all much more than I can do justice to in this short space. In particular, Keith Neilson has travelled the interwar years with me, sharing his vast knowledge of British imperial defence, reading variations of this manuscript, offering honest, informed advice, and providing a constant inspiration upon which I could depend. To him I give special thanks.

Without adequate funding no serious investigation of this nature can be undertaken. Therefore, I would like to thank the University of Alberta for their grants and fellowships; the Herbert Hoover Presidential Library Association in West Branch, Iowa; the Franklin and Eleanor Roosevelt Institute, Hyde Park, New York; and the Canadian Department of National Defence for their investment in my work. In particular, I would like to thank the History and War Studies Departments of the Royal Military College of Canada (RMC) for the opportunity to gain access to their outstanding resources. I would also like to extend my thanks to the staff at the Massey Library at the RMC, as well as those at the Hoover and Roosevelt Presidential Libraries, Hoover Institute, Naval Historical Center, Nimitz Library, US Army Military History Research Collection, the Library of Congress, the National Archives in Washington, the Public Record Office, University of Birmingham Library, Roskill Archives Churchill College Cambridge, University Library Cambridge, National Maritime Museum, British Library, Bodleian Library Oxford, Middle East Studies Centre, St Antony's College Oxford, and SOAS Library University College London.

Finally, but by no means least, I would like to thank my lovely wife Frankie and our daughters Megan and Jenna for their inspiration and patience. There is nothing as wonderful as coming home to them after a day of research or writing. They make it all worth while. Thank you for your understanding and sacrifice.

As always, the final responsibility for what has been written here and any errors and omissions that have been made are the author's, and his alone.

# Abbreviations

| | |
|---|---|
| AD | American Department of the Foreign Office |
| ADM | Admiralty |
| *AEHR* | *Australian Economic History Review* |
| *AFS* | *Armed Forces and Security* |
| *AHR* | *American Historical Review* |
| *AJPH* | *American Journal of Political History* |
| *BDFA* | *British Documents on Foreign Affairs* |
| *BISA* | *British International Studies Association* |
| *BJIS* | *British Journal of International Studies* |
| BL | British Library |
| BLINY | British Library in New York |
| *BNA* | *Brassey's Naval Annual* |
| BoT | Board of Trade |
| C.-in-C. | Commander-in-Chief |
| CAB | Cabinet |
| CAS | Chief of Air Staff |
| CC | Cabinet Conclusions |
| CCA | Churchill College Archives |
| CID | Committee of Imperial Defence |
| CIGS | Chiefs of Imperial General Staff |
| *CJH* | *Canadian Journal of History* |
| CNO | Chief of Naval Operations |
| CNS | Chief of Naval Staff |
| COS | Chiefs of Staff Committee |
| CP | Cabinet Paper |
| *CR* | *Contemporary Review* |
| CSDCF | Confidential State Department Central Files |
| *D&S* | *Diplomacy & Statecraft* |
| *DBFP* | *Documents on British Foreign Policy* |
| DCNS | Deputy Chief of the Naval Staff |
| DFEA | Division of Far Eastern Affairs (State Department) |
| *DH* | *Diplomatic History* |
| DNI | Director of Naval Intelligence |

| | |
|---|---|
| DO | Dominions Office |
| DOT | Department of Overseas Trade |
| DPR | Defence Policy and Requirements Sub-Committee |
| DPR(DR) | Defence Policy and Requirements (Defence Requirements) Sub-Committee |
| DRC | Defence Requirements Sub-Committee |
| *DUJ* | *Durham University Journal* |
| EAC | Economic Advisory Committee |
| *EcHR* | *Economic History Review* |
| *EEH* | *Explorations in Economic History* |
| *EHQ* | *European History Quarterly* |
| *EHR* | *European History Review* |
| *EJ* | *Economic Journal* |
| *EnHR* | *English Historical Review* |
| *FA* | *Foreign Affairs* |
| FAA | Fleet Air Arm |
| FDR | Franklin D. Roosevelt |
| *FDRFA* | *Franklin D. Roosevelt and Foreign Affairs* |
| FDR–OF | Franklin D. Roosevelt–Official Files |
| FDR–PPF | Franklin D. Roosevelt–President's Personal Files |
| FDR–PSF | Franklin D. Roosevelt–Private Secretary's Files |
| FED | Far Eastern Department of the Foreign Office |
| FO | Foreign Office |
| FPC | Cabinet Committee on Foreign Policy |
| *FRUS* | *Foreign Relations of the United States Diplomatic Papers* |
| GB | General Board |
| GC | General Correspondence |
| *H* | *The Historian* |
| *HJ* | *The Historical Journal* |
| *HR* | *Historical Research* |
| *IA* | *International Affairs* |
| *IHR* | *International History Review* |
| IIC | Industrial Intelligence Centre |
| *IJ* | *International Journal* |
| IJN | Imperial Japanese Navy |
| *INS* | *Intelligence and National Security* |
| *IPSR* | *International Political Science Review* |
| *IS* | *International Studies* |
| *JAH* | *Journal of American History* |
| *JAS* | *Journal of American Studies* |
| *JCEH* | *Journal of Contemporary European History* |
| *JCH* | *Journal of Contemporary History* |
| *JEEH* | *Journal of European Economic History* |
| *JEH* | *Journal of Economic History* |

| | |
|---|---|
| *JGO* | *Jahrbücher für Geschichte Osteuropas* |
| *JICH* | *Journal of Imperial and Commonwealth History* |
| *JMH* | *Journal of Military History* |
| JPC | Joint Planning Committee |
| *JRIIA* | *Journal of the Royal Institute of International Affairs* |
| *JSAS* | *Journal of Southeast Asian Studies* |
| *JSMS* | *Journal of Slavic Military Studies* |
| *JSS* | *Journal of Strategic Studies* |
| LNC | London Naval Conference, 1935–36 |
| *MAS* | *Modern Asian Studies* |
| MI | Military Intelligence |
| *MM* | *The Mariner's Mirror* |
| MT | Ministry of Transport |
| NA | National Archives, Washington, DC |
| NAC | National Archives of Canada |
| NCM | Naval Conference Ministerial Committee |
| *NM* | *The Northern Mariner* |
| *NWCR* | *Naval War College Review* |
| ONI | Office of Naval Intelligence |
| *PHGB* | *Proceedings and Hearings of the General Board of the US Navy* |
| *PHR* | *Pacific Historical Review* |
| PREM | Premier Papers |
| PRO | Public Record Office |
| PSF | Private Secretary Files, for FDR |
| PSOC | Principal Supply Officers' Committee |
| *PSQ* | *Political Science Quarterly* |
| PUS | Permanent Under-Secretary (Foreign Office) |
| RAF | Royal Air Force |
| RG | Record Group |
| *RIS* | *Review of International Studies* |
| RN | Royal Navy |
| *SEER* | *Slavonic and East European Review* |
| *S&T* | *Strategy and Tactics* |
| T | Treasury |
| *TCBH* | *Twentieth Century British History* |
| *TMM* | *The Mariner's Mirror* |
| USN | United States Navy |
| USNGB | United States Navy General Board |
| *USNIP* | *United States Naval Institute Proceedings* |
| *WH* | *War in History* |
| *WMQ* | *William and Mary Quarterly* |
| WO | War Office |
| *WP* | *World Politics* |
| *WS* | *War and Society* |

# Introduction

... action is far the most difficult point on which to make recommendations, for America is the despair of the diplomat. In her remoteness, both physical and political, she resembles a prize fighter with a very long reach. He stands with his left arm stretched far out, and the opponent may dance round and round in the ring and never come to close quarters.[1]

Interwar Anglo-American strategic foreign relations, in the sense of any significant commonalities in foreign or defence policy, were centred primarily around Far Eastern issues. Isolated from European affairs after the First World War, American foreign and military interests focused on the possibility of a threat to world peace emanating from the Pacific. Based on a desire to establish an international acceptance of its view on how international relations were to be conducted (the Wilsonian legacy), the United States possessed a philosophical empire in the Far East that required defending, as it denounced the use of naked aggression by nations for their own benefit. Japan's use of force to expand its territorial possessions in China in 1931 and 1932 was a direct challenge to those American ideals. That challenge created a need for the United States to develop a Far Eastern policy: would it become more active in Far Eastern affairs or would it abandon the region to its own fate? However, because of the United States' military weakness and its diplomatic isolation from the League of Nations, the Roosevelt administration would have to rely on an old-fashioned balance of power approach to dealing with the Far Eastern crisis. Naturally enough, because of its predominant position as a major trading power in China and the Far East, as well as a protector of Far Eastern Dominions, Great Britain's position in that balance of power scheme was a key consideration in the construction of the United States' Far Eastern strategic foreign policy.

After 1932, the British Empire also saw itself facing the possibility of attack from an ambitious Japan. With the Soviet Russian empire incapable of checking Japanese expansion on the mainland, with the Chinese divided and industrially weak, and with the empire hobbled by the horrors of the First World War and constant, unreasoning cries for disarmament and peace, British strategic policy-makers also realized that the survival of British interests in the Far East required a balance of power in that area. For the Foreign Office, the primary creator and conductor of British strategic policy, the question was, how did the United States fit into that regional balance of power, as well as the global balance of power which was used to protect the entire empire? Thus, for Britain, the United States, as a potential major naval power in the Pacific, as a major trading nation, as a democratic, capitalist country dedicated to the ideals of individual freedom, and as a nation with economic and strategic interests in the Far East, was an important element in the final formulation of that strategic balance.

This study charts how the two nations' individual strategic needs created a 'parallel but not joint' relationship towards the Far East as the crisis in international relations evolved in that region. In short, it is a look at how the two nations developed similar views of the Far Eastern crisis and 'got along' with respect to accommodating one another on certain strategic and diplo-matic issues so that they could become more confident of one another in any potential showdown with Japan. The evidence presented reveals that, because of the Far Eastern question, the 'special relationship' between the United States and Great Britain was indeed a reality before it was allowable even to admit that such a relationship existed. With parallel goals, similar strategic evalu-ations and common approaches to the problem of what to do about Japan, the British Empire and the United States began to work together towards establishing and maintaining that balance-of-power scheme in the Far East. Those ties, forged in the troubled waters of the Pacific, were the first crucial steps in the construction of the more famous Churchill–Roosevelt 'special relationship' and as such are the true origins of the Grand Alliance.[2] For the purposes of this study, the 'special relationship' refers to the long-lasting circumstances that created friendship through understanding, networking, intellectual affinity, financial ties, family or blood relations, empathy and mutual fear of deception, but remained only a sentiment, not a formal or public expression of policy.

Why should a study of Anglo-American relations in the Far East concentrate on the period from 1933 to 1939? There are several reasons. First, there is little to be gained from studying, as is often done, the development of Anglo-American relations in that region from 1937 to 1941. Such an approach denies the reality of the development of that special relationship before 1937 and jumps ahead in its analysis because of the historian's certainty that the Second World War will definitely arrive.[3] The Eurocentric, as well as inevitable, aspects of such an approach has led to a simplification of the international situation in the period from 1933 to 1939. In that paradigm Germany is the only enemy Great Britain and the United States considered as being worthy of serious attention as a threat to global peace, and all other possible conflicts except the

European are relegated to second-class status. While Japan was indeed a second-class power in terms of industrial ability and modern war-fighting when compared to Germany, the historical record cannot assume glibly that the Far East did not consume an equal or even greater share of the time of British, and certainly American, strategic planners in those six years.

Second, while one could plausibly look at Anglo-American relations either from the point of view of separate administrations (either British or American) or through the lens of major international crises, one cannot cross over the divide which is the outbreak of the Second World War in Europe. Once a European war became a reality, all prewar contingency planning was subject to the exigencies of that new reality. Likelihoods were actualities and relations with non-combatants, such as Japan, the United States and the Soviet Union, would have to be made within that wartime context. Finally, there is a more reasonable way of looking at the development of Anglo-American strategic relations in the Far East: acknowledging that the period 1933 to 1939 forms a discrete contextual unit.

The creation of such a unit was the result of interwar events. From 1919 to 1931 a state of relative calm existed in the Far East. But, after 1932, in the aftermath of a failed attempt at cooperation by the Americans and British to check Japan's first aggressive moves in the region, a number of changes took place that make the period from 1933 to 1939 a separate block, as far as strategic foreign policy planning within a Far Eastern balance of power environment is concerned.[4] The coming to power of a new administration in the United States, a British move to rearm (with the Far East being the catalyst for that rearmament), a continuity of personnel and personalities in the policy-making elites on both sides of the Atlantic, and the absolute change brought about in strategic planning by the outbreak of a European war all combine to prevent the historian from linking events before September 1939 with the eventual bombing of Pearl Harbor. The period from September 1939 to December 1941 is a distinct era with some ties to the prewar era, but, when considered with respect to the efforts made by Great Britain and the United States to create and maintain a balance of power in the Far East to contain Japan in the preceding six years, it is one which must be seen in the context of an entirely different set of circumstances. The Nazi–Soviet Agreement of August 1939, the Tripartite Pact of September 1940, the fall of France in June 1940, the Soviet–Japanese Neutrality Agreement of April 1941, British warship losses in the first two years of the war, the US embargoes against Japan and the German attack on the Soviet Union in June 1941 were some of the 'new realities' that forced both American and British policy-makers to modify their Far Eastern policies. Therefore, pre-war Anglo-American ideas of working together to contain Japanese expansion can only be understood when they are left in the natural historical and chronological period bounded by the years 1933 to 1939. Understanding the difference between that period and the two years that followed also helps explain the reasoning behind some of the policies that did emerge from September 1939 to December 1941.

Many of the questions surrounding the study of Anglo-American relations and events in the Far East in the 1930s are rooted in a even more difficult argument: was Great Britain still *the* only global power throughout this period? Any discussion of this argument demands a renewed and rigorous investigation. A greater depth of analysis is particularly important when the comparison that is being drawn is between Britain, one of the prewar great powers, and the United States, the acknowledged superpower since 1945. To make such a comparison, one needs to consider economic, military, diplomatic and social matters, as well as personal perceptions and cultural elements. Only then can one gauge accurately what were the essential indicators of power and their affect on relationships. Here, Paul Kennedy is to be congratulated for his attempt to outline these elements in a comprehensive form. Kennedy argues that Britain's status as a great power was in a state of steady and inevitable decline following the turn of the century. He sees faster-growing, younger, expanding nations, such as the United States, Germany and Japan, overtaking the tired, inefficient and obsolescent British Empire in financial and industrial terms.[5] However, the 'declinist' interpretations of Kennedy and other scholars of a similar mind have been the object of a recent challenge over the nature of power and the relationship between Great Britain and other nations in the twentieth century.

This new school takes many of Paul Kennedy's conclusions to task, particularly his economic determinist approach to Britain's status during the interwar period.[6] In particular, this school points out that the declinists do not address adequately the issues of policy-makers' perceptions, circumstances and national will, all elements that make power a relative matter. Critics charge that the declinist model does not consider the broader criteria that make a nation a pre-eminent power. This caveat is especially true with regard to the elements required for a nation to be a pre-eminent maritime power. However, is the anti-declinist model, which attempts to find a point of transition (when did the United States take from the failing hand of Great Britain the trident of world power?) and argues for a 'supreme' power, really adequate for the multipolar situation which was the reality of the interwar period?

The answer is no. The argument that Great Britain was the greatest of the great powers is largely a false one. Great Britain existed as a great power in the 1930s precisely because of the balancing forces exerted by the other European great powers. As David French and others have argued, Great Britain was never really able to stand *alone* against any other great power, and certainly not against any combination of powers.[7] However, no other power was able to stand alone against a coalition either. The very nature of the great-power system was such that it demanded alliances and balance-of-power combinations that ensured that no one nation could remain above the others. Here, Britain was fortunate at the end of the First World War to be left stronger than the other European nations. But, as Italy and Germany regained their strength and continued to claw their way further up the great power ladder, Britain was forced once again to look for allies. By 1933 – in sharp distinction to the years before 1914 – Britain faced a hostile Japan and an unreliable Soviet Russia. Further, its remaining pre-1914 partner, France, was weak and hesitant. Given this alignment, the British Empire's search for allies or friends amongst the more powerful nations of the world naturally tended towards the United States, Britain's last First World War ally.

What needs to be considered is where was the focus of Anglo-American relations. The enormous economic, financial and potential military power displayed in the First World War by the United States was not a permanent part of the European great-power system. This divorced position made the United States only a potentially effective force in European wars. However, in the Far East, the United States was a vital military element in the Far Eastern balance of power.[8] The United States had no interest in becoming involved in European affairs and often was reluctant even to acknowledge the need to deal with Far Eastern matters during the interwar period.[9] This situation makes it necessary to return and consider once more another aspect of the declinist versus anti-declinist debate. Many historians fail to recognize that Anglo-American relations in the interwar period did not have any solid foundation, with regard to European affairs, until well after Roosevelt's re-election in the autumn of 1936. Europe did not matter for the Americans in terms of a global balance of power until well after that point because the isolationist tendencies that made the United States so very different from European nations were still dominant.[10] The United States was not thinking of a global balance of power. It is only after 1936 that one can begin to detect the emergence of a process of education in the United States, aimed by the Roosevelt administration at the American public in the hope of awakening the masses to the need to participate in global matters, particularly the Far East.[11] It would take a Europe suffering from the Abyssinia problem, the Spanish Civil war, German expansion, and finally Munich, to build a momentum that could shift the United States from its indifference towards the continent. Instead, it was the Far East that was the critical common ground for Anglo-American relations in the interwar period because that region was really the only one in which the United States was engaged in any military or diplomatic initiatives that placed them side by side with the British Empire, both facing a potential threat.

Another problem with the existing studies is one quite distinct from arguments about decline. Many non-American historians, critical of the United States' lack of support for the British Empire in the interwar period, have laboured under a number of mistaken liberal notions. Those range from the assumption that the United States was under some common cultural obligation to cooperate with the British in all circumstances, to the idea that there was some form of common outlook or formula among British and American policy-makers that could be applied in all circumstances to all Anglo-American interactions. While many who follow this type of analysis claim to be furthering the study of the role of personality along the lines of the work pioneered by Donald Cameron Watt and J.-B. Duroselle,[12] what in fact happened was the creation of generalized archetypes – Atlanticists, imperialists, anti-American, anti-British, pro-American, pro-British, and so on – into which people are thrust in Procrustean fashion. This method is simplistic. For example, was Sir Robert Vansittart, the Permanent Under-Secretary (PUS) of the Foreign Office from 1933 to 1938, anti-American? The answer is yes, with regard to the American refusal to become engaged in the European balance of power, a fact which annoyed Vansittart immensely. However, Vansittart could not be called anti-American in all situations and circumstances, particularly those concerning the Far East. The question is thereby clouded by the reality of the historical record: on some matters and in certain situations Vansittart was hostile to and suspicious of the United States, on others he was not. Alternatively, was Stanley K. Hornbeck, Chief of the Far Eastern Division of the State Department, anti-British? The answer is no, but Hornbeck was at all times aware of how American interests would have to take priority over British concerns, for in his eyes Anglo-American relations were second in importance to the protection of American interests in the Far East.[13] However, he also realized that good Anglo-American relations in the Far East would in fact further American interests in that region and thus was a solid supporter of working towards a mutually useful Anglo-American relationship in that region.

Both Vansittart and Hornbeck formulated their attitudes towards each other's Far Eastern policy around the desire to protect national self-interest through the maintenance of a balance of power. Therefore, both men were flexible in their assessments and attitudes towards the other's strategic foreign policy. Those strategic requirements made both men complex, multifaceted characters, and not simplistic, one-dimensional administrators. What is required instead of a simple labelling is a careful look at the individuals involved in, and the exact circumstances surrounding, a given issue, so that an accurate policy-making picture can be taken without implying that some permanent pattern or scheme existed. It was in this environment, of individual prejudices and biases, departmental directives and political desires, that American and British strategic foreign-policy planners created the 'mental maps' of each other and their Far Eastern policies. Those charts and the pictures that they drew were crucial to the creation of any 'special relationship' between 1933 and 1939.

It is not only the periodization of Anglo-American relations that needs to be determined, but also the nature of the relationship itself. The mental map that a nation's policy-making elite develops of another country determines the basis of international relations.[14] That relationship is ultimately concerned with the power of a nation and how that nation will utilize its power. The elements influencing how a nation's power manifests itself include domestic, foreign and defence policies; economic, financial and trade issues; ideological, political, religious and cultural systems of belief. These elements also influence the relationship that is the working reality when nations attempt to create mental images of one another.[15] From 1933 to 1939, the United States and Great Britain developed mental maps charting each other's Far Eastern policy and how the other would meet the perceived crisis in the Far East. Would the other nation use its power to meet the Japanese threat and, if so, how? Would each nation use its power in conjunction with the other, or would it be used separately? These are questions related to the formulation of British and American mental maps of one another that are dealt with in the chapters that follow. Also found below, however, are two other sets of mental maps, interwoven as a sub-text into the tracing of that strategic foreign-policy construction process. One of those sub-texts is the tangential recognition of the similarity between British and American policy-makers and their mental maps of Japan's strategic foreign policy. The other, less traditional usage of the idea of mental maps, concerns British attempts to manipulate Japan's mental map of the Anglo-American relationship. British Far Eastern policy-makers were concerned constantly with how Japan viewed the balance of power in the region. They manipulated continually the Japanese fear of a possible British alliance with the United States, and the Soviet Union, in order to create a deterrent to further Japanese expansion and aggression.[16] That manipulation was in fact one of the key elements of the 'no-bloc' policy of the British Foreign Office, which is discussed in greater detail below. Within that no-bloc policy, the British were not averse to attempting to make the Japanese believe that the Anglo-American relationship in the Far East was perhaps more than it officially appeared, so long as that perception would not panic the Japanese into an attack designed to prevent encirclement.

Also, for the purposes of this study, the mental-mapping process must be seen to take place on a number of sub-levels, such as at the Departmental and Embassy level, as opposed to just at the Cabinet or presidential or secretary of state level. That also means that the idea of a policy-making elite must be traced down through departmental and staff levels to see where ideas and policy originate, why they are either accepted or rejected and at what level. High-level officials rarely 'make' policy, they simply approve or disapprove of recommendations. Only by adopting this method of investigation can a complete picture of who formed policy and why they did so be determined. To do this, many detailed issues need to be considered: Who knew whom in the various embassies? Were they friends or antagonists? Who was a friend of which important civil servant? What groups or individuals could get information out of or into the right office or department? The answers to such questions determine the nature of an 'informal relationship' and these are the type of personal relations that need to be explored if a clear picture of how and why particular attitudes and policies were formed is to be gained. 'Great Man' appreciations of such complex and intricate interactions will simply not suffice.

How mental maps were formed and how they affected policy is complicated and took place over time. In this period, both the United States and Great Britain were conscious of the need to support each other at the most fundamental level, but also were aware of the various strengths and weaknesses of their own and their neighbour's position. In practice, from 1933 to 1936, what existed were strained but not ruptured Anglo-American relations. During this time, the British government came to grips with Roosevelt's foreign and domestic policies and their ramifications for the British Empire, while the Roosevelt Administration decided what its Far Eastern policy was to be and how best to go about achieving that policy. Ray Atherton, a very astute and accurate assessor of the British government's attitude and policy, on staff throughout the period under study at the US Embassy in London, summed up the circumstances nicely in March 1933:

> In conversations it is frequently brought out that the British Cabinet is increasingly conscious of England's political responsibilities as a European nation and, after surveying the field for Anglo-American cooperation, has reluctantly come to the conclusion that while Anglo-American aims may coincide in their general outlines, any policy of effective cooperation is practically unattainable in view of conflicting interests. 1. Thus, England and the United States both desire peace, but they have so far failed to agree on the nature of the cooperation essential to maintain peace. 2. England and America are both seeking a revival of world propriety. However, the more important methods whereby England hopes to raise world commodity prices seem directly to clash with the interests of the United States.[17]

All this changed in the period from 1936 to 1939. By early 1936, the two sides had been forced to forge new bonds of trust that helped overcome those differences. Also, as a second-term president, Roosevelt was much more confident of his ability to push the isolationist United States towards greater involvement in Far Eastern matters, as were the State Department and other American defence planners, particularly in the Navy. By 1936, those three groups were very aware of the fact that they would require British assistance in the Far East if American interests and Far Eastern foreign policy were going to survive and succeed.

Given the above, how did the creation of this special and informal relationship proceed? In order to dissect some of the forces working on the formulation of Anglo-American relations in the Far East, this study focuses on three major areas of Anglo-American relations: maritime-naval relations; foreign-policy-making elite relations; and assessments of the strategic situation in the Far East. The first has been chosen because of the geographic realities of fighting a war in the Far East.[18] If there were to be any meaningful cooperation between the two nations, at either a formal or informal level, then each had to come to an acceptance of both the other's naval strength and its security needs.[19] Therefore, John Hattendorf's observation that, 'In the twentieth century, both Britain and America have used maritime strategy as a subset of grand strategy in order to deal with balance of power issues', must be put at the core of Anglo-American relations for the Far East.[20] Achieving maritime harmony was not easy. As Britain and the United States had been bitter naval and shipping rivals in the period immediately following the end of the First World War, Anglo-American naval relations had been sorely tested up to 1933. However, under the pressure of having to react to Japan's aggressive actions, the United States and Great Britain established an informal, but solid, acceptance of and respect for each other's maritime strength, acknowledging the need to accommodate one another in order to meet the strategic challenge in the Far East.

Linked to this is the need, when assessing Anglo-American relations in the Far East 1933–39, to establish a more comprehensive definition of maritime power than that which is usually implied by the terms 'naval power' or 'sea power'. While many non-American efforts to do so have been enlightening,[21] most studies have suffered from conceptual problems, mainly an over-dependence on declinist theories and an over-reliance on the assumption of an inevitable war in Europe.[22] On the other hand, American attempts to write the history of their maritime efforts, especially in the Far East during the interwar period, have been totally unsatisfactory.[23] These failures were the product of several things: an attempt to project into the past certain perceptions of US power during the Cold War, a backlash against military and diplomatic studies in the 1960s and 1970s, and a refusal to leave behind narrow Mahanian ideas concerning the definition of maritime power. Thus, it is necessary that US maritime strength in the interwar period, especially with regard to the Far East, be properly re-evaluated. Further, because of the unbreakable link between a nation's naval policy and its foreign policy, the foreign-policy-making elites of the two countries must also be paid more attention.[24]

American and British foreign-policy-makers had developed a healthy distrust of one another between 1919 and 1932. Woodrow Wilson's delay in entering the First World War, the failure of the United States to join the League of Nations, and the inability of Sir John Simon and Henry L. Stimson to form a united front to contest Japan's actions in Manchuria rekindled, on both sides of the Atlantic, suspicions of the other's motivations, especially amongst non-elected officials in the Foreign Office and State Department. As a result, these governmental organs, the two most responsible for the development of mental maps and strategic foreign policy, had to overcome that legacy of distrust and suspicion if a 'special' relationship was to be established.[25]

A final matter that needs attention is the issue of how both nations saw the balance of power in the Far East. One strand of this concerns American and British views of Japan. Both the United States and Great Britain made assessments of Japanese intentions and power, and both had a sound respect for Japanese military and naval strength.[26] While, when discussing Japan's pre-1941 ability to make war, some historians have confused tactical or operational competence and innovation with strategic superiority,[27] the primary documentation leaves little doubt that British and American interwar planners accurately gauged the industrial, resource, economic and financial weaknesses that plagued Japan's strategic planning in the age of total war.[28] More importantly, British and US policy-making institutions recognised what most historians of the interwar Far Eastern situation did not: that the primary adversary for the Japanese was Russia, that the main theatre of operations would be China, and that the main naval foe for the Imperial Japanese Navy, until 1939, was the Royal Navy.[29] Whether policy-makers in either Western nation acted on or believed such information is another, albeit crucial, matter. A consideration of this latter point leads to the question of why it was that such information was not acted on or accorded greater significance. The oft-cited and simple answer, that all resulted from racial prejudice, does not bear the test of empirical evidence.[30]

A second strand of American and British thinking about the balance of power in the Far East is their less well known but more important evaluation of the role of the Soviet Union. The literature dealing with either American or British views of Soviet Far Eastern policy is very scanty.[31] However, since the Soviet Union was an important, if not the most important actor, in the Far Eastern balance of power, such an historiographical blank spot is a serious omission. The significance of the Soviet Union's place was not lost on American and British assessors of the Far East. And, significantly, the two Western powers shared their views about the worth of the Soviets with one another. What did the Anti-Comintern Pact of 1936 between Japan and Germany mean for the balance of power in the Far East? What effect did the Soviet military purges have on the Russians' ability to act as a strategic counter-weight to Japan's desire for further expansion on mainland China? These were some of the questions that both American and British strategic planners had to consider. They did so individually, but also in a cooperative manner that helped give each nation a better appreciation for the other nation's overall view of the Far East.

British and American views of Japan and Soviet Russia are part of the basis then for an exploration of how the strategic policy-makers of the two nations saw the Far East. Was their vision sufficiently similar to allow avenues of co-operation to be explored, in an attempt to counter Japan's expansionist policies? For, if cooperation between and coordination of Anglo-American Far Eastern policies could exist, then an informal, yet stable alliance relationship could be formed. Therefore, understanding the consensus created over these three separate areas in the strategic policy-making bodies of the American and British systems, creates a clear evaluation of the nature of Anglo-American relations towards the Far Eastern crisis and how that specific relationship provided the basis for the growth of the 'special relationship'.

## NOTES

1. FO 371/20651/A2378/38/45, very confidential despatch from Sir Ronald Lindsay (British Ambassador to the United States) to Anthony Eden (Secretary of State for Foreign Affairs), 22 Mar. 1937.
2. The literature on the 'special relationship' is immense. Some of the standard works are: Martin Gilbert, *Road to Victory: Winston Churchill, 1941–1945* (London, 1986); Winston S. Churchill, *The Gathering Storm* (Boston MA, 1948); Herbert Feis, *Churchill–Roosevelt–Stalin: The War They Waged and The Peace They Sought* (Princeton, NJ, 1967); Joseph P. Lash, *Roosevelt and Churchill, 1939–1941* (New York, 1976); Francis L. Lowenheim, Harold D. Langley, and Manfred Jonas, eds, *Roosevelt and Churchill: Their Secret Wartime Correspondence* (New York, 1975).
3. Works specific to the Far East in this vein are Ann Trotter, *Britain and East Asia, 1933–1937* (Cambridge, 1975); Peter Lowe, *Britain in the Far East* (London, 1981); idem, *Great Britain and the Origins of the Pacific War: A Study of British Policy in East Asia, 1937–1941* (Oxford, 1977); Aron Shai, *Origins of the War in the East: Britain, China and Japan 1937–1939* (London, 1976); Stephen Lyon Endicott, *Diplomacy and Enterprise: British China Policy, 1933–1937* (Vancouver, 1975); R.P.T. Davenport-Hines and Geoffrey Jones, *British Business in Asia since 1860* (Cambridge, 1989); Donald Cameron Watt, 'Chamberlain's Ambassadors', in Michael Dockrill and Brian McKercher, eds, *Diplomacy and World Power: Studies in British Foreign Policy, 1890–1950* (Cambridge, 1996), 136–70.
4. In fact, this thesis can best be understood as a continuation and elaboration of Thorne's very early work, 'The Shanghai Crisis of 1932: The Basis of British Policy', *AHR*, 75 (1970): 1616–39.
5. The declinist school includes Paul M. Kennedy, *The Rise and Fall of British Naval Mastery* (New York, 1976); Kennedy, *The Rise and Fall of the Great Powers: Economic Change and Military Conflict from 1500 to 2000* (London, 1988); Correlli Barnett, *The Collapse of British Power* (London, 1972); Aaron Friedberg, *The Weary Titan* (Princeton, NJ, 1988); Michael G. Fry, *Illusions of Security: North Atlantic Diplomacy 1918–22* (Toronto, 1972); Max Beloff, *Britain's Liberal Empire, 1897–1921* (London, 1969); Christopher Hall, *Britain, America and Arms Control, 1921–37* (London, 1987); Bradford A. Lee, *Britain and the Sino-Japanese War, 1937–1939: A Study in the Dilemmas of British Decline* (London, 1973).
6. This new school is loosely referred to as the London School, but it may be more precisely seen as the anti-declinist coalition. See bibliography for the works of John Ferris, B.J.C. McKercher, Keith Neilson, David French, Gordon Martel, Greg Kennedy and Michael Roi.
7. David French, *British Way in Warfare, 1688–2000* (London, 1990).
8. That fact was acknowledged by the need to include the United States in the Washington Treaty system of 1921–22.
9. Important works for the purposes of this investigation, from the Traditional, Realist, Revisionist or 'Wisconsin School', and Soft-Revisionist schools, as well as on the various debates concerning the state and focus of American diplomatic history can be found in the bibliography.
10. On the isolationist attitude of the United States, see R.A. Divine, *The Illusion of Neutrality* (Chicago, IL, 1962); Wayne S. Cole, *Determinism and American Foreign Relations During the Franklin D. Roosevelt Era* (Lanham, MD, 1995); R. Powaski, *Toward an Entangling Alliance: American Isolationism and Europe, 1901–1950* (New York, 1991); J.D. Doenecke and J.E. Witz, *From Isolationism to War, 1931–1941* (Arlington Heights, VA, 1991); W.L. Langer and S.E. Gleason, *The Challenge to Isolation* (Gloucester, 1970);

M. Jonas, *Isolationism in America, 1935–1941* (Chicago, IL, 1990); G. Kahn, 'Presidential Passivity on a Nonsalient Issue: President Franklin D. Roosevelt and the 1935 World Court Fight', *DH*, 4 (1980): 183–205; P.G. Boyle, 'The Roots of Isolationism: A Case Study', *JAS*, 6 (1972): 41–50.

11. On Roosevelt's use of the media to educate the public to the world's problems, see Richard W. Steele, 'The Great Debate: Roosevelt, the Media, and the Coming of the War, 1940–1941', *JAH*, 71 (1984): 69–92; Steele, 'Preparing the Public for War: Efforts to Establish a National Propaganda Agency, 1940–1941', *AHR*, 75 (1970): 1640–53; Michael Leigh, *Mobilizing Consent: Public Opinion and American Foreign Policy, 1937–1945* (Westport, CT, 1976), 1–41. On the British attempts to influence the American public favourably towards aiding Britain, see John Nicholas Cull, *Selling War: The British Propaganda Campaign Against American Neutrality* (Oxford, 1995).

12. For an explanation of their legacy, see B.J.C. McKercher, '"Our Most Dangerous Enemy": Great Britain Pre-eminent in the 1930s', *IHR*, 13 (1991); D.C. Watt, 'America and the British Foreign-Policy-Making Elite, from Joseph Chamberlain to Anthony Eden, 1895–1956', in D.C. Watt, ed., *Personalities and Policies: Studies in the Formulation of British Foreign Policy in the Twentieth Century* (London, 1965).

   On the American side, see, Frank Costigliola, *Awkward Dominion: American Political, Economic, and Cultural Relations with Europe, 1919–1933* (Ithaca, NY, 1984); Carl P. Parrini, *Heir to Empire: United States Economic Diplomacy, 1916–1923* (Pittsburgh, PA, 1969); Akira Iriye, *Power and Culture: The Japanese–American War 1941–1945* (Cambridge, 1981). For a most concise and enlightening discussion of 'the special relationship' see David Reynolds, 'Rethinking Anglo-American Relations', *IA*, 65 (1988–89): 89–111.

13. On the debate over Vansittart's position in British foreign-policy-making see Chs 5 and 6 below. For a very pro-Chinese view of what Hornbeck should have done to help China, see Shizhang Hu, *Stanley K. Hornbeck and the Open Door Policy, 1919–1937* (Westport, CT, 1995). Hornbeck held both the thinking and views of Sir George Sansom and Harold Nicolson in the highest regard and used them as a guide in his own thinking. See Stanley K. Hornbeck Papers [SKH], Hoover Institute, Stanford University, Box 454, Chronological Day File, Folder: Jan.–Apr., 30 Mar. 1935; Box 260, Subject and Correspondence Files, Folder: 1934, letter from Johnson to Hornbeck, 12 Feb.

14. On the idea of mental maps and international relations see: Keith Neilson, *Britain and the Last Tsar: Anglo-Russian Relations, 1894–1917* (Oxford, 1995), xi–xii, 3–50; Zara Steiner, *The Foreign Office and Foreign Policy, 1898–1914* (Cambridge, 1969); Steiner, 'Elitism and Foreign Policy: the Foreign Office Before the Great War', in B.J.C. McKercher and David J. Moss, eds, *Shadow and Substance in British Foreign Policy, 1895–1939: Memorial Essays Honouring C.J. Lowe* (Edmonton, Alberta, 1984), 19–56; Paul M. Kennedy, *The Realities Behind Diplomacy: Background Influences on British External Policy, 1865–1980* (London, 1981); A.K. Henrikson, 'The Geographical "Mental Maps" of American Foreign Policy Makers', *IPSR*, 1 (1980): 496–530.

15. Three outstanding authors, whose works and attitudes towards the writing of history serve as models for this study, are Donald Cameron Watt, *How War Came* (London, 1989); David Reynolds, *The Creation of the Anglo-American Alliance, 1937–1941* (London, 1981); and Christopher Thorne, *Allies of a Kind: The United States, Britain, and the War Against Japan, 1941–45* (London, 1978); Thorne, *The Limits of Foreign Policy: The West, The League and the Far Eastern Crisis of 1931–1933* (London, 1972). For the best definition of power and its implications for relations between nations see David Reynolds, *Britannia Overruled: British Policy and World Power in the Twentieth Century* (London, 1991), 5–37.

16. Michael A. Barnhart, 'Driven By Domestics: American Relations with Japan and Korea,

1900–1945', in Warren Cohen, ed., *Pacific Passage: The Study of American–East Asian Relations on the Eve of the Twenty-First Century* (New York, 1996), 190–212.

17. Confidential US State Department Central File, Great Britain, 1930–39, 711.41/261, despatch from Atherton to Hull, 9 Mar. 1933. See also ibid., 711.41/275, memo of conversation by Western European Division of the State Dept., 14 July 1934.

18. Emily O. Goldman, *Sunken Treaties* (Pennsylvania, PA, 1994); Malcolm H. Murfett, 'Look Back in Anger: The Western Powers and the Washington Conference of 1921–1922', in B.J.C. McKercher, ed., *Arms Limitation and Disarmament* (New York, 1992), 83–104; Stephen W. Roskill, *Naval Policy Between the Wars*, Vol. I (London, 1968), 70–5; J. Kenneth McDonald, 'The Washington Conference and the Naval Balance of Power, 1921–22', in John B. Hattendorf and Robert S. Jordan, eds, *Maritime Strategy and the Balance of Power* (London, 1989), 189–213; Erik Goldstein and John Maurer, eds, 'Special Issue on the Washington Conference, 1921–22: Naval Rivalry, East Asian Stability and the Road to Pearl Harbor', *D&S*, 4 (1993).

19. John B. Hattendorf, 'The Anglo-American Way in Maritime Strategy', *NWCR*, 63 (1990): 90–100.

20. Ibid., 98.

21. Some of the better works on maritime strength are Lawrence R. Pratt, *East of Malta, West of Suez* (Cambridge, 1975); Stephen Roskill, *The Strategy of Seapower: Its Development and Application* (London, 1962), G.A.H. Gordon, *British Seapower and Procurement between the War: A Reappraisal of Rearmament* (London, 1988); Orest M. Babij, 'The Second Labour Government and British Maritime Security, 1929–1931', *D&S*, 6 (1995): 645–71; J.T. Sumida, 'Forging the Trident: British Naval Industrial Logistics, 1914–1918', in John A. Lynn, ed., *Feeding Mars: Logistics in Western Warfare from the Middle Ages to the Present* (Boulder, CO, 1993); J.A. Lynn, 'British Naval Operational Logistics, 1914–1918', *JMH*, 57 (1993): 447–81; and David F. Trask, *Captains and Cabinets* (Columbia, MI, 1972).

22. Kennedy, *The Rise and Fall of British Naval Mastery*; Roskill, *Naval Policy Between the Wars*, Vols 1 & 2; Arthur J. Marder's *Old Friends, New Enemies: The Royal Navy and the Imperial Japanese Navy* (Oxford, 1981).

23. For a complete and full criticism of the various US and British schools of naval history, how, where and why they need to improve their craft see: James Goldrick and John B. Hattendorf, eds, *Mahan is Not Enough: The Proceedings of a Conference on the Works of Sir Julian Corbett and Admiral Sir Herbert Richmond* (Newport, RI, 1993); John B. Hattendorf, *Ubi Sumus: The State of Naval and Maritime History* (Newport, RI, 1994); Hattendorf, *Doing Naval History: Essays Toward Improvement* (Newport, RI, 1995).

24. On the practice and writing of US military and diplomatic schools of thought over this 30-year period and their attempts to explain US international relations, see B.J.C. McKercher, 'Reaching for the Brass Ring: The Recent Historiography of Interwar American Foreign Relations', *DH*, 15 (1991): 565–98, particularly 589–98; Jerald A. Combs, *The History of American Foreign Policy*, Vol. II (New York, 1986), Chs 13 and 14; Charles S. Maier, 'Marking Time: The Historiography of International Relations', in Michael Kammen, ed., *The Past Before Us: Contemporary Historical Writing in the United States* (Ithaca, NY, 1980), 355–87; multiple authors, 'Responses to Charles S. Maier, "Marking Time: The Historiography of International Relations"', *DH*, 5 (1981): 353–82 and subsequent responses to this debate in *DH* throughout the 1980s.

25. See: J.B. Crowley, *Japan's Quest for Autonomy: National Security and Foreign Policy, 1930–1939* (Princeton, NJ, 1966), 82–180; I.C.Y. Hsu, *The Rise of Modern China* (New York, 1975), 656–63; I.H. Nish, *Japan's Struggle With Internationalism. Japan, China and the League of Nations, 1931–1933* (London, 1993): 23–43. For the American side of the falling out between the United States and Great Britain over the Manchurian Crisis see

Christopher Thorne, *The Limits of Foreign Policy*, 135–62; James C. Thomson Jr, 'The Role of the State Department', in Dorothy Borg and Shumpei Okamoto, eds, *Pearl Harbor as History Japanese–American Relations, 1931–1941* (New York, 1973), 92–4; Dorothy Borg, *The United States and the Far Eastern Crisis of 1933–1938* (Cambridge, MA 1964).

26. Papers of the Chiefs of Staff Sub-Committee (hereafter COS papers), CAB[inet] Office Records, Public Record Office (PRO), London, 53/19, Imperial Defence College Exercise, No. 4, 1932; Captain A. W. Johnson, USN, Director of Naval Intelligence, 'Naval Policies of Maritime Powers: United States–British Empire–Japanese Empire', a paper presented to the Army War College, Washington, DC, 3 Dec. 1928, file no. 351-A-3, G-2 Course No. 3, 1928–29, US Army Military History Research Collection, Carlisle Barracks, Pennsylvania; Proceedings and Hearings of the General Board of the US Navy, 100–1950 (hereafter PHGB) (on microfilm, National Archives, Washington, DC), 'Characteristics of Battleships, 1941 Building Program', 28 June 1939, and 'Battleship X', 5 Dec. 1939; memo from Chairman of the General Board to the Secretary of the Navy, 16 Sept. 1932, General Board (hereafter GB) 420-2-1578, RG 80, Box 61, Folder 1931–32, National Archives, Washington, DC; Monthly Intelligence Summaries Issued by the General Staff the War Office, Vol. 22, No. 3, Jan. 1933, 98–9 (National Archive of Canada, Ottawa), RG 25, Vol. 1716, File 1934-865 part o; ibid., Vol. 24, No. 4, 28 Feb. 1934, 89; John Ferris, '"Worthy of Some Better Enemy?": The British Estimate of the Imperial Japanese Army, 1919–1941, and the Fall of Singapore', *CJH*, 28 (1993): 223–56; Borg, *The United States and the Far Eastern Crisis of 1933–1938*, 116.

27. Peter Lowe, 'Great Britain's Assessment of Japan Before the Outbreak of the Pacific War', in Ernest May, ed., *Knowing One's Enemies: Intelligence Assessment Before the Two World Wars* (Princeton, NJ, 1984), 456–75; Wesley K. Wark, 'In Search of a Suitable Japan: British Naval Intelligence in the Pacific Before the Second World War', *INS*, 1 (1986): 189–211; and Lee, *Britain and the Sino-Japanese War*, 1–23.

28. See Strategic Planning in the US Navy: Its Evolution and Execution, 1891–1945, Navy Basic Plan-Orange, Vol. 4, on microfilm, National Archive, Washington, DC, Change No. 3, W.P.L. 16 July 1933; War Office (hereafter WO) (PRO, London), 106/5136, Imperial Defence College, Exercise No. 3, 1934; D.E.H. Edgerton and S.M. Horrocks, 'British Industrial Research and Development Before 1945', *EcHR*, 67 (1994): 213–38; and for a post-war confirmation of those prewar assessments see 'Reports of the US Naval Technical Mission to Japan, 1945–1946', on microfilm, Operational Archives, US Naval History Division, Washington, DC.

29. Imperial Defence College, Exercise No. 3, 1934, WO 106/5136; 'Monthly Intelligence Summaries Issued by the General Staff the War Office', Vol. 26, no. 4, 1935, 189–94 in RG 25, Vol. 1716, National Archive, Ottawa; Alvin D. Coox, *Nomonhan: Japan Against Russia, 1939*, Vols I and II (Stanford, CA, 1985); Edward J. Drea, *Nomonhan: Japanese–Soviet Tactical Combat, 1939* (Fort Leavenworth, KY, 1981).

30. John Dower, *War Without Mercy: Race and Power in the Pacific War* (New York, 1986); Akira Iriye, *After Imperialism: The Search for a New Order in the Far East, 1921–1931* (New York, 1965).

31. See Jonathan Haslam, *The Soviet Union and the Struggle for Collective Security in Europe, 1933–1939* (London, 1984); Haslam, *The Soviet Union and the Threat From the Far East, 1933–1941* (London, 1992); Coox, *Nomonhan*; James W. Morley, ed., *Deterrent Diplomacy: Japan, Germany and the USSR, 1935–1940* (New York, 1976); Keith Neilson, '"Pursued by a Bear": British Estimates of Soviet Military Strength and Anglo-Soviet Relations, 1922–1939', *CJH*, 28 (1993): 189–222; R.J. Pritchard, *Far Eastern Influences upon British Strategy towards the Great Powers, 1937–1939* (New York, 1987); Michael J. Carley, *1939: The Alliance That Never Was and the Coming of World War II* (Chicago, IL, 1999).

# 1

# Anglo-American Intelligence, War Planning and Naval Cooperation, 1933–39

For many historians, interwar attempts to create Anglo-American naval cooperation and intelligence sharing begin and end with the less-than-spectacular efforts of Captain Ingersoll's mission to England in January 1938.[1] The Far East itself and intelligence sharing in the region between the two future allies have seldom been acknowledged as a worthwhile medium for looking at the development of Anglo-American relations. Instead, the focus of such studies has been attempts to prove that American and British intelligence gathering and distribution systems suffered from a narrow, racist, anti-Oriental approach, and therefore were either incompetent or inaccurate. And those studies which wish to start in 1937, after the Japanese attack on China that summer, fail to appreciate the true nature of the ongoing relationships that already existed between the various intelligence and planning groups that were involved in the policy-making process.[2] Tied into the two other issues of intelligence sharing and cooperation, the idea of naval planning for a war in the Pacific has often, unfortunately, revolved around only such ideas as the preparation of the Singapore base or the American revisions to their War Plan Orange. There have been, fortunately, a few forays into the industrial planning for a war with Japan, which have given some additional insights.[3] But the net result is a historiography that in most instances does not start early enough in its assessment, and misses the key regions and areas of cooperation.

There are four main geographic locations where sensitive information was passed between Americans and Britons. In Japan, the embassies constantly shared economic, strategic and naval information concerning their host nation. This was particularly true of the naval attachés, as well as of the ambassadors themselves. Close personal and professional ties, in some cases stretching back for decades, were the cement that allowed delicate intelligence and strategic appreciations to pass back and forth.[4] In London and Washington, the

US and British embassies were another avenue for the exchange of material. The US and British naval and military attachés were given special consideration by their host countries, and allowed to venture to places and see things that their foreign counterparts could not. These special considerations also worked to create a sense of trust and cooperation over what were at times delicate and sensitive issues. The Foreign Office and State Department and the various officials within those institutions also passed along information through private channels, at times dropping simple hints or confirming queries. In other instances, open and complete exchanges of positions or appreciations were passed, with the professional understanding that no other foreign service was being given access to such exclusive treatment. In this arena, various intelligence agencies could intermingle, trading bits and pieces for gain, or attempt to trap and deceive the other in tests of faithfulness. Was the other side telling the truth about Japan? Did they know what we knew and did they know we knew? If so, should we tell them? These were the types of question asked as the two sides attempted to formulate Far Eastern strategies against Japan, all the while keeping a wary eye on one another. Finally, there was the Chinese theatre itself, where both American and British diplomats and naval officers made individual decisions to trust one another and share secrets. There, close bonds and solid relations, based on shared dangers and a proven ability of one set of representatives to be able to trust the other, created important and lasting cooperation based on common cause. Therefore, it is logical to start the exploration of this process at one of the crucial pivots in that system of information gathering and sharing, the US and British embassies in China.

The head of the US mission in China, Minister Nelson T. Johnson, respected the British position in that region and liked his British opposite number, Sir Miles Lampson. Both men worked constantly to ensure that Anglo-American relations and cooperation on their stations was a reality.[5] It was Johnson's opinion that, 'The evidence of cooperation between the two countries which we were able to present was very gratifying to us, for we are both committed to the feeling that the United States and Great Britain can and should be together in the work of stabilizing the world conditions.'[6] When asked whether the British sharing of information and close coordination of tactics in the region were really signs of a willingness to cooperate with the United States or rather simply the artful playing of a waiting game that would protect their imperial interests, Johnson revealed an insightful and lucid understanding of the British situation in the Far East:

> so far as Great Britain's representative in China was concerned, he and I worked together very intimately and closely throughout all of this difficulty. There is in England ... a body of conservative opinion which has, and still regrets [the end of] the Anglo-Japanese Alliance. There is no

doubt in my mind that the British Government has had to carry water between that camp and the other camp which has been playing the game with us.[7]

Other British officials in China were in close and intimate contact with the US legation, sharing confidential and secret information about the deliberations of the Lytton Commission in 1932. The Commission, set up by the League of Nations to investigate the origins of the Sino-Japanese dispute of that year, was chaired by Britain's Lord Lytton. During its deliberations (which eventually reached the same conclusion as the British Foreign Office and branded Japan as the aggressor nation in that dispute[8]), Lord Lytton's secretary leaked confidential documents concerning the Commission's debates, through an American advisor to the Commission, Dr G.H. Blakeslee, to Johnson.[9] Johnson then commented on the Commission's proposals, allowing Blakeslee to take his unofficial 'American' perspective back with him for the group to consider. The close communications between the Commission and the American diplomats in China allowed that British-dominated body to have the unofficial, yet useful, exchanges of opinion that helped them avoid antagonizing the Americans, or proposing anything that would be unacceptable to the United States' Far Eastern foreign policy.[10] Johnson, in particular, counselled the Commission not to entertain the idea of a Sino-Japanese alliance over Manchuria based on the idea of one coming to the other's aid if attacked by a third party. That proposal was obviously aimed against the Soviet Union, and Johnson's argument was that any such action was dangerous and would result in creating a position that was 'a challenge and a certain invitation to war'.[11] American concerns and pressures were, therefore, displayed through a discreet route while the Commission went about its task.

That sort of exchange of information, useful for keeping the other nation in the game and allowing it to voice any concerns unofficially before anything became policy, also occurred in Japan between the British and US Embassy staff. In July 1933, for example, the Foreign Office was concerned that the Americans might have been negotiating an arbitration treaty with the Japanese. The US Embassy alleviated those fears by allowing one of its Counsellors, Edwin L. Neville, to show a British Counsellor, Mr Cunningham, the telegrams which had been passing back and forth between Ambassador Grew and the State Department.[12] That openness, and the evidence in the confidential memoranda and telegrams, not only convinced the British that there was no plot on the part of the US State Department, but also reinforced the traditional strong ties of cooperation and liaison that had existed between the two embassies. Neville also maintained close and intimate contact with T.M. Snow, Counsellor in His Majesty's Embassy in Tokyo, whose views on Japan and the Soviet Union were held in high regard by the Foreign Office and other Embassy members, including Sir Francis O. Lindley, the British Ambassador. The maintenance of such lines of communication allowed the British embassy to assess confidently what the US Ambassador, Joseph Grew, was trying to do in his dealings with Japan. Snow, after many discussions with Neville, wrote a widely read and valued report that outlined how the Americans were trying to improve US–Japanese relations, indicated what the US Embassy's views were on whether the United States should be involved in the Pacific, and illuminated how Britain's position and relations with Japan might be affected.[13] Even after Lindley returned to England on 18 May 1934, his replacement, Sir Robert Henry Clive, maintained very warm and close relations with Grew.[14] Armed with these insights from Tokyo, the Foreign Office could compare notes with other departments and sources, and try to put together an accurate map of American perceptions of the region. A similar process occurred in the State Department and between the Royal and US Navies.

Both the British and American representatives in Japan and China kept in close and constant touch with their respective senior naval commanders in the region. Lampson, Lindley, Johnson and Grew all maintained good relations with such admirals as Frank Brooks Upham (USN), Commander-in-Chief (C.-in-C.), Asiatic Fleet, and Sir Frederic C. Dreyer (RN), C.-in-C. China Squadron.[15] The close working relationship between the naval and political representatives was also continued by the men who succeeded to these posts. Lampson, and later Sir Alexander Cadogan, kept Johnson well informed of Admiral Dreyer's study of the Anglo-Japanese question and his attempts to foster better relations between the Royal Navy and the Imperial Japanese Navy (IJN). The Americans were interested in knowing whether the Royal Navy was willing to accommodate Japanese demands for a larger navy. By keeping a watch on Dreyer and how he approached the Japanese, intelligent deductions about British naval policy towards Japan could be made by the Americans.[16] The US and British navies also had their own strong tradition of informal cooperation in the Far East.[17]

In late 1933, Dreyer and Upham had collaborated to construct a simple code for communication between themselves in the event of any trouble arising.[18] The two Admirals felt that 'we should have at our disposal a ready means of concerting action for the protection of our respective national interests without first announcing to all the world what we intended to do'.[19] The need for such a code was related to trouble not only with the Japanese, but also with the Chinese. It was a distinct, independent attempt for the two navies to cooperate in the face of threats to common interests at a local level. However, a fear that such collaboration would be seen by other powers as indicating a more significant pact or formal agreement than was the case caused Dreyer to ask Upham to forgo the idea of using the code and to destroy his copy of it.[20] There were other instances of such cooperation.

Upham was also privy to the discussions held in Singapore on 23 and 24 January 1934, which saw Royal Navy and Dominion senior naval officers and staffs debate whether the British should withdraw from Hong Kong and

Singapore. Those talks had larger consequences. The British decision to bring forward the completion date for the Singapore naval base to 1938, and the Royal Navy's fears of an American withdrawal from the Philippines and the resulting decline of the United States as a naval power in that region, were relayed by Upham to Admiral William H. Standley, the Chief of Naval Operations (CNO).[21] Upham's recommendations to Standley and his assessment of how to deal with Japan reflected several themes which were common to US Asiatic Fleet commanders: the United States should make a firm commitment to establishing itself as a serious naval power in the Pacific, or, failing this, withdraw; force would be required to meet the Japanese threat and that threat would be met best in conjunction with the British and any other powers with interests similar to those of the Americans.[22] Clearly, early in Roosevelt's first administration, there was a desire on the part of the two Western navies to make an accommodation with each other and to cooperate to a wide extent, even if their national visions were not identical. Service rivalry and the need to protect sensitive technical and strategic information were still obstacles to complete Anglo-American naval cooperation in 1933, but they were obstacles which were being continually eroded.[23]

During the first year of Roosevelt's presidency, the Admiralty extended 'exceptionally unrestricted latitude to visit activities in the shore establishment of the Royal Navy ...' to the US Naval Attaché and his staff in London.[24] The British Director of Naval Intelligence (DNI), Sir Oswyn A.R. Murray, and others in charge of the Admiralty's intelligence organization, in accordance with general Admiralty policy, were determined to make Anglo-American naval relations, at this informal level, as close and cooperative in tone as possible.[25] The Admiralty gave many special courtesies and made gestures to the US Naval Attaché, Captain A.L. Bristol and his Assistant, Captain H.S. Howard in 1933, gestures ranging from visits to facilities to offers of cruises on Royal Navy vessels. Bristol was wary of the attention, fearing that he might be placed in a compromising position. He, as well as Captain (USN) Hayne Ellis, the Director of Naval Intelligence, were concerned that if Bristol accepted too many of these 'generous' offers, then the US Navy would be put in the position of having to offer reciprocal visits.[26] Taken on a tour of the Gunnery School (Whale Island), the battlecruiser *Nelson*, the Torpedo School (*Defiance*), and given a thorough look around the heavy cruiser *Dorsetshire* (just shortly after presenting himself to the Admiralty), Bristol wrote to Ellis specifically to let him know that 'there was no particular request for these inspections on my part'.[27] When a suggestion of a short cruise on a Royal Navy ship was hinted at by Bristol's friends in the Admiralty, he asked Ellis for clearance and explained the Admiralty's thinking about their relations with him:

> The farther one gets from London the more free and easy the British Navy becomes, particularly towards Americans. Here in London, the idea is

constantly to the fore that anything that they do for me will be found out and they will be in the position of having to extend the same to the Naval Attachés of other countries. Such a visit, if I accepted, would unquestionably carry with it reciprocity treatment at some time in the future.[28]

Ellis informed Bristol that the DNI was not worried about the reciprocity aspect and that such a cruise would be good for relations.[29] The Admiralty's desire to woo Bristol also extended to his being allowed to tour the Royal Navy aircraft carriers *Courageous* and *Furious* in December 1933.[30]

In return, Captain (RN) A.R. Dewar, the British Naval Attaché in Washington, asked Ellis for permission to visit the New York Navy Yard. Ellis had no objection to reciprocation, and quickly gave his consent, with the proviso that Dewar not be shown anything of a secret nature or any 'late types of confidential material'.[31] The DNI specifically instructed the Commandant of the Third Naval District to withhold information concerning

(1) Remote control searchlight installations or developments. (2) All matters connected with radio and sound equipment and developments. (3) Remote control of AA guns. It is planned to negotiate an exchange of information with the British Admiralty in regard to the following: (a) Latest British practice with respect to air pressure in firerooms, pressure drop through burners, oil pressure used, etc. Also on British water gauges, draft gauges, feed regulators and $CO_2$ indicators. Also difficulties of operation or maintenance of British boilers. (b) British condenser installations, operations difficulties, etc. (c) British propeller design for high speed ships, all types. (d) British submarines; and conversations on these subjects should be limited to matters of general nature.[32]

In an effort to benefit from the high standard of British naval construction and expertise, close technical cooperation was certainly on the mind of the DNI and others within the US Navy.[33] On the other hand, the Admiralty was more interested in trying to get a handle on whether the US Navy was capable of fighting a war in the Pacific.[34]

In late 1933, Dewar approached the Americans about a tour of various industrial plants and naval facilities on the West Coast and Hawaii.[35] The object of the tour was to ascertain the ability of the US Navy to support a Fleet in the Pacific. Dewar wished to begin his tour in late February 1934 and to continue on until the end of May.[36] Japanese requests to see Pearl Harbor had just been denied by the DNI, but Ellis was quick to make special arrangements for the British Attaché.[37] On 4 December 1933, Ellis informed Dewar that all the installations the Attaché wished to see were approved unconditionally, except Pearl. Ellis did not, however, close the door on the British request. If certain conditions were met, then Dewar would be allowed access to that sensitive base:

It is our policy to not grant permission for foreign officers to visit those stations. However, I have discussed the matter with the Chief of Naval Operations and we have decided that in view of the friendly relations existing between our two countries and in anticipation of similar exceptions from your government to our Naval Attaché, we will be glad to arrange for you to make those visits. We ask, however, that you give as little publicity as possible to the fact that you are being permitted to visit Pearl Harbor.[38]

In preparation for Dewar's tour, and to improve Anglo-American naval relations for that future exchange of information, Ellis helped pave the way for the Attaché, sending personal requests to the Commandants of various Naval Districts to give special treatment to the RN Captain. He informed Rear Admiral D.F. Sellers, the C.-in-C., US Fleet, that it would be all right to show Dewar through the aircraft carrier *Saratoga*, because the American Attaché in London had been granted a visit to one of the British carriers, during which 'he went over it very thoroughly'.[39] The DNI also hinted to Rear Admiral W.T. Tarrant, Commandant of the 11th Naval District, that regarding Dewar's visit to facilities in San Diego it would be acceptable to give him special treatment in this case, because, 'For your information only – we work very closely with the British Attachés.'[40] The granting of these exceptions, especially with regard to allowing a foreigner to tour one of the large aircraft carriers and its sensitive technical equipment (especially anything to do with the arresting gear), signalled that a very special relationship at this informal level was a reality indeed.[41]

The tour itself allowed for a fairly free exchange of information and certainly allowed the affable Dewar the opportunity to establish a personal relationship with various high-ranking US naval officers. During his visit to the US Naval Air Station in San Diego, Dewar confirmed a number of facts about British carrier operations for the Commanding Officer of the Station, even though the latter did not think Dewar knew or was particularly interested in aviation matters.[42] Dewar was reported to have confirmed that the British were somewhat behind the Americans in the development of arresting gear and had recently resumed development of such devices along the lines utilized by the US Navy. Some of the results of that development were already in service, but not in any general way. Dewar also informed the Americans that the new carrier under construction would be probably around 20,000 tons, similar to the *Yorktown* and *Enterprise* in size. In addition, on the matter of flush deck versus island construction, he was of the opinion that the latter was the style preferred by the Royal Navy. As for the tactical use of carriers with the British fleet, the Attaché had revealed that

they [the British] had been much concerned over the necessity for launching carrier airplanes into the wind when tactical considerations were such as to make this a most undesirable direction into which to steam. The impression was obtained that as a matter of policy they had adopted a compromise of keeping their carriers sufficiently remote from the battle line to permit such maneuvering.[43]

Reports from Pearl Harbor, Mare Island, Puget Sound, and San Diego indicated that Dewar was interested in information that would allow him to judge the level of support the Americans had prepared on the West Coast for the Pacific Fleet. He asked for, and was given, information on labour forces, new shore construction, dredging work, dry docks, shop areas of the bases, technical details of ship construction, plant production capacity, funding schemes, and building programmes. At the same time, he golfed and dined in the company of the US naval officers, spreading the message of good relations between, and common interests of, the US Navy and Royal Navy.[44] The relationship between the British naval officers in the United States and the US naval officers with whom they came in contact appeared to be based, even as early as 1933–34, on a mutual trust that neither afforded any other nation's naval representatives. If matters were sensitive they were avoided. For the Americans, at least, the general tone of the informal Anglo-American naval relationship was one in which the British were almost always as honest and forthcoming as they could be. That sense of trust and confidence certainly carried on into 1935, even when the incumbent British Naval Attaché and US DNI changed.

The Admiralty's appointments to the Washington embassy were usually divided into two groups: a 'salt' sailor and an engineering officer. The Naval Attaché was the 'salt', while the Assistant Naval Attaché was the engineering officer. In September 1935, Captain F.C. Bradley became the British Naval Attaché. His Assistant, replacing Orr in December 1934, was Commander A.L.P. Mark-Wardlaw.[45] Captain W.D. Puleston had become DNI by December 1934. Under this new regime, the British Attachés were still given access to aircraft and naval plants, as well as to industrial laboratories. The nature of their visits suggests that their efforts were aimed not so much at the collection of specific technical data, but, instead, at an ongoing attempt to evaluate the US Navy's mobilization plans and infra-structure developments for fighting a war with Japan.[46] Certainly, the Foreign Office had requested the Washington Embassy to find out whether the official American position was to 'scuttle' out of the Far East or to stay and fight to defend the Philippines and their other interests in the region.[47] Puleston was aware of this ongoing assessment process, and did a great deal to make the task as easy as possible.[48] While an unwillingness to divulge all technical or policy information was present in relations between US Navy and Royal Navy representatives, a willingness to work with one another, much more so than with any other navy, was present in the relationship. British actions designed to establish sympathetic relations with US naval officers were also aimed at countering the increased Japanese propaganda campaigns, which all had an anti-British tone. These Japanese productions caused some concern among Foreign Office officials, but were thought to be containable, especially given the lack of fertile ground in the United States from which any pro-Japanese movement could sprout.[49]

By the end of 1934, the Industrial Intelligence Centre (IIC), under the leadership of Major (later Sir) Desmond Morton, an organization under the umbrella of the Committee of Imperial Defence that utilized material from political as well as from service departments, was able to submit a detailed evaluation of the United States' ability to mobilise its industry in time of war.[50] The IIC was of the opinion that in a Far Eastern war the Americans possessed the natural and industrial resources to maintain a large navy with no serious difficulty. If a large military effort, that is to say, the raising of a great army were required, then some difficulties could arise. The key problems for the Americans, according to the IIC, were limitations in certain capacities: a shortage of precision instrument and optical industries, a deficiency in railway rolling stock, a lack of a proper appreciation of the financing necessary for a national mobilization scheme, no educational or preparatory orders for armament stores placed with civil industry in peacetime, small reserves of finished armaments, and no reserves at all of special purpose machine tools, jigs and gauges. These factors all combined to create the possibility of a great time-lag occurring in US mobilization before the required levels of output could be achieved. In short, there was some doubt as to how seriously the United States approached the idea of naval and industrial rearmament, especially given the natural safety provided by geography.[51] If properly organized, especially in manpower and material production, the United States would have no equal. Such a power, especially in the age of industrialized warfare, was not a force to be ignored or alienated. During the preliminary and actual discussions of the 1935 London Naval Conference, those British agencies tied to manufacturing and to monitoring Anglo-American relations, especially naval relations, were well aware of the vast naval potential that lay dormant in the United States. That latent strength would mean nothing, however, if the Americans were not aligned in some fashion with British interests.

In November 1934, American policy-makers felt that there was some chance that Great Britain was attempting to recreate the Anglo-Japanese Alliance, in order to protect imperial interests in the Far East.[52] This was a critical period in the development of Anglo-American naval relations, as both sides worked to establish a sense of trust and security in the other's Far Eastern policy and naval position. Rear Admiral G.C. Dickens (RN), the DNI, warned the British Broadcasting Corporation (BBC) against letting pro-Japanese commentators attack the course of the preliminary naval conversations. He feared that such commentary, if aired, would add fuel to the fire of American suspicions. The BBC agreed with his attempt to prevent the talks from being permanently damaged, and also offered to use any person that the Admiralty wanted to talk on the naval conversations.[53] Aware of the chance to counter anti-British American newspapers publicly, the Foreign Office prepared a speech for the Secretary of Foreign Affairs, Sir John Simon, in case such action was required. He gave the speech in mid-December as the preliminary stages of the talks were being wrapped up, attempting to ensure that an image of progress and cooperation was presented to both the British and American public.[54] Any possibility of a public display of pro-Japanese or anti-American sentiment was avoided, thus allowing the further development and improvement of Anglo-American relations.

US naval intelligence sources in Great Britain responded well to British initiatives to create a friendly and cooperative atmosphere. While various American political and diplomatic sources were catering to the idea that there was a great risk of the British and Japanese reuniting, Captain W.S. Anderson, now the US Naval Attaché in London, reassured the US Navy that there was probably not that much to worry about. Anderson told the DNI:

> Not just in connection with the approaching conversations, but in general, there seems to be a current belief that the British policy at present contemplates paying particular attention to friendship and good under-standing with the Japanese. To my mind this does not mean that the British are entirely pleased with everything the Japanese have said or done, but that the British propose to follow what seems to them the only practicable policy, that is, friendship – what may be called stressed friendship.[55]

Anderson, like so many US officers who had any sustained contact with their British counterparts, was willing to grant a certain degree of sympathy towards Great Britain's naval situation. Indeed, by the end of 1935, Anderson was of the opinion that the Admiralty offered him better access to officers of high rank than was afforded his counterparts in Washington:

> Summing the whole situation up, so far as I am personally concerned I have found the higher officers and officials the most communicative, as there is a zone of rank below senior Captains down to, say, Lieutenant Commanders which, if at the Admiralty, apparently feels some inhibitions in talking with a Naval Attaché on certain subjects. It is difficult to make comparisons, but I believe our relations with officers of authoritative rank and position surpasses those enjoyed by our opposite numbers in Washington, whereas they have probably more intercourse with officers of more junior ranks.[56]

But, if good relations between the two navies were important, it was equally vital that the American politicians were subjected to a similar dose of kindness by the British Admiralty, so that they, too, might develop that spirit of acceptance of Britain's strategic requirements.

Dickens and the Admiralty intelligence community were instrumental in wooing President Roosevelt himself in 1935, in order to garner what goodwill they could. Their approach was not to lecture on or promote the British position to the President. Instead, they catered to one of his private loves: naval history. Roosevelt was very interested in the British expedition of 1777, which had gone down the Hudson River and bombarded what was now Hyde Park and burnt part of Kingston, New York. In December 1933, Roosevelt had asked the US Ambassador to England, Robert W. Bingham, if he could get the documents and logs of HMS *Preston* and *Dependence*. The President hoped to recreate the movements and campaign of the British warships, which had left a number of cannon balls planted in his ancestral grounds.[57] Dickens and the Admiralty complied with Roosevelt's request, providing the logs and documents in question. Those actions earned Dickens and his colleagues the President's undying gratitude, as he raved about the material and instructed Bingham to take advantage of Dickens' generous nature and to secure more information.[58] That exchange, while not a supreme act of intelligence sharing or Anglo-American cooperation, came at a critical time, when Roosevelt was reflecting on whether to accept and trust Great Britain's naval and Far Eastern position. While a direct connection between any later acceptance of the British situation cannot be shown, it is not unnatural to credit these small acts with having some effect on how Roosevelt viewed the Royal Navy and its strategic needs.[59]

In the Philippines, relations between the British Consulate in Manila and various US military and diplomatic figures stationed there provided the Admiralty and Foreign Office with another source of information and an avenue for the dissemination of opinion. Not under the watchful eye of a full Ambassador and his staff, and removed from close control by the Foreign Office or State Department because of its secondary status in the region, Manila provided a Far Eastern equivalent to Lisbon, as a place where free, if discreet, conversations could take place. In May 1935, Foreign Office officials were still trying to assess whether the United States planned to abandon the Philippines and scuttle out of the Far East, or whether it would challenge Japan's expansion. The British Acting Consul-General, A.P. Blunt, conducted confidential discussions with Major-General Frank Parker, the General Officer Commanding United States troops in the Philippines, in order to try to clarify the picture. The General informed Blunt that it was his opinion that the US flag would remain in the Philippines for some time to come. Parker also was emphatic in his statements to Blunt about how the Anglo-Saxon races needed to cooperate in their Far Eastern policies.[60] Those views were echoed by Rear Admiral A.H. Allen (USN), who commanded the US naval base at Cavite, and Joseph R. Hayden, the Acting Governor-General. Both men expressed the belief that it would be at least ten years before any American withdrawal from the Philippines was achieved.[61] Furthermore, both Parker and Allen offered Blunt 'access to any "intelligence" at their disposal'.[62] By August, that offer had been translated into action. During a call on Colonel J.B. Richardson, the Chief of the Intelligence Section of the US Army HQ in Manila, Blunt was told how and why General MacArthur was coming to the Philippines and what the future military strength of the islands was to be. Because of his good relations with Parker, Blunt believed that he was being told the truth, as did the American Department of the Foreign Office, which placed great store in Blunt's ability to procure accurate information.[63] Such close relations allowed both nations to draw a clearer map of where their paths in the Pacific were leading.

In 1936, after the successful conclusion of the Second London Naval Conference, Anglo-American cooperation, at the formal and informal levels, on Far Eastern and naval matters increased. Now driven by concerns over possibly having to deal with the Italian and German navies in Europe, British strategic planners hoped to get a firm commitment from the United States to help safeguard the Far East, thus allowing the Royal Navy to concentrate on European waters.[64] Therefore, Admiralty and Foreign Office officials kept the US Embassy informed of the technical aspects and developments of the Anglo-Soviet bilateral naval agreement talks, which began in March 1936.[65] The new British DNI, Rear Admiral J.A.G. Troup, also maintained a close relationship with the US Naval Attaché, discussing problems of mutual interest.[66] Captain Anderson was treated to a Mediterranean cruise by the Royal Navy in the spring of 1936, although with certain conditions:

> When this trip was broached to the Admiralty and their approval requested, it was represented that the Naval Attaché would exercise great reserve in speaking about the trip, that it would ostensibly be a holiday trip, and that if ever forced into a position in which he had to speak about it to his colleagues or anyone else he would adhere to the proposition that it was a holiday trip. These reports are accordingly all confidential and it is hoped that nothing will be said about this trip in Washington which might compromise it. The Admiralty distinctly desire that they not be approached for approval of similar trips by all Naval Attachés.[67]

In particular, the Admiralty did not want to have to fend off requests from the Japanese Naval Attaché for similar tours. Nor did they wish to arrange a reciprocal exchange of information on the methods of detecting and destroying submarines as Anderson had also suggested.[68] However, the US Attaché's cruise had more to do with Anglo-American relations than simply with making better contacts with the Royal Navy.

In setting up the cruise, Anderson had met with the British DNI. During that meeting, he had broached the idea of increased cooperation in intelligence between the Royal Navy and US Navy, mentioning the reciprocal visit and submarine ideas. Besides those two rejected proposals, which had been 'informal and unauthorized requests', Anderson made specific requests for the reciprocal exchange of information on the Japanese Mandated Islands in the North Pacific, and unexpected movements of the Japanese Navy or mercantile fleet which might give a warning of an impending war. The Admiralty had no objection to such an arrangement, as it was seen to be 'advantageous from the strategical point of view'.[69] There was, of course, the danger that the Japanese would find out about the arrangement and take offence. Although the Admiralty thought the risk of such discovery was slight, they desired the Foreign Office's view.

The American Department led the debate within the Foreign Office as to whether this was a good time to move closer to the United States through such action. P.H. Gore-Booth, a senior official in the American Department whose views on the United States were well respected within the Foreign Office, started the ball rolling with a paper outlining the pros and cons of taking up Captain Anderson's offer. On the con side, Gore-Booth pointed to the American idea of trying to manufacture an Anglo-American joint policy or declaration aimed specifically at Japan. Norman Davis, the chief negotiator for the United States during the 1935 London Naval Conference, had been particularly insistent on trying to get such an arrangement.[70] There was also the fear that the State Department would leak the news of such intelligence cooperation to the press in order to further their own position: 'the United States would not fear the consequences of a disclosure of such an arrangement, since the Americans are not particularly popular in Japan anyhow, whereas we have still some capital of friendship to lose in that country, and discriminatory measure by us would be ill-received and to some extent harmful'.[71] On the pro side, Gore-Booth summed up the general Foreign Office attitude towards the United States admirably, arguing that

> It is a broad political fact that there is a constant danger of our acting on the once-bitten-twice-shy principle and taking United States suggestions of this kind too pedantically. I venture to think that sooner or later what might be called 'special relations' ought to and will subsist between the British Commonwealth and the United States, if indeed they do not subsist already, and anything which tends to further this special relationship, be it assistance in the suppression of liquor smuggling or exchange of naval information, seems to merit consideration from a general as well as the special point of view. For that reason it would be a pity, I suggest, to reject any suggestion of this kind from the United States side out of hand, on grounds of an appearance of immediate impracticability, – and one cannot believe that this suggestion is just a bright idea of Captain Anderson's.[72]

Gore-Booth's suggestion for working around the dual problems of the Japanese discovering matters or the State Department trying to steal a march was to have a verbal understanding only. The extent of information that would be exchanged would be left open, with much of the maintenance of the agreement left to the personalities of the attachés. J.M. Troutbeck (who would become head of the American Department in 1937 when Sir Robert Craigie left to become the Ambassador to Japan), thought that the paper did not sufficiently emphasize the advantages to be had by moving closer to the United States. It was his view that, given Great Britain's need for an ally in the Pacific, it would be foolish to refuse the American offer.[73] Other departments in the Foreign Office concurred. The Far Eastern Department rejected the idea of a formal agreement to exchange information, but it too favoured dealing frankly with the Americans in an informal and safe fashion that avoided the usual diplomatic machinery.[74]

Others emphasized caution. Sir Robert Vansittart, the permanent under-secretary of state, objected most strenuously, calling such a move dangerous. His suspicions of the United States caused him to believe that sooner or later the arrangement would be given away by the Americans. Without any formal agreement from the United States to give support in the Far East, Vansittart was unwilling to chase too far after better relations if there was any danger that Great Britain might find itself facing an irritated Japan alone. However, he, too, was torn, as he desired better relations with the United States in order to alleviate Great Britain's strategic difficulties around the globe. His suggestion was simply to let the matter drop and wait to see if Anderson returned to the matter. If the US Naval Attaché brought it up again, Vansittart then agreed to follow Robert Craigie's suggestion as to what action to take.[75] Craigie acknowledged Britain's need to keep its distance from the United States on matters regarding Japan, but argued in favour of cooperating with the Americans at some level. He suggested that Great Britain had just as much to gain from such an arrangement as the United States and that an oral exchange was best. Tied to the understanding that had been reached with the Americans during the Second London Naval Conference talks, such an exchange, Craigie felt, could be justified as being beneficial to the empire. What was important was not to let a situation be created where it appeared as if Japan were being singled out by both Western nations.[76] The Parliamentary Under-Secretary of State, Lord Stanhope, also agreed with Craigie, cautioning the new Secretary of State, Anthony Eden, not to be put into a position where the United States could leave Britain 'holding the baby' in the Far East.[77] The end result was that Eden approved of letting the matter drop temporarily because of the uncertainty of whether the Americans were really serious about cooperating with Great Britain against Japan. He acknowledged the benefits such actions could have on Anglo-American relations, but was still concerned about Japan appearing to be the target of such cooperation. If Anderson brought the matter up again, however, then the Attaché would simply be informed orally that the recent conclusion of the London Naval Treaty, coupled with the re-affirmation of the intention of the United States and the United Kingdom to abstain from any form of naval competition, appear to His Majesty's Government to justify a free exchange of information between both countries on all questions which seem likely to affect that Treaty.[78]

While this settled matters at the Foreign Office, other service departments had similar problems. For its part, the Admiralty also avoided being drawn into any exact definition of the scope of any information to be exchanged.

Apart from prodding the Foreign Office into having to think about greater intelligence sharing with the United States, Anderson's cruise with the Royal Navy was a very useful exercise. The Royal Navy allowed Anderson to inspect a triple 16-inch turret on the *Nelson*, a double 15-inch turret on the older battleship *Barham*, a double 8-inch turret on the heavy cruiser *London*, and a double 6-inch turret on the light cruiser *Galatea*.[79] The US Attaché also asked about and was given information on developments in British anti-submarine warfare. The responses he received made him believe that the Royal Navy, like the US Navy, had not solved the problem of detecting and destroying of the undersea vessels and it remained a troublesome problem. Anderson also discussed gunnery fire-control methods, spotting, doctrine and camouflage paint, and visited the bases at Gibraltar, Alexandria, Haifa and Malta. Despite the Admiralty's rejection of the idea of closer, open relations, Anderson was much impressed by his special treatment and the information and insights afforded him. His report to the DNI included information on valuable and open talks with senior British officers on a variety of topics. Overall, his assessment was that

In general it can be said that the trip was highly satisfactory. The Naval Attaché received every possible courtesy and consideration. He feels his knowledge of the British Navy has been definitely increased by the enlarged circle of contacts and the numerous visits to British ships resulting from this trip. It is suggested that a similar visit to the British Mediterranean Fleet and Bases, including at least Gibraltar and Malta, could with advantage be made by each Naval Attaché accredited to London, say, after he had been at this post in London for about a year to establish acquaintances which would be of value to him on such a trip … It is proper to state that the British had their necessary reserve with regard to what was shown, just as we have. For example, at Gibraltar the vessels went out for a 'Queen Bee' firing which the N.A. had no opportunity of witnessing. It is a fact, however, that the N.A. was on various occasions shown particular items which our Regulations do not permit to be shown to foreigners or others than individuals in our military service.[80]

Anderson's criticism of the level of access given his British counterparts in Washington certainly applied to the Admiralty's attempts to acquire information on US carrier operations.

In mid-1936, in the midst of the Ethiopian crisis, in the aftermath of the 1935 Anglo-German Naval Agreement, and with Anglo-Soviet naval discussions ongoing, the First Sea Lord, Admiral A. Ernle M. Chatfield, began to push for great improvements to the Royal Navy's Fleet Air Arm (FAA).[81] To help in the fight to strengthen the FAA, the Royal Navy attempted to obtain as much information as it could from the US Navy on its carrier operations, particularly on technical items such as aircraft design, arresting gear and catapults.[82] As a first step, then, and as a *quid pro quo* for the openness shown to Captain Anderson, the Admiralty directed the Naval Attaché and his staff in Washington to ask for admittance to the US vessels. How this initiative was dealt with was representative of the ongoing exchange between the Royal Navy and US Navy of technical information on battleships, cruisers, destroyers and submarines, as well as naval bases and support facilities, that grew in size and scope from 1936 until September 1939, after which it expanded even more rapidly.

Captain Anderson and his staff in London had been very careful to avoid touring on British carriers specifically, in order to be able to avoid setting a precedent for reciprocity.[83] However, the previous visits by Captain Bristol had to be acknowledged by the US Navy. The CNO, Admiral William H. Standley, knew that US naval personnel in London had visited the British carriers, and therefore did not hesitate to allow Captain Bradley to visit two older carriers, the *Lexington* and *Saratoga*, a privilege not extended to any other nation's Naval Attaché. While the British Naval Attachés were being given preferential treatment, they were still not allowed on board the new *Ranger* or any other US carrier. Even on the old carriers, 'The chief of the Bureau of Aeronautics has no objection to such an inspection provided details of arresting gear are not shown and no information be given as to time factors involved in getting off and taking on planes.'[84] The DNI, Puleston, contacted Anderson to fill him in on the special treatment being given to the British and what they were being allowed to see. He instructed the Attaché:

> In general, it is the policy of the Navy Department not to authorize visits of foreigners to aircraft carriers. Special circumstances may arise however where it appears advantageous to make a particular exception in the case of the older carriers, but no exceptions whatever will be made in the case of new carriers, including the RANGER.[85]

Puleston told Anderson that, therefore, it would be a good idea not to encourage any attempt by the Admiralty to get him aboard a British carrier. However, this attitude would change quite dramatically over the next two and a half years, especially after the Japanese invasion of China in July 1937 and Hitler's aggressive moves in Europe in 1938. But, in the meantime, other attempts were made to garner information about the performance of American carriers.

Captain Bradley did indeed visit the *Saratoga* in 1936 and again in 1937, but he was not the only British naval officer to 'pump' the Americans for information on carrier operations.[86] In February 1938, Group Captain G.C. Pirie, the British Air Attaché, paid a visit to the *Lexington*. He compared notes with the Americans, commenting particularly on the larger complement of aircraft on the US carriers. Pirie told the Americans that British carriers operated with their aircraft on the hanger deck due to the more severe weather conditions under which they operated. The Americans could keep their aircraft on deck because of the relative calm of the Pacific, their main theatre of operations.[87] Admiralty attempts to unearth insights into planned US carrier operations in the Pacific continued with the visit of Captain Lord Louis Mountbatten (RN) to the US Air Station in Pensacola in May. Mountbatten told his hosts that British torpedo planes were considered to be a very valuable tactical asset, and was quite open in the information that he provided his host about the Royal Navy's utilization of such aircraft:

> He stated that the British had an extremely satisfactory torpedo but had been generally unsuccessful in coordinating attack with surface light forces. He thought that torpedo planes were very vulnerable during attack and doubted the value of smoke in masking attack … The Captain said that British were taking steps to increase the number of planes on board their carriers. He further stated that we change personnel of carrier squadrons much oftener than in British practice and that our squadrons do not spend so much time embarked. He wondered if our carrier squadrons could be considered ready for war according to European standards.[88]

Immediately following Mountbatten's visit, Commander John Caspar (RN), a member of the British Air Mission touring the United States under Lord Weir, also visited Pensacola. He, too, was most interested in naval aviation, especially in American training and operational procedures. Caspar continued to question the Americans along the same lines as had Mountbatten. How could the Americans think that they were ready to fight a war in the Pacific when so much of their training and time was spent on shore, especially when compared to the British system? Caspar was also very free in his discussions of the operations of the new British carrier, the *Ark Royal*. According to Caspar, the new carrier contained no catapults and had arresting gear and a barrier, a new departure for British carrier operations.[89]

These types of visit and exchange of technical and operational data, as well as the increased fear of Japanese and German aggression, paid off for the British. By the summer of 1939, Admiral D. Leahy, the CNO, was allowing

British naval officers full access to formerly secret carrier operation information. In July, Captain R.M. Ellis (RN) was allowed to spend time in the carrier gear section of the Bureau of Aeronautics, going through plans and talking to experts.[90] This gear, improved by the US Navy's years of experimentation on the *Ranger*, was a vital part of US carrier operations, especially with regard to the speed with which landing aircraft could be captured and then stowed, making way for the next plane to land. After his time in the Bureau, Ellis believed that he needed a demonstration, in order to monitor flight operations and the arresting gear on the *Saratoga*. The American response underlined the high level of Anglo-American cooperation. Leahy instructed the C.-in-C. US Fleet that:

> He [Ellis] believes that a two day demonstration of actual flying on and off the SARATOGA will be all that he needs and that one or two days inspecting the gear and its plan, while SARATOGA is at anchor during the following week, will be sufficient. Whether the above days of actual demonstration and of inspection of the gear prove sufficient will, of course, depend on the facility with which he learns. As stated in paragraph 4 of reference (a), he is at liberty to witness flight operations and to inspect the gear until satisfied.[91]

The years of informal cooperation and information sharing by the various Naval Attachés and their respective navies had paid off. By the summer of 1939, Anglo-American naval cooperation was a reality. But, more importantly for Anglo-American relations as a whole, this type of sub-official liaison and cooperation had also been encouraged in other areas.

In China, Nelson T. Johnson had had some trouble adjusting to the departure of Lampson. Lampson's replacement, Sir Alexander Cadogan, and his councillor, R.G. Howe, had not immediately established the same intimate relations with the resident Americans as their predecessors had. Instead, Johnson thought that the British Embassy (the American and British missions were given embassy status in 1936) was not as communicative as it had once been. Part of the reason for this was the lack of knowledge and experience the two new British officials had of China. This was also due 'partly to the fact that they were both fresh from Europe where the relations between our several representatives are perhaps not as informal and cordial as they were here under the Lampson regime'.[92] Johnson felt that Cadogan, while always showing the Americans the files or documents requested, never ventured to give out such information on his own. While confidential information still continued to pass between the two embassies and there was not a rift between them, the free and open atmosphere that had been a hallmark of Anglo-American relations in China at that level were strained. Johnson looked forward to a new British representative arriving in late 1936 to replace Cadogan, who had been called back for bigger and better things in the Foreign Office.[93] For his part, Cadogan thought Johnson a very interesting and pleasant person, with whom he attempted to coordinate matters as much as possible.[94] On the other hand, in London, relations between Ambassador Bingham and his chief liaison with the British, Ray Atherton, had continued to improve. The Second London Naval Treaty talks and ongoing naval and Far Eastern matters were topics about which the Foreign Office, usually through Sir Robert Craigie, had no trouble talking openly and confidentially to the Americans.[95] Now, with the spirit of trust and cooperation created by those talks (as well as the increasing importance of the United States in the global balance of power that was being challenged by Germany, Italy and Japan), when the US Army approached Sir Ronald Lindsay, the British Ambassador in Washington, about information sharing, the response was rather different than that given to Captain Anderson just six months earlier.

In October of 1936, the US War Department initiated informal conversations with Lindsay and his Military Attaché, Colonel W.W.T. Torr, about the possibility of exchanging material on mechanization and other technical subjects, including the newest information on the latest models of tanks.[96] This was not entirely a new initiative. Lindsay had acted as an unofficial link between the War Department and the British War Office for some time, sending a good deal of information to the Director of Military Operations and Intelligence (MI2) over the preceding months.[97] The Americans were now pushing harder to see whether the British would be willing to begin a large-scale exchange, particularly on information concerning industrial mobilization.[98] Once again, the question of 'what if Japan found out' came up in the debate as to whether such an exchange was warranted. This time, however, the Foreign Office had no hesitation about proposing to the War Office that the American offer should under no circumstances be rebuffed. Troutbeck, Craigie and Vansittart, all were animated in their desire to see such cooperation take place. Gone were fears of leaks to the Japanese or the dangers of being left 'holding the baby'. Instead, Vansittart wrote to the to Chief of the Imperial General Staff (CIGS), Field Marshal Sir Cyril J. Deverell himself, emphasizing the political importance the Foreign Office placed on accepting the American advances.[99] Vansittart's friend, Lindsay, had himself petitioned the Permanent Under-Secretary to ignore any reservations from Colonel Torr about the Americans not having much to trade or leaking material to other countries, and to press the War Office to agree to cooperate.[100] It was the Ambassador's belief that, 'By and large, if Anglo-American cooperation is important, as I believe it is, the most promising way to get the most of it is to foster it carefully in all those fields where Congress does not have direct control. Cooperation between Government Departments is one of the most important of those fields.'[101] Anthony Eden lent his hand to the effort to ensure that greater Anglo-American cooperation became a reality by lobbying both the Secretary of State for War, A. Duff Cooper, and the Chancellor of the Exchequer, Neville Chamberlain, to support the American offer.[102] The Foreign Office's efforts were rewarded in late November 1936, when the Minister for the Coordination of Defence, Sir Thomas Inskip, informed Eden that the War Office had agreed to go ahead with the exchange. In fact, the CIGS had no misgivings or doubts about the validity of such an endeavour and had in fact already initiated 'action to meet the United States' views in the more strictly military matters'.[103] The final details of the actual information sharing needed to be worked out and put into effect, but the important decision had taken place. Both sides had shown themselves willing to be forthcoming and open about cooperating at the departmental level, an act, as Lindsay had pointed out, that was sure to make for better overall relations.[104]

Those relations became even closer after the Japanese attack on China in July 1937. During that crisis, British naval forces on the Yangtze River earned the respect and admiration of many US diplomats, naval officers and civilians. Both Ambassador Johnson and Admiral Harry E. Yarnell, C.-in-C. Asiatic Fleet, worked very closely with the British Ambassador, Sir Hughe Montgomery Knatchbull-Hugessen, and Admiral Sir Charles J.C. Little, C.-in-C. China Squadron, during and after the emergency. When Sir Hughe was shot by strafing Japanese aircraft, it was a US marine who supplied the blood for a transfusion. For his part, Yarnell was very impressed with the response of the HMS *Cumberland* in assisting the American merchant ship *Herbert Hoover*, when the latter was bombed.[105] As the crisis continued, Yarnell and Little shared information and ideas about their own plans and their nations' attitude towards the Japanese. According to Yarnell, the two worked 'like two kittens in a basket'. He thought the British Admiral was a fine officer, of rare good judgement, and delightful personality: 'There is about the British naval officer an aura of solidity and reliability which is a great comfort to those who are associated with them in times of stress.'[106] That respect was returned by Little in his views of Yarnell.[107] Because of his close association with senior British naval commanders, Yarnell continuously prodded both the Navy Department and the State Department to work closely with the British in the Far East. It was his belief that

> With reference to our own policy, it is my firm conviction that we should stick with England and France. It is inconceivable to me that we as a nation are going to give up our rights of trading or living in China and confine our activities to our own continental limits. As for pulling chestnuts out of the fire, England stands to pull just as many out for us as we do for her. If these three countries stand together they can dominate the situation in the Far East. If they do not, they will be defeated singly and in detail.[108]

Yarnell was aware of the need to be careful in dealing with the British, in order to avoid provoking State Department officials, some of whom still were worried about being trapped into 'pulling Britain's chestnuts out of the fire'.

Embarrassing his political masters would not help his position. But Yarnell did not hesitate to give Admiral Little his views on the need for continued closer RN–USN relations as the latter was leaving his post. Yarnell's motivation was obviously the hope that such a clear declaration of friendship and cooperation would be passed on to other senior Royal Navy officers in positions of authority back in London. The C.-in-C. Asiatic told Little that the cordial relations that had existed between the two fleets were one of the most pleasant features of his cruise.[109] The CNO, Admiral Leahy, was also advised of Yarnell's views of Little.[110]

Out of the fires of the undeclared war in China came closer and better Anglo-American naval relations, based on shared dangers and a mutual hatred of Japanese actions and policies. Leahy's own attitude about whether or not he thought there was close cooperation with the British against Japan was revealed in February 1938, during questioning by the Congressional Naval Committee. The CNO, under oath, intimated the same view that he had earlier in the month disclosed to William Castle: that there was an understanding between the Royal Navy and US Navy; that each would have its special duties in case of war. Secretary of State Cordell Hull and Roosevelt were forced to limit the damage such an intimacy might do in the hands of isolationists and denied such a relationship, even though the truth of the matter was not acknowledged.[111] The two navies now began to share even more information about their building programmes, as well as information about and opinions on Japanese ship-building and modernization.[112] Because of the inextricable link between naval and foreign policies, that cooperative spirit also spilled over into the strategic and political realms, working to soften attitudes that had previously been hardened against Anglo-American cooperation in the Far East. The process was, however, a difficult one.

In November 1937, after an hour-long discussion with Secretary Hull, the CNO, Admiral William D. Leahy, had a completely informal unofficial talk with the British Naval Attaché, Captain Bradley, about the possibility of a joint naval demonstration in Asiatic waters.[113] The idea of naval planning discussions never materialized, but the simple act of thinking about such a project created tensions on both sides of the Atlantic.[114] Both the State Department and the Foreign Office were frightened of revealing too much, for fear of allowing the other side a glimpse of their own sensitive code-breaking abilities.[115] Progress was being made, however, in the area of the informal exchange of sensitive information between the two groups. For example, Sir Alexander Cadogan, who took over as PUS from Vansittart on 1 January 1938, was authorizing the release of secret Foreign Office papers and reports on Britain's assessment of Japan's southward expansion to the US Embassy in London. This was thought necessary in order both to gain the trust of the State Department and to educate that institution about the British view of the Far Eastern situation.[116] Cordell Hull was also doing his own informal feeling out of the British. In January 1938, the Secretary of State had a long and confidential chat with Lindsay on Anglo-

American relations and the Far Eastern situation. As both sides were unwilling to allow the public to see the drawing together of the two nations in opposition to Japan, such unofficial methods became the normal substitute for regular diplomatic channels.[117] The same was true in Japan, where both embassies worked together to oppose Japanese actions, bringing their respective staffs into even closer proximity.[118] In fact, the new British Ambassador, Sir Robert Craigie, had a long history of working with the Americans, from his time as Britain's chief naval negotiator. The US Embassy had a useful agent of its own, in the form of Counsellor Eugene Dooman, a man whose career had paralleled Craigie's closely, the pair moving from naval conference to naval conference from 1927 to 1936. Craigie and Dooman's knowledge of one another certainly did not hurt the ability of the two embassies to communicate with one another easily and confidentially, even if they held very different views of how best to deal with Japan.

Ease of communication at the informal level took great steps in 1938 and 1939, especially in the areas of sharing information and code breaking. The flow of material from the United States to the IIC allowed that body to make some very detailed examinations of the United States' war-making potential.[119] As for the Americans, their Naval Attaché accompanied the Royal Navy on exercises in the North Sea, observing anti-submarine operations.[120] The US Naval Attaché in Japan was also doing his bit to further better Anglo-American relations, sharing with his British opposite number information on the two new, and very large, battleships the Japanese were building. The Foreign Office was most careful to ensure that no questioning of the Japanese about the two vessels would lead to their intelligence source being compromised.[121] In March 1938, the Foreign Office and the Admiralty, in a highly confidential manner, let the US Chargé d'Affaires, Herschel Johnson, 'know' that they were able to read some of the Japanese diplomatic codes.[122] A year earlier, the War Office had told the US Military Attaché in London that the American consular messages were being tapped by the Japanese.[123] The Americans repaid the favour in March 1938, by letting the British embassy in Washington know that the Japanese were reading Great Britain's diplomatic codes in the Far East. While the accuracy of the information was in question, there was no doubt that the Americans were repaying the British for their confidence of a year earlier. The American information confirmed something the Foreign Office had suspected for some time: that the Japanese could read the 'R' cyphers used in diplomatic communications. An exchange of secret code-breaking information had been established, and another measure of confidence building established in the Anglo-American strategic relationship.[124] Such a willingness to allow an intimacy of this sort signalled that a solid, stable relationship had been developed between the two nations with regard to strategic planning for the Far East. Further evidence of the closeness of that relationship came about in 1939, as the British tried to re-establish naval conversations with the Americans.

In March of that year, the Secretary of State for Foreign Affairs, Lord Halifax, instructed Lindsay to inquire if the United States Government was willing to resume an exchange of naval views in a continuation of Captain Ingersoll's mission.[125] Halifax was anxious to have the Americans understand clearly that His Majesty's government, with its involvement in any conflict in Europe, 'might not be able at once to reinforce on a large scale their naval forces in the Far East, and that might affect US naval dispositions'.[126] Two days later, Lindsay reported that Under-Secretary of State Sumner Welles had made a secret visit to the British embassy to give him President Roosevelt's reply. The President was indeed anxious to have the talks resumed, but the open procedure used i n 1938 could not be repeated. Fears of the press finding out about Anglo-American naval cooperation demanded that the utmost secrecy had to be maintained. If word of such talks got out, the leak would compromise seriously the pending neutrality legislation. Roosevelt suggested that an officer ranking not higher than Captain be sent as the Naval Attaché to Washington to conduct the conversations along the lines of talks the President had witnessed between the Royal Navy and US Navy in 1915.[127]

Roosevelt's quick agreement to talks had caught the Admiralty and Foreign Office by surprise. Neither department had any solid plan for how such talks were to be conducted, as the initial query had been made as an almost reflexive action by Sir Alexander Cadogan, when asked about the idea by Halifax.[128] The Naval Attaché position had been filled just six months previously, so any change would engender immediate suspicion from the press, as well as amongst foreign observers. Lindsay told Welles of this concern, but to no avail. Lindsay then suggested that the Admiralty consider sending an officer with no connection to the embassy, to live in another nearby town, communicating with the Americans through the embassy, while the present Naval Attaché, Captain L.C.A. Curzon-Howe, was recalled temporarily to London on the pretence of taking leave.[129] No action was taken on the matter for a month, however, while the Admiralty tried to establish what the object of such talks would be, and then to find a suitable method for conducting the talks.[130] Also, President Roosevelt's agreeing to send the US Fleet ahead of schedule back to the Pacific after exercises in the Atlantic, as a warning to Japan, had raised questions as to whether such talks were necessary.[131] Lord Chatfield, now Minister for the Coordination of Defence, considered the American decision to move the Fleet back to the Pacific a clear and very welcome warning to the Japanese. His opinion was that now, after such a signal had been given, there was a need to discuss two areas concerning that American action: a precautionary deployment of the US Fleet to Hawaii; and what to do in case of an actual war. Chatfield was willing to abide by the instructions Welles had given to Lindsay, as well as by the suggestions made by the Ambassador on how such talks could be arranged. The point of greatest concern to Chatfield was, however, that 'as it was we who are most anxious for these conversations, we should make every effort to be accommodating. If we did not and simply raised objections the Americans might say that perhaps it would be better not to hold conversations just now.'[132] While the debate continued in London, Lindsay, impatient and annoyed that Roosevelt's initiative had been ignored for so long, demanded, on 2 May, to know why nothing was being done on such an important matter.[133] Three days later, the Admiralty and Foreign Office finally instructed Sir Ronald to tell Welles that they were most willing to establish talks, but that the method of removing the Naval Attaché and replacing him with another was not sound. Instead, they were willing to abide by Lindsay's plan or to wait until June, when a vacant post might be filled at the US Embassy in London by a new Naval Attaché capable of continuing the 1938 discussions.[134] Lindsay was to sound out the Americans on which method they preferred and then get the ball rolling to establish talks.

On 8 May, Lindsay told Welles of the above, and Welles in turn informed the British Ambassador that the Americans did not wish to hold the talks in London. To ensure the secrecy of the talks only three or four officers in the USN were allowed to know what was happening. The need to communicate from London would widen the circle of US Navy officers who would know about the talks and the danger of a leak would be increased considerably. Such a leak would be fatal to the development of Anglo-American naval cooperation, said Welles. Lindsay then proposed that a

> Competent officer should come from the Admiralty if necessary under false name. Plausible pretext for the journey should be provided, e.g., he might appear as official of some shipping company or as an officer sent to inspect munitions on order here for His Majesty's Government. His papers should be sent separately by bag to New York but on the same ship as himself. His headquarters in America might shift, sometimes in Baltimore. No objection to a night or two in Washington. He could safely use the telephone for communicating with Naval Attaché about appointments etc. Actual conversations would take place in private house of American naval officer. His papers might have to be kept in the Embassy or by the Naval Attaché. … my Naval Attaché should return to London for a short visit … that it might be useful for him to have a spell in the plans division so as to be able to continue conversations later.[135]

The Under-Secretary of State agreed with the plan, as did President Roosevelt. The President did not want the British officer to travel under a false name, however, but did suggest that the visit of the British cruiser *Exeter* to Baltimore on 7 June might be a useful screen.

On 22 May, the Foreign Office informed Lindsay that Commander T.C. Hampton would travel to the United States in early June as Mr Hampton, a land agent going to the United States on business. It was expected that the talks would begin after the Royal visit to the United States was complete, around 11 June, and that the discussions would be done by 21 June at the latest.[136] The maintenance of absolute secrecy was of the utmost importance to both Americans and British, as arrangements for the talks were to be made directly with Admiral Leahy, and the US Director of Naval Intelligence was not to be informed of the visit.[137] Hampton's instructions from the Admiralty were straightforward and wide-ranging. He was to explain to the Americans how the changing situation in Europe was affecting Britain's ability to send a major Fleet to the Far East, if Japan decided to take advantage of a war in Europe. Under no circumstances was he to propose an initiative for a combined strategy. That sort of proposal had to come from the Americans. If the US authorities did ask about the possibility of naval cooperation aimed at Japan, he was to inform them that British policy-makers preferred that the Americans concentrate their naval forces in the Pacific. Singapore would be made available for their use, if it was required, and Great Britain would also welcome any assistance the US Navy could give to putting cruiser forces in the Western Atlantic.[138] Hampton began his talks with US naval officers on 12 June.

The talks took place at Admiral Leahy's home, with Leahy, Admiral R.L. Ghormley (Director of Plans), Captain Curzon-Howe and Hampton. No one else, except Welles and Roosevelt, knew anything about the talks. Hampton told the Americans that if Japan took aggressive action in the Far East, the Admiralty did not know when they would be able to send a fleet to the Far East, nor what the composition of such a fleet would be. This was a change from the talks held with Captain Ingersoll in 1938. Leahy told Hampton that it was his opinion that if a war broke out in Europe, it was the President's intention to move the US Fleet to Hawaii as a deterrent to Japan. That action would prevent the Japanese from attacking New Zealand and Australia, said the CNO, but he agreed that the US Navy was not in a position to conduct offensive operations against Japan itself. Questions about the distribution of signal books and cyphers were also brought up at this first meeting.[139] On 14 June a second meeting was held, with the same participants. This time Leahy and Ghormley told Hampton that they were satisfied that the exchange of signal books and cyphers that had taken place would 'enable all US units to cooperate with British units throughout the world in case of necessity. Some further copies of signal books, codes and cyphers would be required as and when US ships in reserve were brought forward.'[140] Leahy then went on to explain his 'personal views' of how the two fleets sould cooperate in case of a war with Germany, Italy and Japan. The United States would concentrate on the Pacific and leave forces in the Atlantic as well. The US Fleet would move to Singapore in sufficient force to defeat the Japanese Fleet, a force that would consist of at least ten capital ships. The CNO was opposed to sending any weak or small force to Singapore. The size of the US Fleet despatched, however, would depend on the size of fleet that the British were willing to send. American public opinion would not tolerate such actions by the US Navy unless there was a suitable British force in the region as well. That British force did not have to be as large, but it had to be an 'adequate token force' containing some capital ships. Ghormley told the British representatives that the US Plans Division was now working on a scheme for the movement of a US Fleet to Singapore, as no such detailed plans had existed previously. As for the time needed to collect and transit such a fleet, Leahy informed Hampton that if the British planned on the Americans relieving Singapore, it would take at least 120 days. The CNO also suggested that any British units working with the Americans in the Far East should be placed under the strategic control of the US Commander-in-Chief, but did not press the point. Hampton told the American naval officers all he knew about the condition of Singapore in terms of docking and repair facilities, hinting that if the Americans based their fleet there approximately 2,500 semi-skilled and skilled personnel and labourers would be required. In return, Hampton was informed that the US Navy expected to fight for the Philippines but not hold them, and therefore, would not base their Fleet in the islands.[141] The talks ended quickly and quietly, as Hampton returned to the Admiralty to relay his findings.

Hampton reported that, overall, he thought that President Roosevelt was far ahead of the public in his desire to assist Great Britain and the other democracies. Admiral Leahy was also thought to be 'extremely pro-British' and was in close and intimate communication with the President. Leahy's being relieved in the near future by Admiral Harold R. Stark as CNO was not seen as an event which would create any change in the Anglo-American relationship, as he also was felt to be pro-British. While the US Navy had no detailed plans for cooperating with the Royal Navy, Hampton's opinion was that there was a fundamental agreement between the US Navy and the Deputy Chief of Naval Staff on the broad conduct of a war at sea.[142] Thus, by the summer of 1939, American and British strategic planners had managed to create an atmosphere of close and friendly exchanges on sensitive information which allowed each to more confidently judge any future actions of the other in the Far East.

While the informal avenues of information sharing in the Anglo-American strategic relationship still contained sensitive areas and some suspicions, a dramatic improvement at all levels had taken place from 1933 to 1939.[143] Both the Royal Navy and the US Navy had moved forward in their ability to share technical and strategic information. As well, the diplomatic machinery of the policy-making process had established a rapport that also allowed for important information on the Far East to be shared in an unprecedented fashion. Such openness had allowed each nation to paint a better mental map of the other's Far Eastern policy and to anticipate how the other would react under certain conditions.[144] At the war-planning level, mobilization techniques and plans had been exchanged, allowing both the United States and Great Britain each a better understanding of how the other would react to a war in the Far East.[145] The net result was that, through a multitude of channels, a system of informal and discreet cooperation on various issues had been established to help coordinate the Far Eastern policies of the United States and the British Empire.[146] By the end of 1939, the cooperation of the two nations in Far Eastern matters, while still tempered by the need to protect national interests, was very close. A parallel but not joint policy was indeed a reality.

That parallel but not joint attitude was also assisted in its development through certain common visions and perceptions held about the condition of the balance of power in the Far East. One of the most important areas of informal agreement for the strategic foreign-policy-making elites of both nations was their shared evaluation of the position and worth of the Soviet Union in that balancing equation. Both nations shared information about the Soviet Union, but, more importantly, came to their own separate conclusions that the Soviet bear was an important part of the overall picture forming in the Far East. Therefore, the manner in which the United States and Great Britain approached the Soviet aspect of the Far Eastern Crisis created a further common basis of assessing developments in that region. Most importantly, because the views of the Soviet Union were shared at the informal level, a sense of common values and approaches was also added to through that experience. In a sense, having to deal with the Soviet Union's role in any Far Eastern matters forced the British and Americans to come to the realization that their positions were similar in more ways than they might have thought originally in 1932.

## NOTES

1. Nicholas Tarling, *Britain, Southeast Asia and the Onset of the Pacific War* (Cambridge, 1996), 18; Richard J. Aldrich, *The Key to the South: Britain, the United States, and Thailand during the Approach of the Pacific War, 1929–1942* (Oxford, 1993), 192; Borg, *The United States and the Far Eastern Crisis of 1933–1938*, 497–9, 509, 512, 542; Roskill, *Naval Policy between the Wars*, Vol. II, 366–8, 460, 476.

2. Two very fine exceptions to that rule are Antony Best, *Britain, Japan and Pearl Harbor* (London, 1995); and Aldrich, *The Key to the South*. John Ferris, 'A British "Unofficial" Aviation Mission and Japanese Naval Developments, 1919–29', *JSS*, 5 (1982): 134–58; Ferris, 'From Briadway House to Bletchley Park: The Diary of Captain Malcolm Kennedy, 1934–46', *INS*, 4 (1989): 48–70; Thomas G. Mahnken, 'Gazing at the Sun: The Office of Naval Intelligence and Japanese Naval Innovation, 1918–1941', *INS*, 11 (1996): 424–41; Jeffery M. Dorwart, *Conflict of Duty: the US Navy's Intelligence Dilemma, 1919–1945* (Annapolis, MD, 1983); Malcolm Muir Jr, 'Rearming in a Vacuum: United States Naval Intelligence and the Japanese Capital Ship Threat, 1936–1945', *JMH*, 54 (1990): 24–36; Geoffrey Till, 'Perceptions of Naval Power Between the Wars: the British Case', in Philip Towle, ed., *Estimating Foreign Military Power* (New York, 1982).

3. See Strategic Planning in the US Navy: Its Evolution and Execution, 1891–1945, Navy Basic Plan–Orange, Vol. IV, on microfilm, National Archive, Washington, DC, Change No. 3, W.P.L. 16 July 1933; Millar, *War Plan Orange*; WO, PRO, London, 106/5136,

Imperial Defence College, Exercise No. 3, 1934; Robert J. Young, 'Spokesmen for Economic Warfare: The Industrial Intelligence Centre in the 1930s', *EHR*, 6 (1976): 473–89; Ian Cowman, 'Defence of the Malay Barrier? The Place of the Philippines in Admiralty Naval War Planning, 1925–1941', *WH*, 3 (1996): 398–417.

4. A very enlightening explanation of how this system worked is given in Sir Victor Wellesley, *Diplomacy in Fetters* (London, 1944), 7–42.

5. Nelson T. Johnson Papers (hereafter NTJ Papers), Library of Congress, Washington, DC, Container 7, letter from Johnson to Sir Harry Armstrong, British Consul-General in New York, 19 Jan. 1928; NTJ Papers, Container 17, Folder A–L, letter from Sir Miles Lampson to Johnson, 3 June 1932; NTJ Papers, Container 17, Folder A–L, letter from Johnson to Lampson, 18 July 1932; NTJ Papers, Container 19, Folder A–G, letter from Johnson to Grew (US Ambassador in Japan), 7 July 1933; Lampson Diaries [Lampson], Middle East Studies Centre, St Antony's College, Oxford, entries for 6, 10, 13, 28 Feb., 11 Mar., 17 May, all 1933.

6. NTJ Papers, Container 18, Folder M–Z, letter from Johnson to Dr Cloyd H. Marvin, President of George Washington University, 19 May 1932.

7. NTJ Papers, Container 18, Folder M–Z, letter from Johnson to Dr Marvin, 18 Aug. 1932.

8. Louis, *British Strategy in the Far East*, 199–201; Trotter, *Britain and East Asia*, 1–22; Nish, *Anglo-Japanese Alienation*, ch. 2.

9. NTJ Papers, strictly confidential record of conversation between Dr G.H. Blakeslee and Johnson, 13 June 1932.

10. The Chinese were also quick to try to play the Americans off against the British, trading secrets for support. For Johnson's intimate knowledge of the complete workings of the Commission, see NTJ Papers, Container 17, Folder A–L, letters from Johnson to Stanley K. Hornbeck, 16 and 30 Aug., 1932; ibid., confidential letter from Johnson to Hornbeck, 13 Sept. 1932; NTJ Papers, Container 18, Folder M–Z, letter from Robert E. Olds to Johnson, 6 July 1932.

11. NTJ Papers, strictly confidential record of conversation between Dr G.H. Blakeslee and Johnson, 13 June 1932.

12. FO 371/16618/A5619/5619/45, confidential despatch from Snow to FO, 1 July 1933.

13. FO 371/16618/A7537/5819/45, despatch from Snow to FO, 15 Sept. 1933 and minutes.

14. Clive described Grew as a 'diplomatist by profession and a man of tact and charm'. FO 371/18169/F5975/57/23, despatch from Clive to FO, 11 Sept. 1934.

15. NTJ Papers, Container 21, Folder O–Z, letters from Johnson to Upham, 8 Aug. and 30 Oct. 1933; Admiralty (ADM), PRO, Kew, 116/2953, China Station Proceedings, letter No. 4, 10 July, and letter No. 5, 8 Aug., both 1933; FO 371/18175/F507/233/23, from ADM, 'Visit of Commander-in-Chief, China to Japan', and FO minutes, 26 Jan. 1934; FO 371/18175/F5028/233/23, from Admiral Dickens to Charles Orde (Head of Far Eastern Department), 'Proposed Visits to Japanese Ports, Autumn, 1934', 22 May 1934; Chatfield Papers (CHT), National Maritime Museum, Greenwich, /4/4, Dreyer to Chatfield, 19 Aug. 1933; ibid., Dreyer to Chatfield, 22 Oct. 1934; Lampson Diary, entry for 5 June 1933.

16. NTJ Papers, Container 19, Folder A–G, letter from Johnson to Grew, 7 July 1933; NTJ Papers, Container 21, Folder O–Z, memo for Secretary of State, Cordell Hull, 12 June 1933; Sir Alexander George Montagu Cadogan Diaries [CAD], 1933–37, Churchill College Archive Centre, Cambridge, entries for 2 and 4 Oct. 1934; Lampson Diary, entry for 8 and 9 June 1933.

17. Admiral M.M. Taylor, Upham's predecessor, had been on very good terms with his British opposite number, Admiral Kelly. On the eve of Kelly's departure as C.-in-C. China Squadron, Taylor reported to his Chief of Naval Operations, Admiral W.V. Pratt,

that 'I'll be sorry to see him go. We have gotten quite close and talk quite freely about our common troubles'. Admiral Montgomery M. Taylor MSS, Library of Congress, Washington, DC, Container 2, Folder Jan.–Feb. 1933, letter from Taylor to Pratt, 28 Jan. 1933.

18. Franklin D. Roosevelt Official Files (hereafter FDR-OF) [Presidential Library, Hyde Park, New York], Navy, Folder: Adm. William D. Leahy, letter from Assistant Secretary of the Navy, H.L. Roosevelt to Marvin H. McIntyre, Assistant Secretary to the President, 16 Mar. 1934. Enclosed were letters from Dreyer to Upham, 13 Jan. 1934 and from Upham to Admiral William H. Standley (USN), Chief of Naval Operation (CNO), 4 Feb. 1934.

19. FDR-OF, Navy, Folder: Adm. William D. Leahy, letter from Dreyer to Upham, 13 Jan. 1934.

20. Ibid.

21. Ibid., letter from Upham to Standley, 4 Feb. 1934.

22. Ibid.

23. Vice Admiral Charles Wellborn transcript, Nimitz Library, United States Naval Academy, Annapolis, Oral History, 48: ADM 116/2952, China Station, Reports and Proceedings of C.-in-C., 1 Apr. 1933; ADM 116/2993, China Stations Proceedings, Letter No. 13, 9 Apr. 1934.

24. RG 38, Office of the Chief of Naval Operations, Division of Naval Intelligence, General Correspondence, 1929–42 (hereafter RG 38, CNO-DNI-GC), Box 15, Folder A2-14/EF/EN3-11, Vol. 4, letter from Ellis to Commandant, Third Naval District, 18 July 1933.

25. Admiral Drax was another important RN senior officer who supported strong Anglo-American relations, Drax Papers [DRAX], Churchill College Archive Centre, Cambridge, 2/4, US, letter from Drax to Hankey, 12 Nov. 1933; ibid., Drax to Winslow, 29 Feb. 1933.

26. Bristol thought Britain was being forced into a position of opposition against Japan in the Far East, a circumstance the British disliked and distrusted. See RG 38, Office of the CNO, Correspondence of the London Naval Attaché, 1927–40 (hereafter CNO-LNA, 1927–40), National Archive, Washington, DC, Box 7, Folder: Office of Naval Intelligence, US Navy Dept., letter from Bristol to Ellis, 21 Feb. 1933.

27. RG 38, CNO-DNI-GC, Box 58, Folder A2-14/EN3-11(X), letter from Bristol to Ellis, 1 May 1933.

28. RG 38, CNO-DNI-GC, Box 58, Folder A2-14/EN3-11(X), letter from Bristol to Ellis, 1 Aug. 1933.

29. RG 38, CNO-DNI-GC, Box 58, Folder A2-14/EN3-11(X), letter from DNI to Bristol, 11 Aug. 1933.

30. RG 38, CNO-DNI-GC, Box 58, Folder A2-14/EN3-11(X), memo from DNI to Commander Battle Force, 27 Dec. 1933.

31. Ibid.

32. Ibid.

33. John C. Niedermair (naval architect) transcipt, Nimitz Library, United States Naval Academy, Annapolis, 140.

34. The good relations between the British embassy's naval representatives and the DNI even managed to weather a minor incident when a retired British naval officer, Hugh Wake, gained entrance to certain US naval facilities under false pretenses. Mr Wake, who it turned out held a subordinate position in the British Consulate in New York, was in desperate financial straits and living with his wife and family in a old chauffeur's lodge on an estate on Long Island. He gained entry to naval ships, establishments and concerns manufacturing for the USN in New York and Philadelphia by representing

himself as a British naval officer. His exploits were seen as being acts of desperation, done for British Admiralty Intelligence in return for money. See RG 38, CNO-DNI-GC, Box 17, Folder A2-14/EF13/OQ, Vol. III, confidential letter from DNI to Commandant, Third Naval District, 19 June 1933; ibid., confidential letter from DNI to Commandant, First Naval District, 14 Aug. 1933.

35. This tour would follow one made by the British Assistant Naval Attaché, Commander J.S. Orr (RN) in early 1933. See RG 38, CNO-DNI-GC, Box 15, Folder A2-14/EF/EN3-11, Vol. III, confidential letter from Orr to Ellis, 15 Feb. 1933.

36. Dewar's list of things to see included: the Naval Operating Base, Fleet Aircraft Base, Naval Training Station and Destroyer Base, all in San Diego; the Fleet Base and Fleet in San Pedro; Mare Island Navy Yard in San Francisco; Bethlehem Shipbuilding Corp. at Hunter's Point; the Naval Operating Base and Naval Air Station at Pearl Harbor; the Bremerton Navy Yard and the Naval Air Station at Puget Sound; the Great Lakes Training Station and Naval Reserve Aviation Squadron in Chicago; and the Ford Assembly Plant and General Motors Laboratory in Detroit. RG 38, CNO-DNI-GC, Box 15, Folder A2-14/EF/EN3-11, Vol. IV, letter from Dewar to Ellis, 21 Nov. 1933.

37. RG 38, CNO-DNI-GC, Box 15, Folder A2-14/EF/EN3-11, Vol. IV, note on file covering slip, 23 Nov. 1933. On US Attachés' exploits in Japan and the effect Japanese attitude towards US Naval Attachés had on Japanese access in the United States, see: RG 38, CNO-DNI-GC, Box 57, Folder A2-14/EN3-11(W), memo from Ellis to Chief Bu-Aero (Ernest J. King), Dec. 1933; ibid., letter from Capt. Fred Rogers, US Naval Attaché Tokyo to Ellis, 9 Feb. 1934.

38. RG 38, CNO-DNI-GC, Box 15, Folder A2-14/EF/EN3-11, Vol. IV, letter from Ellis to Dewar, 4 Dec. 1933.

39. RG 38, CNO-DNI-GC, Box 15, Folder A2-14/EF/EN3-11, Vol. IV, letter from Ellis to Rear Admiral D.F. Sellers, 17 Feb. 1934.

40. RG 38, CNO-DNI-GC, Box 15, Folder A2-14/EF/EN3-11, Vol. IV, letter from Ellis to Rear Admiral W.T. Tarrant, 17 Feb. 1934.

41. Dewar was not shown anything to do with the arresting gear or catapults at this time, nor anything of a confidential nature, but he did go through the stack and bridge structures, the flight deck, the main deck, officers' quarters, sick bay, the hanger deck, the main control room, one fireroom and the general machine shop. See RG 38, CNO-DNI-GC, Box 15, Folder A2-14/EF/EN3-11, Vol. IV, confidential letter from Commander R.K. Turner to DNI, 31 Mar. 1934.

42. RG 38, CNO-DNI-GC, Box 15, Folder A2-14/EF/EN3-11, Vol. IV, confidential letter from Commanding Officer, US Naval Air Station, San Diego to DNI, 27 Mar. 1934.

43. Ibid.

44. RG 38, CNO-DNI-GC, Box 15, Folder A2-14/EF/EN3-11, Vol. IV, confidential letter from Commandant Fourteenth Naval District, Navy Yard Pearl Harbor to DNI, undated; ibid., confidential letter from Commander E.D. Almy, Commandant's Office, Mare Island Navy Yard to DNI, 26 Apr. 1934; ibid., confidential letter from Capt. H.M. Cooley (USN), of Puget Sound Navy Yard to DNI, 7 May 1934.

45. RG 38, CNO-DNI-GC, Box 15, Folder A2-14/EF/EN3-11, various.

46. On one occasion, Commander Mark-Wardlaw toured the building ways at Mare Island, showing a particular interest in welding techniques. He informed his hosts that they were far in advance of Great Britain in that method of construction. The RN was experimenting with a combination of welding and rivetting in the construction of some of its new destroyers, where the first 100 feet of the those ships was being constructed almost entirely by welding. He also told the Americans that the Royal Navy was endeavouring to reduce weight in some of their latest ships, particularly destroyers, using a method which required thinner shell plating and framing of special alloy steel

that reduced the weight of the ship without necessarily sacrificing strength. After that exchange, the US Assistant Naval Attaché, Capt. H.S. Howard, was allowed to see an all-welded cargo ship under construction at Swan, Hunter and Wigham Richardson Limited at Wallsend-on-Tyne. See RG 38, CNO-DNI-GC, Box 15, Folder A2-14/EF/EN3-11, Vol. VI, confidential report from Commandant, Mare Island Navy Yard to DNI, 25 Apr. 1935; RG 38, CNO-DNI-GC, Box 58, Folder A2-14/EN3-11(X), letter from Anderson to Sir Oswyn Murray, 13 June 1935.

47. FO 371/18186/F2996/652/23, draft of secret telegram from Charles Orde (Head of Far Eastern Department of the FO) to Osborne (Chargé d'Affaires, Washington), 28 Aug. 1934.

48. RG 38, CNO-DNI-GC), Box 15, Folder A2-14/EF/EN3-11, Vol. V, report from Inspector of Naval Material, Schenectady, New York, to DNI, 29 June 1934; ibid., Vol. VI, letter from Mark-Wardlaw to Puleston, 18 Feb. 1935.

49. FO 371/18184/F546/546/23, letter from A. Fletcher (British Library of Information, New York) to R.A. Leeper (Head of News Department of the FO), 19 Jan. 1934.

50. Robert J. Young, 'Spokesmen for Economic Warfare'. The views of this group were circulated to the Admiralty, War Office, Air Ministry, Foreign Office, Department of Overseas Trade, Board of Trade, MI5 and other lesser departments.

51. FO 371/17590/A7943/428/45, IIC Report, 'Industrial Intelligence in the United States', 5 Oct. 1934.

52. See Chapter 5 below.

53. FO 371/17602/A10254/1938/45, letter from Dickens to Robert Craigie (Head of American Department in the FO), 14 Nov.,1934.

54. Ibid., copy of speech, delivered 19 Dec. 1934.

55. RG 38, CNO-LNA, 1927–40, Box 7, Folder: Office of Naval Intelligence, US Navy Dept., letter from Anderson to Puleston, 11 June 1934.

56. RG 38, CNO-DNI-GD, Box 58, Folder A2-14/EN3-11(X), letter from Anderson to Puleston, 21 Dec. 1935.

57. FDR, President's Personal File, 1933–45 (hereafter, FDR–PPF), Presidential Library, Hyde Park, New York, PPF file 716, Robert W. Bingham, letter from FDR to Bingham, 15 Dec. 1933.

58. FDR–PPF 716, Bingham, letters from FDR to Bingham, 11 June and 5 July 1935.

59. The RN's attitude to give all assistance to such projects was still in place in July 1939. A US Reserve Intelligence Major, George F. Eliot, had come to Britain to interview and write about European personalities connected with defence. The views of Liddell Hart had done great damage to how Americans perceived Britain's defence policy-makers, seeing them largely as fools. Eliot's mission was to correct that image in order to create a greater sympathy in the United States for Britain's defence position. The Admiralty were most willing to give all assistance to his efforts. Cunningham Papers, British Library and Museum, London, 52568, letter from Stanhope to Cunningham, 31 July 1939.

60. FO 371/18763/A5630/722/45, very confidential despatch from Blunt to FO, 15 May 1935.

61. Ibid.

62. Ibid.

63. FO 371/18764/A7829/722/45, secret telegram from Blunt to FO, 5 Aug. 1935; ibid., Craigie minute, 12 Sept. 1935. Charles Orde (Head of the Far Eastern Dept. of the FO) did not agree with Parker's ideas on the Far East, thinking the General simple-minded in his views. Parker had a long conversation with Admiral Dreyer on the Pacific situation during the C.-in-C. China Squadron's visit to Manila in late January 1935. See FO 371/19359/F2366/483/23, 'Secret: Notes of some remarks made by Major-

General F. Parker to Admiral Sir Frederic Dreyer at Manila in January, 1935', 8 Apr. 1935; ibid., Orde minute, 16 Apr. 1935.

64. See Chapter 6 below.

65. Those talks eventually led to an agreement which allowed the Soviets to build freely against the Japanese but restricted the size of the fleet they would build against any European power, especially Germany. See RG 38, Records of the Chief of Naval Operations, Record of the Deputy Chief of Naval Operations (Operations), 1882–1954, Office of Naval Intelligence, 1882–1954, Intelligence Division – Naval Attaché Reports, 1886–1939 (hereafter DCNO-ONI-NA, 1886–1939), National Archives, Washington, DC, Box 456, Folder: London Treaty, 1936, for Limitation of Naval Armament, US Naval Attaché's report, 14 June 1936; ibid., US Naval Attaché's Report, 1 Aug. 1936; ibid., memo from Secretary of State Cordell Hull to Bingham, 20 Sept. 1936.

66. Ibid., Box 457, memo for DNI, Report on England by Commander Baker (USN), 4 Apr. 1936.

67. RG 38, CNO-LNA, 1927–1940, Box 11, Folder: Naval Bases – Great Britain, Naval Attaché's Report, 9 June 1936.

68. FO 371/19836/A2494/2494/45, secret letter from Phillips War Plans to Under-Secretary of State for Foreign Affairs, 25 Mar. 1936.

69. Ibid.

70. FO 371/19836/A3291/2494/45, FO minute by Gore-Booth, 30 Mar. 1936.

71. Ibid.

72. Ibid.

73. Ibid., Troutbeck minute, 31 Mar. 1936.

74. Ibid., Orde minute, 1 Apr. 1936.

75. Ibid., Vansittart minute, 10 Apr. 1936.

76. Ibid., Craigie minute, 9 Apr. 1936.

77. Ibid., Simon minute, 9 Apr. 1936.

78. Ibid., draft of secret letter to Admiralty from FO, 24 Apr. 1936.

79. RG 38, CNO-DNI-GC, Box 16, Folder A2-14/EF13/EN3-11, Vol. VII, confidential memo from CNO (William H. Standley) to C.-in-C., US Fleet, 27 June 1936.

80. RG 38, CNO-LNA, 1927–1940, Box 11, Folder: Naval Bases – Great Britain, Naval Attaché's Report, 9 June 1936.

81. Roskill, *Naval Policy Between the Wars*, Vol. II, 392–415; Lord Chatfield, *It Might Happen Again*, Vol. II (London, 1947), 102–10; Pratt, *East of Malta, West of Suez*, 8–62; CAB 53/28, Chiefs of Staff Papers (hereafter COS Papers), PRO, Kew, London, No. 477, 'Problems Facing His Majesty's Government in the Mediterranean As A Result of the Italo-League Dispute', 18 June 1936; CAB 53/31, COS Paper No. 571, 'Review and Organisation Of And Responsibility For Naval Air Work', 4 Apr. 1937; CAB 53/7, Minutes of the Meeting of the Chiefs of Staff (hereafter COS Meeting), PRO, Kew, London, No. 205, 6 May 1937; CAB 53/7, COS Meeting No. 206, 18 May 1937.

82. The Americans were well aware of the fight between the RAF and RN for control over the FAA, as well as a great deal about the performance of British aircraft and equipment. See material in RG 38, Records of the Office of the Chief of Naval Operations, Security Classified Records of the London Naval Attaché, 1937–53, National Archives, Washington, DC, Box 25, Folder: 'Fleet Air Arm – Organization, Control, Etc.', and Folder: 'Aircraft, Fleet Air Arm'; ibid., Box 26, Folder: 'Fleet Air Arm – Personnel, Admiralty'.

83. RG 38, CNO-DNI-GC, Box 16, Folder: A2-14/EF13/EN3-11, Vol. VII, confidential letter from Anderson to DNI, 3 Aug. 1936.

84. RG 38, CNO-DNI-GC, Box 16, Folder: A2-14/EF13/EN3-11, Vol. IV, confidential memo from Standley to C.-in-C. US Fleet, 27 June 1936.

85. RG 38, CNO-DNI-GC, Box 16, Folder: A2-14/EF13/EN3-11, Vol. VII, confidential letter from DNI to US Naval Attaché, London, 2 Sept. 1936.
86. RG 38, CNO-DNI-GC, Box 16, Folder: A2-14/EF13/EN3-11, Vol. VII, confidential letter from US Fleet Aircraft Battle Force to DNI, 2 Sept. 1937.
87. RG 38, CNO-DNI-GC, Box 16, Folder: A2-14/EF13/EN3-11, Vol. VII, confidential report from US Fleet Aircraft Battle Force to DNI, 24 Feb. 1938.
88. RG 38, CNO-DNI-GC, Box 17, Folder: A2-14/EF13/OQ, Vol. VI, confidential letter from Rear-Admiral William H. Halsey, Commandant US Naval Air Station, Pensacola to DNI, 2 May 1938.
89. RG 38, CNO-DNI-GC, Box 17, Folder: A2-14/EF13/OQ, Vol. VI, confidential letter from Commandant US Naval Air Station, Pensacola to DNI, 19 May 1938.
90. RG 38, CNO-DNI-GC, Box 18, Folder: A2-14/EF13/OQ, Vol. VII, confidential memo from Leahy to C.-in-C. US Fleet, 26 July 1939.
91. Ibid.
92. NTJ Papers, Container 29, Folder: A–E, 1936, letter from Johnson to Hornbeck, 25 Aug. 1936.
93. Ibid.; *Foreign Relations of the United States* (hereafter *FRUS*), Vol. IV, *The Far East, 1936*, despatch from Johnson to Hull, 1 Apr. 1936, 95–8.
94. CAD, entries for 3, 27 Apr., 14 June 1934.
95. Some examples of that relationship are: *FRUS*, Vol. IV, memo by Atherton, 13 July 1936, 241–3; FO 371/19829/A9447/180/45, record of conversation between Craigie and Bingham, 19 Nov. 1936; FO 371/20286/F7926/303/23, record of conversation between Cadogan and Atherton, 22 Dec. 1936.
96. FO 371/19842/A9153/8480/453, secret letter from Lindsay to Vansittart, 10 Nov. 1936. See also, Richard A. Harrison, 'Testing the Waters: A Secret Probe towards Anglo-American Military Co-operation in 1936', *IHR*, 7 (1985): 214–34.
97. FO 371/19842/A8480/8480/45, no distribution telegram from Lindsay to FO, 24 Oct. 1936.
98. FO 371/19842/A9036/8480/45, secret letter from Torr to MI2, 27 Oct. 1936.
99. Ibid., secret letter from Craigie to Major-General R.H. Haining at the War Office, 23 Nov. 1936; ibid., Troutbeck minute, 18 Nov., Craigie minutes, 19 and 20 Nov. and Vansittart minute, 20 Nov. 1936; FO 371/19842/F9193/8480/45, Vansittart minute, 18 Nov. 1936; ibid., letter from Vansittart to Deverell, 19 Nov. 1936.
100. FO 371/19842/F9193/8480/45, secret letter from Lindsay to Vansittart, 10 Nov. 1936; ibid., personal letter from Lindsay to Vansittart, 10 Nov. 1936.
101. Ibid.
102. FO 371/19842/A9193/8480/45, letter and attached copy from Eden to Duff Cooper, 18 Nov. 1936; ibid., note and attached copy from Eden to Chamberlain, 18 Nov. 1936.
103. FO 371/19842/A9471/8480/45, letter from Inskip to Eden, 26 Nov. 1936; ibid., draft of secret telegram from FO to Lindsay, 7 Dec. 1936. See also FO 371/19842/A9486/8480/45, letter from G.D. Roseway of the War Office to Hoyer Millar, FO, 27 Nov. 1936.
104. The American mission that was supposed to come to England for the exchange was cancelled because of changes to the American Industrial Mobilization scheme. While some suspicion existed that the US Army had gone too far too fast for its administration, in the FO the delay was not seen as being anything significant. See FO 371/19842/A10126/8480/45, no distribution telegram from Lindsay to FO, 22 Dec. 1936; FO 371/20659/A3212/228/45, confidential letter from Haining to Troutbeck, 29 Apr. 1937.
105. RG 38, CNO-DNI-GC, Box 117, Folder: A4-5/FF6, restricted report from Yarnell to CNO, 31 Aug. 1937.
106. Rear Admiral Harry E. Yarnell Papers (hereafter the Yarnell Papers), Library of

Congress, Washington, DC, Container 4, Folder: C.-in-C. Asiatic Fleet, Far Eastern Situation, 121–35, letter from Yarnell to Admiral Sir Lewis Bayly (RN) ret., 28 Nov. 1937. Bayley had pushed through the idea of offering the US squadron in the Mediterranean the use of Malta and Gibraltar as bases for their ships with the free use of the dockyards. The idea passed through the Admiralty and Foreign Office without a hitch, with only passing remarks on not playing the matter up too much in order to avoid giving American isolationists any ammunition. See FO 371/20662/A5298/228/45, letter from Bayley to Admiralty, 26 July 1937; ibid., A6519/228/45, letter from ADM to Under-Secretary of State, 8 Sept. 1937.

107. CHT/4/8, Little to Chatfield, 18 Feb. 1937.
108. Yarnell Papers, Container 3, Folder: Leahy 37–45, letter from Yarnell to Leahy, 22 Dec. 1937.
109. Yarnell Papers, Container 4, Folder: C.-in-C. Asiatic Fleet, Far Eastern Situation, 146–60, letter from Yarnell to Little, 2 Jan. 1938.
110. RG 38, CNO-DNI-GC, Box 117, Folder: A4-5/FF6, restricted report from Yarnell to CNO, 16 Jan. 1938.
111. Castle Diary, entry for 19 Feb. 1938.
112. FO 371/20649/A7332/6/45, Fitzmaurice (American Department) minute, 12 Oct. 1937; FO 371/20649/A8110/6/45, letter from ADM, Captain Phillips (War Plans) to Under-Secretary of State, 11 Nov. 1937; FO 371/20650/A9302/6/45, telegram from Lindsay to FO, 22 Dec. 1937; FO 371/20650/A9363/6/45, note from Herschel V. Johnson (Chargé d'Affaires US Embassy) to Eden, 28 Dec. 1937; CAB 4/27, CID Paper 1389-B, 'Size of Japanese Capital Ships', 28 Dec. 1937; RG 38, DCNO-ONI, 1882–1954, Box 456, Folder: London Treaty, 1936, for Limitation of Naval Armament, Confidential US Naval Attaché Report, 26 May, 1938; ibid., confidential US Naval Attaché Report, 13 Apr. 1938.
113. William D. Leahy Diary (hereafter Leahy Diary), entry for 28 Nov. 1937.
114. Leahy Diary, entry for 29 Nov. 1937.
115. FO 371/21028/F10616/26/23, N.B. Ronald minute, 4 Dec. 1937; ibid., telegram from Lindsay to FO, 30 Nov. 1937.
116. FO 371/21041/F11265/615/23, secret despatch from Consul-General Fitzmaurice (Batavia) to FO, 12 Nov. 1937; ibid., Cadogan minute, 16 Jan. 1938.
117. FRUS, Vol. III, The Far East, memo of conversation between Hull and Lindsay, 20 Jan. 1938, 38–9; FO 371/21525/A651/64/45, secret despatch from Lindsay to FO, 26 Jan. 1938.
118. NTJ Papers, Container 33, Folder: A–C, despatch from Grew to Hull, 15 Sept. 1937; FRUS, Vol. III, The Far East, telegram from Hull to Grew, 2 Sept. 1937, 505–8; FRUS, Vol. III, The Far East, telegram Grew to Hull, 18 Aug. 1938, 265–6; FO371/22181/F10611/71/23, telegram from FO to Craigie, 13 Oct. 1938.
119. FO 371/21490/A1469/1/45, IIC report, 'US material resources and industry in their bearing upon national war potential', 24 Feb. 1938; FO 371/21546/A9426/1202/45, IIC Report, 'Economic situation in the US in the event of war,' 14 Dec. 1938; FO 371/22813/A2173/98/45, IIC report, 'US Protective Mobilisation Plan', 21 Mar. 1939; CAB 56/2, Joint Intelligence Committee Papers (hereafter JIC Papers), PRO, Kew, London, Most Secret No. 28, 'Far Eastern Appreciation', 5 Mar. 1937.
120. RG 38, CNO-LNA, Box 1, Folder: British Naval Exercises and Maneuvers, US Naval Attaché's Report, 27 July 1938.
121. FO 371/21518/A426/55/45, J.G.S. Beith (American Dept.) minute, 19 Jan. 1938; ibid., A537/55/45, confidential telegram from Craigie to FO, 21 Jan. 1938; ibid., A552/55/45, Vansittart minute, 24 Jan. 1938; FO 371/21519/A644/55/45, Vansittart minutes, 22 Jan. 1938.

122. RG 38, DCNO-ONI, 1882–1954, Box 456, Folder: London Treaty, 1936, for Limitation of Naval Armament, confidential US Naval Attaché's Report, 15 Mar. 1938.
123. FO 371/21494/A2548/1/45, letter from Capt. Little (WO) to A. Holman (American Dept.), 1 Apr. 1938.
124. FO 371/21493/A2458/1/45, letter from Torr to the WO, 18 Mar. 1938; ibid., most secret letter from Gladwyn Jebb (Cadogan's Private Secretary) to Lindsay, 23 Mar. 1938.
125. Lawrence Pratt, 'The Anglo-American Naval Conversations on the Far East', *IA*, 47 (1971): 745–63.
126. FO 371/23560/F2879/456/23, telegram from FO to Lindsay, 19 Mar., 1939.
127. FO 371/23560/F2880/456/23, telegram from Lindsay to FO, 21 Mar. 1939.
128. FO 371/23560/F2943/456/23, Cadogan minute, 2 May 1939.
129. Ibid., most secret telegram from Lindsay to FO, 25 Mar. 1939.
130. Ibid., N.B Ronald minute, 28 Apr. 1939.
131. FO 371/23560/F2942/456/23, important, most secret telegram from Lindsay to FO, 24 Mar. 1939; FO 371/23560/F2963/456/23, draft telegram from FO to Lindsay, 24 Mar. 1939; FO 371/23560/F2943/456/23, N.B. Ronald minute, 28 Apr. 1939. See also Leahy Diary, entries for 11 Apr. and 14 Apr. 1939.
132. FO 371/23560/F2943/456/23, Ashley Clarke minute, 1 May 1939.
133. Ibid., secret telegram from Lindsay to FO, 2 May 1939.
134. FO 371/23560/F2943/456/23, most secret telegram from FO to Lindsay, 5 May 1939; CAB 2/8, Committee of Imperial Defence (hereafter CID), Minutes of Meetings, PRO, Kew, London, 355th meeting, 2 May 1939.
135. FO 371/23561/F4366/456/23, most secret telegram from Lindsay to FO, 8 May 1939.
136. FO 371/23561/F4519/456/23, draft of most secret telegram from FO to Lindsay, 22 May 1939. On the Royal visit and its impact on Anglo-American relations see: Benjamin D. Rhodes, 'The British Royal Visit of 1939 and the "Psychological Approach" to the United States', *DH*, 2 (1978): 197–211; David Reynolds, 'FDR's Foreign Policy and the British Royal Visit to the USA, 1939', *Historian*, 45 (1983), 461–72.
137. Reynolds, *The Creation of the Anglo-American Alliance*, 61–2; Leutze, *Bargaining for Supremacy*, 33–6; FO 371/23561/F7010/456/23, most secret report of meeting on 14 June 1939.
138. FO 371/23561/F4962/456/23, most secret orders for Commander T.C. Hampton, 22 May 1939. Hampton was to destroy these orders before he sailed from England.
139. FO 371/23561/F7010/456/23, most secret report of meeting held on 12 June 1939.
140. FO 371/23561/F7010/456/23, most secret report of meeting held on 14 June 1939.
141. Ibid.
142. Ibid.
143. An example of the reluctance to go too far in information sharing involved an American request for statistical data on the supply capability of Singapore. Because the Americans had no similar operating base in the United States (San Francisco being in embryonic stage) they were cautious in their request. Their fears were justified when the British approved their request, but only if the British were allowed a tour of Pearl Harbor in return. The Americans refused to go along with the trade. See RG 38, CNO-LNA, Box 11, Folder: Singapore Supply Facilities, letter DNI to US Naval Attaché in London, 30 June 1938; ibid., letter DNI to US Naval Attaché in London, 19 Oct. 1938. As well, it was highly unlikely that the British told the Americans that they could read the Dutch codes, and thereby gained information on American naval movements through that method. The Chief of Intelligence Staff, Singapore, reported to the Admiralty, who then passed it along to the FO, that the USN was sending the carrier *Langley* and 12 submarines to the Philippines to preserve US neutrality in October 1939. That information came from Dutch sources. See FO 371/22802/A6911/63/45,

copy of telegram from Chief of Intelligence Staff, Singapore, from DNI to FO, 6 Oct. 1939. The two navies did share information over German U-boat sightings however. See RG 38, DCNO-ONI, 1882–1954, Box 481, Folder: American–British relations various, 1935–39, US Naval Attaché's Report, Brazil, 1 Nov. 1939.

144. FO 371/21536/A1229/293/45, despatch from Lindsay and attached note from Hull, 8 Feb. 1938; DRAX 2/8, War Plans, 1938–39, Secret Notes on War Plans, 21 Oct. 1938.

145. An American mission sailed to England in August 1939, to gather information regarding Britain's plans for industrial mobilization. The outbreak of the war in Europe in September interrupted the mission, which did a quick survey and returned as soon as possible. See RG 38, DCNO-ONI, 1882–1954, Box 493, Folder: Comments on Geneva Protocol, confidential report of American mission to Britain, 25 Nov. 1939.

146. CAB 56/1, Minutes of Meetings of Joint Intelligence Committee (hereafter JIC Meetings), PRO, Kew, London, Meeting No. 30, 7 July 1939.

# 2

# British and American Views of the Soviet Union's Role in the Far East, 1933–39, I: The British

> History and geography combine to make Japan regard Russia as her permanent rival for the hegemony of East Asia, which is the goal of Japanese ambitions.[1]

By 1933, diplomatic relations among the great powers relied on a balance of power to sustain the peace in the Far East. Thought long dead and gone after the First World War and the Treaty of Versailles, balance-of-power diplomacy and the shadowy uncertainty of old-style great-power diplomacy were major elements of the day-to-day reality of US and British Far Eastern policy. Between 1933 and 1939, both the United States and Great Britain made certain assumptions about the usefulness of the Soviet Union in their strategies for dealing with Japan. British and US diplomacy utilized Japanese fears both of the Soviet bear and of diplomatic isolation, used to contain Japanese expansion.[2] Thus, it is important to understand what role the two Western nations thought the Soviet Union might play in the Far East.[3] Before this can be done, it is necessary to consider the situation prior to the United States' recognition of the Soviet Union in late 1933.

Britain's view of what this meant was an important issue for the Foreign Office. Earlier in the year, in April 1933, Sir Robert Vansittart, the Foreign Office's Permanent Under-Secretary (PUS), had visited the United States. Through this fortunate circumstance, the chief civil servant in the Foreign Office was able to provide a first-hand assessment of the US attitude towards the Soviet Union.[4] Prior to the Metro-Vickers Affair, considerable pressure had been brought to bear on Roosevelt for recognition, and recognition was thought to be imminent. Vansittart reported that there had been a feeling in the United States that recognition was imminent, but the Metro-Vickers Affair had, in the words of the Under-Secretary of State William Phillips, 'put the clock right back'.[5] Sir Ronald Lindsay, the British Ambassador to the United States, and Vansittart agreed that the State Department had always been opposed to recognition of the Soviet Union and now its hand had been greatly strengthened. However, despite the Vickers affair, pressure on Roosevelt for recognition continued to come, particularly from American industrial interests that saw an opportunity to profit greatly from trade with the Soviet Union.[6] Lobbying on behalf of the Soviet cause also emanated from William C. Bullitt, a close personal advisor to the President and a future US Ambassador to Soviet Russia.[7]

On 25 April, President Roosevelt had expressed his own views on the matter to Prime Minister Ramsay MacDonald; 'though recognition did not appear to be matter of immediate moment he hoped that we would not take it as an unfriendly action on his part *if* it eventually took place'.[8] The US position towards the Soviet Union was obviously still unresolved, but it was attracting the attention of enough high-ranking policy-makers to indicate that it was of some importance.[9] Such continuous pressures worked away on the Roosevelt administration until 17 November, when the White House finally announced that diplomatic relations with the Soviet Union were now a reality.[10]

One of the main British concerns about this new development was what would be the effect on Japan? The common view of the British diplomatic personnel at the embassy in Tokyo was that recognition would cause a set-back in US–Japanese relations and that US diplomatic officials in Japan knew that this would be the case.[11] The British view was reinforced by statements attributed to Maxim Litvinov, the Soviet Foreign Commissar who had negotiated the final terms of recognition with President Roosevelt. Sir Ronald Lindsay reported that 'In private conversation on the ship which brought him he [Litvinov] spoke, I hear from a trustworthy source, with the greatest candour. Recognition of the USSR by the United States, he said, would be welcome to the former, chiefly because it would give Japan seriously to think.'[12] Ironically enough, one of Roosevelt's motives for recognition was the hope that such a move would act as a brake against Japanese aggression in the Far East, particularly against China and Russia.[13] Both the United States and the Soviet Union had reason to feel that better relations between them would have a positive influence on Japanese aggression. Neither power seemed to give consideration to the outcome which the British Foreign Office thought likely: that recognition would make Japan more suspicious of both and less likely to want to work towards any constructive agreements with either the United States or the Soviet Union.[14] The recognition of the USSR by the United States marked the beginning of informal policies emanating from both London and Washington, not coordinated in any way, yet parallel in nature, which were directed at assessing and evaluating how the Soviet Empire in the Far East could be used as a counter-balance to Japanese aggression in the region.

In 1933 Great Britain viewed the Soviet Union as a large but militarily weak power in the Far East.[15] While preparing their pivotal Annual Review of Imperial Defence for 1933, the Chiefs of Staff (COS) received the Foreign Office's view of the Soviet Union.[16] The Foreign Office held that, as far as Soviet relations with Japan were concerned,

> Towards Japan, indeed, their recent policy has been so forbearing, in the face of a clearly concerted effort by the Japanese and Manchukuo authorities to undermine their position in North Manchuria, as to give rise to a general (though perhaps ill founded) belief throughout the Far East that they will never face a war in that region.[17]

As to Sino-Soviet relations and what effect that would have on Japanese policy, the accepted view at the Foreign Office was that 'It is too early at present to estimate the possible results of China's resumption of diplomatic relations with the USSR. It is not anticipated, however, that there will be any considerable swing over towards communism. As regards Manchuria, the USSR, though deeply resenting Japan's aggression is likely to continue to play a passive role.'[18]

As a result of this lack of appreciation for the Soviet bear's worth in any military considerations of the Far Eastern theatre, the COS made the defence of India against Soviet aggression its third and last priority in the Annual Review.[19] However, a change in perspective on the role of the Soviet Union in Far Eastern affairs was not long in coming.

By May, 1933, a division of opinion over the true nature of the Soviet regime existed in the Foreign Office between Laurence Collier, the head of the Northern Department (which dealt with the Soviet Union), and Sir Lancelot Oliphant, assistant under secretary of state. Both men expressed their views about the role the Soviet Union could be expected to play in the Far Eastern balance-of-power scheme in a Foreign Office discussion of the COS Annual Report and its ranking of the empire's strategic concerns. While Collier questioned the COS's labelling of the Soviet Union as Britain's 'avowed enemy', Oliphant held strongly to the anti-communist feeling that had for so long been a fixture of British foreign policy.[20] Collier's argument acknowledged that the Communist Party was Britain's avowed enemy in the Far East, but questioned the strategic placement that the COS gave the USSR in Far Eastern matters. He saw the Soviet Union as a nation desperately seeking allies to aid it against an encircling group of traditional enemies. And he thought that this traditional Russian fear of encirclement could be used to Britain's global strategic advantage:

> they are bitterly opposed to Japanese ambitions, and are likely to remain so, as long as Japanese policy remains what it is. We consequently seem

more likely than not to find ourselves one day in the position where we and the Soviet Government will have a common enemy, though we are not perhaps likely both to be fighting him at the same time. This may seem strange to the CID; but after all, as Palmerston said: 'We have no eternal friends nor eternal enemies. Our interests only are eternal.'[21]

Collier also saw Japan as a power similar to the Germany of 1914, one ruled by militarists and seeking complete regional dominance. In order to protect its interests from the expansionist tendencies of such a power, Britain once again would have to operate in a balance-of-power environment that afforded it both formal and informal allies.[22] On the other hand, Oliphant believed that Soviet Russia had not been substantially affected by any recent developments, and, therefore, believed the COS position to be sound.[23] His view was unsupported by any other important members of the Foreign Office.

Charles Orde, head of the Far Eastern Department, considered tension and antagonism to be the day-to-day norm for Soviet–Japanese relations in the future. His department was undertaking a survey of the Far Eastern situation at that very moment, with the objective of creating a document that could guide British foreign policy in the Far East.[24] Orde strongly supported the COS's rankings of defence problems and stressed the need for real military force in the Far East to counter the growing Japanese aggression. He felt that Great Britain could not depend on the United States to assist it in defending its imperial interests, but believed that Soviet Russia could be counted on to remain a constant counter-balance to any Japanese southern advances:

> an alliance between Japan and Russia is not a probable contingency; if and when Japan secures Vladivostok it might become one; but even then the outlook of the Soviets will have to change considerably before they abet the most imperialist country in the world in extending her power in China and give up their ambitions of spreading Communism, which is anathema to Japan, in the hopeful field, as the Soviets regard it, of China. Japan, for her part, not only detests Communism as a political force, but regards it as a hindrance to the development of the Chinese market which is all important to her.[25]

The Far Eastern Department's view of Japan was echoed by Sir Victor A.A.H. Wellesley, Deputy Under-Secretary of State and a close monitor of Far Eastern affairs. He, too, stressed the desire of Japan to establish a hegemony in the Far East and Pacific at China's expense.[26] This could lead only to continued confrontation with other powers, one of those powers being presumably the Soviet Union. Wellesley did not endorse the COS report's ranking of threats, as he saw the threat from Japan being primarily an economic and not a military one. His analogy between the Japan of 1933 and the Germany of 1914 stated that:

It does not seem to me likely that she is going to make the mistake which Germany made of trying to accelerate the pace by resorting to arms in order to get what can equally be obtained by economic pressure unless we are to assume that we are dealing with a nation of madmen.[27]

He wanted the Committee of Imperial Defence (CID) to wait for the final findings of the review of Far Eastern policy that was under way before implementing the COS's recommendations. The main reason he preferred the delay was that he questioned when the Japanese would choose to attack British interests in the Far East: '1. if she were attacked by us and 2. if we were engaged in war with another great Power and then only if she were convinced that we were going to be defeated.'[28] This questioning of the timing of a Japanese attack against Britain allowed Vansittart an opportunity to try to turn the COS report from a 'Far East-first' recommendation into a 'Germany-first' declaration.

Vansittart objected to the report putting Japan first, arguing that it presupposed that Japan would attack British interests in the Far East only after Britain became involved in difficulties elsewhere.[29] As he then argued: 'It seems to be generally agreed that Japan is unlikely to attack us, unless we are engaged elsewhere. Very well then. That puts "elsewhere" first. And elsewhere is Europe and Germany.' One of the main reasons why Vansittart argued that the threat from Japan could be relegated to second place behind European considerations was his perception of the state of Soviet–Japanese relations. He believed that Japan had no desire to provoke a war with Britain, especially while the Japanese were not on better terms with the Soviet Union. As he read the situation, the available evidence pointed to no decrease in the tensions between the two Asian powers, and, therefore, no improvement in Soviet–Japanese relations was likely. Vansittart recommended that the Singapore base be completed as soon as possible, but concluded that 'If therefore we cannot cover the *whole* ground, first things must come first, and we must begin 'a day's march nearer home' … we must begin at the centre, and spread as we can afford it.' He also called for a speedy delivery of the Foreign Office's Far Eastern review, in order that a more accurate appreciation of the defence needs of Great Britain in that region could be made.

The need to establish Britain's defence priorities clearly resulted in the establishment of the Defence Requirements Sub-Committee (DRC) of the CID, on 15 November 1933. The immediate topic for the committee, and certainly the service chiefs, was the situation in the Far East. For Vansittart and Sir Warren Fisher, Secretary to the Treasury, other ideas about the priority of British defence preparations were at play in their minds, but the resulting recommendations, apart from identifying Germany as the 'ultimate potential enemy', clearly were concentrated on Japan and the growing dangers in the Far East.[30]

The DRC was quick to place the Soviet Union in the strategic scheme of things. In fact, for those, like Fisher and Vansittart, concerned primarily with European issues, the state of Soviet–Japanese relations was a critical factor if the debate was to shift towards Germany. Expressed in a statement that was a cross between the arguments of Orde and those of Neville Chamberlain, the Chancellor of the Exchequer, who was reluctant to identify any threat which would require money being spent and favoured the re-establishment of the Anglo-Japanese alliance, the DRC's opinion was:

> In the meantime, Japan's relations with Russia in the Far East have deteriorated and should incline her to seek improved relations with other Powers generally and ourselves in particular. This inclination is at present confirmed both by letters and despatches from our Embassy at Tokyo and by outward and visible signs, among which may be quoted the successful issue of the Indo-Japanese cotton negotiations and the speech of the Japanese Foreign Minister in the Diet on the 23rd January, when he said that 'the traditional friendship with Great Britain remains unshaken and the two island empires can by wholehearted collaboration effectively serve the cause of universal peace.'[31]

This statement represented a compromise between the Treasury's desire for the re-establishment of some kind of relationship akin to an Anglo-Japanese alliance and the Foreign Office's belief that Anglo-Japanese relations were still in a steady state of decline, requiring security to be provided by a Far Eastern balance of power. It also represented the influence Vansittart had on the formulation of the DRC report.

At the third meeting of the DRC, on 4 December 1933, Vansittart had brought his objection to the COS's annual report to the attention of the committee.[32] Repeating the arguments he had made in the Foreign Office discussion of the COS Annual Review, Vansittart argued for a greater concentration on the German problem. He again placed the strained Soviet–Japanese relations in a prominent position in any evaluation of the Far Eastern situation:

> for some time both Japan and Russia had been apprehensive that the next clash would be between those two countries, and Sir Francis Lindley, in Tokio, had often confirmed the existence of this apprehension. If the view was held that Japan came first in order of priority it pre-supposed that Japan would not expect any trouble with Russia, as she would be unlikely to embark on any offensive action *vis-à-vis* ourselves, if, at the same time, she was expecting or preparing any trouble with Russia. If it was believed that we were to have a settled period as between Russia and Japan, then a more serious view must be taken of the position as regards India ... he felt that if our economic policy – and by that he had in mind such issues as the present cotton dispute – allowed the Foreign Office a reasonably free hand, the Foreign Office should be able to prevent our diplomatic

relations with Japan from deteriorating into a rupture so long anyhow as accounts with Russia were unsettled ... In his opinion the danger of being drawn into a European War provoked by Germany was a nearer menace than that from Japan, though the latter undoubtedly existed too, and would be brought nearer by the necessities of our economic policy, which must necessarily affect the internal situation here, and weight with our Government.[33]

Vansittart's attempt to use the Soviet bear as a guarantor of Britain's position in the Far East met with a cool response from his DRC colleagues. General Sir Archibald A. Montgomery-Massingberd, Chief of the Imperial General Staff (CIGS), Admiral Sir A. Ernle M. Chatfield, First Sea Lord and Chief of Naval Staff, and Sir Warren Fisher, all viewed the Japanese menace as one which required a strengthening of Britain's military and naval strength in the Far East.[34] Unable to put forth a solid argument as to why Germany should be considered the greatest *immediate* threat, Vansittart's attempt to make the DRC report a 'Germany first' document failed, and preparations for improving Britain's defensive position in the Far East, particularly with regard to naval preparations, remained the first priority.[35]

By early 1934 it was not yet clear how far the Soviet Union could be included in any Far Eastern strategy. While militarily and politically not a formal ally, the impact of the Soviet 'loose cannon', in the Far East remained an important factor.[36] The Foreign Office, particularly the Far Eastern and Northern Departments, continued to monitor the USSR's relations with Japan closely. The Departments' objectives with regard to protecting British interests in the Far East were two-fold: first, to assess the Soviet Union's military and diplomatic capabilities and, second, to keep an eye on the state of Soviet–Japanese relations, in order that Britain's Far Eastern foreign policy could exploit any underlying fears, uncertainties or tensions to its own benefit.[37] It was not long before the Soviet bear took a greater place in British diplomatic and defence plans concerning the Far East.[38] Much depended on Soviet strength.

Military assessments of the Soviet Union's forces in the Far East were positive, if reserved. The Northern Department noted a growing Soviet military capability, especially in armoured and aviation units, which it attributed to a direct fear of Japanese aggression in the Far East. In the 1933 Annual Report on the USSR, the British embassy concluded that:

The increased concentration on armaments, possibly to the prejudice of other industrial developments, which was shown during the year, was certainly the direct result of the Japanese menace in Manchuria. Reliable evidence was obtained in the spring ... that submarines were being assembled at Vladivostok and the defences of the port overhauled. According to information received from Harbin, twenty submarines had been commissioned by April. Meanwhile, during the spring and summer the strength of the Far Eastern Army ... was brought up to between 200,000 and 250,000 men. Evidence of troop movement to the Far East was obtained from widely separate parts of the country, and the withdrawal of forces from European Russia was reported to have been compensated for by the formation of five new infantry divisions.[39]

In January 1934, the COS prepared a paper on Russian military efficiency and capability,[40] which was approved by the CID on 31 May without any comment. The report suggested that the Red Army was becoming a modern fighting force, although it still had a long way to go to reach the operational and mechanical efficiency of the British Army. More encouraging was the evidence that a modern, productive and efficient industrial base was being set up to support a vast army and air force.[41]

British Army and Royal Navy intelligence sources also attempted to ascertain what the nature of the Soviet–Japanese tension was and how it affected British interests. In early February 1934, Rear-Admiral G.C. Dickens, Director of Naval Intelligence (DNI), received secret information from Captain J.P. Vivian, the Naval Attaché in Tokyo.[42] Vivian was responding to Dickens' request for more information and for the views of the Naval Attaché on the possibility of another Soviet–Japanese war. In Vivian's opinion, there was little chance of Japan's declaring war on the Soviet Union in the next three to four years, although the attitude of younger, more aggressive, Japanese army and naval officers made such prophecy an uncertain science.[43] That view was also held by the First Sea Lord, Admiral Ernle Chatfield, who informed Admiral Dreyer in the Far East that:

> I feel that Japan is no more anxious to push us to extremes than we are to be involved in any war with her ... Japan is in difficulties with Russia and hostilities with that country are no doubt her most pressing anxiety at the moment. Russia and the United States have come closer together. It is, therefore, all to Japan's interest to keep us quiet so that she has not to look for war on two fronts, if not three, at the same time.[44]

Dickens immediately forwarded a copy of Vivian's assessment to his good friend 'Dillo', Major-General J.G. Dill, Director of Military Operations and Intelligence.[45] Dill informed Dickens that the army agreed with Vivian's opinions on the unlikelihood of an immediate war and the influence of the 'Young Officers'.[46] A consensus of opinion between the army and navy intelligence community then existed, for Dicken's views were in accord with Dill's:

> My reading of the situation is: – Japan knows exactly what she wants to get from Russia and she intends to have it – one day. No one knows when that day will be. The Japs don't. They will watch the situation patiently

and intently. The moment the best possible combination of circumstances shows itself – it may be this year or in 2 or 3 – they will act quickly
and God help the Bolos![47]

The Northern Department agreed with the bulk of this assessment, pointing
out that there were particular problems with supplies and foodstuffs being
made available to the Soviet forces in the Far East.[48] The British Ambassador
Lindley added perspective with information garnered from influential Japanese
sources. Commenting on discussions held between the British Military Attaché
in Tokyo, Colonel E.A.H. James, and Colonel M. Homma, former Japanese
Military Attaché in London and now close advisor to General Araki, the
Japanese Minister of War, on the inevitability of a Soviet–Japanese war, Lindley
concluded:

> It will be observed that the Colonel [Homma] regards a conflict with
> Russia as inevitable, and is preoccupied with the possibility of Japan being
> faced with hostility from some other quarter while such a conflict is in
> progress. It is generally recognised amongst responsible Japanese that
> Japan's success against Russia was due to the fact that Great Britain held
> the ring; and the General Staff are naturally concerned with the isolation
> of their country at the present time. Although it is doubtless to British
> interests that a second war between Japan and Russia should be avoided,
> I cannot help feeling that the conviction of its inevitability, prevailing at
> army headquarters, which are, at present, so influential in directing
> Japanese foreign policy, will be of not little assistance to our diplomacy
> so long as it persists.[49]

That threat of an increased Soviet military capability, and Japan's perception
of its own isolation, was already felt to be having its effect on Japanese attitudes
towards Great Britain, according to other Foreign Office assessments.

The Far Eastern Department and the British Embassy in Tokyo commented
frequently on the state of Soviet–Japanese relations in 1934, and the possible
repercussions they might have on the British Empire. Lindley thought that the
Soviet military build-up in the Far East was acting as an effective corrective to
Japan's aggressive tendencies. The increase in Russian military might corres-
ponded with a deterioration of the Japanese diplomatic position, said Lindley,
creating a feeling of anxiety in the Japanese that made them careful to 'avoid a
breach with any great power at a time when American recognition of Soviet
and universal outcry against Japanese trade competition have emphasised her
isolation'.[50] Orde agreed, crediting the increased fear of Soviet Russia for Japan's
increased willingness to foster better relations with Britain in upcoming trade
talks between the two.[51] The increasing flow of information on Soviet–Japanese
tensions from such various sources had created a sense of opportunity and

change within the higher circles of the Foreign Office. In early February an attempt to take a clearer view of the situation was made by A.W.G. Randall, a Far Eastern Department officer. He produced a memo, at Vansittart's request, on what impact a Soviet–Japanese war would have on British interests in the Far East.[52]

Randall's views indicated that the probability of such a war was not great at that moment or in the near future, but it was a distinct possibility for the remoter future. The reason the idea of such a war could not be submerged easily was that

> there is no reason to suppose that Japan has given up her ultimate aim of domination of the Asiatic continent, or that Soviet Russia has abandoned her fundamental policy of undermining all bourgeois States and using them to spread the Communist idea. Between these two imperialisms there seems little chance of permanent accommodation ...[53]

He argued that, as far as British interests in the Far East were concerned, if such a war did occur, a Japanese victory would be less harmful than a Soviet one. In Randall's opinion, in most circumstances, such a war would be won by the Japanese. As matters stood at the moment, the best the Soviets could do was to win a defensive war. If such was the case, then all was well, as both Soviet Russia and Japan would be greatly weakened.[54] While Orde and the rest of the Far Eastern Department supported Randall's analysis, other Foreign Office departments were not so certain about many of his conclusions.

Laurence Collier disagreed with the insinuation that Soviet Russia was a greater threat to British interests than Japan. Using arguments similar to those he had expressed earlier in his evaluation of the COS's Annual Report, Collier pointed out that the Soviets were interested in maintaining the status quo in the Far East. Therefore, Soviet interests coincided with the British desire to prevent Japan from dominating mainland China.[55] If this analysis were correct, Collier argued, then

> I feel that we must take the facts as we find them, and that, since we live among a number of Powers, few of whom really wish us well but some of whom have the same interests as ourselves, we should, whenever possible, encourage the latter to join with us in defending the *status quo* against those whose interests ... demand its overthrow.'

Citing past Japanese aggression and the probability of greater demands for expansion due to an increasing population, Collier considered the Japanese a far greater threat to British commercial interests than the Soviets could possibly be.[56]

Vansittart took favourable note of his friend Collier's difference of interpretation, and was very pleased with the viewpoint taken, using it to help guide

Britain's relations with China. His own view of how continued Soviet–Japanese tensions played to the British benefit was

> that no clash between Russia and Japan is anticipated anyhow for some years to come. Since tension produces good, or better, behaviour on both sides, it is in our interest that there should be tension but not blows for as long as possible. Were the latter to come about, it is clear of course … that a draw would be the best result. If that could not be, the choice would be difficult between the two evils.[57]

On 31 May, Sir George Mounsey, Assistant Under-Secretary of State, passed Vansittart's view along to Sir Alexander Cadogan, head of the British Legation in Peking. The Chinese had been trying to pin down Cadogan on what he thought British and US attitudes would be towards a Soviet–Japanese war.[58] Vansittart thought it would be useful for Cadogan to know his personal views, in case the matter came up again. Mounsey described those views as:

> it would best suit our interests in the Far East that war between Russia and Japan should not occur; but that the reciprocal antipathies of the two races should restrain both of them from doing actual harm to our interests which depend upon peace and the absence of any one-sided predominance.[59]

Vansittart's approval of the memo and the approach that it advocated were echoed by the Foreign Secretary, Sir John Simon. But, while the Foreign Secretary approved of the general tone and direction of the memo, he was concerned about the timetable of events proposed by Randall. In Simon's view, as soon as Japan was finished digesting Manchukuo and Jehol, a task that would take some four to five years, Japan would be prepared to take on Soviet interests once more.[60] If that happened, Simon was of the opinion that Japan would win such a contest, causing Soviet Russia 'to try to regain cast by successes elsewhere …', most likely in the direction of Afghanistan and Persia.[61] The prospect of facing a Japan flushed with victory also did not sit well with the Foreign Secretary.[62] His fears of what a frustrated Japan might do if it were denied the ability to expand on the mainland also were applicable to the perils that the southern regions in the Far East might someday also face in such circumstances. The informal policy of trying to sail a course between Soviet–Japanese tension was one fraught with great dangers for the British Empire in the Far East.

In these circumstances, the Foreign Office attempted to pursue what can be called a 'no bloc' policy. It was, however, one which was consistent with the 'no bloc' policy British diplomacy was trying to implement generally.[63] The 'no bloc' was a strategy to balance various Far Eastern powers against each other, with Great Britain making no formal commitment that would endanger its interests. That opportunistic approach of the Far Eastern Department's strategy served three purposes: to protect British trade and commerce against Japanese and Chinese pressures; to exert diplomatic influence on both Japan and China in the balance-of-power environment, and to act as a shield, utilizing the balance of power in the region to buy time for the rearmament and reorganization of the defence forces of the empire. As long as this balance of power continued in the Far East, two elements of the traditional 'British way in warfare' (both the creation of a dominant maritime force for use in Europe and the Far East and the use of time, over which perhaps a new government or fiscal problems would temper Japan's aggressive attitude) had an opportunity to take effect. Such insights and information on Soviet–Japanese tensions became even more important to British policy-makers after the Japanese Amau declaration of April 1934.[64] This Japanese-style Monroe Doctrine created concerns about what Japan's attitude would be towards British interests in the Far East.

Sir Robert Henry Clive replaced Lindley as the British Ambassador to Japan in May 1934. Clive's initial attitude towards the role of Soviet Russia in regard to British interests was the same of that of his predecessor. In his view, the Japanese had missed their chance to do anything about Soviet Russia, now that the Soviet forces had been increased and improved. But, while a war was not likely, tensions would remain high.[65] However, by September, Clive had reassessed the matter and concluded that the possibility of a Soviet–Japanese war was greater.[66] Out of his concern about the possible escalation of tensions, Clive recommended to London that he should approach the Japanese and warn them against going to war with the Soviet Union. The Ambassador's proposal was met by a solid negative reaction, primarily at the War Office (WO), the Foreign Office and the Treasury.[67] The main problem with such action was felt to be the fear of antagonizing the Japanese General Staff, which was believed to be in favour of an early war with the Soviet Union.[68] Both the FED and the War Office held this opinion. However, the WO's private view of what might happen if such a war took place was not shared by the FED or Foreign Office.[69] The War Office's position reflected that department's view of the advantages accruing to Britain from a possible Soviet–Japanese war. While agreeing that the risk of antagonizing Japan was a possibility that had to be avoided, Colonel Ismay, MI2, GSO1, at the War Office also held that:

> It is of course a truism that, from the ethical and economic standpoint, peace throughout the world is to be desired. But viewed solely from the military aspect, we cannot altogether agree with Sir R. Clive. Soviet Russia and Japan are both potential enemies of the British Empire. The result of a war between them is problematical, but there seems a fair chance of a draw or a stalemate resulting. Such a result would remove the potential danger from both of them for many years and thus give us time to complete our own preparations. The defeat of one or other side would suit us

less well, but the enormous strain of a modern war would impoverish both sides and again neutralize our danger for a long time even from the victor. Moreover, we should then only have one instead of two possible enemies to guard against.[70]

Some of the military advantages referred to by Ismay were already paying dividends for the British strategic planners. The Joint Planning Committee (JPC) and the COS, when considering the defence requirements for Hong Kong, factored in the Japanese preoccupations with Soviet Russia.[71] It was their contention that, as far as air attack against Hong Kong was concerned:

Japan does not normally maintain any air forces within effective striking range of Hong Kong and units required for attack would have to be drawn from those stationed in Japan, Manchukuo, Korea, Formosa, etc. In deciding the size of the forces which she could use for this purpose, Japan will be influenced by such factors as the Soviet Air Force and by a desire not to commit too large a proportion of her Air Force to operations at a distance from Japan.[72]

The Admiralty had similar views. The Director of Naval Intelligence (DNI) received information in late 1934 that supported the idea that the build-up of Russian naval and air forces in Vladivostok was holding the Imperial Japanese Navy (IJN) somewhat in check. At a farewell party held by Captain Vivian for the Japanese naval officers going to London as part of a naval conference delegation, he was informed by Captain Iwamura, ADC to the Japanese Minister of Marine:

that the Russians are building submarines at Vladivostok and … that he, Iwamura, fully realised that in the event of a Soviet–Japanese war, Japan's international position would be a difficult one. Capt. Iwamura is a man who holds broadminded views and he probably reflects the opinions of the Minister of Marine. The Vice-Minister informed me that Iwamura is an exceptionally able officer.[73]

The Vice-Minister of Marine, Vice-Admiral Hasegawa, told Vivian at the same party that a Soviet–Japanese war, '"is the last thing we want and the Army is not ready", he then hastily changed the subject'.[74] Clearly, then, by the end of 1934, while no move was being made to warn the Japanese against going to war with the Soviet Union, British assessments of the Soviet–Japanese relationship were undergoing continuous modification and the usefulness of continued Soviet–Japanese tensions was being constantly monitored.

A large part of that modification was the result of the continued build-up of Soviet military and naval strength in the Far East. Ismay had alluded to this increase in strength in his discussions with the Foreign Office and it was a view also held at the Tokyo Embassy and the COS. Completed in early January 1935, the Embassy's Annual Report on Japan opened the section on Japan's relations with the Soviet Union with the comment that 'The world may congratulate itself that the year passed without a war between Japan and the USSR.'[75] By 1935, and in comparison to 1933, the Soviet Army was much larger, more technologically advanced and in a solid defensive position. The Soviet Navy and the large fleet of submarines in Vladivostok were a more serious threat to lines of communication between Japan and its armies on mainland China. Most important, however, was the Japanese fear of massive air attacks on their wooden cities.[76] As far as British interests were concerned, the military aspects of Soviet–Japanese tensions were favourable in 1935.

The delicate diplomatic balance that was required between Japanese, British and Soviet perceptions, tensions and positions was difficult to maintain. It almost collapsed under pressures brought on by Italian and German challenges to Britain's security in Europe.[77] Equally, that critical Far Eastern balance of power was threatened in 1935 by an incident of the Foreign Office's own making: the suggestion of creating closer relations with Russia through the granting of a loan, a suggestion followed by a mission of the Lord Privy Seal, Anthony Eden, to Moscow in March.[78] The Treasury stirred the pot as well, ruminating over the possibility of bilateral Anglo-Japanese action to rehabilitate China's struggling currency situation. There was also the possibility of the Soviet Union finding some terms of agreement with Germany, but the close ties between Germany and Japan cast many doubts upon such a likelihood. All of the above aside, because it was viewed as both a European and an Asian power, the Soviet Union posed a unique problem for British strategic planning in 1935.

The usefulness of the Soviet Union to British interests in both Europe and the Far East had been clearly defined during discussions in early January 1935, surrounding the up-coming London naval talks. When the chief British naval negotiator and head of the American Department, Sir Robert L. Craigie, indicated that he was not overly concerned whether or not Britain was particularly tender towards the Soviet Union's fears of an Anglo-Japanese entente arising out of the conversations, Collier quickly pointed out the strategic place the Soviet Union occupied in British global defence considerations.[79] Referring to an appreciation of the issue prepared by himself and Frank Ashton-Gwatkin, an economic advisor in the Foreign Office, Collier pointed out that there was indeed some reason 'for not letting Russia assume that we are particularly anxious to cooperate with the Japanese'.[80] The two argued that the Soviet Union had what it considered to be two main enemies: Germany and Japan. It considered Japan the more dangerous of the two, and, therefore, any policy of British cooperation with Japan could not be considered in the Far Eastern context only. They pointed out that the Soviet government was intensely nervous about any moves made by Great Britain or Japan towards each other as a result of the legacy of the Anglo-Japanese Alliance – an alliance formed to resist possible Russian expansion in the Far East in 1902. Owing to that history, the Soviet Union watched Anglo-Japanese relations very closely and was convinced that Japan would join others in actions designed to rehabilitate China only if Japan could use such actions to help further its aim of excluding the Soviet Union, Great Britain and all other powers from China. On the grounds that British cooperation with Japan would signal to the Soviet Union that Great Britain was a willing partner in the ousting of all other powers from China, Collier and Ashton-Gwatkin argued against any strict bilateral cooperation with Japan to aid China's currency problems.[81] In addition, they argued that the Soviets were now definitely opposed to any change in the status quo in both Europe and the Far East. Collier and Ashton-Gwatkin concluded that the lesson to be remembered at all times was that:

> Russia cannot afford to have an enemy East and West. The coming together of Russia and Germany is Europe's greatest danger, so long as there is possibility of war. The flirtation of Germany and Japan is obviously a lesser danger so long as Russia is hostile to both. The situation in Europe must once again dictate our policy in the Far East. It should forbid us from gratuitously antagonising Japan; but it also forbids us from approaching Japan beyond the limit where such an approach would alarm Russia and throw her into the arms of Germany. Joint action by the Consortium Powers to assist the Chinese currency situation would be on the right side of this limit; joint action with Japan alone for the same purpose would be getting dangerously near to it; and it might be actually crossed as the scope of the rehabilitation programme, the closeness of the cooperation, and the price of Japanese support became more clear. A good deal of the above argument applies equally to our relations with the United States in this matter ... a policy of exclusive collaboration with Japan in China would make us Japan's supporter in the opinion of the rest of the world, and particularly of the Soviet Government; and that, in view of the paramount importance of maintaining and strengthening every factor in Europe which tends to the consolidation of the status quo and in particular to check the ambitions of Germany, we cannot afford to take any action in the Far East which would antagonise one of the most important of those factors and perhaps turn it in a direction opposed to our own.[82]

This view was supported by Victor Wellesley and Vansittart. They feared that the Treasury was indeed working towards just such a disastrous bilateral Anglo-Japanese solution. On the basis of the arguments put forth by Collier, Ashton-Gwatkin and others, Vansittart had informed Sir Warren Fisher that the Foreign

Office was 'irrevocably opposed to any deal à *deux* with Japan', and he hoped that the United States and France would also be asked to join with Great Britain and Japan in any such currency schemes.[83]

Collier put the situation clearly once again in late January:

> There is, however, a possibility that, if M. Litvinov who is already somewhat disgruntled at recent developments in Europe, makes up his mind that the French and ourselves are going to leave him without support in face of German 'Drang nach Osten', he may throw in his hand altogether in the Far East in order to be able to turn his undivided attention to the West. This, of course, would not suit our book at all, any more than the reverse situation – which is also a possibility though a more remote one – in which a Soviet–German detente in Europe might be brought about through Soviet fear of isolation in the face of Japan in the Far East. The moral for us seems to be that we should handle M. Litvinov very carefully in the next few months.[84]

Both Vansittart and Eden agreed with Collier's analysis of how the Soviets worked into Britain's strategic scheme. Still, under pressure from what he perceived was a worsening European situation, Vansittart was determined to attempt to reach some sort of understanding with the Soviet Union over Germany.[85] Vansittart's Europe-first vision posed a serious threat to the very fabric of the 'no bloc' strategy that safeguarded Britain's Far Eastern interests.

Because Soviet Russia held such an important position as a deterrent to Japanese aggression in China, a continued threat from that flank was vital, if British diplomacy were to balance the one against the other. However, any British arrangement with Soviet Russia over any issue, no matter if it was economic, commercial, political or military, would also give Japan cause to fear the beginning of an anti-Japanese bloc being created by Britain. The result would in all likelihood be a Japanese move southward against British interests.[86] Vansittart's attempts at securing European security through an agreement with Soviet Russia cut across this 'no bloc' strategy of opportunism that the FED was trying to keep in play. His approach tended towards trying to create a sterile environment around the disease (Japan), rather than dealing directly with the problem, as was Simon's wish to do through the multilateral approach.[87] Given the importance and vulnerability of the Far East in imperial affairs, the perception of greater volatility from Japan, and the need to respect the coming of the critical year 1936, such a disruption of the balance of power in the Far East could not be tolerated.[88] Just as an Anglo-Japanese *rapprochement* would have increased suspicions of Britain in Moscow, thereby perhaps eliminating a potential British ally in the containment of Germany, Vansittart's ambitions on this matter had little chance of success due to the *absolute* importance of a 'loose' Soviet Russia at this time in the Far Eastern balance of power. The

Treasury and Board of Trade, who both desired an improvement in relations with Japan, were also opposed to the risks inherent in such a venture with the Soviet Union.[89]

This reliance on an unaligned Soviet Union coincided with the need to avoid any unnecessary action that might possibly provoke Japan. The solution was to avoid any bilateral agreements with powers involved in the Far East so that there could be no grounds for charges of collusion between one power or group of powers against another. In his discussion with Litvinov on 28 March, Eden explained that the British position towards the situation in the Far East was 'that mutual relations should be as good as possible, as, amongst other reasons, freedom from anxiety in the Far East made a greater possibility of British influence being usefully exercised in Europe'.[90] Eden assured the Soviets that the British government's policy was that it had no intention of signing a bilateral non-aggression pact with Japan, nor did it intend to establish a special relationship with any single power in the Far East at the expense of any other.[91] This attitude was reflected in the manner in which the British had dealt with the Chinese loan issue, said Eden, a clear indicator of the cooperative and joint-approach policy Britain would like to see utilized in dealing with Far Eastern matters. Furthermore, he made it clear that Great Britain considered close communications with the Soviets and a clear understanding of Far Eastern matters to be very important to the British government. Eden told Litvinov that if there ever was a time when the Soviet government required information on British policy towards Far Eastern matters, they only had to ask Lord Chilston or the Soviet Ambassador in London, Maiski, to enquire and the information would be provided, because, 'His Majesty's Government wished that there should be no cloud in the relations between the two countries on grounds of mere misunderstanding.'[92] Finally, in a gesture meant to solidify Anglo-Soviet understandings about the situation in the Far East, Eden put Stalin and Litvinov at ease over their fears of Britain granting possible loans to Japan. According to Lord Chilston, Eden 'had given a formal promise to Litvinov and Stalin that no loans were now contemplated and that if any loans from Great Britain to Japan should be contemplated in the future the Soviet Government would be fully informed in advance.'[93] Litvinov expressed his gratitude for the offer, and told Eden that he too considered the Japanese problem to be one that required collective, and not independent, action.[94]

That policy of not formally favouring one power over another in the Far East of course also applied to the British treatment of the Soviet Union. However, while not taking an overt and active attitude towards the balance-of-power predicament in the Far East, the Foreign Office, through acts of omission, could attempt to create an atmosphere more conducive to British interests. Victor Wellesley's instructions to Ambassador Clive, in the spring of 1935, summed up the situation regarding the attitude of Britain towards the Soviet Union and its place in the Far Eastern strategy for defending the empire. In the most diplomatic of terms, Wellesley, at Orde and the Northern Department's request, instructed Clive to not promote the idea of better Soviet–Japanese relations to the Japanese during this 'critical' period:

> War between Japan and Russia is of course far from our desire. Apart from the evils resulting by repercussion from any war a Soviet–Japanese war would destroy for the time being a balancing factor against Germany, our greatest source of anxiety. Our desire to maintain good relations with Russia, both for their own sake and from the standpoint of her influence against Germany, has caused us to assure her in all sincerity, that we do not wish Japan to attack her. We also of course are most anxious to maintain good relations with Japan but she is a danger to our interests in the Far East and it is difficult at present to see how she is to be checked. We can place no reliance on American co-operation against her or, in spite of Litvinov's language to Eden, on concerted help from Russia. But nervousness in Japan about Russia may be useful as a check on Japanese aggression further South and the ideal state of things seems to us to be one in which such nervousness should continue but without any commitment of Russia's strength in the Far East which could not quickly be liquidated should the situation in Europe render this desirable. We think therefore that it will be best not to go out of our way unnecessarily to sooth Japan's fears of Russia, though naturally we must be careful to negative any impression that we *want* ill-feeling between them. Apart from special circumstances this is the general line we should like you to follow.[95]

Vansittart understood what Orde meant, writing later that, 'They [Japan] will probably have to become more frightened of trouble with Russia before they really try to earn our friendship.'[96]

The Lord Chancellor, Viscount Hailsham, pointed out the same strategic realities to the Cabinet during the final discussions in early 1936, over whether the Soviet Union should receive a loan. He explained most clearly that such a disruption of the balance of power would involve not only Far Eastern questions, but also the links of the three countries to Germany, all with serious and unwelcome consequences for the defence of Britain's Empire.[97] The Far Eastern Department's 'no bloc' strategy had survived another challenge, as the loan discussions floundered in the face of such forceful opposition to any bilateral actions throwing the delicate Far Eastern balance out of its natural rhythm. The need for Great Britain to keep all nations with Far Eastern interests 'in play' continued to be the central pillar of imperial foreign policy.

The subtlety of the 'no bloc' balance-of-power approach was not to the liking of the CIGS, Field Marshal Sir Archibald Montgomery-Massingberd, and the Secretary of State for War, Duff Cooper. Working from incomplete information provided by the Military Attaché in Tokyo and scraps of Foreign Office despatches from Clive, Montgomery-Massingberd argued to the Cabinet that the Japanese Foreign Office desired better relations with Britain.[98] Given that the stated desire of British foreign policy was to ensure that the British Empire never faced simultaneously a coalition of Germany, Italy and Japan, Montgomery Massingberd advocated that the Foreign Office should attempt to take advantage of the Japanese offer and formally improve relations between the two countries.[99] The CIGS's attempt to dictate British foreign policy in the Far East was quickly rejected by the Foreign Office, although Chatfield supported the CIGS's position.[100] Starved of crucial defence monies, the service chiefs rallied around the idea of diplomacy keeping the strategic commitments to a minimum. Their linear thinking saw alliances as a natural choice. It was not the Foreign Office's preference.

Charles Orde launched a scathing attack, placing the Soviet factor as one of the most prominent reasons why such an event could not take place. He argued that, if Britain should now attempt a closer relationship with Japan, the United States and the League of Nations would view the British as selfish opportunists and 'traitors to the cause of international morality', and, such action would encourage the Japanese to take aggressive action against the Soviet Union.[101] Of the utmost importance was the need to keep the larger strategic picture in view. Citing Clive's most recent reports, Collier emphasized that any Anglo-Japanese political agreement would 'fall like a bombshell on Russia'. Such a consequence needed to be very carefully considered, argued Collier, in order to avoid anything which might alienate the Soviet government and weaken it as a counterweight against Japan in the Far East or Germany in Europe. He acknowledged that uneasy relations between Japan and the Soviet Union were to Britain's advantage as a check on Japanese aggression; however, he did not think it wise to do anything to encourage hostilities between the two, as that could hardly fail to have the result of making Japan feel that it had made the initial step to closer Anglo-Japanese relations. His final analysis was that Japanese action against the Soviet Union was likely unless the USSR became so involved in the affairs of Europe and liquidated its position in the Far East by meeting all Japanese requirements. There was, he judged, no imminent danger of a conflict at the time. Japan would wait to rebuild and reorganize its army. Soviet Russia in the meantime would grow strong as well, and as it became stronger Japan would be more likely to wait until Germany was ready to strike at that end. As for a German–Japanese agreement, Collier thought:

> The danger of an agreement between Japan and Germany, to which the CIGS draws attention, is only too real, but it is difficult to agree to the suggestion that Anglo-Japanese friendship will diminish the danger. Japan will pursue her primary aims, which must include any help she can obtain in a possible struggle with Russia, regardless of our wishes, and an

agreement with us will in no way diminish the attraction of an agreement with Germany. The most that can be said is that it would diminish the risk of a Japanese attack on British possessions when we were at war with Germany. Obviously this would be an object worth securing, but the price to be paid for it indicated above would surely be excessive ... Good relations with both China and Japan should be our basic policy, and cooperation with both if the Sino-Japanese link in the circle can be brought into existence.[102]

Orde's position was fully supported by the rest of the key members of the Foreign Office. Victor Wellesley contended that Orde had disposed of the CIGS's fallacies admirably.[103] This admiration was continued in Vansittart's commentary on the issue, as he exclaimed that he agreed with the whole of it, but added

Perhaps the true situation can be summed up still more tersely. Germany wants to attack Russia. Japan wants to attack Russia and China, when Germany is ready. So long as these wholly immoral ... ambitions are entertained, it is of no use to expect any permanent or real settlement with either. And if we tried, we should lose more ... than we won ... These remarks apply equally to Germany and Japan, and will apply for some time yet to come. But they need not at all necessarily apply, when we have hastened to repair our strength.[104]

Vansittart was also aware, from information provided by Sir Eric Drummond, the British Ambassador in Rome, that Japan was indeed worried that Russia's relations with France and Great Britain would make the Soviets unstoppable in the Far East.[105] Lord Stanhope, another of the Foreign Office's senior Deputy Under-Secretaries of State, lent his support to the cause. He commended Orde's report, and suggested that the case could be made even stronger against the army, because, in his view, the General Staff tended to paint the Japanese as supermen and ignored the changed strategic, domestic and commercial realities of Japan.[106] In the final analysis, he found the CIGS's assessment of the situation out of date, and warned: 'It is not difficult even for an ordinary civilian to see the advantages from a military point of view of an agreement between the UK and Japan, but it is not sound strategy to disregard, as I think our General Staff has, all other considerations.'[107]

Anthony Eden, the newly appointed Secretary of State for Foreign Affairs concurred.[108] He pointed out to both the CIGS and the First Sea Lord that, while he shared their desire to improve Britain's relations with Japan, 'It was easier to desire them, however, than to find in current events a good opportunity for promoting them in the general interest.'[109] In May, Eden expressed further his whole-hearted support of the 'no bloc' strategy for the Far East. In a private and confidential letter to Orde, Clive had reported repeated Japanese attempts to further better relations with Great Britain.[110] Clive held that this change in the Japanese military's attitude towards Britain was due to Japan's isolation and desire to confirm that the British Empire would, at worst, be a benevolent neutral in any Japanese war with Russia. Clive's opinion of the matter was that, 'So far as we are concerned it is not a bad thing that both the Japanese and the Russians should be feeling anxious as to where our sympathies lie and uncertain as to what line we should adopt ...'[111] Orde replied to Clive's letter in June, informing him that Eden was in full agreement with his assessment and that

> the Secretary of State observed that the first few lines of the penultimate paragraph represent the right position for us to be in. In our present state of inadequate armament and vast commitments we haven't got the straw necessary for all the bricks we should like to make.[112]

Indeed, by mid-1936, conditions in Europe, and British preoccupations with the continent, made the Soviet bear an even more necessary part of the overall British strategic considerations for the Far East.[113] Japanese fears of a possible Anglo-Soviet rapprochement were having the desired effect of making that island nation anxious as to what action to take next in China.[114] S.G. Harcourt-Smith, a member of the FED, provided a useful commentary on the issue when he observed that Japanese fears of an Anglo-Russian understanding, embracing Far Eastern matters, was 'almost the only adequate protection available for our Pacific interests', given the growing British concern with European problems. He wished that the Japanese fear could be stimulated further, in order that Japan could be brought to heel.[115] Orde cautioned that while the desire to further stimulate Japan's apprehensions of Russia was an easy card to play, 'It is satisfactory to see this preoccupation with Russia, which is the best brake on Japan. But it is too uncertain a field to interfere in with the object of increasing the application of the brake.'[116] British opinions of Russia's worth as a military power, and its effectiveness as a brake, were upgraded in September 1936, with the visit of Major-General Archibald Wavell's military mission to the Soviet Union. After careful observation of Red Army manoeuvres, Wavell's conclusion was that the Red Army was a formidable defensive force, but it was not an effective offensive instrument.[117] Wavell's evaluation of the Russian military machine was lent strong support by a report submitted by the Indian General Staff on Japanese aggression against India.[118] The report maintained that, 'Even if there were no formal alliance between Russia and the British Empire, Russian interests would remain diametrically opposed to those of Japan, and Japan would be compelled to take account of possible Russian action.'[119] In an Anglo-Japanese war, Japan's fears of Russian opportunism would cause the Japanese to retain a large part of their air force in home regions for potential operations against Russia. This would allow Britain's military preparations to counter

71

effectively the minor Japanese air attacks that could therefore be expected.[120] In a war which saw the Soviet Union and the British Empire allied against Japan, the report was positive that the results would be even more favourably inclined towards the protection of British interests in the Far East.

These evaluations suited the Foreign Office's plans for the Far East well enough; a strong Soviet Union that could act as a brake on Japanese aggression, yet was not strong enough to threaten British interests was indeed a case of the bear's porridge being not too hot, nor too cold, but just right.[121] However, that Far Eastern balance of power was put in jeopardy by two important events in 1936 and 1937: the signing of the Anti-Comintern Pact by Germany and Japan, on 25 November 1936; and the devastating Stalinist purges of the Soviet Red Army in June 1937.

The Anti-Comintern Pact was viewed by some in the Foreign Office as a signal that Japan could now disregard the threat from the Soviet Union because the USSR would now have to concentrate more of its energies on Germany and the European front.[122] This analysis was quickly rejected by the FED, by Craigie, and by the new Deputy Under-Secretary at the Foreign Office, Sir Alexander Cadogan, all of whom argued to the contrary: since Japan had declared itself openly as an antagonist of the Soviet Union, it would have to be even more wary of its adventures in the Far East.[123] In late October, Clive had warned the Foreign Office that since the Japanese bluff in the Far East had been called by the Soviet military build-up, the Japanese now realized that they had missed the opportunity to deal the Russians a quick, decisive blow. This realization was making an improvement in Soviet–Japanese relations possible.[124] Orde and Cadogan thought the chances of such an understanding occurring were slight. Both held to the belief that Japan was still most concerned with its interests in China and that any rumoured Soviet–Japanese rapprochement was a temporary condition brought on by Japan's desire not to provoke the Soviets unnecessarily.[125] More important, as far as Britain's interests in the Far East were concerned, was the disquieting point brought up by Harcourt-Smith, who argued that if Japan were stymied by the Russians in the North, it would then most likely turn its attention to the South.[126] Both Orde and Cadogan acknowledged the possible dangers that lay in having the Soviet Union present too formidable a position to the Japanese, and Vansittart summed it up well as being: 'Very interesting ... and potentially disquieting.'[127]

In view of the creation of the Anti-Comintern Pact and the impact it might have on the normal tensions that had been the mainstay of Soviet–Japanese relations, the situation now seemed to warrant a formal reassessment.[128] In November, Vansittart asked Orde for a memorandum on the Japanese attitude towards other powers and an evaluation of whether Japan was satisfied enough with its relations with the Soviet Union as to contemplate a strike southward. Orde repeated that he believed that the Japanese Army still had its eye firmly fixed on the Soviet Union.[129] He thought it unlikely that enough evidence of a pacific attitude would be forthcoming from Soviet Russia to make Japan move from that assessment. Russian increases in their military strength had allowed them to meet Japanese border pin-pricks with great force, said Orde, causing Japan to have to re-evaluate its chances of success in any military adventure. As for the Anti-Comintern Pact, it had disposed of any chance of a *rapprochement* between the two. There was something to be said for the fear of Japan turning southward, Orde argued, but it was still a distant problem, although a growing concern that required careful attention.[130] Cadogan and Vansittart both thought the memo a wise summary, with Cadogan adding that the Japanese had a growing fear of the Soviet bomber forces in Vladivostok. Both appreciated that the Anti-Comintern Pact was perhaps not an entirely disadvantageous agreement from the British perspective.[131] The full spectrum of advantages and disadvantages of the Pact were analysed at the end of the year.

In December, the Far Eastern Department, in consultation with the Central and Northern Departments, produced a definitive report on what the Japanese–German agreement meant to British interests in the Far East.[132] Their combined opinion was that the agreement was ill-advised on the Japanese side. The agreement did nothing to strengthen Japan's strategic position, while at the same time the psychological effect on Russia was tantamount to creating the same impression a German–Japanese military alliance would have. Because of that perception being created, Japan's strategic position was weakened rather than strengthened. The three Foreign Office Departments believed that the Soviets had been irritated rather than frightened. Soviet forces in the Far East were now considered strong enough to meet any Japanese threat and were rapidly approaching a state of organization where they would be entirely self-supporting and independent of European Soviet Russia. The agreement would give an extra boost to that Russian rearmament. The report also contended that, with the agreement with Germany, Japan had confirmed existing Soviet suspicions. That meant the Soviets would be unlikely to move any considerable forces from the Far East to the West. Moreover, Japan's aim to create a curtain along the Mongolian–Manchurian frontier of the USSR to prevent 'dangerous thoughts' of communism penetrating into Manchukuo, Korea or China was now threatened. Had an accommodation with the Soviets been reached, Japan might have been able to secure an undertaking that would have helped check that flow of subversive thought. However, by irritating the Soviet Union, Japan had made it necessary to reinforce that border area with more troops and resources. That situation made it all the more improbable that Japan would have the resources available for adventures outside Mongolia and Manchukuo. Most importantly, consensus within the Foreign Office and among elements of the British Cabinet was growing over what these new developments meant for Anglo-American relations. Overall, Anglo-American relations were thought to have been brought closer together by the events. Indeed, even the Japanese Minister for Foreign Affairs, Mr Arita, admitted as much to Clive on 2

December 1937. China would also now be driven to work more closely with precisely those countries with whom Japan did not want it to have better relations. Most importantly, the agreement would have a serious impact on the conditions within which Britain had crafted its naval disarmament strategy:

> The Russian reply has been the announcement of a large naval building programme. This will inevitably react through its effect on our naval agreement with Germany and endanger the whole labouriously constructed system centring round the London Naval Treaty. Apart from this and the introduction of a fresh disturbing factor into world politics the consequences of the agreement for us would not appear to be serious. We might indeed derive some small advantage if Japan finds it more instead of less necessary to watch Russia, and if annoyance with the Germans on top of her fears of Japan leads China to divert some of her orders from Germany to the United Kingdom. And if Japanese fears expressed in their press have any foundation in fact we may arrive at closer and harmonious collaboration with the USA in the Far East.[133]

The memo received solid support from Cadogan, Vansittart and Eden, the latter deciding that the Anti-Comintern Pact was something he could not take too seriously.[134]

The Far Eastern Department's analysis of the Pact was also reinforced by secret intelligence gathered from broken Japanese diplomatic codes, which added to the Foreign Office's overall picture of relations between Great Britain, Soviet Russia, Japan and Germany.[135] Evidence of the continual improvement in the Soviet bear's military capability was also reflected in the Review of Imperial Defence, prepared by the COS and Joint Planning Committee for the 1937 Imperial Conference.[136] According to that review, the Soviet Union possessed the largest army and air force in the world, and a growing submarine fleet, with much of that force being directed at the Far East. In fact, the formal British military view of the usefulness of the Soviet Union in any Far Eastern conflict was that

> the Soviet military preparations are rapidly being completed, and include the location of a large force of long-distance bombing aircraft in the Maritime Province, which constitutes a serious threat to Japan. The Soviet submarine forces in the Far East, moreover, are a factor which cannot be disregarded. Consequently, in the event of war between the United Kingdom and Japan, the assistance of the USSR might be of considerable value.[137]

The Soviet Union remained, therefore, a strong semi-formal component of British diplomatic and military strategic planning for any conflict in the Far

East, a role fostered by continuing favourable reports from the COS and CID about the increasing military strength and capability of the USSR.[138] But that faith in the Soviet Union's strength was shaken, in June 1937, by a series of purges in the officer corps of the Soviet military establishment.

The possible repercussions from the purges on British foreign policy and strategic planning were immediately recognized by members of the Foreign Office, as well as by military planners.[139] In the Far East, the impact was not so disastrous. The importance that the Soviets placed on being prepared to meet any Japanese threat was underlined by the fact that Marshal Blucher, commander of the Soviet Far Eastern Army, was the only commander of a military district left untouched at his post.[140] However, some feared a Soviet withdrawal into isolationism. This was an especially worrisome prospect, as it would send a clear signal to the Japanese that they could act without fear of Soviet reprisals.[141] Fortunately, the Soviet purges coincided with the new Japanese campaign against China. The Soviet purges, combined with the reorganization and strain in the Japanese army, reduced the chances of the Japanese taking advantage of a weakened Russia.[142] Despite reassurances to this effect from Tokyo, the FED thought it best that the Japanese not be allowed to acquire any British views or information as to the possible damage done by the purges to the Soviet military presence in the Far East.

Therefore, the FED cautioned Collier not to not divulge any information on British assessments of the Soviet military capability to Japanese officials. In particular, the Northern Department was not to let Japanese military attachés or embassy staff in London get the impression that the purges had created a serious crisis in the Soviet military. It was feared that if the Japanese perceived the Soviets to be severely weakened then Japan might adopt a more forward policy in the region.[143] Collier followed the FED's advice, as he, too, believed that the Japanese assessment of the situation should be kept as confused as possible for as long as possible. When the counsellor from the Japanese Embassy called to enquire as to the Northern Department's views on the consequences of the Soviet purges, Collier told him,

> that while it would seem as he suggested, that the immediate effects on the upper ranks of the Army must be unfavourable, we had no evidence of serious discontent in the Army as a whole or among the population in general and could only assume that Stalin's recent actions had been prompted by a desire to remove possible future dangers to his power, rather than by the discovery of any actual plot. Baron Tomi said he agreed generally with this diagnosis and certainly did not believe that the Generals had been actually plotting with the Germans. He himself thought Stalin's actions were the usual precautionary measures of a dictator who thought to strengthen his own position by the elimination of all possible opposition; and he supposed it was possible that in a

country like Russia the regime might actually be strengthened by such measures in the long run. I hastened to agree with this view and to point out that if the regime were strengthened and the army became more reliable politically, the Soviet States and its power of resistance against foreign attack would be strengthened generally, although the technical efficiency of the Army might temporarily suffer. I then added, in accordance with Mr Ronald's suggestion ... that these developments would at least ensure that Soviet policy in the Far East would be strictly defensive for the next few months at least, which should give the Japanese Government the opportunity to reduce their forces in Manchuria. This produced the expected burst of laughter, followed by remarks to the effect that a mutual reduction of forces might be considered ...[144]

The War Office was also in accordance with the measures taken by the FED and Collier, as the former also wished, for obvious reasons, to keep the Japanese guessing on the matter as long as possible.[145] While the impact of such a disinformation campaign on Japanese intentions in the Far East is not clear, the escalation in border incidents between the Soviet and Japanese forces, in 1938 and 1939, reflected the Japanese need to test the USSR military, since there was no clear consensus in Tokyo on the state of the USSR's defences.[146]

Craigie, who took over as Ambassador to Japan on 4 August 1937, reported six months later that the Japanese military had lost some of their fear of the Soviet bear both because of the purges and as a result of the lack of any aggressive action being taken by the Soviets while the Japanese were tied up in China.[147] That lack of fear of Soviet Russia had allowed an increase in the anti-British attitude of Japanese officials, in both the army and the navy, as well as in the government. Craigie also pointed out that it was only now, when the USSR had reacted to various border tensions with obvious military strength and political determination that Japan was once more approaching Britain in a more conciliatory attitude.[148] In his view, Japan was still not strong enough, in 1938, to risk the simultaneous antagonism of any two of the three great powers – the Soviet Union, the United States and Great Britain – arrayed against it. Therefore, with an increase in anti-Japanese feeling on the rise in the United States, and, with Russia still viewed with great anxiety, the only option available to the Japanese was to try to get on better terms with Britain.[149]

The Soviet Union's role as a 'loose cannon' was modified to a large extent after the Japanese attack on China in 1937 to a position of predominant military advisor to the Chinese.[150] The Soviets quickly became one of the main sources of military assistance and supplies to China, a nation whose strategic position in the Far Eastern balance of power was also of great importance to the British position.[151] Britain's service chiefs were not able to reach a definite conclusion regarding the extent to which British assistance should be offered to China.[152] Air Chief Marshal Sir Cyril L.N. Newall, Chief of Air Staff (CAS), saw the situation in the Far East as going from bad to worse. He advocated supporting the Nationalist leader, Chiang Kai-Shek, and the Chinese war effort against Japan, in order to (a) secure China's goodwill; (b) keep China from turning to the USSR for more help, and (c) to prevent China seeking an accommodation with Japan.[153] The CIGS, General the Viscount Gort, and the First Sea Lord, Admiral Sir Roger Backhouse, both disagreed with Newall's vision, citing a lack of faith in China's ability to resist Japan, and a belief that Japan had already bitten off more than it could chew on the mainland. In the face of such deadlock, the COS refused to interject their voice into the Cabinet's debate over how much aid was to be given to China.[154] No such reluctance over aid to China existed within the Soviet Union.

Between September 1937 and June 1941, the Soviet Union supplied 904 aircraft, 82 tanks, over 1,500 automobiles, over 600 tractors, 1,140 heavy guns, over 9,000 machine guns (both light and heavy), 50,000 rifles, over 31,000 bombs, 2 million shells, 180 million cartridges, as well as over 3,600 military advisors and specialists.[155] Soviet military support to China, along with lesser material aid provided by Great Britain, and the financial aid of the United States, was seen as an integral part of the Foreign Office's 'stalemate' policy, which was aimed at containing any further Japanese aggression in the Far East through weakening it by attrition in a stalemated Chinese adventure. Seen by most Far Eastern experts as the great, unconquerable mass, China was thought to have the potential to be the Japanese equivalent of Napoleon's march on Moscow.[156] The enormous financial and military effort Japan was forced to make in China, combined with the traditional tensions and fears of the Soviet Union, created a real balance of power for the British Empire in the Far East.[157] The usefulness of a strong Soviet Union and a Soviet-backed China providing a deterrent to Japanese aggression against British Far Eastern interests continued to be a viable part of British Far Eastern strategy well into 1939, as the clouds of war grew darker over Europe. There were divided opinions as to how best to achieve this goal.

In mid-1938, in response to continued misguided pleas from Craigie for Britain to strike a deal with Japan over the China issue and thus attempt to buy Japanese goodwill, the FED and the Foreign Office outlined their views of how a long Japanese struggle in China, and continued fears of the Soviet Union, worked to Britain's advantage.[158] Sir John Brenan, a senior Far Eastern Department official, demolished Craigie's arguments and suggestions, painting a clear picture of the realities facing British policy-makers concerned with Far Eastern matters:

> The truth of the matter is that we acquired our dominant position in China as the result of our wars with that country in the nineteenth century and we can now only keep it by the same or similar methods. We must either use force, or otherwise bring sufficient pressure to bear on the

Japanese authorities to compel them to relinquish in our favour what they regard as the spoils of victory. We may, without fighting ourselves, be able to apply that pressure if the Japanese are exhausted by a long war with the Chinese, but it is futile to expect that we shall get what we want for the mere asking, or by protests about the infringements of our 'rights', or by a more friendly attitude ... there is no prospect of obtaining anything of permanent value by abandoning China and cooperating with Japan – at least, not yet. The 'stalemate' policy still offers the best hope for the survival of our influence in China.[159]

Cadogan, who took over as PUS from Vansittart on 1 August 1938, agreed entirely with Brenan's assessment. On 15 September, he repeated Brenan's analysis as the instructions Craigie was to follow from that point on in any discussions with the Japanese, making Brenan's views official Foreign Office policy on the matter.[160]

In April 1939, as discussions took place in the Cabinet Committee on Foreign Policy (FPC) over whether or not Great Britain should join France and the Soviet Union in another Grand Alliance, the question of the Far East, and Britain's interests there, was also taken into consideration.[161] The role, capabilities and intentions of the Soviet forces in the Far East held an important place in how the FPC viewed the situation in the Far East at this crucial juncture.[162]

The COS were tasked with providing the necessary appraisal of the Soviet Union's military capability and attitudes, primarily with the European situation in mind. The underlying question that was being asked and required an answer was, could the Soviet Union help Britain in any way if Japan threatened to take advantage of a general European war to further its position in the Far East at Great Britain's expense? The COS's initial evaluation was to repeat to the FPC that,

> In the Far East Russian intervention on our side would quite possibly delay and might even deter Japan from entering the war against us. Japan's preoccupation in China and the possibility of Russian action in Manchukuo would almost certainly prevent Japan from carrying out large-scale seaborne expeditions against either Singapore or Australia and New Zealand.[163]

The COS returned to the FPC six days later with a more comprehensive position.[164] In their view, the Russian Navy's two light cruisers, two large destroyers, nine small destroyers and large number of submarines (estimated at close to 80) were an important deterrent against the Japanese attacking Australia, New Zealand or Singapore with any sizeable, large-scale military force, especially an expeditionary force. The Red Army in the Far East was estimated at 5 cavalry and 32 infantry divisions. It had enough reserves for the first six months of a war, although there were some fuel supply problems. The opinion was that such a force would 'at least exercise a containing influence on Japan in Manchukuo and China, particularly in support of the Chinese 8th Route Army'. In the air, the Soviet air force east of Lake Baikal was composed of over 1,000 aircraft of various types. That force was economically independent of Western Russia, and it, too, had at least a six months' reserve of planes, parts and aviation fuel. In the COS's opinion, the general level of efficiency of the force was

> equal to, if not better than, the Japanese. A number of heavy type bombers in this force, although obsolete, can reach Tokyo, a threat which we understand the Japanese consider with some trepidation. The presence of this Russian air force in the Far East would have a restraining influence on the Japanese, would contain some Japanese air force, and might afford valuable assistance to China.[165]

While the Soviet 'steamroller' was plagued with traditional organizational, supply and transport problems in the western theatre, the overall picture of the Soviet's capability in the Far East was much more promising and helpful.[166]

This deterrent value of the USSR against Japan was not lost on Sir Thomas Inskip, the Secretary of State for Dominion Affairs. He and the rest of the FPC did not dispute the fact that Soviet forces would be able to exercise a restraining influence on Japan and were therefore a valuable element in ensuring that the strategic nightmare of Italy, Germany and Japan simultaneously attacking the British Empire did not become a reality.[167] That was also the strategic view held by Chatfield, now the Minister for the Coordination of Defence, when he questioned the COS as to the need for an Anglo-Soviet agreement covering the Far East.[168] The COS did not respond to this request because of other, more pressing planning matters. The Foreign Office and FED did not support a hard line against Japan in the negotiations with the Soviet Union, acknowledging the nervousness with which Tokyo was watching the process.[169] They were wary that the formalization of an alliance with the Soviet Union would cause Japan to panic and strike out against British interests. This view was also held by other high-ranking British officials, but there were other views as well.[170]

Sir Horace Wilson, Chief Industrial Advisor to His Majesty's government and a confidant of Prime Minister Chamberlain, was willing to sell out the Soviets in order to get the Japanese to accept some sort of arrangement. In a conversation with the US Ambassador to Great Britain, Joseph Kennedy, Wilson told him that the Soviet military was worthless and therefore there was nothing the Soviets had to offer. As well, 'he [Wilson] said the Japanese are beginning to indicate some willingness to play ball with Great Britain if no pact is concluded with Russia and have also indicated their willingness to break away from the Axis'.[171] Reports from the US Ambassador in Warsaw also suggested Neville Chamberlain was indecisive as he tried to balance European needs with Far Eastern interests and patch together an Anglo-Russian agreement:

> Though for some time it had become clear that British public opinion desired an alliance with Russia Chamberlain has been seeking a formula to circumvent the Far Eastern implications of a three-cornered full military alliance (reportedly desired by Moscow) for Chamberlain wished to minimize the risk of throwing Japan into military alliance with the Axis. Accordingly Beck [Jozef, Polish Foreign Minister] was now under the impression that Chamberlain was suggesting formula entailing: (a) mutual Anglo-Russian assistance (somewhat along the lines of the French–Soviet alliance)in the event of a European conflict; and (b) British assistance for Russia in the Far East in the event Russia were attacked there by a third party while engaged in honoring her pledge in Europe. Beck felt moreover there was room for hope that arrangements along these lines might not throw Japan into an Axis alliance.[172]

Such reports reveal clearly the serious indecision resulting from fears of the potentially major dislocation of the balance of power that would occur if the Soviet Union sided with the Axis powers. The references to Britain making a deal with the Japanese certainly could not have done much to strengthen the US view of London's determination to stand firm against the Japanese, and such rumours most certainly must have created great suspicions of Great Britain's real intentions towards the Far East.

The signing of the Nazi–Soviet Pact, on 23 August 1939, quickly ended any further speculation about the role the Soviet Union would play in conjunction with Great Britain in the Far East. At that point, the entire strategic position of the British Empire in the Far East required a serious re-evaluation.[173] However, even after the signing of the Pact,[174] the Japanese did not feel secure in their ability to turn southward against British and American interests. This was because of Tokyo's Chinese entanglements and its fear of the Soviet Union.[175] The FED and Foreign Office continued to believe, correctly, that the innate qualities that had long characterized Soviet–Japanese tensions remained beneficial to Britain's long-term interests. When Craigie informed the Foreign Office that he had information that Japan and the Soviet Union were working towards a non-aggression pact, his views were characteristically dismissed by Brenan and other FED members.[176] Brenan quickly dismantled Craigie's argument that Soviet Russia would throw over the Chinese for better relations with Japan:

> I suggest that it would not suit her purpose because of the difference, from the Russian point of view, between the European situation and that in the

Far East. It is not unlikely that the Kremlin looks at things somewhat as follows. The non-aggression pact with Germany will encourage the latter to embark on a war which will involve the Western European Powers and possibly the United States. From this war Russia can remain aloof, but whatever the outcome it will leave Germany exhausted and eliminate the German menace to Russia for a long time to come. It may also produce revolution in Germany, and other countries, and prepare the ground for the spread of communism. There is quite another outlook on the other side of the world. Russia's chief enemy in the Far East is Japan. But Japan is already at war with China and, if assured of a free hand by a non-aggression pact with Russia, the Japanese may well consolidate their position on the mainland and become a much graver menace to Soviet Russia than they were before. Whether or not, therefore, the Soviet Government are encouraged by their German pact to embark on a direct war with Japan, or, shall we say, enlarge the hostilities already in progress on the Mongolian border, it must be to Russia's interest to assist the Chinese in prolonging their own campaign against Japan. The longer China continues the war with Russian help, the greater the Soviet hold over the Chinese Government; and the more exhausted Japan becomes the less of a danger she is to Russia and the more chance of internal trouble and the emergence of a Japanese socialist regime.[177]

Collier supported Brenan's argument that the Soviet Union was not likely to agree to a non-aggression pact with Japan, as did R.A. Butler, the Parliamentary Under-Secretary of State.[178]

Further enquiries of Craigie by the FED and Foreign Office, as to the possibility of a Soviet–Japanese non-aggression pact, were answered initially that such an occurrence was indeed likely and that, therefore, a greater effort was needed to create better Anglo-Japanese relations.[179] The British Ambassador's stance on the matter soon crumbled under a devastating barrage of information and argument put forth from the FED experts, old Far Eastern hands, such as Brenan and Sir George Sansom, as well as the Political Intelligence Department.[180] Craigie's credibility, already damaged by his lack of Far Eastern knowledge and languages, and heavy reliance on the Japanophile Military Attaché, Major-General F.S.G. Piggott, had suffered one more devastating blow. He attempted to backtrack on his previous position and to repair the damage done to his credibility, but as far as his views on a Soviet–Japanese entente were concerned, it was too late.[181]

As 1939 came to a close, the Soviet bear held a vital position in the strategic and diplomatic manoeuvring of British Far Eastern policy-makers. Japan's insecurity concerning its isolated political position and economic instability brought on by the prolonged campaign in China, made it even more susceptible to the usual Japanese fears of the USSR and communism. Those fears would not be put to rest until Nazi Germany commenced Operation 'Barbarossa', in June 1941. Then, and only then, was the Russian 'loose cannon' in the Far East firmly lashed down in Eastern Europe. But, in December 1939, British interests could still be protected by a Far Eastern balance of power that used the Soviet bear and the Chinese panda as powerful levers against Japan. A reliance on Soviet–Japanese tensions was a vital factor used by British strategic policy-makers to ensure that Germany, Italy and Japan did not all declare war on the British Empire simultaneously. Fascinatingly, the Japanese fear of the Soviet Union also benefited the United States in its attempts to protect American interests in the Far East. This common strategic vision of the balance-of-power dynamic in the Far East helped move Anglo-American strategic foreign-policy relations closer together towards, if not a formally cooperative, at least a mutually supporting informal relationship.

## NOTES

1. FO 371/23559/F13004/347/23, 'Political Intelligence Report: The Foundations for a Japanese–Russian Entente', 21 Dec. 1939.
2. Studies of the attitudes towards and perceptions of Soviet Russia, as a major player in Far Eastern affairs in the 1930s are almost non-existent. A few works that touch on the subject are Haslam, *The Soviet Union and the Struggle for Collective Security in Europe, 1933–1939*; Haslam, *The Soviet Union and the Threat From the Far East, 1933–1941*; Coox, *Nomonhan*; I.H. Nish, *Japanese Foreign Policy 1869–1942* (London, 1977); Morley, ed., *Deterrent*; Roy H. Akagi, *Japan's Foreign Relations 1542–1942: A Short History* (Tokyo, 1936; Washington, DC, 1979); Neilson, 'Pursued by a Bear'; Pritchard, *Far Eastern Influences upon British Strategy towards the Great Powers*.
3. Lee, *Britain and the Sino-Japanese War*. For evidence that the US Far Eastern Division requested the US Embassy in London to keep a close eye on British announcements and discussions of the Soviet Union in the Far East, see Confidential US State Department Central File, Great Britain – Foreign Affairs, 1930–39 (hereafter CSDCF), on microfilm, National Archive, Washington, DC, 741.61/403, letter from Pierrepoint Moffat, Chief, Division of Western European Affairs, to Ray Atherton, US Embassy, London, 13 Jan. 1934. In the letter Moffat told Atherton that, with regard to a 1 Dec. 1933 despatch that contained a record of a debate in the House of Lords on the British government's policy in China, the Far Eastern Division appreciated the record and its information on British views of the Far East and Russia. They also wanted more information on the speakers recorded in future despatches so that weight could be given to specific comments. For the despatch, see ibid., despatch and enclosure from Raymond Cox, First Secretary of Embassy to Hull, 1 Dec. 1933.
4. FO 371/17263/N3090/1149/38, telegram from Sir R. Lindsay, 25 Apr. 1933. See also Simon Bourette-Knowles, 'The Global Micawber: Sir Robert Vansittart, the Treasury and the Global Balance of Power, 1933–35', *D&S*, 6 (1995): 91–121, 99.
5. See G.L. Owen, 'The Metro–Vickers Crisis: Anglo-Soviet Relations between Trade Agreements, 1932–1934', *SEER*, 114 (1971): 92–112; Neilson, 'Pursued by a Bear', 207; Neilson, 'A Cautionary Tale: The Metro–Vickers Incident of 1933', in Greg Kennedy and Keith Neilson, eds, *Incidents and International Relations: Personalities, Perceptions and Power* (Westport, CT, 2001); FO 371/17263/N3090/1149/38, telegram from

Vansittart, 25 Apr. 1933.

6. FO 371/17263/N3231/1149/38, telegram from Vansittart to FO, 28 Apr. 1933, and minutes of Lawrence Collier (Head of the FO Northern Dept.) and Robert L. Craigie (Head of FO American Dept.), both 29 Apr. 1933. See also James K. Libbey, 'The American–Russian Chamber of Commerce', *DH*, 9 (1985): 233–49; and Edward M. Bennett, *Recognition of Russia* (Waltham, 1970).

7. FO 371/17263/N3231/1149/38, telegram from Vansittart to FO, 28 April 1933, and minutes of Collier and Craigie, both 29 April 1933. See also, Andrew J. Williams, *Trading with the Bolsheviks: The Politics of East–West Trade, 1920–39* (Manchester, 1992), 169–70.

8. FO 371/17263/N3231/1149/38, Vansittart telegram; see also Robert Dallek, *Franklin D. Roosevelt and American Foreign Policy, 1932–1945* (New York, 1979), 39–40.

9. Karl A. Bickel, President of the United Press Association, confided to his friend Nelson T. Johnson, US Minister in China, on 30 Sept. 1932, that his sources caused him to believe that if FDR were elected, he would probably do something to regularize relations with Soviet Russia soon after his election because of the role Russia could play in the Far East due to the Russian–Manchurian situation. Nelson T. Johnson MSS (hereafter NTJ Papers), Library of Congress, Washington, DC, Container 17, letter Bickel to Johnson, 30 Sept. 1932.

10. Dallek, *Franklin D. Roosevelt and American Foreign Policy*, 78–81.

11. FO 371/17263/N7829/1149/38, telegram from T.M. Snow to FO, 26 Oct. 1933; FO 371/17263/F6784/614/23, telegram from Snow to FO, 26 Oct. 1933. See also Malcolm D. Kennedy, *The Estrangement of Great Britain and Japan, 1917–35* (Manchester, 1969), 270–1.

12. FO 371/17263/N8492/1149/38, despatch from Lindsay to Simon, 16 Nov. 1933.

13. Dallek, *Franklin D. Roosevelt and American Foreign Policy*, 78.

14. FO 371/17263/N7726/1149/38, telegram from Snow to FO, 26 Oct. 1933. Snow reported that the Japanese FO feared that such recognition would add fuel to the fire of hot-headed anti-Soviet and anti-Western/US groups in general, because the perception was that recognition would strengthen the Soviets' position in the Far East against Japan.

15. CAB 21/395, 'The Munition Industry' ns, 20 May 1932, ICF 313, with 'an appreciation by the Technical Consultant to the I.I.C., Mr G.S. Whitham (A.D.O.F. War Office)'; ibid., 'USSR Present Capacity of Railways to Maintain an Armed Force in the Far East', ICF 14, 4 Apr. 1933; ibid., 'USSR The Shipbuilding Industry', ICF 31, 1 May 1933.

16. CAB 4/22, Committee of Imperial Defence Papers (hereafter CAB 4/), Paper 1112–B, 30 June 1933, 'Imperial Defence Policy', FO memo.

17. Ibid.

18. CAB 53/23, Chiefs of Staff Committee Minutes of Meetings and Papers (hereafter COS), Paper No. 307, 'Imperial Defence Policy', 20 May 1933.

19. CAB 53/23, COS Paper, No. 310, 'Imperial Defence Policy', 12 Oct. 1933.

20. FO 371/17388/W11987/11987/80, Collier and Oliphant minutes, 2 Nov. and 8 Nov. 1933. For the anti-Communist tradition in British politics, see Michael Jabara Carley, '"A Fearful Concatenation of Circumstances": the Anglo-Soviet Rapprochement, 1934–1936', *JCEH*, 5 (1996): 36–44.

21. FO 371/17338/W11987/11987/50, Collier minute, 22 Nov. 1933.

22. Ibid.

23. Ibid., Oliphant minutes, 8 Nov. 1933.

24. Ibid., Orde minute, 27 Oct. 1933; Lampson Diary, entry for 13 Nov. 1933.

25. Ibid.

26. Ibid., Wellesley minute, 8 Nov. 1933.

27. Ibid.
28. Ibid.
29. Until otherwise indicated, the following is based on ibid., Vansittart minutes, 30 Nov. 1933.
30. CAB 16/109, Defence Requirements Committee Minutes and Papers (hereafter CAB 16/), DRC Report 14, 28 Feb. 1934. D.C. Watt, 'Work Completed and Work as Yet Unborn: Some Reflections on the Conference from the British Side', in Nish, ed., *Anglo-Japanese Alienation, 1919–1952*, 291–2.
31. CAB 16/109, DRC Paper 14, 28 Feb. 1934.
32. CAB 16/109, minutes of the 3rd DRC Meeting, 4 Dec. 1933.
33. Ibid.
34. Ibid.
35. Lord Vansittart, *The Mist Procession: The Autobiography of Lord Vansittart* (London, 1958), 443.
36. For a look at the Soviet's equivalent of the DRC, see Lennart Samuelson, 'Mikhail Tukhachevsky and War-Economic Planning: Reconsiderations on the Pre-war Soviet Military Build-Up', *JSMS*, 9 (1996): 804–47.
37. Evidence of the need to consider Soviet–Japanese tensions in the formulation of British Far Eastern strategic policy at the highest level is available in CAB 23/78, Minutes of Cabinet Meetings (hereafter CAB 23/), Cabinet 9(34), 14 Mar. 1934, when the viability of making closer relations with Japan a formal policy were discussed.
38. Neilson, 'Pursued by a Bear', 207–9.
39. FO 371/17256/N8770/3632/38, 'Annual Report on Russia', 5 Dec. 1933.
40. CAB 53/23, COS Paper No. 316, and also, CAB 4/22, Paper No. 1127–B, 'Russian Preparations for War'; CAB 2/6, CID Minutes of meetings (hereafter CAB 2/), Meeting No. 264, 31 May 1934. See also Neilson, note 83.
41. CAB 4/22, Paper No. 1127–B, 'Russian Preparations for War'.
42. War Office (WO), PRO, Kew, London, 106/5499, secret letter from Vivian to Dickens, 19 Jan. 1934.
43. Ibid.
44. CHT/4/4, secret and personal letter from Chatfield to Dreyer, 2 Feb. 1934.
45. WO 106/5499, note from Dickens to Dill, 20 Feb. 1934.
46. WO 106/5499, secret letter from Dill to Dickens, 28 Feb. 1934.
47. WO 106/5499, holograph from Dickens to Dill, 1 Mar. 1934.
48. FO 371/18301/N489/4/38, T.A. Shone and R.G. Howe minutes, commenting on CID paper 1127–B, 17 Jan. 1934.
49. FO 371/18176/F639/316/23, despatch from Lindley to FO, 26 Dec. 1933.
50. FO 371/18166/F27/24/23, telegram from Lindley to FO, 1 Jan. 1934.
51. FO 371/18166/F731/24/23, Orde minute, 11 Jan. 1934.
52. FO 371/18176/F823/316/23, Foreign Office memo by A.W.G. Randall, 9 Feb. 1934.
53. Ibid.
54. Ibid.
55. Ibid., Collier minute, 16 Feb. 1934.
56. Ibid.
57. Ibid., Vansittart minute, 22 Feb. 1934.
58. FO 800/293, Cadogan MSS, PRO, Kew, London, China file 1934–36, private and confidential letter from Mounsey to Cadogan, 31 May 1934.
59. Ibid.
60. FO 371/18176/F823/316/23, Simon minute, 26 Feb. 1934.
61. Ibid.
62. Ibid.

63. For the full description of this 'no bloc' policy see Greg Kennedy, '1935: A Snapshot of British Imperial Defence in the Far East', in Keith Neilson and Greg Kennedy, eds, *Far Flung Lines: Essays in Honour of Donald M. Schurman* (London, 1997), 190–216.

64. Louis, *British Strategy in the Far East*, 222; Trotter, *Britain and East Asia*, 58.

65. FO 371/18169/F5943/57/23, very confidential letter from Clive to Wellesley, 23 Aug. 1934.

66. FO 371/18177/F5371/316/23, telegram from Clive to FO, 4 Sept. 1934.

67. Ibid., Orde minutes, 5 Sept.; S. Harcourt-Smith minute, 5 Sept.; Sir George A. Mounsey minute, 5 Sept.; Vansittart minute, 5 Sept.; Simon minute, 7 Sept.; and letter from Neville Chamberlain (acting PM) to Simon, 10 Sept., all 1934; see also WO 106/5396, 'A Review of the Far Eastern Situation' prepared by MI2, 31 Dec. 1933.

68. FO 371/18177/F5371/316/23, personal letter from Simon to Chamberlain, 7 Sept. 1934.

69. Ibid., Harcourt-Smith minute, 5 Sept. 1934, on conversation that he had with Col. Ismay and a Col. Grimsdale on the matter. Ismay requested the meeting and revealed that the WO felt Russia was improving its military position in the Far East faster than Japan could, and that this fear of being over-matched was causing some groups in Japan's military to call for a pre-emptive strike. The WO did not think that the Japanese General Staff was so inclined at the moment.

70. WO 106/5499, telegram Clive to FO, 4 Sept. 1934; Ismay minutes, 7 Sept.

71. CAB 53/24, COS Paper 344 (JP), 'Hong Kong – Plans for Defence, Relief or Recapture', 11 July 1934.

72. Ibid.

73. FO 371/17600/F6006/537/23, Secret Report from DNI to FO, 6 Oct. 1934; ibid., Naval Attaché's Report, 5 Sept. 1934.

74. Ibid. Hasegawa had been Naval Attaché at Washington from 1923 to 1926 and Chief of Staff in 1932 to the Naval delegation to the Geneva Disarmament Conference. He was appointed Vice-Minister of Marine in early 1934. The British assessment of him was that he spoke good English, was very friendly and fond of the sake bottle. It was expected that he would go far in the service because of his political capabilities. See FO 371/19361/F1104/1104/23, despatch from Tokyo to FO, on leading personalities in Japan, 18 Jan. 1935.

75. FO 371/19360/F1086/1086/23, Annual Report on Japan for 1934, 1 Jan. 1935.

76. Ibid., and Neilson, 'Pursued by a Bear', 210.

77. On the European crisis, see Pratt, *East of Malta, West of Suez*, 8–21; R.J.Q. Adams, *British Politics and Foreign Policy in the Age of Appeasement, 1935–39* (London, 1993); M.I. Roi, 'From the Stresa Front to the Triple Entente: Sir Robert Vansittart, the Abyssinian Crisis and the Containment of Germany', *DH*, 6 (1995): 61–90; R.A.C. Parker, *Chamberlain and Appeasement: British Policy and the Coming of the Second World War* (London, 1993); Gaines Post, Jr, *Dilemmas of Appeasement: British Deterrence and Defense, 1934–1937* (Ithaca, NY, 1993).

78. Robert Manne, 'The Foreign Office and the Failure of Anglo-Soviet Rapprochement', *JCH*, 16 (1981): 725–55; R. Vansittart, *The Mist Procession*, 454–5; FO 371/18826/N1339/55/38, Vansittart to Chilston (British Ambassador to Moscow), 21 Feb. 1935; FO 371/19447/N281/1/38, Vansittart minute, 21 Jan. 1935; Greg Kennedy, '1935', 285–91; Neilson, 'Pursued by a Bear', 209; Roi, 'From the Stresa Front to the Triple Entente', 82–3; Bourette-Knowles, 'The Global Micawber', 114–17; Carley, 'A Fearful Concatenation of Circumstances', 29–36.

79. FO 371/18731/A127/22/45, despatch from Chilston to FO, 5 Jan.; Craigie minute, 9 Jan.; Collier minute, 9 Jan., all 1935.

80. Ibid., Collier minute; Collier/Ashton-Gwatkin memo, 7 Jan. 1935.

81. Ibid., Collier/Ashton-Gwatkin memo, 7 Jan. 1935. On the British attempts to help

rehabilitate China's currency see Trotter, 'Dominions and Imperial Defence', 132–46; Lowe, *Britain in the Far East*, 150–1; Endicott, *Diplomacy and Enterprise*, 82–100.

82. FO 371/18731/A127/22/45, Collier/Ashton-Gwatkin memo, 7 Jan. 1935.
83. FO 371/18731/A127/22/45, Wellesley minute, 10 Jan. 1935; Vansittart minute, 11 Jan. 1935.
84. FO 371/19347/F632/13/23, Collier minute, 29 Jan. 1935.
85. FO 371/19460/N927/135/38, Minute by Vansittart and memo from Collier, Wigram and Orde, 12 Feb. 1935; Roi, 'From the Stresa Front to the Triple Entente', 84–5; Bourette-Knowles, 'The Global Macawber', 105–16; David Carlton, *Anthony Eden* (London, 1981), 62–4; R. Rhodes-James, *Anthony Eden* (London, 1986), 140–5.
86. FO 371/19347/F4366/13/23, despatch, Clive to Simon, 'Soviet–Japanese Relations', 6 July 1935; FO 371/19349/F4646/29/23, despatch, 'Political Situation in Japan', 20 June 1935; FO 371/19349/F2908/55/23, 'Press Summary', 3 Apr. 1935.
87. Kennedy, '1935', 266–9.
88. 1936 was considered a critical year by British strategic planners because it was the year in which the Japanese obtained a number of naval aircraft squadrons and new vessels into the Japanese Fleet; the Japanese were likely to withdraw from the Washington and London naval treaty system that year; it was a year before the base at Singapore could be completed; and, it marked the beginning of British naval rearmament programmes, all of which combined to create a very unfavourable position for the Royal Navy in the Far East as a guarantor of imperial interests. Kennedy, '1935', 283–4.
89. Kennedy, '1935', 259–61; Roi, 'From the Stresa Front to the Triple Entente', 82–3.
90. FO 371/18733/A3755/22/45, copy of record of conversation from Central Dept. file, C2726/55/18 dated 1 Apr., 5 Apr. 1935.
91. CSDCF, 741.61/456, telegram from Bullitt to Hull, 1 Apr. 1935.
92. FO 371/18733/A3755/22/45, record of conversation, 5 Apr. 1935.
93. CSDCF, 741.61/476, confidential letter from Bullitt to Hull, 22 Apr. 1935, underlining in the original.
94. FO 371/18733/A3755/22/45, record of conversation, 5 Apr. 1935.
95. FO 371/19347/F4837/13/23, memo on 'Soviet–Japanese relations', Orde and Dodds minutes, 6 June 1935.
96. FO 371/19357/F8065/376/23, Vansittart minute, 12 Dec. 1935. See Coox, *Nomonhan*.
97. CAB 23/83, Cabinet meeting 6(36), 12 Feb. 1936.
98. CAB 24/259, Cabinet Papers (hereafter CP), CP12(36), 'Memorandum by the Chief of the Imperial General Staff', 17 Jan. 1936.
99. Ibid.
100. FO 371/20279/F607/89/23, 'Cabinet Conclusion Extract', 29 Jan. 1936.
101. FO 371/20279/F701/89/23, 'Orde Memo', 22 Jan. 1936.
102. Ibid., Collier minute, 22 Jan. 1936.
103. Ibid., Wellesley minute, 22 Jan. 1936.
104. Ibid., Vansittart minute, 25 Jan. 1936.
105. Anthony Eden MSS, FO 954/6, PRO, Kew, London, folder – The Far East, letter from Drummond to Vansittart, 21 Feb. 1936.
106. FO 371/20279/F701/89/23, Stanhope minute, 23 Jan. 1936.
107. Ibid.
108. Ibid., Eden minute, 23 Jan. 1936.
109. FO 371/20279/F607/89/23, 'Cabinet Conclusion Extract', 29 Jan. 1936.
110. FO 371/20279/F2872/89/23, private and confidential letter from Clive to Orde, 22 Apr. 1936.
111. Ibid.
112. Ibid. Eden's view of Anglo-Soviet relations was, 'I want the footing to be friendly as

befits two fellow-members of the League but I have no intention of hugging the bear too closely for I am fully conscious of what happens to people who hug bears. Moreover, I have no illusions as to the real feelings of the Soviet Government towards the capitalist State.' Phipps [PHPP] Papers, 1/16, private letter, Eden to Phipps, 28 Feb. 1936.

113. Eden MSS, FO 954/7, note and memo by Secretary of the CID (Hankey) to Eden, 11 Aug. 1936 (the memo is dated 8 June). Hankey sees the role of Russia as being critical to Britain's Far Eastern strategy given the military weakness of the empire in that region: 'it is difficult to make a helpful suggestion, except that we should do all we can to avert war between China and Japan (which would probably precipitate the situation in which Japan will be free to pursue her "*Drang nach Suden*") and to maintain as satisfactory relations with her as we can. Our best hope for the present lies in the balance of power between China's neighbors – Japan and Russia. The longer it can be maintained without war the better.'

114. FO 371/20279/F3900/89/23, despatch from Clive to FO, 3 July 1936.

115. Ibid., S.G. Harcourt-Smith minute, 15 July 1936.

116. Ibid., Orde minute, 16 July.

117. Neilson, 'Pursued by a Bear', 212–13.

118. CAB 53/29, COS Paper No. 523, 'The Vulnerability of Burma in a Far Eastern War', 27 Oct. 1936.

119. Ibid.

120. Ibid.

121. The Cabinet desired an appreciation of where Great Britain's military preparedness stood so that the Dominions could be apprised of the imperial defence situation at the 1937 Imperial Conference. The COS produced a number of reports, one of which revealed how the Royal Navy was fearful of Russian involvement in a European war against Germany lest such action would bring Japan into the fray. This would cause the RN to have to send a large portion of the fleet to the Far East, a delicate point in Britain's strategic planning. The Navy preferred Russian neutrality to intervention in the case of a European war. CAB 53/29, COS Paper No. 539(JP), 'Comparison of the Strength of Great Britain with that of Certain Other Nations as at May 1937', 22 Dec. 1936; CAB 53/30, COS Paper No. 551, 9 Feb. 1937 (also CAB 4/26, CID paper No. 1311–B, 25 Feb. 1937).

122. Neilson, 'Pursued by a Bear', 214.

123. FO 371/20348/N5886/287/38, minutes, 19 Nov. 1936.

124. FO 371/20286/F6478/539/23, despatch from Clive to FO, 26 Oct. 1936.

125. Ibid., Orde minute, 1 Nov., Cadogan minute, 5 Nov., both 1936.

126. This point was brought up in the CID and at the Imperial Conference of 1937, when, in outlining the Review of Imperial Defence the COS stated that as far as the situation in the Far East was concerned Sino-Japanese tensions continued to create risks for British interests in that region, but 'On the other hand, the increase of Soviet strength in the Far East may act as a check on Japanese activities, though it may deflect them further southward, when they would come into more direct conflict with our interests.' CAB 53/30/COS 561 and 562. 'Review of Imperial Defence', 11 Feb. 1937 for both.

127. FO 371/20348/N5886/287/38, Vansittart minute, 5 Nov. 1936.

128. On the impact of the Anti-Comintern Pact on Japan and its thinking, see Ohata Tokushiro, 'The Anti-Comintern Pact, 1935–1939', in J.W. Morley, ed., *Deterrent Diplomacy*, 20–1.

129. FO 371/20287/F7146/553/23, Orde memo, 19 Nov. 1936.

130. Ibid.

131. Ibid., Cadogan minute, 19 Nov. 1936.

132. The following is based on FO 371/20286/F7504/303/23, secret FO memorandum, 4 Dec. 1936.
133. Ibid.
134. Ibid., Eden minute, 8 Dec. 1936.
135. John R. Ferris, 'Indulged in All Too Little?: Vansittart, Intelligence and Appeasement', *D&S*, 6 (1995): 122–75, 134–6; David Dilks, 'Appeasement and "Intelligence"', in David Dilks, ed., *Retreat From Power: Studies in Britain's Foreign Policy of the Twentieth Century* (London, 1981), 139–69, 142. The standard work on British intelligence does not take the interwar Far East and intelligence work into account in any relevant way, preferring to write it off as 'The Japanese intercepts thus merely helped Britain keep track of a menace to which she was in no real position to respond.' See Christopher Andrew, *Her Majesty's Secret Service: The Making of the British Intelligence Community* (London, 1986), 353. For a more thoughtful accounting of the role of intelligence in the formulation of Britain's Far Eastern policy in this period see Antony Best, *Britain, Japan and Pearl Harbor: Avoiding War in East Asia, 1936–41* (London, 1995), 27–9; Best, 'Constructing an Image: British Intelligence and Whitehall's Perception of Japan, 1931–1939', *INS*, 11 (1996): 403–23.
136. CAB 53/30/COS 561 and 562, 11 Feb. 1937.
137. Ibid.
138. CAB 4/25, CID Paper 1305–B, 'Review of Imperial Defence by the Chiefs of Staff Sub-Committee', 22 Feb. 1937. Also, FO 371/22190/F2286/2286/23, 'Annual Report on Japan for 1937', 1 Jan. 1938; and FO 371/22299/N961/961/38, 'Annual Report on Russia for 1937', 9 Feb. 1938.
139. Neilson, 'Pursued by a Bear', 215–16.
140. FO 371/22299/N961/961/38, 'Annual Report on Russia', 9 Feb. 1938. The Soviet Navy also was beginning to play a more important role in British considerations of the Far East at this time, 'it is difficult to say where Russian naval policy is leading; but, in view of the insistence with which the Soviet Union maintained that her Far Eastern forces should not be governed by the Anglo-Soviet Naval Treaty, it is conceivable that all her "large navy" talk is directed towards Japan, and that it is in the Far East that her primary naval strength is now most urgently required'.
141. FO 371/22288/N97/97/38, letter Collier to Col. Hayes, DMI, WO, 14 Jan. 1938; FO 371/22288/N748/97/38, letter from Chilston (British Ambassador in Moscow) to Collier, 1 Feb. 1938.
142. FO 371/21041/F8128/609/23, Orde minute, 20 Oct. 1937; FO 371/21041/F10924/609/23, 'Confidential, Military Attaché's despatch', 17 Nov. 1937.
143. FO 371/21104/N3447/461/38, A. Walker minute, 3 July 1937.
144. Ibid., Collier minute, 3 July 1937.
145. Ibid., WO minute, 3 July 1937; see all of WO 106/5626 and WO 106/5631.
146. Hata Ikuhiko, 'The Japanese–Soviet Confrontation', in Morley ed., *Deterrent Diplomacy*, 115–79.
147. FO 371/22185/F2844/152/23, despatch from Craigie to FO, 12 Feb. 1938.
148. Ibid.
149. Ibid.
150. Shai, *Origins of the War in the East*, 120, 163.
151. Jonathan Haslam, 'Soviet Aid to China and Japan's Place in Moscow's Foreign Policy, 1937–1939', in Ian Nish, ed., *Some Aspects of Soviet–Japanese Relations in the 1930s* (London 1982), 35–58; Haslam, *The Soviet Union and the Threat From the Far East, 1933–1941*, 88–135.
152. CAB 53/10, COS Minutes, 263rd meeting, 23 Nov. 1938.
153. Ibid.

154. Ibid.
155. Haslam, 'Soviet Aid to China and Japan's Place in Moscow's Foreign Policy', 38–9; Haslam, *The Soviet Union and the Threat from the Far East*, 88–111.
156. FO 371/22183/F6419/103/23, 'Annual economic report on Japan', 20 May 1938; FO 371/22183/F6424/103/23, 'Visit of Mr Hall Patch to Tokyo', 20 May 1938; Kennedy, '1935'.
157. Here the German–Soviet non-aggression pact of 23 Aug. 1939, and the resulting anti-German, anti-Russian fears it created in Japan, worked in Britain's favour. See Nish, *Japanese Foreign Policy, 1869–1942*, 230–3; WO, 208/847, comments of N.B. Ronald and others, 23–24 Aug. 1938.
158. FO 371/22181/F8961/71/23, letter from Craigie to Cadogan, 27 July 1938; ibid., Sir John Brenan minute, 25 Aug.
159. Ibid., Brenan minute.
160. Ibid., secret letter from Cadogan to Craigie, 15 Sept. 1938.
161. CAB 27/624, Committee on Foreign Policy, Proceedings, 43rd and 44th meetings, 19 and 25 Apr. 1939.
162. Neilson, 'Pursued by a Bear', 217–18.
163. CAB 27/624, FPC, 43rd meeting.
164. CAB 24/285, CP 95(39), 'Military Value of Russia, Report by the COS', 25 Apr. 1939; also CAB 53/48, COS Paper 887, 'Military Value of Russia', 24 Apr. 1939.
165. CAB 24/285, CP 95(39), 'Military Value of Russia'.
166. For a contrary view of British assessments of the Russian military in the Far East, see Paul W. Doerr, 'The Changkufeng/Lake Khasan Incident of 1938: British Intelligence on Soviet and Japanese Military Performance', *INS*, 5 (1990): 184–99.
167. CAB 27/624, FPC, 43rd and 44th meetings.
168. CAB 53/11, COS minutes, 305 meeting, 28 June 1939. The question had been raised in an indirect way at the 17 May Cabinet Meeting, when in response to questions on how Japan would react to an Anglo-Soviet agreement aimed at Germany, Lord Halifax had replied, 'he thought the effect would be bad, but not catastrophic. Japan would, no doubt, be annoyed; but he doubted whether Japan's actual course of action would be greatly affected provided that our agreement with Russia did not extend to the Far East. When the time came the Japanese Government would do what suited them, whatever their commitments.' CAB 23/99, Cabinet meeting, 17 May 1939.
169. FO 371/23555/F4419/176/23, 'Record of conversation', Ashley Clarke minutes, 10 May; E. Dening minutes, 11 May; Sansom minutes, 12 May; R.G. Howe minutes, 13 May; Cadogan minutes, 15 May; Halifax had read this as well on 15 May with no comment, all 1939; Inverchapel Papers, Bodleian Library, Oxford, Box 1939 and undated 1930s papers, memo of conversation between Inverchapel and Generalissimo Chiang Kai-shek, 29 Apr. 1939.
170. Premier [PREM] Files, PRO, Kew, 1/409, note from Stanhope to Halifax, 19 May 1939.
171. CSDCF, 741/61/629, strictly confidential telegram from Kennedy to Hull, 19 May 1939.
172. CSDCF, 741.61/645, strictly confidential telegram from Biddle (Ambassador to Poland) to Hull, 25 May 1939.
173. CAB 53/11, COS Minutes, 312 meeting, 24 Aug. 1939. See also, Brock Millman, 'Toward War with Russia: British Naval and Air Planning for Conflict in the Near East, 1939–1940', *JCH*, 29 (1994): 261–83.
174. Hosoya Chihiro, 'The Tripartite Pact, 1939–1940', in Morley, ed., *Deterrent Diplomacy*, 191–258; Nish, *Japanese Foreign Policy*, 231–45; David Bergamini, *Japan's Imperial Conspiracy*, Vol. II (New York, 1971), 861–920; Haslam, 'Soviet Aid to China and Japan's Place in Moscow's Foreign Policy, 1937–1939'.
175. FO 371/23555/F11481/23/23, Simon note on letter from Peir Groves, 11 Oct. 1939;

ibid., Brenan minute, 2 Nov. 1939; FO 371/23556/F11063/176/23, 'Record of Conversation between R. Butler and Japanese Ambassador, Shigemitsu', 13 Oct. 1939, and minutes of Ashley Clarke and George Sansom, both 19 Oct., and R.G. Howe (now head of the FED), 21 Oct., all 1939.

176. FO 371/23558/F9456/347/23, telegram from Craigie to FO, 25 Aug. 1939.

177. Ibid., Brenan minute, 29 Aug. 1939.

178. Ibid., Collier minute, 30 Aug.; Butler minute, 1 Sept., both 1939.

179. FO 371/23559/F11426/347/23, telegram from FO to Craigie, 23 Nov. 1939; FO 371/23559/F12088/347/23, telegram from Craigie to FO, 23 Nov. 1939.

180. FO 371/23559/F12088/347/23, Dening minutes, 23 Nov.; R.G. Howe minute, 27 Nov.; Cadogan minute, 28 Nov. (This particular telegram was also read by George Sansom, Vansittart and Halifax, who all seemed to accept the above minutes and offered no support to Craigie's views), all 1939. FO371/23559/F12129/347/23, telegram from Sir W. Seeds (Moscow) to FO, 25 Nov. 1939; Brenan minutes, 2 Dec.; and FO 371/23559/F13004/347/23, 'Political Intelligence Report: The Foundations for a Japanese–Russian Entente', 21 Dec. 1939. The conclusion of the lengthy report was that:

> The liquidation of outstanding disputes between Japan and Russia for the sake of their mutual convenience, is possible and not improbable. On the other hand, the conclusion of a fundamental agreement, such as could radically affect the position of the Western Democracies in the Far Eastern areas and influence the issues of the European war, opens up very great difficulties.
>
> History and geography combine to make Japan regard Russia as her permanent rival for the hegemony of East Asia, which is the goal of Japanese ambitions. That rivalry is, at the present time, chiefly active in China, where Russia is thwarting Japan's efforts to acquire political and economic control in the face of Chinese resistance …
>
> The principal advocates of a 'pro-Russian' policy for Japan are an extremist minority group. It is only if this group succeeds – as is possible but not, on the whole likely, – in wresting the governing power in Japan from the hands of the relatively moderate element who are at present in office that there would be imminent danger of Japan turning decisively in the direction of Russia. Drastic action against Japan by the US might drive Japan further in that direction, but at the present time the Government in Washington, although taking a firmer line with Japan, show no intention of proceeding to extremes.
>
> As for Russia, one can see no adequate inducement for her to enter into a non-aggression pact with Japan which would crystallise the position in East Asia and fetter Russia's freedom of action in that region. Any motives which Moscow might have for binding herself to Japan would be motives of pure opportunism arising out of her attitude towards the world situation as a whole.

181. FO 371/23559/12287/347/23, telegram from Craigie to FO, 30 Nov. 1939; Dening minute, 5 Nov.; Howe minute, 6 Dec. all 1939.

# 3

# British and American Views of the Soviet Union's Role in the Far East, 1933–39, II: The Americans

The Roosevelt administration's attitude towards the usefulness of the Soviet Union in Far Eastern strategic matters underwent some modification from 1933 to September 1939, primarily on issues related to the actual worthiness of Soviet Russia's military forces in that region. Yet, overall, the basic goal of using the Japanese fear of a joint Soviet–US, and possibly British, front to keep Japanese aggression in check remained a constant factor in American Far Eastern policy, closely monitored and exploited by the US Far Eastern Division of the State Department, the Secretary of State, Cordell Hull, and Roosevelt.[1] There were various channels through which information on the Soviet Union and how it affected US interests in the Far East reached these decision-makers.

One of the early, important commentators on the increasing importance of the Soviet Union in Far Eastern affairs was the talented US Ambassador to China, Nelson T. Johnson. An academic, professional diplomatist and the recognized expert on Chinese language, government and culture, Johnson was a valuable 'old China hand'.[2] He was also the type of diplomatic official least likely to make an impression on President Roosevelt, who fancied the informal style of a William C. Bullitt, the US Ambassador to the Soviet Union. In fact, in Roosevelt's view, too many State Department career men lost their common touch and became snobs. His belief that they would benefit from consular or business experience eventually led to a shake-up within the State Department ranks in 1935, which resulted in the likes of J. Pierrepont Moffat, Chief of the Division of Western European Affairs, being assigned to head the legation in Australia for two years. In Roosevelt's view, Bill Bullitt was a refreshing contrast to such correct diplomats. The recognition of Soviet Russia was an example of what could be done if the diplomat's code of endless talking and sparring was ignored.[3] An experienced veteran of the diplomatic game, Johnson, on the other hand, had the consular advantage. But, given Roosevelt's personality and attitude towards the diplomatic corps, Johnson, like so many other State Department members, would have to be content to let his expertise support his views and ideas as they percolated through the State Department apparatus. Influencing policy construction, as opposed to making policy decisions, was the role of men such as Johnson during this difficult period.

The specialized requirements of the Far Eastern Division and the close relations of its staff, allowed Johnson and the US Ambassador to Japan, Jospeh Grew, the chance to have their ideas drift through the policy-making process, finding allies to support and advance them to the next highest level. This was in contrast to Bullitt's style, which attempted to bludgeon his ideas into actual policy.[4] This difference in style and procedure was a reflection of the uniqueness of the Far Eastern Division, a situation resulting from the language skills, cultural knowledge and specialized training that was required by the majority of its staff.[5] As was the case for Great Britain's policy-making elite, the strangeness and foreignness of the Far East made policy-makers in the United States very dependent on those few individuals who had the necessary skills, contacts and training to enable them to give an accurate picture of Far Eastern affairs.

Johnson's view of the role of the Soviet bear in the Far East fluctuated in 1932. In the early months of that year he thought that the Soviet Union was very weak militarily in the East, and that Japan could have taken Vladivostok and the Maritime Provinces at any time.[6] However, although militarily weak, there were certain historical pressures that continued to make the Soviet Union a key element in any American policy aimed at securing peace in the Far East. In a January letter to the then Secretary of State, Frank B. Kellogg, Johnson gave a clear expression of the relationship between Japan and the USSR:

> The more I think about the situation in Manchuria and Japan's recent activities there, the more convinced I am that the whole matter must be interpreted in the light of Japan's traditions with Soviet Russia … The interest of Russia in Manchuria is strategic. Manchuria is stretched directly across Russia's highway to Asia and Pacific waters. The vast and fertile steppes of Siberia, destined some day to be the bread basket of European Russia, need access to the Pacific. The only power that challenges this need is Japan, which Fate has placed directly in front of Siberia's front door, Vladivostok. Japan's interest in Manchuria is both strategic and economic. It is strategic because a powerful and growing Russia threatens Japan; it threatens Japan because Japan is completely dependent upon the mainland for her supplies of iron and coal, resources so necessary to the successful life of a modern nation in this age of steel ships … A strong and growing Russia threatens this freedom of access so necessary to Japan's existence. Therefore, it seems to me that there can be

no final settlement, nor settlement calculated to ensure peace in the Far East, that does not take into consideration the vital interests of these three nations: China, Russia, and Japan.[7]

According to Johnson, US foreign policy would have to take into account this three-sided structure in any policy it made for the Far East. He advocated strongly the idea that it was indeed in the United States' self-interest to stay involved in Far Eastern matters, even though it would have to play the loathsome 'balance of power' game in order to keep the peace in the Far East.[8] His argument was that the United States, China and Japan were jointly responsible for the future of the Pacific area, but the growing power of Russia was something that none of the other powers could afford to ignore. Any solution to the struggle taking place in the Far East was bound to fail if it did not recognize the need to consider the Soviet Union.[9]

Stanley Hornbeck, the Chief of the State Department's Division of Far Eastern Affairs, also recognized the changing face of relations in the Far East and his views coincided exactly with Johnson's. Writing in February, 1932, Hornbeck pointed out that Great Britain needed to reestablish the balance of power in northern China using the Soviet Union and suggested what this meant for US Far Eastern policy:

> The balance of power has again been destroyed, this time by Japan, and Great Britain is becoming conscious of her need for diplomatic reinsurance in the Far East ... But in Northern China, there is only one Power which could counter-balance the rising power of Japan: the Soviet Union; and it is in Northern China that the balance of power has been destroyed ... So long as the United States is dealing with the defense of international rights and interests in Central China, it may be assumed that the British Government will cooperate. It is not certain that they will follow us with any conviction so far as concerns Manchuria, where their inclination will be to accept a special Japanese position as a *fait accompli* of which they can say that they regret the fact but that they can do nothing to undo it. It should, therefore, be the objective of our Far Eastern policy, so to link the situation in the Yangtze with our policy in Manchuria as to bring basic Russian and British interests simultaneously into the balance against such features of Japanese policy as are subversive of the Nine-Power Treaty, the Kellogg Pact and the international policy relative to China which is commonly known as the open door policy.[10]

Hornbeck's analysis of the world situation, plus his special interest in the Far East, required him to see how the Soviet bear played into the wider aspects of US interests. Here, Hornbeck believed firmly that only a combined front of Soviet Russia, Great Britain and the United States could force the Japanese from

Manchuria.[11] If such a harmonization of interests could not be achieved, then he believed that only a general Far Eastern war would stop Japan.[12] Clearly, by the time the new Roosevelt administration took over the reins of power in Washington, the Far Eastern Division of the State Department recognized the pivotal role that the Soviet Union played in Far Eastern affairs.[13]

The Division did not take long getting those views into the hands of the key foreign policy-makers of the new administration. Johnson's consideration on the Far Eastern situation in general was put before Cordell Hull in June 1933 in a memo prepared specifically for the new Secretary of State entitled 'Japanese Activities on Asiatic Mainland. Probable Effect on American Interests in the Pacific Area.'[14] Johnson's critique of possible problems facing American interests in the Far East started with an assessment of Soviet–Japanese relations. Citing the Soviet Union as the power most immediately concerned with Japan's expansion in Asia, Johnson proposed that the Soviets would seek to avoid antagonizing the Japanese but that continual tensions and conflict were indeed possible as the Japanese threatened Soviet Russian interests in Inner and Outer Mongolia.[15] Grew's assessments of Soviet–Japanese relations in early 1933 agreed with this view of the strategic situation, and confirmed that the Japanese could indeed be influenced through their fear of a possible Soviet–American alliance.[16] By late 1933, because of growing rumours and fears that the two Asian rivals would perhaps be going to war in the near future, the assessments from China and Japan of Soviet–Japanese relations became even more important. It was Grew's belief that the Soviets had built up a large and powerful military force in the Far East, and that they were becoming much more resistant to Japanese attempts to bully them.[17] His conclusion and forecast for the future was:

> While the situation between the two countries does not at the present moment appear to be critical, foreign observers in Tokyo are very nearly unanimous that, with a continuance of present political conditions, eventual war between Japan and Soviet Russia is inevitable, such differ-ences of opinion as arise being concerned more with the probable time of the eventual clash than with the inevitability of its occurrence. The majority of observers see the spring of 1935 or the spring of 1936 as the most likely dates, basing their opinion on the fact that Japan will then be fully prepared to strike, but it is obviously recognized that unforeseen developments may alter these predictions. The foregoing opinions are based to some extent on the following factors: (1) The Chinese Eastern Railway controversy. (2) The continuance of petty but irritating incidents. (3) Japanese ambitions in Kamchatka and Mongolia. (4) Soviet military preparations and increasing indications of Russian intransigence … In conclusion therefore, it appears reasonable to believe that for the present Japan will devote her energies to the exploitation of Manchuria, to the

94

North China situation, to the modernization of her army and the building of her navy, and to her manifold trade problems, although, it may be said, the possibility certainly exists that a crisis may result from the Chinese Eastern Railway situation. For the future only time will tell whether a war will fulfill the logic of the evidence or whether unforeseen forces will obviate a struggle generally predicted for two years hence.[18]

For American interests in southern China and in the south Pacific, this continual Japanese preoccupation with its northern flank was a strategic asset, at least until 1935 or 1936, at which time many believed the inevitable Soviet–Japanese war would take place.[19]

The views of the Division of Far Eastern Affairs on the Far Eastern balance of power and the Soviet Union's place in it were passed along to the Roosevelt administration by Hornbeck in October 1933. Writing in reply to Japanese overtures for an anti-war pact, the Far Eastern Division chief painted a clear picture of where American interests fitted into the overall Far Eastern situation. He established that geographical location dictated the linkage between the interests of the United States, China, the Soviet Union and Japan in the Far Eastern problem:

> The Far Eastern problem of course revolves around China. What happens in China is of concern not only to China but to Russia and to the United States. Japan wishes to deal with China in her own way and without restrictions … To any definite proposal from Japan for the conclusion between Japan and the United States of such an agreement, an expedient rejoinder might be the suggestion that there be concluded such a pact not on a bilateral but on a quadrilateral basis, the four parties to be the United States, Japan, Russia and China. Such a counter-proposal would, of course, be rejected by Japan.[20]

This balance-of-power approach advocated by Hornbeck and the rest of the Far Eastern Division was certainly part of the reason for the American recognition of Russia in November 1933. A need for both closer relations with this important Far Eastern power and more information about Soviet designs and capabilities in the Far East, was part of the reason for recognition.[21] That act signalled that the Roosevelt administration saw the connection between the Soviet Union and the protection of American interests in the Far East. Further, it signalled that the United States was willing to follow a balance-of-power policy to contain Japanese aggression in the Far East.

Confirmation of the usefulness of the American recognition to US strategic planners did not take long. Ivan Maiski, the Soviet Ambassador in London, congratulated Robert W. Bingham, the US Ambassador in London, on the United State's vision in the matter. Maiski confided to Bingham that the Soviet

Union was sure that it was going to have to fight a war with Japan in the spring of 1934. However, now that the United States had recognized the Soviet Union, the Japanese were having a change of heart in their attitude towards the USSR, for fear that they might be caught between the Soviets and the Americans.[22] US reports from the Far East and the Soviet Union confirmed that US recognition of the USSR had indeed created a stir in the Far Eastern balance of power and that these shifting currents would have to be watched closely.

Various groups within the US policy-making elite watched events in the Far East unfold in early 1934, and all, including President Roosevelt, did so with the Soviet Union in mind. In January, the Office of Naval Intelligence (ONI) prepared a memo for the Chief of Naval Operations (CNO), Admiral W.H. Standley, as to what were the pertinent factors in the Soviet–Japanese situation.[23] The ONI believed that the militaristic leadership of Japan required a foreign threat to hold steady their domestic support among various Japanese groups. To that end, a successful campaign against the Soviet Union seemed the logical choice, given the Japanese fear of communism; their desire to seize rich Soviet fishing grounds; the high probability that Japan would win such a war; and the need to pre-empt the growing military power of the Soviet Union in the Far East.[24] Admiral Standley relayed this information to William Bullitt, telling him that Japan would fight a limited war in Asia.[25] As for the effect of this rivalry on the US Navy, Standley believed that:

> Japanese naval preparations are without doubt for the purpose of making any intervention in a Soviet–Japanese war by the United States or Great Britain an unattractive proposition. If the Japanese Government esti-mates that the United States or Great Britain might intervene in such a war, then Japan will not take any measures that will lessen the advantage of Japanese naval preparedness. Japan will retain its naval force concen-trated in a manner best calculated to deter intervention on the part of the United States or Great Britain. Control of the sea in the Western Pacific, as against Russia, is essential to Japan to guard her commerce and to move troops overseas without interference from Russia. The naval force of Japan will undoubtedly remain concentrated in Japanese home waters, with observation and patrol forces in the Marshalls, the Bonins, the Pescadores Islands and off the eastern coast of Honshu.[26]

Hornbeck's views on the escalating tension between Japan and the Soviet Union were not as pessimistic when he laid out what the United States' response to a Soviet–Japanese war should be. Stating that he thought the trend in Soviet–Japanese relations was away from rather than towards armed conflict, Hornbeck repeated his views on the balance of power in the Far East between Japan, China, the Soviet Union and Great Britain. He also pointed out that the United States did not have any vital interests at stake in the region, except a general desire for world peace.[27] The possibility which worried Hornbeck would occur if Japan fought Soviet Russia and won. Then, Japan could potentially emerge from the conflict stronger than ever and even more capable of disrupting the balance of power in the Far East. The solution, argued Hornbeck, was for the United States to safeguard its interests through ensuring a perpetuation of the rough balance between China, the Soviet Union and Japan. To that end, he suggested:

> This is likely to be achieved only if China grows stronger, Russia remains at peace, and the military spirit and power of Japan are kept in check. It should therefore be the intent and effort of the United States: 1. To help China towards internal improvement; 2. To help the Soviet Union likewise; 3. To discourage the militarism of Japan; 4. To work towards preventing war; 5. In the event of there beginning a war to which Japan is one of the parties, to see to it that Japan does not emerge the victor.[28]

Also incorporated into this grand strategy were the twin features of a strong, rebuilt US Navy that would be able to stand up to the Japanese fleet, and some form of cooperation with Great Britain. However, the latter would have to take the lead in any initiatives, as American public opinion was still not ready to acknowledge the realities of global balance-of-power diplomacy.[29]

In China, Johnson's view continued to correspond with Hornbeck's, and vice versa. The Ambassador saw the Soviet Union as being an inward-looking state, one bent on completing the great 'ten year plan' as soon as possible and thus not willing to jeopardize the gains made over the previous few years in a war with Japan.[30] Similarly, Japan was also taxing its population severely with efforts to modernize and expand its army and navy for the coming year of crisis, 1936.[31] Time, Johnson predicted, was on Soviet Russia's side. The longer the Japanese waited, the stronger would be the Russian air, army and naval forces in Vladivostok and other regions. These forces, along with the uncertainty created by the Japanese perception of increasing Soviet–US friendship resulting from US recognition of the Soviet Union, would play havoc with Japanese strategic considerations.[32]

These views were supported by Ambassador Grew in Tokyo. In February 1934, Grew reported to Hull that he considered a war between the Soviet Union and Japan to be very unlikely in the next six months, although there were always likely to be tensions between the two rivals.[33] Militarily, he believed that the Japanese Army was still confident that it could take Vladivostok and the Maritime Provinces, but the Soviet defences had grown much stronger in the previous six months. The Japanese Army would reach its peak in 1935, said Grew, citing the views of the military attachés in Tokyo, and after that 'time will tell in favor of Soviet Russia in point of lines of communication, organized man power, fortification and equipment'[34] Those military experts also believed that

Manchuria, the Maritime Provinces and Eastern Siberia were the main strategic goals of Japan. Because the Soviet Union stood in the way of that expansion, the Japanese would be forced to deal with the Soviets at the first favourable moment.[35] Grew's own opinion differed from that of the military observers, whom he considered too pessimistic. Unlike them, while he thought the situation between the two nations fraught with tension, he did not believe that a Soviet–Japanese war was inevitable.[36] His own opinion was that

> their [Russia's] defenses in the East have been materially strengthened, and their air forces in Vladivostok and elsewhere along the frontier constitute a serious threat to Tokyo and other important Japanese cities. Furthermore, American recognition of Soviet Russia has injected an important psychological element into the situation and gives pause to those in authority in Japan, for regardless of the pacific policy of the United States, American action in the event of a Japanese–Soviet conflict would be to the Japanese an unknown and disturbing factor ... Military plans may be regarded as infallible; but the attitude and possible action of the United States constitutes an element of uncertainty and therefore an unknown hazard. American recognition has increased self-confidence and bluster in Moscow, but no one believes that the Soviet Union will commence hostilities. I therefore believe that our recognition of the Soviet Union has injected into the situation a restraining influence ...[37]

This new Soviet military strength, now bolstered by the American recognition of the Soviet Union, was sure to confuse, and therefore slow down, Japanese aggression without the United States having to risk a direct confrontation with Japan.

By the summer of 1934, even American policy studies groups and academic gatherings were considering how the United States could or should utilize the Soviet bear in the Far East. At a round table conference on 'Currents of Conflict in the Far East', held at the Institute of Public Affairs at the University of Virginia, the group recommended three possible methods for ensuring peace in the Far East.[38] Those recommendations were to retreat gradually from the field and let Japan do as it wished; to establish a balance of power in the Far East between Japan and the Soviet Union; and to establish a Far Eastern regional organization.[39] All demonstrated the central importance of the Soviet Union in Far Eastern matters. This was especially the case for the second solution:

> Assuming that there is a general desire for peace, stability and economic development in the Far East, how can peace machinery best operate to achieve these results? ... A second possibility is the establishment of a far Eastern balance of power, with Japan and Russia as the principal pro-tagonists. Such a balance was doubtless a major factor in maintaining the

stability of the Far East from 1894 to the World War, and the ambitious policy of Japan may be attributed to the serious weakening of Russia as the result of the Bolshevist revolution. It seems not improbable, however, that this weakening is temporary, and that the balance will eventually be restored ... The danger of such balance, however, is that it could only be maintained through periodic wars, in the course of which Manchuria and China would undoubtedly suffer. The balance, however, might eventually be made more stable through the development of greater internal strength in China itself, thus establishing a balance of the three powers surrounding Manchuria, a consummation which could easily be further stabilized through a Far Eastern Locarno.[40]

This view that the Soviet Union was able to balance or control Japanese aggression was confirmed and supported by both Hornbeck and Johnson. Their assessment was that time was on the Soviet Union's side and Japan was developing a healthy respect for the USSR's air and naval forces in Vladivostok.[41]

Ambassador Bullitt added his voice to the chorus of experts on the Soviets' importance. He wrote to the State Department about a possible Anglo-Soviet rapprochement, mistakenly taking the British contentment with a 'loose' Soviet Russia, for more, arguing 'that the British no less than the Russians now regard the establishment of close relations between the British Empire and the Soviet Union is a primary object of foreign policy'.[42] According to Bullitt, who was receiving his information directly from the Soviet Foreign Commissar, Maxim Litvinov, Simon had assured the Soviets that the British would under no circumstances aid Japan in an attack on the Soviet Union. Litvinov's response to Simon's declaration was to tell Bullitt that for the first time since Great Britain had recognized the Soviet Union, there were now actual diplomatic relations between the two countries. The apparent reversal in British policy, said Litvinov, was a response to the threat posed by German aviation and the Japanese threat to British interests in Northern China, which, combined with Japanese dumping in British markets, had made British cooperation with Japan impossible.[43] Bullitt also commented on the effect that this change of policy would have on British Far Eastern policy. In a conversation with the British Chargé d'Affaires, Bullitt was told that Britain desired Japan to be 'firmly planted between the Soviet Union and China as a bar to Soviet advance and to have the eyes of the Japanese directed towards the continent of Asia rather than towards the Southern Pacific'. Bullitt took this statement to be authoritative, given that the Chargé had just returned from a long visit to London where, Bullitt assumed, he had been made privy to official policy.[44] Copies of Bullitt's conversation were immediately sent to the US offices in Japan and China for their information.[45] The idea of the possibility of a Soviet–Japanese war, and the effect such a war would have on American interests in the Far East, created a clear picture for President Roosevelt of what Anglo-Soviet relations meant to

American interests in that region. There were, however, many subtle interpretations of that image,

In a September interview with a Mr Streit, a reporter for the *New York Times*,
Roosevelt was asked what he would do if a Soviet–Japanese war broke out. The
President replied 'Nothing. We shall provide material etc. to both sides and we
shall strengthen our naval bases, but beyond that nothing.'[46] Roosevelt was
more than willing to utilize the Japanese fear of the Soviet Union as an indirect
method of guaranteeing continued good behaviour from the Japanese. The
British Foreign Office and Admiralty certainly accepted that Roosevelt's most
likely response to any Soviet–Japanese troubles would be to sell war material
to both parties and let them bludgeon one another into a weaker state, a situation that was advantageous for US interests in the region.[47] William Bullitt's
reports to the State Department (which eventually found their way through a
circuitous route from Assistant Secretary of State, Judge Walton Moore, to
Roosevelt's Secretary, Miss Le Hand, and finally to Roosevelt) confirmed that
even the Soviets did not think that the Americans would intervene in a
Soviet–Japanese conflict. At the same time he informed the President that the
honeymoon with the Soviet Union was now over because:

> The Russians are convinced that Japan will not attack this spring or
> summer and, as they no longer feel that they need our immediate help,
> their underlying hostility to all capitalist countries now shows through
> the veneer of the intimate friendship. We shall have to deal with them
> according to Claudel's formula of the donkey, the carrot, and the club.[48]

Bullitt explained, however, that the Soviets expected that, if such a war
occurred, the United States would inevitably be drawn to the Soviet side no
matter 'whether our relations with the Soviet Union prior to such an event were
warm, tepid or cold'.[49] But, these Soviet beliefs were not shared by Roosevelt.
Instead, he followed the balance-of-power argument put forth by Hornbeck
and Hull about the correct approach the US government should take towards
the Soviet Union and what the latter's role was in US Far Eastern interests.[50]
This view – that the Soviets were a useful and relatively cheap foil to the
Japanese – was refined throughout 1935.

In early January 1935, Hornbeck produced a seminal policy declaration for
the State Department entitled 'Relations between the United States and
Countries of the Far East – Especially Japan – in 1935'.[51] At the same time, Grew
had submitted his own lengthy analysis of the situation, 'The Importance of
American Naval Preparedness in connection with the Situation in the Far East',
which also contained a section on the role of the Soviet Union in the Far East.[52]
The Secretary of State agreed entirely with the contents of both documents,
thinking so much of their analysis that he sent them directly to the President.
Hull had also given copies to Norman Davis, Roosevelt's advisor and roving

negotiator, and to Bullitt for their appraisal. Both men agreed with the contents of the memos, and Roosevelt was so informed by Hull.[53] A clear consensus of opinion on Far Eastern issues and possible policy options had emerged from the two papers.

Grew's principal point about the Soviets was that their approach to dealing with the Japanese was a useful one that the US government would be wise to consider. Citing discussions with the Soviet Ambassador in Tokyo and the results that the latter had achieved over the previous two years, Grew's opinion was that the hardline and rearmament strategy adopted by the Soviet Union had proved very effective in making the Japanese respect the Soviet position. The Soviet method could be applied by strengthening the US Navy, said Grew, thereby creating the military force required for duplicating the Soviets' success.[54] Hornbeck's attitude towards the US Navy was identical to Grew's, but his main focus was to outline what possible favourable diplomatic avenues were open for US policy-makers in their future dealings with Japan.

The Hornbeck policy established foreign relations with Japan as the most important problem facing the United States in 1935. The paper was divided into eleven sections that discussed both what possible unilateral actions the United States could take in the Far East and the various multilateral US options in that region.[55] The idea of close cooperation with the Soviet Union was explored, with Hornbeck stating clearly that the best course would be a cautious economic cooperation with the Soviets rather than any closer political rapprochement between the United States and the Soviet Union.[56] Such economic and commercial cooperation would keep the Japanese guessing as to the true nature of the Soviet–US relationship.[57] Cooperation would also help the Soviets continue their military programme in the Far East: 'Increments of economic strength by the Soviet Union will tend to divert the attention of Japan and to discourage reckless adventuring on Japan's part.'[58] On the diplomatic front, however, caution had to be employed in order to avoid causing a panic in Japan, a panic brought on by the perception of a united Soviet–US front:

> We should be cautious, however, about any movement toward the developing of political bonds or appearance of diplomatic rapprochement between ourselves and the Soviet Government. Developments of those types would give us nothing upon which we could definitely rely and would, on the other hand, increase suspicion among the Japanese of our intentions with regard to the Far East, thereby injecting a new cause of irritation into our relations with Japan ...[59]

In April, this line of argument was repeated by Hornbeck to Assistant Secretary R. Walton Moore, at which point Hornbeck summed up his attitude towards the Soviet Union: 'We should therefore be friendly with but not unduly cordial towards the Soviet Union.'[60] Hornbeck's need for caution, tinged with hopeful-ness for continued Soviet–Japanese tension, was a sentiment shared by the War Department, who also considered a war between Japan and Soviet Russia to be inevitable and set to begin possibly some time in 1935.[61] Slowly but surely the Far Eastern Division and its views were becoming the stuff of recognized wisdom in such strategic foreign policy matters.

In February 1935, Ambassador Grew submitted a lengthy report on the Soviet Union's military forces in the Far East, their build-up and the potential impact for the United States.[62] His opinion was that the Soviets had little to fear from the Japanese at present. Indeed, Grew believed that Soviet–Japanese relations would 'crystallize' along the lines established during the sale of the Chinese Eastern Railway in 1934, a sale which saw the Japanese buy the railway from the Soviets in order that both countries could consolidate their strategic positions in Manchuria.[63] It was Grew's fear that the sale might inaugurate a cooperative, or at least less tumultuous, relationship between the Soviet Union and Japan which could bode only ill for American interests. He believed that the Japanese fear of Soviet Russia was forcing Tokyo to consider expanding in central and southern China, an act that would be distinctly detrimental to US and British interests.[64] Grew also acknowledged that the Soviet–US honeymoon was over, leaving Japan willing either to oppose the Soviet Union or to try coming to terms with it on conflicting items.[65] Still, no matter how much some of the external issues surrounding Soviet–Japanese relations changed, no matter what changes were made in the Japanese government, Grew believed that the Japanese Army would continue to see the Soviets as their greatest menace and would take the first opportunity afforded to them to strike decisively against the Russians.[66] Clearly the Soviet presence in the Far East was a double-edged sword for the United States. Needing to protect American interests in China, trying to contain any further Japanese aggression, and, attempting to avoid the unattractive possibility of having a communist nation dominant in the region, US Far Eastern policy was indeed a delicate balancing act. That act involved playing on Japanese fears of their traditional enemy, Soviet Russia, while at the same time trying to establish better relations with Japan itself.

Many of the US military and diplomatic appreciations of Soviet–Japanese relations in the first half of 1936 commented on two themes: (1) the feeling in both Japan and Soviet Russia that Soviet military forces were superior to the Japanese forces immediately facing them (meaning that if there was to be a war it would be a long and costly one, an action that Japan was loath to begin unless absolutely certain of victory), and (2) the assumption that Japan was perhaps going to have to try to come to an understanding with the Soviet Union, if only for a short time, because of Tokyo's military inferiority.[67] Johnson's position in China gave him a particularly good position from which to comment on the situation. Replying to queries from newspaper editor Roy

Howard as to whether or not the Soviet Union was washed up in the Far East,[68] Johnson stated:

> There is no doubt in my mind that at the moment the Japanese are more afraid of Russia than they are of anyone else. It is the Russian situation which is moving Terauchi and his colleagues to recommend the placing of an increased financial burden upon the Japanese for the purpose of permitting them to buy a new defensive outfit. It has seemed to me that a clash between Russia and Japan is almost inevitable … I believe that Japan will precipitate such a clash because Japanese leadership is actively interested in Japan's expansion on to the continent. For the moment Russian leadership is not interested in Russian expansion anywhere, but Japanese leadership at present does not feel itself prepared for the clash. Russia is the only country in a position to strike Japan, but Russia is held back by the situation in Europe which has not been improved by the revolution now going on in Spain.[69]

Seeing clearly the ties that joined Soviet Russia to both the Far East and Europe, Johnson believed that fear of the Soviet bear was still potent, even though there had been some sign of improved relations between the two traditional rivals.

Corroborating evidence of Japan's new-found respect for Russia was provided by Norman H. Davis, after he had talks with the Japanese Ambassador to Great Britain, Shigeru Yoshida. Davis reported to Hornbeck that Yoshida had confirmed that the Japanese Army had been taken by surprise by how well prepared Russia was militarily. The Ambassador intimated to Davis that the Japanese Army's leadership were having to rethink their approach to the Soviets: should they make greater military preparations to combat the Soviets or should they try diplomacy? Above all, the Japanese hoped that the Soviets would not join with anyone, and, if it was at all possible, the Japanese desired to get an alignment with some other power against Russia.[70] In talks with British officials, Ray Atherton, the Chargé d'Affaires at the US Embassy in London, confirmed that the Soviets were more and more becoming an important part of Britain's balance-of-power policy in the Far East. He reported to the State Department that British foreign policy was now based on the idea of temporization while rearmament went on. The British had created a policy which 'circumstances have rendered appealing to Eden who is anxious to belie Tory criticism of [his] youthful impetuousness and impractical idealism'.[71] Atherton explained Eden's attitude towards Japan:

> Since Japan's position and attitude renders Great Britain very vulnerable in the Far East, England will, through temporization, strive to prevent any issue from arising with Japan so long as the German situation remains unsolved. Indeed, there are influential elements here which continue to

advocate the consideration of a policy of rapprochement with Japan. In answer to a question it was stated to me that the present surface friendliness between London and Moscow, born of mutual support for the League is viewed merely as a feature in the present British policy of temporization, since it tends to ease France's position in pursuit of her Danubian policy, where England has no commitments of her own outside the League, and also it has a restraining influence in Berlin and Tokyo.[72]

Any fears that the Americans might have had that the Japanese and Soviets were moving closer to each other were not confirmed by such insights. The final evidence that such a Soviet–Japanese rapprochement was unlikely came in November, when the German and Japanese governments signed the Anti-Comintern Pact.

The Pact was an immediate source of tension in Soviet–Japanese relations, a point not lost on the Americans. The Tokyo Embassy reported back to the State Department that the signing of the pact was a severe set-back to the efforts of the Japanese Prime Minister, Koki Hirota, to improve Soviet–Japanese relations. It had been the embassy's opinion that until then Hirota had indeed been having some success in creating an atmosphere favourable to better Soviet–Japanese relations.[73] Now, however, the falling out of the two signalled a renewed effort on the part of Japan to create better Japanese–US relations. Grew's analysis was that

> there is very good reason to feel that the Japanese Government values American friendship, especially in view of Japan's increasing difficulties with other nations, and will not purposely alienate the United States unless situations arise where Japan considers her own national interests to be acutely involved.[74]

In addition, Grew pointed out the increased pressure that was being brought to bear on the Japanese by their fear of a combined Anglo-Soviet front in the Far East.[75] The shift in Soviet–Japanese relations, according to Grew, ensured that:

> the die is now cast and it is obvious that Japan's relations with Soviet Russia have suffered a rude setback which is not likely to be overcome in the near future. Moreover we may be sure that the Soviet Government will continue to act on the principle that the only language understood by the Japanese is force, and that when struck whether by a minor frontier incursion or by some broader form of aggression, the wisest policy to follow is promptly to strike back with double the force.[76]

Nelson Johnson agreed with Grew's assessment of the situation, believed that the Japanese military had acted stupidly, and felt that Japan had now ensured continued animosity from the Soviets.[77] That animosity was intensified by the start of the undeclared war between China and Japan in the summer of 1937. Faced with a lack of military resources in the region and having limited diplomatic leverage to employ against the Japanese, the United States scrambled to establish a strategy for dealing with the emergency in the Far East. One avenue of approach was to attempt to manipulate the Japanese fear of Soviet Russia, and in particular the fear that there might be grounds for a combined Soviet–US front. This diplomatic foray required the assistance of the US Navy.

Members of the American naval and maritime communities had observed the development of the Soviet naval forces in the Far East closely after 1933. In a well-publicized essay on America's naval policy in the Pacific, Rear Admiral Yates Stirling Jr reflected on how navies, including the Soviet Navy, might fight Japan in any Far Eastern conflict. His conclusion was that naval weakness in the region meant that:

> The situation thus becomes one that our statesmen must solve. Reciprocal trade treaties and carefully forged friendly relations between Japan, Russia, and the United States under the circumstances will give us more lasting and better results than any amount of saber rattling and for the present it is along that line that our Far Eastern policy should lie.[78]

Captain Dudley Knox, noted American naval publicist, Intelligence Officer and general Navy Department booster, also called for the US Navy and the American public to recognize the worth of the Soviet Union for the protection of American interests in the Far East, particularly the Philippines. Knox made the connection between Japanese fear of Soviet Russia and its reluctance to challenge the United States: for Japan to do so, he argued, would be to commit strategic suicide by courting a two-front conflict.[79] This modest yet informed interest shown by American navalists in the Soviet Far Eastern Fleet increased in 1936.

The signing of that Anglo-German naval agreement and the after-glow of the London Naval Conference generated enough interest in the United States about naval matters that leading US newspapers, along with those groups which had a traditional interest in American naval affairs, began to consider some of the maritime strategic questions facing US Far Eastern policy. The *Baltimore Sun* reported that the Soviet Union was determined to create an impenetrable wall of submarines to the north and south of Vladivostok. The aim of this deployment was to deter the Japanese from making an attack on the Soviet Pacific port and thus occupy the Japanese fleet far from any important strategic areas.[80] In November the *Washington Star* reported that the Soviet Navy had made their Pacific bastion impregnable to Japanese attack through an extensive naval building programme.[81] Soviet naval preparations hit closer to home in the United States in the spring of 1937, when reports emerged that the Soviet Union had approached the State Department with a request that it be permitted to ask shipbuilding companies to construct a 16-inch battleship for the Soviets.[82] In attempting to gain support for the project, the Soviet Ambassador, Alexander Antonovitch Troyanovsky, assured the US Chief of Naval Operations, Admiral William D. Leahy, that American support for the Soviets building a strong Pacific fleet would go a long way towards ensuring peace between the Soviet Union and Japan.[83] While the battleships and super-destroyers requested were never completed, the debate that surrounded the building of the 'X' ships for the Soviets illustrated not only the desire of the State Department and President Roosevelt to exploit the Soviet–Japanese tensions, but also how the Soviet question created linkages in Anglo-American strategic relations.[84]

Anglo-American naval discussions on how to respond to Japanese escalation in its capital-ship building programme in May and June of 1938 were affected by the American agreement to build such vessels. In August 1938, a Mr Pell, who had been part of the US State Department's naval affairs team, told A. Holman, a senior official in the American Department of the Foreign Office, that the reason the US government had hesitated in giving its support to Britain for new upper limits for capital ship construction was related to the US government agreeing to build these ships for the Soviet Union. Pell revealed that the US Navy had agreed to build a 62,000 ton aircraft-carrying ship for the Soviets. The plans had been prepared, but the President had not been aware of the obligations of the United States under the 1935–36 London Naval Treaty. This embarrassing situation had created a delay while the State Department squared away an explanation for the Soviets. While not a serious matter, the incident revealed how the Soviet naval question was interwoven into the fabric of Anglo-American Far Eastern policy.[85]

The Japanese attack on China, in July 1937, created another situation where American reaction to Japanese aggression was predicated on the traditional Soviet–Japanese friction. The Commander-in-Chief of the US Asiatic Fleet, Admiral H.E. Yarnell, was scheduled to make a visit to Vladivostok in the flagship *Augusta* during the summer of 1937.[86] The original plans for the visit had been designed to send the same force that went to Vladivostok on to Japan, in order not to raise any unnecessary Japanese suspicions.[87] Yarnell reported that the Japanese seemed overly interested in this trip, and wrote that, 'They feel no doubt that this visit which is the first that a U.S. Naval vessel has made for many years is a sure sign of more friendly relations between the United States and Soviet Russia.'[88] Reports by the US Naval Attaché in Tokyo, Captain Harold Bemis, on Soviet–Japanese relations confirmed Yarnell's latter observation. The Tokyo reports to the Office of Naval Intelligence revealed that:

> There is no doubt that the adjustment of Soviet–Japanese relations is the most urgent issue facing Japanese diplomacy. That negotiations are

resumed after being virtually abandoned with the conclusion of the Anti-Comintern Pact, shows a more conciliatory attitude. Japan is suspicious that the USSR has some underlying motive in its peaceful proposals to nullify the efficacy of the German–Japanese pact, Russia realizes that Japan has waited too long to be able to successfully attack the maritime provinces and having practically consolidated her position in the Far East is maneuvering to break the encircling ring of the anti-comintern signatories. If Russia proposes a non-aggression pact, Japan will have to show her hand in refusing.[89]

With the outbreak of the July crisis, thinking on the proposed naval visit was reversed completely, and it was decided to exploit the tensions expressed in the Naval Attaché's reports. Yarnell immediately informed Johnson that he was willing to cancel the trip to Vladivostok and had informed the State and Navy Departments to that effect. Instead, at the direction of both the State and Navy Departments, the Asiatic Fleet was ordered to visit the Soviet Union, but not Japan, in a deliberate attempt to stall further Japanese aggression by preying on their fears that such an act could be interpreted as the making of a Soviet–US front.[90] As a valuable strategic aside, Yarnell arrived in Vladivostok on 28 July and was able to get a first-hand feel for the Soviet Navy in the Far East. He was impressed by the Soviet forces in Vladivostok, reporting that:

> the Russian Army in Siberia is undoubtedly well provided with tanks, artillery, and war munitions. The Russians place great reliance in their air force, and this is probably well justified. We saw a number of submarines in Vladivostok and they appeared to be well trained. The Russian seamen on these ships were a fine looking body of men. Just how many submarines the Russians have in the Far East is not known. They have at least thirty and may have many more. If they have any ability at all, and I think they have, it will render the problem of the Japanese far more difficult than at present were they to have perfect freedom of the seas.[91]

That appreciation for Soviet military force did not, however, extend to a love of the Soviet form of government. Yarnell's comment on the communist system itself was:

> It is, of course, not possible to generalize about Russia from what is seen of this one city. However, I can not but believe that while general conditions here are worse than they are in other sections of Russia the general appearance of the people and the attitude of the officials is perhaps typical, and if it is, God save us from communism. In order to make a success of this form of government the following requisites seem to be necessary: first, kill off all the intelligentsia of the country; second,

destroy all churches and deny all religion; third, discourage family life; fourth, have one half the people watch the other half.[92]

Throughout the crisis, as they monitored and assessed the situation, both Yarnell and Johnson were constantly aware of the Soviet factor in the developing China crisis and the impact Soviet issues had on Japanese actions. Their observations were passed along all the way up to Roosevelt himself when warranted.

Johnson reported his views on Soviet Russia and its continuing role in the Far Eastern situation directly to the Secretary of State in February 1938. He told Hull that he considered Russia the 'Brer Fox' of the Far East:

> Japan is driving China into a chaos, which may be called communism, through the same door of misery through which Russia entered into that land of promise. Of course Communist Russia is interested in seeing China prolong this conflict. You know Uncle Remus' story of the 'Tar Baby'. China is the 'Tar Baby', Japan is 'Brer Rabbit', and Russia is 'Brer Fox'. And 'Brer Fox ain't saying' nothin'' in this quarrel between 'Brer Rabbit' and the 'Tar Baby'. Communist Russia is not going to assist China by coming in on China's side. Communist Russia expects to profit by the chaos that Japan is creating, and sees safety for itself in a Japan that is exhausting itself in China … If Japan does attack Russia … the first two weeks of the war will be the bloodiest and most terrible that the world has seen. Japan's bombing of Chinese cities far behind the lines has set the tune, and the Russians know that they must get there first or have the Japanese bombers all about them. There is little for Japan to destroy in Siberia, but Russian bombers can get at the very heart of Japan in no time, and Tokyo and Osaka will not be nice places to live in.[93]

Such a view was welcome in Washington. Hull was fearful of the effect in the Far East if Japan faced a Soviet Union that was only inward-looking.[94] That fear of an isolationist Soviet Union was shared by Hornbeck, Herbert Feis (the State Department's Economic Advisor), and Jay Pierrepont Moffat (Chief of the Division of European Affairs), all of whom hoped that the Russians would continue to act as the proverbial fly in the Japanese–Chinese soup.[95] The reports of US officials in Shanghai, in other Chinese centres and in Europe, noting the large amount of Soviet material that was flowing into China from the Soviet Union, supported Johnson's analysis and allayed any fears that the Soviets would withdraw from China.[96]

Such reports were known not only to the Secretary of State, but also to President Roosevelt, who monitored closely the situation and the strategic position of the Soviets in that region.[97] By early 1938, both the US Navy and State Department were informing the White House that expert opinion felt that Japan was not going to be able to consume China; that the Soviet Union was pleased with the weakening of Japan due to its operations in China; that, even though the purges had led to some doubts as to the effectiveness of the Soviet forces, Soviet Russia was still Japan's biggest fear and most formidable military foe: and that the danger of a possible conflict between them was still high, if not higher than before.[98] Clearly, the idea that American interests could be protected by continued Soviet–Japanese tensions was now commonplace in the Roosevelt administration. The monitoring of those tensions and the calculation of how they affected American Far Eastern policy would continue right up until the outbreak of war in Europe, in September 1939. Of course, what impact the Soviet Union would have in the Far East depended on Soviet strength.

The US Army produced detailed military estimates of the Soviet Union's military worth in mid-1938.[99] Their findings noted that, while the Soviet military establishment was the largest in the world, it also had the largest geographic area to protect. As for the Far Eastern forces:

> In 1935 the Transbaikal Military district was formed from the eastern part of the Siberian Military District and the western part of the Special Far Eastern Army Region; apparently another countermove to check the Japanese advance into Mongolia. The combined strength of the two districts is believed to be about: 4 corps headquarters, 15 infantry divisions, 3 cavalry divisions, 7 air brigades, 2 seaplane brigades, 10 separate air groups, 3 medium field artillery regiments, coast and AA artillery units, and numerous engineer, technical, combat vehicle, OGPU and irregular units. Approximate strength: 200,000 infantry and cavalry, 150,000 other troops, 1,000 airplanes, 1,000 combat vehicles, 1,250 field guns.

That land force was supported by the Pacific Fleet, which was composed of 12 obsolete *Stalin* class destroyers, 50 new submarines (of between 200 and 800 surface tons), and approximately 20 patrol and river vessels. The intelligence report concluded that Soviet Russia was the strongest military power in the world, with some logistical, training and equipment problems, but, like the British assessments, the Americans doubted whether the Soviets could produce an effective offensive effort. As well, the purges were not thought to have been very detrimental to Russian defensive power in the region.[100] Strategically, and despite the fact that it was now faced with the possibility of a two-front war, the Soviet Union was in a better position in the Far East than it had been in 1937 because Japan was in a weaker state after its Chinese adventure.[101]

The US Army was not the only US military institution that had made this type of strategic appreciation of the USSR. American Far Eastern observers in the State Department and elsewhere concurred with much of what the intelligence report had to say, continuing to rank the Soviet Union as Japan's number-one enemy in 1939.[102] Early in that year, Admiral Yarnell was one of the most informed sources of information on Soviet military and diplomatic capabilities for American policy-makers. Tied into Nelson Johnson's organization, and with access to information provided by the other powers' naval commanders in China, Yarnell had a very clear insight into how the Soviet bear fitted into the growing Far Eastern crisis. His views often percolated through the Navy Department and Leahy right to the President himself.[103] By February, it was Yarnell's opinion that, if there were a general war in Europe, the Japanese would make short work of American and European interests in the Far East. The only thing that would control them or give them pause was the Soviet Union and fears of how it would react to such Japanese actions.[104] Yarnell's belief was that the Soviet Union could not be conquered in the Far East, nor bought off, by the Japanese.[105] Similar observations and beliefs prevailed within the State Department's core of Far Eastern analysts.[106]

Joseph Grew counselled the State Department that now, perhaps more than ever, under Prime Minister Hiranuma, the Japanese were more likely to go to war with the Soviet Union.[107] The Ambassador's reasoning was that Hiranuma would have a difficult time keeping the military hard-liners from launching a pre-emptive strike against the Soviet Union. The Japanese military leadership thought that the Soviets had been weakened by the purges, said Grew, and thus were more likely to favour a quick strike. As well, the Japanese military were anxious to settle the Chinese matter and to do so needed to eliminate Soviet support to the Chinese. These factors had the potential to create a crisis in Soviet–Japanese relations.[108] Further, talks between Great Britain and the Soviet Union were making the Japanese anxious lest they be faced by a Soviet–British combination.[109] While Eugene Dooman, the Chargé d'Affaires at the US Embassy in Tokyo, ventured to suggest that such anxiety was good for US–Japanese relations, the destabilizing influences were judged to be greater, as such Japanese fears could result in a general Far Eastern war breaking out.[110] Working together closely, Dooman and the British Ambassador, by now Sir Robert Craigie, came to the conclusion that Japanese fear of the Soviet Union's military presence in the Far East, combined with the possibility that the Russians might be allied with the British and French, was forcing the Japanese closer to the German–Italian Axis.[111] While it was not clear whether a war in the Far East was imminent, or even who the main characters in such a conflict would be, both the British and American views held that the Soviets would continue to be at the centre of things for some time to come.[112] However, with the possibility of a European war looming, American Far Eastern policy-makers had to evaluate whether the Japanese would ever be able to work with the Soviets, or whether the Soviets would be a *perpetual* loose cannon in Japanese strategic plans for the Far East.[113]

The signing of the Nazi–Soviet Pact and eventual outbreak of a general war in Europe, while changing some of the circumstances in which Soviet–Japanese relations and the balance-of-power dynamic in the Far East had to be considered, did not alter key American views on matters. On 12 September 1939, Dooman addressed the problem fully for Hull, advocating that:

> The considerations which force on me the belief that Japan would not entertain in the present circumstances a proposal for a non-aggression treaty with the Soviet Union prevail over the reasons which might be brought forward to support a contrary view. There will immediately occur to mind the basic conflict between the interests of Japan and Russia in the Far East, especially in China, the irreconcilability of militant bolshevism with Japanese imperialism, the paradox in the Japanese insistence on the one hand on maintaining troops in Manchuria in violation of the Portsmouth Treaty and claiming on the other hand fishing rights in Soviet waters and so on. But a more important consideration than all these is the fact that the Soviet Union has, like Germany, given evidence of the ephemeral character of any undertaking given by a nation which is ruled by a dictator. The one great advantage which a non-aggression pact with Russia could be expected to bring would be the relaxation of Russian pressure along the Manchurian border, thus enabling Japan to give greater attention than hitherto to her conflict with China. It is I think unlikely that, if the suggested treaty were concluded, Japan would have sufficient confidence in Soviet good faith to divert to China the substantial forces now being maintained in Manchuria to offset Soviet pressure.[114]

Two months later, as Roosevelt pondered the strategic balance of a world now at war, Grew used Dooman's report as his official appreciation of the situation in the Far East and asked President Roosevelt to keep it in mind during his strategic deliberations.[115] Hull and the State Department concurred with both Grew and Dooman, also arguing that the differences between Japan and the Soviet Union were too fundamental to ever permit a comprehensive *rapprochement*.[116] Furthermore, the US State Department was convinced that the Japanese government recognized the strategic role the Russians played in British and American attempts to isolate Japan. The Department contended, therefore, that the Japanese were attempting to obtain concessions from the Western powers by threatening to effect a *rapprochement* with the Soviet Union and thereby putting American and British Far Eastern interests in jeopardy. The State Department's recommendation to Great Britain and its own government was to continue to monitor the situation and not surrender any material interests in the hope of keeping Japan and the USSR from forming an accord. To do so at that point would be to abandon any hope of ever making Japan realize it could not continue to gain by flaunting international law and treaties. The Department advised:

Furthermore, if Japan is actually intending to effect a rapprochement with the Soviet Union, it means that control of the Government is in the hands of extremists. In such circumstance it could reasonably be expected that an accord effected by the Government of the Soviet Union on the one hand and Japanese extremists on the other could endure only for a short period of time.

This attitude of wringing as much respect from the Japanese by utilizing their fear of encirclement and Soviet Russia was also the one being proposed by the US Naval Attaché in Tokyo to the US Navy.[117] By the end of 1939, the Soviet loose cannon was clearly still a vital factor in any US Far Eastern policy attempting to check further Japanese aggression.[118] The United States believed that as long as the Japanese feared the Soviet bear, and feared that the bear might someday find allies, the Japanese would have to move cautiously in their attempts to expand in the Far East.

Neither the United States nor Great Britain wished to see Japan crushed in a war with the Soviet Union. Their desire to see the military strength of the Soviet bear control, drain and deter Japanese aggression was derived from their imperative to see the Far East, and particularly China, remain free of Japanese control while at the same time China also remained independent of communist dominance.[119] And therein lay the dilemma for American and British foreign-policy-makers: how could the Japanese be utilized in the fight against the spread of communism and at the same time be deterred from dominating China? Which was the greater threat: communism or Japanese militarism and aggression? Such complex questions could not be answered by the State Department or Foreign Office with great confidence or surety. Indeed, while both US and British policy-makers recognized the similarities of and variances between their views of the Soviet Union in the Far East, there was no conscious attempt on the part of those nations to coordinate their efforts towards the Soviets. The problem was made even more difficult by the dual position the Soviet Union held in the global balance of power: for Moscow was a counter-weight to both Germany and Japan. This particularly affected the British, who often could find a useful role for the Soviet Union in the Far East, only to realize that it would serve only to complicate or endanger the strategic situation in Europe. Therefore, Soviet–Japanese tensions and problems were merely something that US and British strategic policy-makers could exploit whenever events allowed them to do so. Those conditions were not elements which either democratic nation had any 'control' over.

Furthermore, for both Western nations, their policy towards the Soviet Union had to be a clandestine one, for neither government could act openly towards the Soviets. In the United States and Britain both, there was a likelihood of a public backlash from the electorates if it was thought that either was practising old-fashioned, pre-First World War balance-of-power diplomacy. Equally, there would be a strong reaction in these countries against open co-operation with the communists. Therefore, the Americans and British instead utilized the Soviets in their relations with Japan like a bogey-man; waiting until the Japanese were isolated, needful or vulnerable and then preying on the historic Japanese fear of finding themselves alone, facing a strong Soviet Russia accompanied by a strong naval ally. This approach was an informal, shadowy and uncertain policy, but one which offered some hope of success, in a period when both the United States and Great Britain were militarily weak in the Far East. This common approach to dealing with the Japanese lent itself well to the informal, parallel style of Anglo-American Far Eastern relations in the period from 1933 to 1939.

Such an approach had a strong strategic advantage for both Britain and the United States. As long as China and Russia were strategic threats to Japan, the latter would spend valuable military resources and money preparing to meet those circumstances, instead of using them to build a bigger navy or to prepare for a southern advance. The efficacy of this approach was underlined by the fact that it lasted even past the signing of the Nazi–Soviet Pact and the outbreak of war in Europe. Indeed, it was not until the Nazi invasion of Soviet Russia in June 1941 that Japan believed itself secure enough to initiate a southern advance. With the Soviet forces finally having to move from the East to meet the German advance in the West, the greatest threat to Japan's strategic position was eliminated. With China now subdued, France out of the war in Europe and Britain battling for its very existence, the opportunity to move south beckoned to Japan like a Siren's song. That need for the Japanese to await the moment when the Soviet Union's attention was distracted from the Far East confirmed how correct British and American interwar strategic foreign policy-makers were in their assessments of the worth of the bear in the Far Eastern balance of power.

## NOTES

1. Edward M. Bennett, *Franklin D. Roosevelt and the Search for Victory: American–Soviet Relations, 1933–1939* (Wilmington, NC, 1990), xxii.
2. Johnson was the head of the State Department's Far Eastern Division from 1925 to 1929. He was then made US Minister to Peiping. A close friend of Stanley Hornbeck (Johnson was, in fact, responsible for Hornbeck getting a job with the Far Eastern Division) and on very good terms with Joseph C. Grew, the US Ambassador to Tokyo, Johnson's wise counsel and advice on Far Eastern matters, especially those related to China and Japan's intentions towards China, often filtered from his desk to that of the Secretary of State and even the President, through Hornbeck and later Maxwell Hamilton, who took over the Far Eastern Division when Hornbeck left that spot to become special advisor. See Borg, *The United States and the Far Eastern Crisis of 1933–1938*, 30; and Russell D. Buhite, 'The Open Door in Perspective: Stanley K.

Hornbeck and American Far Eastern Policy', in Frank J. Merli and Theodore A. Wilson, eds, *Makers of American Diplomacy* (New York, 1974), 431–58.

3. Wilson Brown Papers, Nimitz Library, USNA, Annapolis, Box 5, Diary entry, 23 July 1934.

4. Grew certainly was not impressed with the idea that Roosevelt's new political appointee to the Secretary of State's job might interfere with Far Eastern matters, commenting to Johnson, 'I hope very much, however, that we are going to be let alone because your work and mine are not the kind of jobs that can be handled by inexperienced "statesmen", no matter how deserving they may be'. Nelson T. Johnson Papers (hereafter NTJ Papers), Library of Congress, Washington, DC, Container 19, folder A-G, letter from Grew to Johnson, 4 Jan. 1933.

5. NTJ Papers, Container 17, Folder A-L, letter from Hornbeck to Grew, 2 June 1932. In it, Hornbeck told Grew how happy he was with the team he had in the Far East, namely Grew and Johnson. He discussed the nature of the Far Eastern division and its workings, and told Grew, 'in the Far Eastern field, we are exceptionally well circumstanced by virtue of the fact that at all of the most important points or offices are men in charge who have had special experience and a lot of it, together with the additional fact that the members of this group, by and large, are to an unusual degree personally acquainted and familiar with each other's psychology, political outlook and thought and methods'.

6. NTJ Papers, Container 17, Folder A-L, letter from Johnson to Dr G.H. Blakeslee (Clark University), 8 Feb. 1932.

7. NTJ Papers, Container 17, Folder A-L, letter from Johnson to Kellogg, 12 Jan. 1932.

8. NTJ Papers, Container 17, Folder A-L, confidential letter from Johnson to Hornbeck, 13 Sept. 1932.

9. Ibid.

10. SKH Papers, Box 453, memo, 'Conflict of British Interests and Policies in the Far East. Russia, India and Communism. The Empire and the United States in the Pacific', 17 Feb. 1932; ibid., Folder: Oct. 1932–May 1933, confidential memo by Hornbeck, 'Manchuria Situation: Constant Factor for Consideration in Connection with Problem of American–Japanese Relations', 14 Mar. 1933.

11. On the centrality of Hornbeck in the formulation of US Far Eastern policy, see Richard D. Burns, 'Stanley K. Hornbeck: The Diplomacy of the Open Door', in Richard D. Burns and Edward M. Bennett, eds, *Diplomats in Crisis* (Santa Barbara, CA, 1974), 90–117; Buhite, 'The Open Door in Perspective'; James C. Thomson Jr, 'The Role of the Department of State', in Borg and Okamoto, eds, *Pearl Harbor as History*, 81–106; Kenneth G. McCarty, 'Stanley K. Hornbeck and the Far East, 1931–1941', PhD dissertation, Duke University, Durham, NC, 1970; Shizhang Hu, *Stanley K. Hornbeck and the Open Door Policy, 1919–1937* (Westport, CT, 1995).

12. SKH Papers, Box 453, memo, 'Europe and the Far East. Europe, Russia, Great Britain and the United States. Germany, Italy and France. The League of Nations in Europe and in the Far East', 19 Feb. 1932.

13. Ibid., urgent memo by L.E. Salisbury to Hornbeck, 16 Mar. 1933.

14. NTJ Papers, Container 21, Folder O-Z, memo from Johnson to Hull, 12 June 1933; *FRUS*, Vol. III, *The Far East*, 1933, 360–2.

15. Ibid.

16. *FRUS*, Vol. III, despatch from Grew to Secretary of State, 9 Mar. 1933, 228.

17. *FRUS*, Vol. III, despatch from Grew to Hull, 29 Sept. 1933, 412–16.

18. Ibid.

19. *FRUS*, Vol. III, letter from Grew to Under-Secretary of State, William Phillips, 6 Oct. 1933, 421–4; ibid., letter from Assistant Chief of the Division of Far Eastern Affairs,

Maxwell Hamilton, to Hornbeck, 6 Oct. 1933, 424–7. Hamilton had just returned from being on special assignment in the Far East.

20. Hull MSS (hereafter Hull Papers), Library of Congress, Washington, DC, Container 35, memo from Hornbeck to Hull, 9 Oct. 1933. See also, SKH Papers, Box 545, Chronological Day Files, memo by Hornbeck, 'Russo–Japanese Conflict, Problem: What Should be the Attitude and Course of Action of the United States', 31 Jan. 1934.

21. Hu, *Stanley K. Hornbeck and the Open Door Policy 1919–1937*, 175; SKH Papers, Box 308, letter and attached Office of Naval Intelligence study of Russia, Capt. Nimmer to Hornbeck, 9 Nov. 1933; Maxwell M. Hamilton Papers, Hoover Institute, Stanford University, Box 1, Trip to Far East, 1933–34, Diary and Reports, entries for 7–12 Nov. 1933.

22. Bingham Diary, Library of Congress, Washington, DC, entry for 11 Dec. 1933.

23. Franklin D. Roosevelt, President's Secretary's File (hereafter FDR–PSF), Franklin D. Roosevelt Presidential Library, Hyde Park, New York, Japan, 1933–34, 'Memorandum for the Chief of Naval Operations Pertinent Factors in Soviet–Japanese Situation', 31 Jan. 1934.

24. Ibid.

25. FDR–PSF, Japan, 1933–34, secret letter and memo from Standley to Bullitt, 3 Feb. 1934.

26. Ibid.

27. FDR–PSF, Japan, 1933–34, memo, 'Russo–Japanese Conflict, Problem: What Should be the Attitude and Course of Action of the United States', 2 Feb. 1934.

28. Ibid.

29. Ibid. See also, *FRUS*, Vol. III, *The Far East*, memo by Hornbeck, 'Our Diplomatic Position, as of Today, in the Far East, with Special Reference to Naval Conference and Need for Naval Construction', 24 May 1934, 189–93.

30. NTJ Papers, Container 23, Folder G-M, letter from Johnson to Roy Howard of Scripps-Howard Newspapers, 13 Jan. 1934.

31. Ibid.

32. NTJ Papers, Container 23, Folder G-M, letter from Johnson to Hornbeck, 23 Aug. 1934.

33. *FRUS*, Vol. III, despatch from Grew to Hull, 8 Feb. 1934, 32–6.

34. Ibid.

35. Ibid.

36. Ibid. This 8 Feb. despatch was sent by the State Department to Ambassador Bullitt for his opinion. He agreed with Grew's assessment of the situation, both militarily and politically. Bullitt thought that while the honeymoon with the United States and the Soviet Union was over, the Soviets were mindful of the restraining influence of US recognition on Japan, and believed that until their military preparations in the Far East were complete, they would not wantonly strain US–USSR relations for fear of provoking a Japanese attack. *FRUS*, Vol. III, despatch from Bullitt to Grew, 16 Apr. 1934, 109–12.

37. Ibid. *FRUS*, Vol. III, despatch and enclosure from Grew to Hull, 8 Mar. 1934, 66–72. The Soviet Ambassador, Youreneff, had accused the British of trying to instigate a war between the Soviet Union and Japan, in order to protect their own interests in the Far East. The Ambassador also tried frequently to influence Grew into believing that the British were extremely pro-Japanese and willing to sell out anyone else in order to protect their own interests.

38. Hull Papers, Container 37, paper, 'The Far East and the World Peace Machinery', sent to Hull by Dr Quincy Wright, University of Chicago, Illinois, 14 July 1934.

39. Ibid.

40. Ibid.

41. NTJ Papers, Container 23, Folder G-M, letter from Johnson to Hornbeck, 23 Aug. 1934

and Container 26, Folder -K, letter from Hornbeck to Johnson, 17 Jan. 1935.

42. CSDCF, 741.61/427, telegram from Bullitt to Hull, 27 July 1934.

43. CSDCF, 741.61/428, telegram from Bullitt to Hull, 30 July 1934.

44. CSDCF, 741.61/432, telegram from Bullitt to Hull, 24 Sept. 1934.

45. CSDCF, 741.61/432, note and enclosure from William Phillips to Edwin L. Neville (Chargé d'Affaires, Tokyo), Willys Peck (US Consul-General, Nanking) and Nelson T. Johnson, all 8 Oct. 1934.

46. FO 371/18177/F6853/316/23, letter from Drummond (British Ambassador in Rome) to Sir Victor Wellesley, 8 Nov. 1934.

47. FO 371/18177/F5809/316/23, FO memo entitled, 'Attitude of United States to an Eventual Soviet–Japanese war', 17 Sept. 1934; FO 371/18177/F7517/316/23, letter from Rear Admiral G.C. Dickens, Head of Department of Naval Intelligence, to Orde, 20 Dec. 1934. See also Lensen, *The Damned Inheritance*, 444.

48. R. Walton Moore Papers, Franklin D. Roosevelt Presidential Library, Hyde Park, Box 3, letter from Bullitt to Moore, 23–24 Apr. FDR–PSF, Confidential Files, Box 50, Folder – Russia, William C. Bullitt, 1933–36, personal and confidential letter from Bullitt to FDR, 13 Apr. 1934.

49. Ibid. See also FDR–PSF files, Confidential Files, Box 49, Folder – Diplomatic Correspondence, Russia, 1934, despatch from Bullitt to Hull, 'Personal Observations of Ambassador William C. Bullitt on Conditions in the Soviet Union', 2 Oct. 1934.

50. The Soviets were not above trying to get the United States to provide them with information about possible British or Japanese intentions and preying on American doubts about Britain's attitude towards Japan. In a private luncheon at the Soviet Embassy in Nanking, on 31 Aug. 1934, the Soviet Ambassador, Bogomoloff, pumped the US Consul General from Shanghai, Clarence E. Gauss, for information as to why the Japanese had not accepted Soviet terms for the sale of the Chinese Eastern Railway. Bogomoloff blamed the British for this, telling Gauss that John Simon and other Conservatives were desirous of the Japanese expanding in northern China at Russia's expense. This fondness for Japan, coupled with such encouraging gestures to the Japanese as the British Industrial Mission, all served to encourage the Japanese into thinking some agreement could be reached with the British and therefore into believing that a harder line could be taken with the Soviets. Gauss was asked if he knew of any secret agreement between the Japanese and British. Clearly the Soviets thought highly of the Americans' access to information from the British and Japanese and hoped that in light of the new spirit of cooperation that existed between the United States and the Soviet Union, they could gain some insights from Washington. CSDCF, 741.61/41, memorandum of conversation from Johnson to Hull, 7 Sept. 1934.

51. FDR–PSF, Japan, 1935, 3 Jan. 1935; *FRUS*, Vol. III, *The Far East*, Hornbeck memo, 3 Jan. 1935, 829–37.

52. FDR–PSF, Japan, 1935, note from Hull with memo enclosed, 22 Jan. 1935; *FRUS*, Vol. III, *The Far East*, despatch from Grew to Hull, 27 Dec. 1934, 821–9.

53. FDR–PSF, Japan, 1935, note from Hull to FDR with memo enclosed, 22 Jan. 1935; *FRUS*, Vol. III, 1935, 842–3.

54. *FRUS*, Vol. III, Grew memo, 27 Dec. 1934, 821–9.

55. FDR–PSF, Japan, 1935, 3 Jan. 1935; *FRUS*, Vol. III, *The Far East*, 3 Jan. 1935, 829–37.

56. Ibid. *FRUS*, Vol. III, 836.

57. For a very able and more specific look at US–USSR trade relations from 1933 to 1939, see Williams, *Trading with the Bolsheviks*, 151–84.

58. *FRUS*, Vol. III, Hornbeck memo, 3 Jan. 1935, 829–37.

59. Ibid.

60. Moore Papers, memo from Hornbeck to Moore, 'Foreign Policy of the United States

and Analysis, with Suggestions for Procedure', 17 Apr. 1935.

61. *FRUS*, Vol. III, memo from War Dept. Assistant Chief of Staff, G-4 to Hornbeck, 7 Jan. 1935, 2–4.
62. *FRUS*, Vol. III, despatch from Grew to Hull, 8 Feb. 1935, 49–54.
63. Ibid. On the sale of the CER see Lensen, *The Damned Inheritance*, 330–3.
64. *FRUS*, Vol. III, 49–54.
65. *FRUS*, Vol. III, despatch from Grew to Hull, 5 Apr. 1935, 106–11.
66. *FRUS*, Vol. III, despatch from Grew to Hull, 31 May 1935, 193–6.
67. *FRUS*, Vol. IV, *The Far East*, memo by Under Secretary of State, William Phillips, of meeting with Russian Ambassador to Washington, A.A. Troyanovsky, 7 Feb. 1936, 40–1; ibid., telegram from Chargé in Moscow (Henderson) to Hull, 13 Feb. 1936, 56–7; ibid., despatch from Bullitt to Hull, 18 Mar. 1936, 78–9; ibid., despatch from Grew to Hull, 18 Mar. 1936, 80–3; ibid., despatch from Grew to Hull, 29 May 1936, 177–80.
68. NTJ Papers, Container 29, Folder F-L, letter from Howard to Johnson, 17 July 1936.
69. Ibid., letter from Johnson to Howard, 15 Aug. 1936.
70. Norman Davis Papers (hereafter Davis Papers), Library of Congress, Washington, DC, Container 27, letter from Davis to Hornbeck, 17 June 1936.
71. CSDCF, 741.65/210, telegram from Atherton to Hull, 13 Feb. 1936.
72. Ibid.
73. *FRUS*, Vol. IV, *The Far East*, despatch from Erle R. Dickover (First Secretary in Tokyo) to Hull, 26 Nov. 1936, 394–6; ibid., despatch from Grew to Hull, 16 Dec. 1936, 426–9; NTJ Papers, Container 31, Folder A-K, letter from Grew to Johnson, 17 May 1937.
74. *FRUS*, Vol. III, *The Far East*, despatch from Grew to Hull, 1 Jan. 1937, 1–11.
75. Ibid.
76. Ibid.
77. NTJ Papers, Container 31, Folder A-K, letter from Johnson to Grew, 4 June 1937.
78. Rear Admiral Yates Stirling Jr, 'Naval Preparedness in the Pacific Area', *USNIP*, May 1934, 601–8, 608. On Soviet–Japanese tensions see Stirling, 'Sea Power', *USNIP*, June 1935, 767–80, 779.
79. Captain Dudley W. Knox, 'The Japanese Situation', *USNIP*, Sept. 1935, 1277–80, 1278. For more on Knox, see Greg Kennedy, 'Depression and Security: Aspects Influencing the United States Navy during the Hoover Administration', *D&S*, 6 (1995): 342–72.
80. Reprinted in *USNIP*, Apr. 1936, 593.
81. Reprinted in *USNIP*, Jan. 1937, 130. See also, *USNIP*, Sept. 1937, 1350.
82. *USNIP*, June 1937, 898. For the full story of this Soviet–US adventure, see Malcolm Muir Jr, 'American Warship Construction for Stalin's Navy Prior to World War II: A Study in Paralysis of Policy', *DH*, 5 (1981): 337–51.
83. William D. Leahy Diary (hereafter Leahy Diary), Library of Congress, Washington, DC, entry for 3 May 1937.
84. Muir, 'American Warship Construction for Stalin's Navy Prior to World War II', 348–9. See also, Proceedings and Hearings of the General Board of the US Navy, 1900–50 (hereafter Proceedings and Hearings), National Archives, Washington, DC, Hearing of the General Board, Vols 1–2, 1939, 'Battleship "X"', 5 Dec. 1939; and ibid., 'Destroyer to Accompany Ship "X"', 11 Dec. 1939; Official Files of President Roosevelt (hereafter FDR-OF) FDR Library, Hyde Park, New York, Navy Dept., letter from Gibbs and Cox INC. to Assistant Secretary of the Navy, Charles Edison, 7 Sept. 1937; ibid., letter from Charles W. Yost, Office of Arms and Munitions Control, State Dept. to Carp Export and Import Corporation, 27 Feb. 1937.
85. FO 371/21523/A6523/55/45, record of conversation, 18 Aug. 1938.
86. Record Group (RG) 38, Office of the Chief of Naval Operations Division of Naval

Intelligence, General Correspondence, 1929–42 (hereafter CNO-DNI General Corr., 1929–42), National Archives, Washington, DC, Box 117, Folder A4-5/FF6, restricted report from Yarnell to CNO, 1 July 1937.

87. Admiral Harry E. Yarnell Papers (hereafter Yarnell MSS), Library of Congress, Washington, DC, Container 3, Folder – Leahy 17-26, letter from Leahy to Yarnell, 30 June 1937; NTJ Papers, Container 32, Folder L-Y, letter from Yarnell to Johnson, 7 July 1937.

88. Ibid.

89. Selected Naval Attaché Reports Relating to the World Crisis, 1937–43, 'Probability of an Outbreak of War' (hereafter US Naval Attaché, 'Outbreak'), on microfilm, National Archive, Washington, DC, Tokyo Naval Attaché report No. 125, 1 May 1937.

90. NTJ Papers, Container 33, Folder U-Z, letter from Yarnell to Johnson, 21 July 1937. Yarnell's observations of the Russians and his trip to Vladivostok were sent along by the CNO, Admiral Leahy, to President Roosevelt for his information. See FDR-OF, Navy Dept., letter from Leahy to FDR, 23 Aug. 1937, and enclosure, private letter from Yarnell to Leahy, 1 Aug. 1937.

91. NTJ Papers, Container 35, Folder U-Y, letter from Yarnell to Johnson, 13 Feb. 1938. For a study of the Soviet Navy's attitude and capability in the Far East during the 1930s see Jürgen Rohwer and Mikhail Monakov, 'The Soviet Union's Ocean-Going Fleet, 1935–1956', *IHR*, 18 (1996): 837–68.

92. FDR-OF, Navy Dept., letter from Leahy to FDR, 23 Aug. 1937, and enclosure, private letter from Yarnell to Leahy, 1 Aug. 1937.

93. Hull Papers, Container 42, letter from Nelson T. Johnson to Hull, 17 Feb. 1938.

94. Henry L. Stimson Diary (hereafter Stimson Diary), Yale University, New Haven, Connecticut, entry for 24 Mar. 1938.

95. Ibid.

96. *FRUS*, Vol. III, *The Far East*, telegram from Bullitt (Ambassador to France) to Hull, 13 Jan. 1938, 19; telegram from Chargé d'Affaires in France (Wilson) to Hull, 5 Apr. 1938, 135; Bullitt was given information on Russian supplies to China from Sun Yat-Sen's son Sun Fo, as well as intelligence on Soviet Far Eastern policy and attitudes towards Japan, telegram from Bullitt to Hull, 9 May 1938, 164; see also the entire section on 'Developments with respect to Border Hostilities between Japanese and Soviet Troops', much of which shows the military superiority of the Soviets in the defence and the amount of worry, tension and uncertainty, as well as a drain on military manpower and resources, that the Soviet Union caused for the Japanese plans for the Far East; memo prepared by Department of Far Eastern Affairs, *FRUS*, Vol. III, 20 Apr. 1938, 595.

97. Hull Papers, Container 42, Report from A. Bland Calder, Assistant Commercial Attaché at Shanghai, 'The Flow of Arms into China', 2 Mar. 1938. This report was sent along by Hull to FDR for his personal information. The report discussed the flow of arms to China from French Indo-China and Hong Kong, with the last part of the report dealing with the vast bulk of war material, especially aircraft, that was coming into China from Russia.

98. RG 38, CNO-DNI General Corr., Box 117, Folder A4-5/FF6, restricted report from Yarnell to CNO, 16 Jan. 1938; ibid., restricted report from Yarnell to CNO, 16 Mar. 1938; NTJ Papers, Container 34, Folder H-I, letter from Johnson to Hull, 27 May 1938; ibid., Container 35, Folder U-Y, letter from Yarnell to Johnson, 3 Jan. 1938; ibid., Container 35, Folder U-Y, letter from Yarnell to Johnson, 13 Feb. 1938; Morley, *Deterrent Diplomacy*, 133.

99. Until indicated, the following is based on: Records of the Strategic Plans Division, Office of the Chief of Naval Operations and Predecessor Organizations, Series III:

Miscellaneous Subject File, 1917–47 (hereafter Strategic Plans Div.) on microfilm, National Archive, Washington, DC, Military Intelligence Division (Army) Studies, OP-12-War Plans, confidential G-2, 'Russian Combat Estimate', 1 July 1938.

100. The effect of the purges on the Soviet Navy in the Far East was debated in articles reprinted from foreign sources in the *USNIP*; See sections on the USSR in the Nov. 1938, Mar. 1939 and July 1939 volumes of *USNIP*.

101. Ibid.

102. See note 66.

103. Yarnell Papers, Container 2, Folder, General 5 June–1 July 1938, letter from retired Admiral A. St Clair Smith to Yarnell, 26 May 1938; ibid., Container 3, Folder, General 25 June–12 July 1939, letter from Leahy to Yarnell, 31 May 1939; RG 38, CNO-DNI General Corr., Box 117, Folder A4-5/FF6, Restricted Report, from C.-in-C., Asiatic Fleet to CNO, 2 Jan. 1939; Thaddeus V. Tuleja, *Statesmen and Admirals* (New York, 1963), 151–77; John Major, 'The Navy Plans for War, 1937–1941', in Kenneth J. Hagan ed., *In Peace and War* (Westport, CT, 1984), 237–62, 238; Robert G. Albion (ed. Rowena Reed), *Makers of Naval Policy, 1798–1947* (Annapolis, MD, 1980), 344–6.

104. Yarnell Papers, Container 3, Folder, General, letter from Yarnell to Admiral Marquart (at the Naval Examining Board), 18 Feb. 1939.

105. Yarnell's views on the matter were relayed to the CNO and other USN policy-making bodies and were supported by the Naval Attaché in Tokyo, see Naval Attaché, Tokyo, 'Outbreak', Report No. 11, 17 Jan. 1939.

106. Observations by Yarnell and Nelson Johnson had convinced the USN to accept the Soviet Russian factor as being a vital element of the Far Eastern balance of power to such an extent that, during a lecture on 'The Present Naval Policy and its Support of our National Policy', given to 35 US Naval Reserve and Army Officers in Baltimore, Commander Leland P. Lovetter, the USN officer in charge of the public relations branch of the Navy Department in Washington, told his audience that 'Russia was also a sealed book. The Japanese were evidently apprehensive of a move by Russia as they had moved 350,000 of their best troops to the Russian Manchuko border. As far as the American Administration was concerned the rule was to keep on as good terms as possible with the Russian Government and its representatives.' The US Navy's attitude towards the Soviets and their usefulness in the Far East was also carefully monitored by the British. See FO 371/22829/A2122/1292/45, confidential report from Hoyer Millar (HM Consul in Baltimore) to J. Balfour (Head of American Dept.), 3 Mar. 1939.

107. *FRUS*, Vol. III, 'The Far East', despatch from Grew to Hull, 13 Jan. 1939, 1.

108. Ibid.

109. *FRUS*, Vol. III, extract from despatch from Dooman (Chargé in Tokyo) to Hull, 7 June 1939, 43.

110. Ibid. *FRUS* Vol. III, telegram from Dooman to Hull, 8 Aug. 1939, 48. For American advances to the Soviets about possible combination of Powers in the Far East see Bennett, *Franklin D. Roosevelt and the Search for Victory*, 3.

111. For aspects of that relationship see: Jacob Kavalio, 'Japan's Perception of Stalinist Foreign Policy in the Early 1930s', *JCH*, 19 (1984): 315–35; Brian Bridges, 'Yoshizawa Kenkichi and the Soviet–Japanese Non-aggression Pact Proposal', *MAS*, 14 (1980): 111–27.

112. *FRUS*, Vol. III, telegram from Dooman to Hull, 8 Aug. 1939, 48. See also Naval Attaché Tokyo, 'Outbreak', Report No. 163, 19 July 1939; David Dilks, ed., *The Diaries of Sir Alexander Cadogan, 1938–1945* (London, 1971), 150–5, 180–9.

113. See Naval Attaché Tokyo, 'Outbreak', Report No. 81, 12 Apr. 1939.

114. *FRUS*, Vol. III, despatch from Dooman to Hull, 12 Sept. 1939, 64. For the Japanese fear of an Anglo-Soviet alliance see CSDCF, 741.61/655, confidential telegram from

Dooman to Hull, 31 May 1939.

115. FDR–PSF, Japan, 1939–40, letter from Grew to FDR, 6 Nov. 1939, in which he told FDR that as far as he was concerned, the Soviet position in the Far East was that, 'The USSR still appears to be helping Chiang Kai-Shek with supplies but it may be significant that Molotov in his recent speech did not mention China at all and made a point of flattering Japan ... There is much speculation as to whether the USSR and Japan are going to get together with a view to dividing up China between them. The German Embassy is working hard to bring the two countries together. But I can't for the life of me see any possibility of a real Soviet–Japanese rapprochement because far too many fundamental differences exist ...'

116. *FRUS*, Vol. III, undated (sometime late Nov. 1939) memo by the State Department, 92.

117. Naval Attaché Tokyo, 'Outbreak', Report No. 184, 24 Aug. 1939.

118. SKH Papers, Box 459, note from Hornbeck to Welles, 6 June 1939, shows that that interest included that of the President himself.

119. CAB 23/96, Cabinet 57(38), 30 Nov. 1938.

# 4

# The Development of Anglo-American Trust and the 1935 London Naval Conference (I)

Personal contact between the leading statesmen of different countries enables friendships to be formed, more intimate relations and better understandings to be established. These in turn create confidence and confidence makes for cooperation.

Victor Wellesley[1]

Nations that do not trust one another are not likely to be able to cooperate effectively. Continued failures to find common ground or mutually satisfactory solutions to international issues affecting Anglo-American relations threatened to create an attitude of suspicion and hostility early in Roosevelt's first term. Such was the attitude of policy-makers on both sides of the Atlantic in 1934 regarding the strategically linked issues of naval arms limitation and security in the Far East. Elimination of the fear and uncertainty over each other's foreign policy and maritime position regarding the Far East was required if Anglo-American relations were to continue to be amicable.[2] By the end of 1936, that suspicion and distrust would be replaced by a concerted effort on behalf of both parties to work more closely together on Far Eastern matters. This new-found sense of trust between the United States and Great Britain was forged in the discussions that surrounded the 1935 Naval Conference, which proved to be the final phase of the Washington Treaty system of 1921–22.

Prior to the 1935 Conference, American sensibilities towards the British in the Far East and the naval issue were tinged with a sense of irritation, reflecting the administration's belief that Sir John Simon, the Secretary of State for Foreign Affairs, had betrayed the Far Eastern policy of US Secretary of State Henry L. Stimson, during the Manchurian Crisis of 1932.[3] Rubbing salt in that old wound was the failure to achieve Anglo-American economic cooperation at the World Economic Conference in 1933, and a continued suspicion that slippery John Simon and the British government would try to put one over on the United States at the naval conference.[4] The State Department's attitude towards Simon and the condition of Anglo-American relations, in May 1933, was reflected in the views held by the Chief of the Division of Western European Affairs, Jay Pierrepont Moffat:

> Anglo-American relations are growing visibly worse. Simon has been up to his old tricks of undoing all the progress that has been made blocking the Tariff Truce Agreement as well as conniving at the Government's attitude in (1) rushing through their trade agreements with the Argentine, Germany, etc., which are at utter variance with the spirit of the MacDonald talks, (2) increasing the British equalization fund, which is a transparent device to gamble with our currency for the greater advantage of English trade …, and (3) listening complacently to the British outcry against our payment in dollars of our internally issued Liberty Bonds when Great Britain did exactly the same thing and the British courts (not our own) had issued a decision that the gold clause did not mean payment in bullion. There is great discouragement in certain quarters here despite a stiff upper lip.[5]

That attitude created fertile ground for the American belief that many senior policy-makers were more than interested in renewing the Anglo-Japanese alliance, at the expense of the United States.[6]

There were other irritations. On the British side, the failed Economic Conference and the branding of Great Britain as a debtor nation over the war debts issue in the Johnson Act of 11 January 1934 had soured many in the policy-making elite who dealt with the United States.[7] Also, there were mutual feelings of frustration in the Foreign Office, the State Department and the Royal and US Navies, over the failed attempt of the MacDonald Mission to the United States, in April 1933, to bring the two nations closer together on world security issues through the disarmament talks being held in Geneva.[8] Finally, the Admiralty and Foreign Office were unimpressed by the Roosevelt administration's designs for building a treaty-strength navy. John Simon, in particular, saw the American action as guaranteeing that Japan would not settle for anything less than naval parity with the United States and Great Britain. If this were the case, then the conference was sure to end in failure.[9] He and Sir Robert Vansittart, the Permanent Under-Secretary (PUS), were anxious to start a public campaign in England, denouncing the US naval increases, as the first step in ensuring that it would not be the British government that was blamed for any failure. Temporarily warned off such action by the British Ambassador to the United States, Sir Ronald Lindsay, both men grudgingly agreed to await further developments before taking any further steps.[10]

Anti-American sentiment ran strongest in the British Treasury, largely because of the many economic tensions between the two nations.[11] The Treasury mentality was best expressed by Sir Warren Fisher, the Secretary to the Treasury, in the defence debates taking place in England in late 1933 and early 1934.[12] During the Defence Requirements Sub-Committee (DRC) meetings, he opined that Britain's defence planning had to reflect that it was not a 'backboneless nation' required to bow down to the United States. Fisher also thought that the worst aspect of British defence deficiencies was Great Britain's entanglement with the Americans.[13] He believed that entanglement had prevented British diplomacy being able to create better Anglo-Japanese relations. During the DRC debates, Fisher put forth the Treasury view as to how Great Britain should deal with the Americans in the naval talks scheduled for 1935:

> it is essential in my view to get clear of our 'entangling' agreement with the USA who should be left to circle the globe with ships if they want, to gratify their vanity by singing 'Rule Columbia, Columbia rules the waves', and to wait and see for how many years the politically all-powerful Middle West will continue to acquiesce in paying a fantastic bill related to not real requirement but primarily to indulge the braggadocio of Yahoodom.[14]

The Treasury's pro-Japanese attitude towards imperial defence questions in the Far East was also reflected in Fisher's strategic vision of the worth of the Anglo-American relationship in the Far East and his fear of German rearmament:

> The American interest in these naval pacts is, in my belief, to keep us on bad terms with the Japanese (and therefore potentially weaker and less able to take an independent line vis-à-vis the USA), and to limit their own expenditure against the bogy which their imaginings make of Japan. As the USA thinks of a first-class war in terms of Japan, she would of course like us involved on her side. (To get us in the meantime to pick the Asiatic chestnuts of the USA out of the fire is a useful preliminary) ... If then we emancipate ourselves from thraldom to the USA (who as an institution – and indeed from Colonial days – never has been friendly to us and never will be) and thus free ourselves to establish durable relations with Japan, we can concentrate on the paramount danger at our very threshold. This of course is in the future; but its likelihood will in my opinion become a certainty unless the Germans have every reason to believe that, if and when it might suit them to force a war, they will come up against our maximum strength, undivided and undistracted by Far Eastern complications.[15]

This attitude towards the United States was unhelpful and meddlesome, and reflected the narrow continentalist views of a Treasury that had no grasp of the imperial nature of the troubles facing British foreign and defence policy.[16] It also served to complicate Foreign Office and State Department attempts to reach a mutual understanding on maritime and foreign policy questions concerning the Far East. It would, however, be overridden and discarded as British policy by the end of the naval talks, a process in which the Treasury played no significant role.[17]

Both the Royal Navy, under the leadership of Admiral Sir Ernle Chatfield, First Sea Lord and Chief of the Naval Staff, and the Foreign Office took a view opposite to Fisher's. Chatfield many times stated clearly in the Committee of Imperial Defence (CID) and during DRC meetings the need for the Royal Navy to maintain good relations with the United States and in particular with the US Navy. Pushed by Japan in the Far East, and with Singapore unfinished and Hong Kong largely undefended, the Royal Navy hoped ultimately for US maritime assistance in a war with Japan. Even if such assistance were not in the form of a formal naval alliance, there was the need for the United States to help enforce a blockade on Japan by being at least a benevolent neutral. The DRC process could reach no solid conclusion, however, regarding Britain's future maritime power because it was the outcome of the 1935 Naval Conference (would Japan be given the same ratios as the United States and Great Britain?) that would decide ultimately the course of the Admiralty's rearmament programme.[18]

Until that disarmament process was either extended or eliminated, Chatfield and the Royal Navy could not safely plan the future development of Britain's fleet.[19] Prime Minister Ramsay MacDonald lent his reduced but still significant weight to the pro-American side. The Secretary of the CID, Sir Maurice Hankey, warned Fisher that this was the case. Hankey told the Treasury official that the Foreign Office position was to continue to attempt to promote friendly relations with the United States and that MacDonald had 'a very warm spot for the Americans generally' and for President Roosevelt in particular.[20] The official view of the Foreign Office on how the United States fitted into Great Britain's strategic balance of power in mid-1933 was that:

> It must be the aim of His Majesty's Government in the United Kingdom to continue the policy they have consistently followed with beneficial results during the last decade of promoting friendly relations with the United States of America. This policy has not entailed, and does not call for the sacrifice of any essential British interest. It does, however, demand the exercise of much patience, for progress must inevitably be slow. But if the United States Government and people can be persuaded that Great Britain is pursing a sane, constructive and progressive world policy, that, in a word, her attitude contrasts favourably with the mutual antagonisms, fears and suspicions of the continental Powers, it will be possible for this country virtually to ensure that the political and economic influence of

the United States is utilised to the best effect, and incidentally to our advantage.[21]

Even Vansittart, who was often very sceptical of the strategic worth of the Americans, still preferred their strategic company to that of the Japanese. He noted during the DRC meetings that,

> no one realised more than he did the paramount necessity for better relations with Japan, especially during our period of weakness. We had, however, made much progress in Anglo-American relations of recent years and, while Anglo-American relations would always be disappointing, he hoped that the benefits of betterment would not all be thrown away in order to run after the Japanese.[22]

But, Fisher's arguments had presented the issue clearly to the British foreign and defence policy-makers: because of strategic and maritime pressures in the Far East, Britain would have to choose between the United States and Japan at the upcoming Naval Conference.

Underlying the mutual feelings of distrust and frustration that existed between the United States and Great Britain was a real desire to cooperate on naval limitation issues, as long as each nation could ensure its security and find applause from their watchful publics and presses. It was during the preliminary talks and resulting negotiation of the Naval Conference that a lasting sense of trust regarding each nation's attitude towards Japan and the Far Eastern situation was established between the British Foreign Office and the US State Department, and also between their respective navies.[23] This confidence-building process was successful – despite painful suspicions – because of predominantly open and honest communication on both sides of the Atlantic, a mutual need to appear to be trying to limit naval arms (this for domestic consumption), and the desire to find some security against Japanese actions in the Far East.

The Foreign Office's early sensitivity to any perceived affronts by the United States was especially apparent in the actions and statements of Vansittart. The PUS was darkly sceptical of American actions in the period from 1933 to early 1936.[24] His attitude was one of severe reaction to any American slight against Great Britain, and, while he had not supported Fisher's anti-American sentiments during the DRC procedures, he had pointed out that, when preparations for the 1935 Naval Conference began, Fisher's points would then be appropriate.[25] Often he was filled with a distrust of, and a blinding mean-spiritedness combined with a sense of superiority towards, those who held office, both politically and professionally, in the United States.[26] This belligerent, biased, at times irrational and unprofessional attitude was the culmination of many years of trying, as head of the Foreign Office's American Department and as PUS, to attempt to create better Anglo-American relations in difficult times.[27] While naturally loyal and devoted to the protection of Britain's imperial interests and the preservation of the empire's position as a great world power, Vansittart's petulant attitude towards the United States often needed to be overridden or ignored by other members of the Foreign Office or such politicians as MacDonald during the naval conversations that took place between 1934 and 1935. Indeed, from the beginning of the process that would culminate in the 1936 London Naval Treaty being signed by Great Britain and the United States, Vansittart found himself at odds with many powerful and influential British policy-makers over how to deal with the Americans on the issue of naval disarmament.

In early January 1934, shortly after the United States passed the Johnson Act, which prevented nations who had defaulted on First World War debts to the United States from borrowing there, Vansittart vented his rage against what he saw as US duplicity. In discussions surrounding the advisability of allowing a US Naval Squadron to visit the Home Fleet, Vansittart revealed fully just how punitive he wished to be. Pent-up frustration with the Americans boiled forth as he proposed to throw overboard attempts to come to some sort of under-standing with them on naval disarmament, and instead to begin preparations for the 1935 Naval Conference by seeking an agreement with the Japanese:[28]

> The visit is definitely off, so far as I am concerned. In the last week alone the US have given an offensively hostile reception to our disarmament plan, and have ranked us as defaulters (according to the *Times* of yesterday). And this despite the President's assurance. The administration has switched and is now behind the Johnson Bill ... I will only repeat my strengthened conviction that we have been too tender, not to say too subservient, with the US for a long time past. It is we who have made all the advances, and received nothing in return. It is still necessary, and I still desire as much as ever, that we should get on well with this untrustworthy race; we shall never get very far; they will always let us down; but I think our methods will obviously have to change, and we shall do no good until they realise that they must make at least some of the running ... Mr Craigie's idea of preparation for the Naval Conference of 1935 has been first to approach the USA. There was much to be said for this, but by no means everything ... Lord Stanhope evidently considers that we should approach Japan independently. I wonder if he considers that we should approach Japan first ... A change of tactics towards America is evidently desirable. This may conceivably be the moment for stimulating her by the change. It is also conceivable at least that to approach Japan first may, in this instance, be the right tactics anyhow. Japan is rather anxious to stand well with us just at present. It may be right to take advantage of this moment, and certainly by ourselves. The universally unpopular US would

be a deadweight ... The Prime Minister was speaking to us a few days ago about the necessity of an early start of preparations for the Naval Conference. He evidently considered that the opening, indeed I think the opening stages, should be conducted with the USA. I do not feel so sure of that.[29]

On 6 February, Vansittart met with the head of the Far Eastern Department, Charles Orde, the head of the American Department, Robert Craigie, and the Parliamentary Under-Secretary of State, Earl Stanhope, to consolidate his position before presenting it to the Admiralty and the Prime Minister as the first steps to take towards the 1935 conference.[30]

Under Vansittart's guidance, the Foreign Office conclusions that emanated from this meeting were: that (1) it was best not to go to the Americans first but instead wait for them to come to the British; (2) no common front was to be established with the Americans against the Japanese, at least not one which the Japanese could detect. Such action would make the Japanese quite intractable and create the worst impression before the conference even got going. No joint Anglo-American approach to Japan would be made, but it was decided it would be useful to know the American position on quantitative limitation before the British approached the Japanese; (3) Great Britain should define its position and objectives for the conference, inform the United States of them, note that they were going to talk to the Japanese government in preparation for the conference and enquire whether the United States had anything to tell His Majesty's government; (4) if the United States made no response in a reasonable time then talks with Japan were to go ahead; and (5) this procedure was to be used if quantitative limitations were to be discussed first. If qualitative issues were to be raised before the quantitative, then it was thought to be desirable to contact the United States first.[31] This plan of attack reflected the influence of the Foreign Office official who would truly run the diplomatic side of the naval talks for the next two years: Robert Leslie Craigie.[32] Craigie was opposed to chasing too far after the Japanese at the expense of relations with the United States. The five initial steps were his way of creating a mechanism for thwarting Vansittart's desire to pursue the Japanese in order to punish the Americans. While no formal approach would be made to the Americans, the offer of inviting talks with His Majesty's government about the Naval Conference would be opening enough to ensure that discussions would take place with the Americans first. As well, the Prime Minster and the Admiralty, the latter the institution that would have the last word on any formulae, timings or proposals concerning the final outcome of the naval talks, had something to say about the idea of not moving towards the United States first.

Before Vansittart had promised Fisher the Foreign Office's closest cooperation in preparation for the naval talks, the Foreign Office and Admiralty had been in close contact on preparatory tactics and procedures. On 19 January,

Vansittart had written Chatfield telling him that the Foreign Office and Admiralty should cooperate in their historic manner and control the process. Most importantly, the PUS wanted to know how the First Sea Lord felt about the usefulness of early private and unofficial conversations with representatives of other naval powers.[33]

Accompanying Vansittart's questions to Chatfield was a Foreign Office memo, prepared by Craigie. It dealt with five main topics: the need for early preparatory work; the need to distinguish between the naval problems of the Disarmament Conference and those of the 1935 Conference; questions of policy development; procedure; and the position of the Dominions.[34] Craigie emphasized the difficult nature of the upcoming talks and the need for thorough, early preparatory planning and a decision as to the policy and strategy which would be used. He acknowledged the Admiralty's right to make definite proposals regarding that policy, but pointed out the need for the Admiralty to keep other questions in mind: how long should the treaty last? what were the minimum requirements in categories during that period? what reductions would be asked for in unit sizes? what should the relative strengths of the naval powers be? and most importantly, what was the likely attitude of the principal naval powers in light of some of the answers to the above?

On the key issue of the American attitude towards the talks, Craigie felt that the United States could be brought into an agreement on the basis of a 'live and let live' approach. He did not want to pressure the Americans into decreasing the size of their ships by challenging the tactical and strategic considerations that underpinned the American position. Similarly, then, he thought, the United States would not press Britain to reduce the number of units below that considered essential for its absolute needs. This belief was especially important for the Royal Navy in its quest to increase its cruiser numbers to an overall strength of 70. As to capital ships, Craigie felt that the British government could not agree to a further shipbuilding holiday because of the age of their ships.

> Once agreement has been reached with the United States on some such plan and assuming that it is not the intention of the United States Government to resume construction of 8" gun cruisers, we should have reached practically complete agreement with that Power and our hands would be greatly strengthened for negotiating with other Powers. An Anglo-American agreement in regard to the maximum displacements in the various categories would, in the nature of things, have to be accepted eventually by the other naval Powers, however reluctantly, because they would not wish to build larger ships than those favoured by the United States and could not risk building smaller ones.

Craigie acknowledged the care that would need to be taken in handling the Japanese during the process to ensure that their nationalistic sensibilities were not aroused. There was even a chance that tripartite conversations with the

Japanese government might eventually be held in Tokyo, but the success of any such talks would be less problematical if the British earlier had managed to exchange views with the Americans and to arrive at a confidential working agreement. He felt, however, that in the end Japan would accept a total tonnage averaging around 70 per cent of that of both the United States and Britain, but might balk at the idea of 12-inch guns for capital ships instead of the 14-inch that they desired. As to procedures, the order of who was to be met first and what early deals were to be struck, he suggested that the United States and France be approached first, as they 'are the key Powers in this business and also, incidentally the Powers with whom it should be the least difficult for us to reach agreement'. Craigie also desired close cooperation between the Foreign Office and Admiralty in preparing a position paper that could be sent along to MacDonald as soon as possible.[35]

John Simon thought the resulting memorandum first-rate, commenting that 'I am hopeful of USA agreeing to a reduction in the size of capital ships – not of cruisers – as she too has now experienced financial difficulties. The approach to Japan will be difficult. If we go hand in hand with USA we shall, I believe, have far less chance than if we take the matter up independently.'[36] The Secretary of State for Foreign Affairs was also worried about the press and other groups in Britain that did not support the Admiralty's desire to build capital ships larger than 20,000 tons.[37] The latter reflected criticism of the naval disarmament process as influenced by Sir Herbert Richmond, a noted naval thinker and educator, and caused Simon to argue that an attempt should be made to strengthen the Admiralty's hand through the setting up of a Cabinet committee. This committee would act as an official sanctioning agent, support-ing the Admiralty and their policy during the upcoming naval debates.[38] Simon, not knowing of the Admiralty's complete victory in the DRC discussions on this issue, was not dogmatic in his desire for such a committee, as long as the British position going into the talks was prepared thoroughly.[39]

Chatfield and the Admiralty quickly replied to the Foreign Office initiative. The First Sea Lord informed Vansittart that the Admiralty had nearly com-pleted their own proposal as to how to approach the upcoming naval talks. He agreed that the two departments should work closely together. A joint memo-randum could be produced, he thought, which could then be sent to the Prime Minister.[40] The Prime Minister could then strike a Cabinet Committee that would use the joint memorandum as the basis for creating a national policy for the 1935 Conference. Chatfield was not enthusiastic about the efficacy or safety of any private or unofficial conversations on such important issues as ratios, numerical strength, total tonnages and so on, until that national policy was determined. Qualitative limitation could be discussed. As for approaching the Americans, Chatfield thought that they could be induced into discussing qualitative matters, but he wanted to do so only after talking to the other signatory powers.[41]

This hesitant attitude towards approaching the United States first in any discussions did not sit well with Craigie. He disagreed with Chatfield's desire to create a coalition of powers to present a unified front against the United States with regard to qualitative limitation instead of dealing with the quantitative limitations first. Craigie felt that such an approach was unnecessary and '… would end by pushing into the forefront of the picture the well worn controversy arising out of the American need for size and our need for numbers'.[42] His preference was naturally for the Admiralty to consider the course of action that he had recommended in the memorandum prepared for Vansittart. These views were taken up with Chatfield by the PUS. Replying to the Admiralty proposal, Vansittart declared how happy he was that the two departments were agreed that they should work together closely and that a British policy for the conference should be devised as quickly as possible. However, he pointed out to the First Sea Lord that he had doubts as to whether separating qualitative and quantitative limitation issues, and moving ahead only in the former, was the best choice.

> The only point on which we feel a little doubtful is whether it would be wise at this stage to attempt to separate the subject of qualitative limitation from that of quantitative limitation and to press ahead with the former subject as being the more urgent. I quite see there are certain advantages in this course, but feel on the other hand great doubt whether the U.S. Government would be likely to agree to it, every indication we have pointing to their determination to reserve any concession as regards qualitative limitation until they know with what they will be faced in the matter of total tonnage. Furthermore, there is a risk that, even if we did succeed in getting a prior agreement as regards qualitative limitation, the prospects of securing a subsequent quantitative agreement on line acceptable to us might be diminished.[43]

The views of both Craigie and the Admiralty reflected the fact that neither knew exactly what the US Navy's position on the matter really was, nor did they know any details of the Roosevelt administration's attitude towards the 1935 Conference. This uncertainty, combined with a more certain belief that the Japanese were going to demand parity with the United States and Great Britain, created a momentum towards holding Anglo-American preliminary talks.

The State Department and the US Navy were in fact becoming both more flexible in their attitude towards Britain's naval needs and more willing to work together with the British to contain the growing Japanese threat. This new flexibility had an unusual genesis. In September 1933, the British government sent an *aide mémoire* to the State Department that made certain suggestions about how the Americans could modify their naval building programme. Such interference in a traditionally sensitive topic had the potential to embarrass the

British government severely, as well as to rekindle Anglo-American antagon-
isms. However, instead of using the gaffe against the British, the State Department defused the situation by sharing the information with the press, who were
thirsting after and speculating wildly about a confrontational story, and then
instructed the press that they could not use this information. The result was
a series of negative editorials that were resentful of the British action but
not inflammatory.[44] The State Department in general also resented the British
act of interference, but still preferred cooperation with the British and therefore made such an attempt in order to control the negotiating environment
as best they could.[45] Norman Davis, naval disarmament expert and special
ambassador-at-large for President Roosevelt, was sure that the British Admiralty, knowing full well what type of reaction the American press would have to
the suggested modifications, had put the Foreign Office up to sending the *aide
mémoire*. Davis believed that the Admiralty planned to use any negative
American reaction to try to gain more funding for a bigger building programme of their own. The naval negotiator trusted the Foreign Office officials,
such men as Simon and Alexander Cadogan (at that point the Foreign Office's
Advisor on League of Nations Affairs), more than he did the Admiralty to deal
openly and honestly with naval disarmament issues. Still, he was surprised that
the Foreign Office had gone along with such a scheme, given the advantages he
saw for the British in Anglo-American naval cooperation in the Far East.[46]

In March of 1933, the Chief of Naval Operations (CNO), Admiral William
V. Pratt, also advocated a more accommodating attitude towards Great
Britain.[47] Both he and Norman Davis agreed that

> the dictates of higher policy made it essential for us to come to a naval
> understanding with Great Britain before the 1935 Conference; that only
> in this way could we prevent the Japanese from succeeding in getting the
> increase of ratio which they desire; that to attain this, some concessions
> towards the British view must be made, though this could not be accepted
> in toto.[48]

Even though such a stand was in direct opposition to the policy of the US Navy's
General Board, Pratt was willing to challenge that advisory body on the
matter.[49] With support for his views coming from such well-respected and
senior Admirals as William H. Standley (Pratt's successor as CNO) and Arthur
J. Hepburn, Pratt's willingness to consider cooperating with the Royal Navy
signalled a coming test of strength over who would formulate US naval policy
at the 1935 London Naval talks: the President, the State Department and the
CNO, or the General Board and isolationist big navy supporters.

Roosevelt, Davis and Standley were all agreed that some sort of accommodation had to be found with Great Britain on the naval arms question.
Reports from the US Ambassador in Japan, Joseph Grew, confirmed suspicions

that the Japanese Navy would not be willing to accept any new treaty terms that offered anything less than parity with the United States and Great Britain.[50] Even Jay Pierrepont Moffat, Grew's son-in-law and a man not normally given to great expressions of warmth for things British, fell in with the opinion that, given the realities of the situation in the Far East, some sort of naval agreement with Great Britain was necessary. In preparing instructions for the US Embassy in London on how to handle the British in questions concerning the Far East and naval limitations, Roosevelt had approved Moffat's suggestion that 'Our whole energy should be centred on reaching a meeting of minds with the British on the specific question of the Far Eastern and naval situation in 1935.'[51] Roosevelt, at a private lunch with the US Ambassador to Great Britain, Robert W. Bingham, confided that he did not believe that the Japanese had any right to parity. He instructed the Ambassador to take the issue up with the British and to try to work out an understanding on naval disarmament which the two nations could support together against Japan's demands. Roosevelt acknowledged that such a unified approach would in all likelihood drive the Japanese from the conference, but 'then the British and ourselves could absolutely control the situation by giving the Japanese to understand that every time they built one ship, we would build two'.[52] The President believed that it was very important to feel out the British attitude towards cooperation with the United States in case a war broke out in the Far East or Europe. His idea was that if the British showed a willingness to consider cooperation, then the two nations could engage in confidential contacts in order to explore the further possibilities of concerted action in order to try to prevent war, or, failing that, to localize it. That was the strategic vision held by the US President when he ordered Bingham to arrange a meeting between Prime Minister MacDonald and Norman Davis as soon as possible.[53]

Of all the important advisors to the President on this matter, the only major dissenting voice was that of the soon-to-be US Ambassador to the Soviet Union (and close confidant of the President), William C. Bullitt. Bullitt agreed that the only long-term solution to the United States' problems in the realm of naval arms limitation and with respect to Great Britain in general, was for the United States to improve and tighten its bonds with England. He did not think, however, that it was the proper time to try to advance this idea of creating closer relations. This hesitation was based on the belief that most of the major officials in the British government – Stanley Baldwin, former Conservative Prime Minister and now Lord President of the Council; Prime Minister MacDonald; Simon; the Chancellor of the Exchequer, Neville Chamberlain; and the President of the Board of Trade, Walter Runciman – were hostile to the United States. However, Bullitt's point of view did not carry the day in the debate over how to go about preparing for the 1935 Conference.[54] Neither the United States nor Britain knew how compatible the other's views would be with their own naval disarmament positions. Instead, each would have to decide how best to approach the coming conference during an initial preliminary stage designed to allow a feeling out of the other's position.

In preparation for those initial talks, the Admiralty returned to the argument with the Foreign Office as to whether qualitative matters could be divorced from quantitative issues in discussions with the United States. In February 1934, the Admiralty informed the Foreign Office that it was vital to get US cooperation on the matter of qualitative limitation, especially pertaining to capital ships, before anything else was discussed. American reluctance to move on such matters as gun size and tonnage restrictions were acknowledged, but the Admiralty argued that cooperation could possibly be achieved by pointing out to the Americans the European aspect of the problem, and how increases in ships and gun size by those powers would force Great Britain and eventually Japan and the United States to follow suit. Then, if such headway were produced, the Japanese could be approached and brought into the mix to face the British and American agreement.[55] Craigie was sceptical of the Admiralty's assumption that it would then prove relatively easy to obtain Japanese agreement to qualitative limitation, especially with respect to gun size. More importantly, while he agreed on the need to approach the Americans first, he pointed out their reluctance to separate qualitative issues from quantitative or to do so before a building holiday was assured. His acceptance of the need to approach the Americans first on the matter underlined his rejection of Vansittart's call to begin preliminary discussions with the Japanese and not with the Americans. Craigie's arguments reflected his superior knowledge – as opposed to Vansittart's entrenched 1930 vision – of the delicate nature of Anglo-American naval negotiations in 1934. He proposed:

> On thinking the matter over carefully I doubt whether this procedure [Vansittart's view on approaching Japan first] would work in regard to the particular matter now under discussion since, if we approach Japan first in regard to *qualitative* limitation, this would destroy such slender chances as may at present exist of our being able to induce the US Government to discuss this matter independently of *quantitative* limitation.[56]

Finally, Craigie described the US government's, especially the State and Navy Departments', perpetual fears of being 'trapped' into a bad deal by perfidious Albion.[57] With Anglo-American tensions still high due to disputes over cruiser matters during the previous summer, Craigie blamed official channels of communication for much of the problem. He now recommended that the best British approach to the Americans on the qualitative position question would be through unofficial methods. A memorandum could be given to the US Chargé d'Affaires and then supplemented with oral explanations.

Vansittart was willing to be overruled by the Admiralty and Craigie on condition that such action was approved by the Parliamentary Under-Secretary of State, Lord Stanhope. It was time, said Vansittart, for the Foreign Office and the Admiralty to go to the Prime Minister, who was very interested in the matter, and establish a clear plan of action.[58] This traditional method of power-brokering on naval matters by the Foreign Office and the Admiralty was interrupted at this point, however, by Vansittart's earlier promise to Fisher in the DRC to keep the Treasury informed of naval disarmament matters. With that promise, Vansittart had brought the Treasury's virulent anti-American attitude into play. Now, with the Treasury involved, the normal lines of com-munication between the Prime Minister, the Admiralty and the Foreign Office would no longer suffice. Thus, a meeting planned with MacDonald, Simon and Sir Bolton M. Eyres Monsell, the First Lord of the Admiralty, to discuss the approach to be taken towards the 1935 Conference was cancelled because now it would have to include Neville Chamberlain. Trapped by his promise to Fisher, Vansittart was forced to allow a Cabinet Committee to be set up to formulate British strategy for the conference.[59] Before that strategy could be finalized, however, MacDonald met with a US delegation in early March to begin the preliminary feeling-out process.[60]

On 2 March the Prime Minister had a two-hour lunch at the US Embassy. As part of the visit he met with President Roosevelt's emissary-at-large, Norman Davis; Ambassador Bingham; and the US Chargé d'Affaires, Ray Atherton, and discussed the upcoming naval talks.[61] During the luncheon meeting, both sides agreed that there was little or no hope that the Japanese would accept any formulae other than parity with the two Western nations. Both also agreed that such an outcome was unacceptable and Japan should be so informed, although independently through separate channels. There was to be no hint of a united front or collusion on the part of Great Britain and the United States.[62] Clearly, Japanese actions would determine which way Anglo-American naval cooperation would proceed. If the Japanese demanded parity, then the United States and Great Britain would be forced to work together against such a programme. If Japan chose a new ratio system that did not create parity, then it would find the two Western nations eager to accommodate it.

British anxiety over incurring Japan's wrath regarding the naval talks was obvious to the Americans, but that did not deter them from thinking that the first steps towards Anglo-American naval cooperation had been taken in the talks with MacDonald. Davis reported to Roosevelt that the British were desirous of having an Anglo-American agreement in order to check Japanese activities:

> The British are unquestionably disturbed as to the far-reaching effect which the present Japanese activities may have, and they are most desirous of reaching an agreement with us, if possible, because of the salutary effect which it might have on Japan. I am informed that they are pushing the work at Singapore as rapidly as possible but that this will not be completed

until 1937. In the meantime their policy will, in my judgment, be to iron out their differences with us with regard to the maintenance of naval parity, to reach a common understanding as to the Japanese demands for an increased ration and even to go further, if we are disposed to do so, for the maintenance of peace and the protection of our respective rights and interests.[63]

Davis also had some idea as to who within the British Cabinet favoured cooperation with the United States on the matter and who did not. He believed that:

while they all want an agreement with us, Baldwin and some of them are fearful that the Senate might upset any agreement that might be made. For that reason they want to be careful in doing nothing to arouse Japan's susceptibilities until they know definitely where they stand. That, I think, is MacDonald's chief reason for insisting that any preliminary negotiations should be most secret.[64]

Bingham reported that he, too, had no doubt that the Prime Minister wanted to cooperate with the United States in dealing with the Japanese on the naval question. The Ambassador's only reservation after the conversation was that he and Davis both felt that there could be some difficulty in the Americans and British coming to an agreement over qualitative matters concerning capital ships.[65] Bingham attempted to follow up the successful talks with MacDonald by going to Sir John Simon to obtain further information on the British position.[66] The Foreign Secretary had earlier had discussions on the golf course with Norman Davis as to what steps needed to be taken in these early stages to ensure a successful naval conference. In his subsequent meeting with the Ambassador, Simon succeeded only in diminishing his already low reputation with the Americans. The Foreign Secretary attempted to make the US Ambassador wait unnecessarily for the appointment to start and was caught out in his petty contrivance, thereby unnecessarily reinforcing the belief that he was rude and insensitive to US officials. When Bingham threatened to leave at once, the 'busy' Simon rushed out of his office and summoned Anthony Eden, Lord Privy Seal and an expert on British disarmament policy, to attend the meeting.[67] Simon tried to explain that he believed the Far Eastern interests of the United States to be greater than those of the British Empire in the Pacific. As well, it was his view that the Japanese presented a greater problem for the United States than they did for Great Britain. Bingham curtly replied that there was not a man, woman or child in the United States who would agree with that kind of analysis.

Simon's obvious attempt to distort the facts simply succeeded in reinforcing the image of perfidious Albion in Bingham's mind. The Ambassador went away from the meeting believing that:

> They [British] are undoubtedly gravely concerned over the situation and
> want to cooperate with us in holding the Japanese naval programme
> down, but they want to avoid offending the Japanese until they can finish
> their great naval base at Singapore, on which we understand they are
> pushing the work with all possible speed. My impression is that they want
> to cooperate with us, but, as usual, they want us to urge it upon them as
> a favor to ourselves.[68]

Bingham reported the incident with Simon to the US Under-Secretary of State,
William Phillips, who relayed it to the President. It was Phillips' view that
this encounter confirmed the State Department's guess that the British were
disturbed over the naval situation and eager to cooperate with the Americans,
but that their desire to cooperate was cautious and somewhat reluctant. He
apprised Roosevelt: 'However that may be, I am confident that the British are
slowly moving towards the realization of the need of a change of front.'[69]

Having been approached by a person of such high rank as the Prime
Minister, and having been told that the strategic visions of both Great Britain
and the United States were similar, US policy-makers expected a cooperative
attitude from the British in any preparatory talks. However, the problem was
that British policy-makers did not yet have a firm plan of action and had not
decided whom to side with – the Americans or the Japanese – should push come
to shove. The struggle among the Admiralty, the Foreign Office, and the
Treasury over the final British position during the naval talks now began in
earnest.[70]

The Treasury, under the guidance of Chamberlain and Fisher, tried to push
British foreign policy towards an attempt to re-establish an Anglo-Japanese
alliance, through the formation of an Anglo-Japanese non-aggression pact.
Their position resulted from both the failure of the Treasury to move the DRC
to a formal denunciation of any cooperation with the United States and a
commitment to maintain limits on defence spending. Now the Treasury, con-
sumed with anti-American bitterness brought on by failed war debt and trade
negotiations, hoped to influence the British position regarding the 1935 Naval
Conference.[71] Through that process, it wished to avoid closer relations with the
United States, consolidate better relations with Japan, and keep naval spending
on new construction and modernization to a bare minimum. In both the
Cabinet and the CID, the Treasury pushed for creating better relations with
Japan as the first and most critical of the steps required to achieve its goals.[72]
Chamberlain laid out his strategic vision to the Cabinet on 14 March, stating
that he desired an Anglo-Japanese non-aggression pact because it would help
trade contacts between the two nations and thereby create better relations,
especially if the agreement contained assurances from Japan about its attitude
towards China. Then, argued Chamberlain, Britain could concentrate on the
serious situation that was developing in Europe. As for the 1935 naval talks, he

was opposed to any alliance with the United States, for he could think of nothing more guaranteed to give offence to the Japanese, and he refused to 'pull the chestnuts out of the fire ...' for the Americans.[73] His final analysis was:

> While recognising that this question was affected by all sorts of technical considerations he put as a basis for discussion the opposite point of view: we should decline to align ourselves with Washington; indicate that we were not prepared to submit ourselves to the limitations of a Treaty, and say that we did not mind what America chose to build. This would free us from the hampering restriction of the Treaty in matters of design and so forth and perhaps enable us to carry out more effectively our obligations for defence at home. At the same time we might go to Japan and say that we had not linked ourselves with America. If this were done Japan would be free from the fear that we might be united with America against her ... A hostile Japan meant a risk to our Possessions in the Far East, a menace to India and Australasia. What we risked by good relations with Japan was (1) trade, (2) deterioration of our relations with America. As to trade, he thought the difficulties were not insurmountable. As to America, what were we going to lose? He doubted if the pursuit of friendly relations with Japan was inconsistent with good relations with the United States.[74]

The Chancellor of the Exchequer's views were supported by the Secretary of State for India, Sir Samuel Hoare; Monsell; W. Ormsby-Gore, First Minister of Works; and J.H. Thomas, the Secretary of State for Dominion Affairs. For the opposition, while agreeing that better relations with Japan were of course desirable, MacDonald, the Secretary of State for War, Viscount Hailsham and Walter Elliot, the Minister of Agriculture and Fisheries were not enthusiastic about formally re-embracing Japan with such an act. Simon waffled. Knowing the Foreign Office's desire to form no alliance with any nation in the Far East in order to play one off against the other, but at the same time personally leaning towards distancing Britain from the United States in Far Eastern matters, the Foreign Secretary did not commit himself. MacDonald summed up the debate by acknowledging that all agreed that something should be done to improve relations with Japan, but how to do so would require very careful consideration, as 'There was first the question of parity, which raised the whole question of naval power in the Pacific. If Japan was not given some idea of our intentions before the Conference a very serious situation would arise. The more quietly we could improve our relations with Japan the better for present.'[75] Chamberlain felt the issue slipping away from his control and insisted that the naval matters should not be left exclusively in the hands of the Admiralty. For the moment, MacDonald ignored Chamberlain's request for a small committee to deal with preparing the British position for the naval talks, and instructed

Monsell and Simon, in consultation with any other ministers they desired, to prepare a definite recommendation on the issue for Cabinet consideration. Time was of the essence, and the Prime Minister wanted the issue of whether to appease the Japanese to be decided before any further serious talks took place with the Americans.

The centre of activity for that preparation was the Foreign Office. Two days prior to the Cabinet meeting, Vansittart had reviewed the numerous memoranda that had been collected and constructed at the Foreign Office by Sir Victor Wellesley, the Deputy Under-Secretary of State, Far Eastern expert, and superintending Under-Secretary for the Far Eastern Department.[76] Wellesley played an important role. He was a link and filter between the Far Eastern Department of the Foreign Office, Vansittart and Simon, and the other government departments. It was Wellesley who would give the lead on Far Eastern issues during the formulation of the British strategy for the Naval Conference.[77] Vansittart used Wellesley's memoranda and material to inform the Admiralty of the Foreign Office view of the situation in the Far East. The six main points of the Foreign Office assessment were: (1) it was inadvisable to tie British foreign policy in the Far East to either Japan or the United States. Japan had aims in Asia which Britain could not support, and the United States, while an important potential ally, was an uncertain factor in the Far East. (2) It was very important for Britain to not antagonize Japan or be made the point-man in any opposition to Japanese aims. The Foreign Office recommended that a liberal economic and trading attitude towards Japan would be useful. (3) All this did not mean that the Japanese were to be given a free hand in trade matters, and, indeed, Britain must defend its trade interests in the Far East vigorously, but always should maintain a moderate and calm manner. (4) Preparations for enhancing the empire's military strength in the Far East, especially the completion of Singapore, were to proceed in an ostentatious fashion. (5) British foreign policy towards China was to continue as previously, promoting goodwill and avoiding antagonizing the Chinese through cultivating Japanese goodwill at China's expense. (6) British foreign policy in the Far East would have to be opportunist, given the variety of nations involved and the intertwining of European, American and Far Eastern interests. Above all else, Wellesley's recommendation was 'that we should leave our hands free to act as impelled by our international obligations and special interests in all such separate problems …'[78] Citing the collection as the definitive work on the matter, Vansittart suggested broadly that no other department stray far from these overall strategic considerations without first consulting closely with the Foreign Office.

The Foreign Office was also busy preparing a reply to the suggestion put forward by Chamberlain for an Anglo-Japanese non-aggression pact. Simon composed a response listing the pros and cons of such a pact, and, then, on 15 March, asked Orde and Vansittart for their views. The Foreign Office believed that the positive attributes of a non-aggression pact were few. First, Japan might, but this was not at all certain, moderate its naval demands if it were clearly shown that Britain would not ally with the United States in any war against Japan. Second, the pact would give Japan a freer hand against the Soviet Union, and it would demonstrate Britain's friendly feeling towards Japan and signal that there was an intention for them to become more so. The cons of the pact were much more complex, and presented a daunting picture for British interests in the Far East. The most important drawback was the negative effect on Anglo-American relations. It was pointed out that such a pact would come as a severe shock to the Americans. There was the chance that the opportunity to take such action and investigate a pact might present itself *during* the naval talks, but to broach the idea before such talks was definitely not good timing. Overall, even though Anglo-American cooperation in the Far East was not seen as an immediate reality, the damage to even that tenuous relationship was not desired. A second problem would be that China would be antagonized and the League of Nations was likely to see the pact as Britain's condonation of Japanese actions in Manchukuo. Finally, Soviet Russia would resent any Anglo-Japanese *rapprochement*, and Britain's previously stated desire to avoid forming pacts that added nothing to the Kellogg Pact would also be shown to be hollow, damaging Britain's credibility. The overall recommendation of the Foreign Office was that the Admiralty's strategic considerations would have to carry the day on the matter. The cons were more important to the empire's overall position than the pros, which were of little worth, especially in the face of the impending naval talks:

> The view of our Admiralty is that Japan, far from hoping to increase her relative strength, must be content with a ratio in cruiser strength slightly inferior to that accorded by the London Naval Treaty. So complete a deadlock cannot be overcome by means of a non-aggression pact – particularly if we pay our price before the bargaining begins. In fact, the conclusion of such a pact without reference to the impending naval negotiations would probably prove to be merely a 'flash in the pan'. If the policy of the non-aggression pact is considered otherwise desirable, the best course would probably be to keep it in reserve pending the progress of the naval negotiations. If at a later stage it were found that Japan might be induced to accept a lower ratio of naval strength in return for a non-aggression pact with this country – and possibly also with the United States – the proposal might then serve a useful and practical purpose.[79]

Simon gave his views, along with the Foreign Office's collection of memoranda on the Far Eastern situation, to the Cabinet on 19 March. That body, still heavily influenced by Chamberlain, decided that continued study of the question was appropriate.

The Royal Navy opened its part of the debate with the drafting of a memorandum designed to explain Britain's imperial position regarding naval commitments and the upcoming conference. In that document, the Chief of the Naval Staff (CNS) outlined the strategic requirements for a Two Power Standard.[80] That standard was to provide a fleet capable of having sufficient strength to be able to send elements to the Far East to counter any Japanese encroachment on Britain's imperial interests there. At the same time, there would also need to be naval forces adequate to protect merchant ships on all sea routes and still leave sufficient forces in European and Atlantic waters to give security against the strongest European naval powers.[81] Chatfield's argument pointed out that the Royal Navy did not measure up to that standard and would not for at least five more years. His message to the government was very clear: if the government were unwilling to contemplate spending money on rearming the Royal Navy, then a different foreign policy would need to be considered; one which eliminated imperial commitments. The CNS recognized that France and the United States were not to be considered as possible threats to the Empire's security. However, the growth of Japanese aggression in the Far East, coupled with the fear of German rearmament, jeopardized Great Britain's naval security seriously. The time had come either to spend more money expanding and modernizing the Royal Navy or to consider withdrawing all naval forces to European waters and trust to a naval combination with some other power to provide security for the rest of the empire. If this were to be the case, then diplomatic measures, such as the upcoming naval talks, had to ensure that countries such as Japan and Germany agreed to a formula that would guarantee Britain's security for a long time (at least ten years). The memorandum argued that negotiations for the 1935 conference should allow the Royal Navy to expand to a 'safer naval strength'. Japan and its reaction to the naval talks was the key to any future Royal Navy planning. If Japan proved to be unwilling to compromise on its demands for parity, then American approval had to be obtained during the negotiations to allow for the necessary expansion of the Royal Navy.[82]

Sir John Simon hesitated to agree with the CNS's view of the matter. He felt that the Admiralty had always had a 'bee in its bonnet' about Japan, but realized that Japan, unlike the United States, could not be disregarded as a potential foe, if for no other reason than the pressures that would be brought to bear by Australia, New Zealand and Canada. As well, Simon acknowledged that domestic political pressures were in favour of naval rearmament and that both the government and the man in the street would be loathe to sign another 1930 London Naval Treaty limiting Britain's freedom to build, no matter what the financial cost.[83] Where cooperation with other nations to protect Britain's Far Eastern interests was concerned, his belief was that Great Britain could expect no help from the Kellogg Pact or other pacts if the situation became tense. As for the United States and Japan, and the maintenance of the existing treaty ratios, Simon thought that if Japan was contacted first then perhaps the ratios could be kept as they were, but, if the British went into the conference allied with the United States then there was no hope that such would be the case. The Foreign Secretary was sympathetic to the Admiralty's needs for rapid and immediate construction and modernization of capital ships, but was of the opinion that the replacement could be spread over one ship every two years, or at the most, two in two years.[84] Despite his less than full support of the Admiralty's position, Simon respected Chatfield's skills, fearing that the new First Lord would be much firmer in driving home the Navy's message and position than was his predecessor.

That respect was repaid, on 20 March, when Chatfield held a meeting at the Admiralty with Vansittart and Craigie. The CNS told the Foreign Office members that it was his belief that Japan would demand either parity or an increased ratio in capital ships at the Naval Conference.[85] It was his hope that the United States would refuse to accept that parity. Chatfield argued that there was no benefit in agreeing to give Japan a higher ratio, as Britain's slender strategic advantage in that region would then be destroyed. If that occurred, Great Britain could meet the threat only 'by weakening our European position and rectifying it in some political manner. In the long run it would be better to let Japan build her capital ships and keep a free hand as to how Britain would strengthen its own naval forces.'[86] When Vansittart suggested that His Majesty's government might be reluctant to fund a massive capital ship replacement programme and would want a continuation of the building 'holiday' which had been in effect since 1922, the First Sea Lord stressed the fact that such an attitude was unacceptable to the Admiralty. Craigie explained that he thought the Americans would also be in favour of a continuation of the building holiday, although naval and political advisors were known to oppose any reduction. He told Chatfield that it was the intention of the Foreign Office to feel out the US position on parity, qualitative and quantitative limitation, but not to obtain any definite agreement until discussions had taken place with the Japanese. Both the Foreign Office and Admiralty representatives agreed that a joint presentation to the Prime Minister would be required to begin the process of arriving at some solid policy before negotiations began. They also agreed that no government could fail to send a fleet to the Far East if necessary. Both felt that if the government did not accept sending a full fleet to the Far East, then the government must state what their policy was. Lastly, it was decided that the Foreign Office and Admiralty would submit the CNS's policy on imperial security and defend it against all comers to try to get as much as possible accepted by Cabinet or any committee that was struck.[87]

On 27 March the CNS's views on the empire's strategic position, along with a Foreign Office critique of the Admiralty's analysis and proposals, were sent to MacDonald and Hankey by Vansittart. The Foreign Office acknowledged that it believed measures should be taken to get on better with the Japanese, but, unless Cabinet ruled that no fleet was to be sent to the Far East in a time of crisis, then the Foreign Office supported the Naval Staff and their basis for their proposals.[88] Craigie was somewhat concerned about the overall cost of the programme, which would be £7,000,000 a year for replacement, over a period of 12 years, and £2,000,000 a year for modernization over a five-year period, but felt that the Navy could justify its case.[89] As for the procedure that was to be followed in preparing for the naval talks, Vansittart and Chatfield reported that

> we think that until the proposals set forth in this memorandum have been considered by a Cabinet Committee, and decisions reached in regard to our future naval policy, little purpose would be served by entering upon exploratory conversations with representatives of foreign Powers. Once such decisions have been reached, it is suggested that an invitation should be sent simultaneously to the United States and Japanese Governments to exchange views on our respective desiderata for the 1935 Conference. As the United States Government have already made the first approach, it will probably be preferable that the first exchange of views should take place with representatives of that Government.[90]

The ball was now squarely in the Cabinet's court. It would have to decide how to proceed with the formulation of a new imperial defence policy.

On the other side of the Atlantic, the Americans also were consolidating their position. Much of the information as to how they were going to proceed issued from the State Department's Division of Far Eastern Affairs (DFEA), the US Embassy in London and Norman Davis. Their goal was to ascertain the true motives behind the British naval position and what the British attitude towards Japan at the conference would be.

Maxwell Hamilton, a senior member of the DFEA, reported in early March that British interests in the Far East were based on trade, and primarily on trade with China. After talks with Charles Orde, Hamilton reported that relations with Japan were important for Britain's ability to protect its trade in China. However, Orde had confirmed that there did not appear to be any truth in the idea that there would be any sort of Anglo-Japanese agreement to that end, and, in fact, 'aside from the considerations of trade and of the Open Door, opportunism was the keynote of British action in reference to situations in and problems presented by the Far East'.[91] William Phillips, along with Norman Davis and Ambassador Bingham, were still impressed with the face the British had presented so far.[92] This sentiment was not held unanimously. Moffat was becoming suspicious that the British were trying to get the United States to take the lead in the naval talks, while at the same time trying to get some sort of agreement with the Japanese. His suspicions were based on the anti-American sentiments and distrust of key American figures that he saw emanating from British leaders.[93] Such concerns were secondary, however, to the key element in

American preparations: to ensure that the strategic interests of the United States were safeguarded.

Stanley Hornbeck, the Chief of the Division of Far Eastern Affairs and chief constructor of US Far Eastern policy, made that point clear to the Secretary of State, Cordell Hull, in late March.[94] Hornbeck was a disciple of the school of power diplomacy and the protection of national self-interest. His view of the British and US positions in the Far East was critical, yet fair, and had been built up over a long period of time in China and as head of the DFEA since 1928. Hornbeck was naturally suspicious that the British would, if US diplomacy was not alert, at times attempt both to get the Americans to take the lead against Japanese actions in the region and to diminish the Americans in the eyes of the Chinese authorities.[95] However, he also recognized that, given the balance of power in Far Eastern diplomacy, cooperation with Great Britain on major issues was absolutely necessary.[96] For Hornbeck, such cooperation was not a blank cheque or a policy that would be automatically activated in every circumstance. Just as the Foreign Office officials described British policy as being one of opportunism, designed to prevent the Japanese from levelling charges of cooperation or complicity against Great Britain, Hornbeck subscribed to the principle of cooperation between the British and US governments only when major interests of both nations were the issue. It was his view that in the past where British interests had been attacked and the United States had no parallel or any interest at all, the United States had naturally not rushed in to Britain's aid: 'A "joint policy" or a "policy of cooperation" do not call for any such thing', he declared, 'We do not expect them to pull our chestnuts out of the fire and they should not expect us to pull theirs.'[97] Analysing the Far Eastern situation, the upcoming naval conference, and how American interests needed to be protected from further Japanese aggression, Hornbeck argued a line of policy similar to that advanced by the Admiralty and the US Navy, declaring that the United States needed to maintain naval strength sufficient to protect its national interests in the region.[98] For Hornbeck, that meant that while adjustment in details within the ratios was possible, the United States had to adhere to the Washington and London Treaty ratios:

> The naval ratios as they now stand were designed, it is believed, on the principle of making it possible, on the one hand, for each of the powers concerned adequately to safeguard its own interests, on a defensive basis, and of making it impossible, on the other hand, for any one of the powers provided that each and all built up to and maintained its allotment of naval equipment, to indulge in aggression against one or more of the others ... The situation has not changed, as regards the rightful interests of the various powers concerned, separately and collectively, from the point of view of problems of self-defense ... since these rations were worked out and agreed upon. It would therefore seem that any alteration

of the ratios in favor, upward, of any one power, would tend towards an upset of the equilibrium and would impair the principle on which the powers have proceeded in the formulating and concluding of naval limitation agreements ... There is perceived no reason why we should discuss or enter into any agreement by and under the provisions of which Japan would, with our assent, become relatively stronger and we become relatively weaker in naval armament.[99]

There were, therefore, similar strategic views of the situation in the Far East held in the two Western navies, foreign offices and executive offices. These views revolved around the untrustworthiness of Japan's word not to interfere with American and British interests in the region, suspicions of the real intentions of American and British Far Eastern policies, and the need for strong navies to protect those interests from further Japanese encroachments. Both American and British policy-makers recognized that such was the case. Now, these first indicators of common views and interests would have to be refined and explored to see where they would could lead.

Craigie, Vice-Admiral C.J.C. Little, the Deputy Chief of Naval Staff (DCNS), Norman Davis and Ambassador Bingham met on 12 April to follow up the discussions begun by MacDonald on 2 March. The technical and ratio sides of the issue were not that far apart, reported Little. Both groups were agreed that Japan should not have parity, aircraft carriers would not be abolished so the status quo on that class was acceptable, there was agreement on destroyer and submarine matters and, according to Davis, a movement was taking place in the US Navy and State Department, as well as in the executive, towards an understanding on the question of cruiser strength.[100] Only in the area of capital ship qualities did the two sides deviate substantially. Davis explained that Roosevelt and the US government wanted a reduction in the number of capital ships from 15 to 12, but, also wanted those battleships to be larger and carry 16- or 14-inch guns.[101] British strategic needs dictated a need for at least 15 capital ships, but they desired smaller vessels (around 25,000 tons as opposed to the 35,000 tons suggested by the Americans) with 12-inch guns.[102]

On the diplomatic side, each party was still trying to get to grips with the other's position. Craigie noted the continued appeal by the Americans for cooperation in a united front against Japan. Bingham assured the Foreign Office representative that the United States was no longer the same nation which had rejected the League Covenant and the Statute of the Permanent Court of International Justice. The Ambassador argued that Roosevelt and the executive were in the ascendant over Congress and things were now quite different, 'and co-operation in all fields should be attended by fruitful results for both countries'.[103] Craigie summed up the discussion and its meaning as he shared these insights with Ambassador Lindsay:

There is a tendency on the part of the Americans to try to get us to pull the chestnuts out of the fire for them in connection with this question of the Japanese ratio. This our people are not in the least disposed to do, and believe in fact that the more solidaire [sic] we and the Americans appear to be on this question at the present juncture the more stiff we are likely to find the Japanese when the time arrives to talk to them. As you will see however, the Americans are most anxious to establish very close co-operation with us at the earliest possible moment so that the situation may at any moment become a little delicate.[104]

On the American side, Davis informed the President that he now did not believe there was going to be any difficulty with the British over the technical naval questions in any discussions. He also mentioned that it had been agreed that, while invitations for talks would be issued to Japan and the United States at the same time, the American delegation was to arrive at least a week before the Japanese so that the former could work out the details and have a prepared position ready before the Japanese arrived.[105] Bingham supported Davis' interpretation of events. The Ambassador informed Roosevelt that the recent Japanese declaration warning all foreign nations not to interfere with affairs in China – the so-called 'Amau declaration' – had made many British policy-makers more receptive to the idea of some sort of Anglo-American naval cooperation at the conference.[106] Simon had warned him that British financial interests would try to bring great pressure to bear on the government to find some agreement with the Japanese, if the Japanese carried out their plan. The Foreign Secretary had expressed his deep desire for cooperation between the United States and Great Britain in handling the whole situation, including the naval aspect. That sentiment for cooperation had been reinforced by talks with the First Lord of the Admiralty and the retired Admiral of the Fleet, and now Member of Parliament, Sir Roger Keyes. In fact, the Ambassador was scheduled to have lunch with Vansittart that Sunday to discuss these new developments and British attitudes towards the upcoming naval talks.[107]

The intricacies of the situation were increasing, as Chamberlain attempted to keep the British government from favouring any Anglo-American co-operative spirit. In response to the discussions held on 12 April, Chamberlain used the pulpit of the Ministerial Committee on the London Naval Conference [NCM(35)] to continue to preach the safer road of appeasing the Japanese. If the conference failed, he argued, then some sort of pact with Japan would protect British interests in China, the only region where Japanese and British interests were in danger of conflict. The British people, said Chamberlain, would be greatly upset at the failure of the Naval Conference as it would signal the beginning of a new naval race. If, however, an agreement with the Japanese could be substituted for a treaty on quotas, then the public discontent would be assuaged. In his view, some sort of division of China could take place.

145

Worries about how such British involvement in carving up China to suit Japanese and British needs would be viewed by the Americans, let alone the British public and other nations, never entered his mind. Simon and the First Lord of the Admiralty pointed out the problems that such actions would cause with regard to the Nine Power Treaty and the Americans' desire to protect the Open Door policy as based on the Nine Power Treaty. However, Chamberlain was willing to cast the Americans adrift over the matter and let them stay out in the cold.[108] The meeting ended with MacDonald, Simon, Chatfield and Monsell stressing that no approach along Chamberlain's lines was to be made before the conference. As well, the Foreign Office and Admiralty had agreed that, given the state of British capital ships, and if the nation were willing to face the expense, the British position regarding capital ships should be to call for at least the maintenance of the 15 already allowed. A new battlefleet was to be achieved through construction, not reconditioning.[109]

The ultimate battle between the Foreign Office and the Treasury as to whether the British position at the naval talks would take an American or a Japanese focus was taken up in earnest on 19 April. Sensing that support for a Japan-first strategy was not making as much progress as was necessary, the Treasury began to prepare its position more carefully. Fisher produced a statement for the NCM on the effect of the London Naval Treaty on Britain's naval strength, and argued that the Washington and London Treaties should be abandoned. He believed that the treaties had subordinated British interests to those of the United States and had obliged Britain to build classes of ships and a fleet that it did not want. The Foreign Office received a copy of Fisher's views before the memo was circulated to the NCM.[110] Craigie and Vansittart both agreed that Fisher's arguments contained many misconceptions and ill-informed ideas about the strategic reality of the Far Eastern balance of power, especially concerning how cavalierly Britain could treat American sensitivities. They headed off Fisher's misguided presentation by preparing their own evaluation, which was sent directly to the Prime Minister and Fisher in late May.[111]

The Foreign Office counter-attack began by agreeing with Fisher that Britain's predominant defensive concern was to ensure that the empire did not become engaged with Germany and Japan at the same time.[112] That did not mean, however, that there was an opportunity to construct a thorough and lasting accommodation with Japan. Vansittart emphasized the opportunism that was at the heart of Britain's Far Eastern foreign policy and discredited Fisher's allegations about the impact of the Washington and London Naval Treaties. The legacy of those treaties was not onerous, he argued, and they had deterred the United States from building a navy larger than Great Britain's. The size of the US fleet was of special importance for the Royal Navy because the size of the US Fleet dictated what the Japanese could build: the bigger the US fleet the bigger the Japanese. That was the reason why the Admiralty, with Foreign Office support, was unwilling to let the United States build whatever they wanted. As for Fisher's espousal of the idea that the Royal Navy had been forced to build a fleet that it did not want, Vansittart laid the blame for any short-comings in the Royal Navy numbers squarely where it belonged: in the lap of the Treasury. He argued that Britain had never shaped its policy out of any sense of subservience to the United States, but, 'If our navy has been reduced during the post-war period to relatively smaller proportions this has notoriously been due far more to motives of economy than to any other vice or virtue.' Further, it was the view of the Foreign Office that Britain would have had to match the United States in building 10,000-ton, 8-inch gun cruisers in any case. It was now unlikely, given Japan's continued aggression in the Far East, that the Americans would reduce the size and gunpower of their ships.

Vansittart pointed out that the Foreign Office and Admiralty agreed with Fisher that there could be no question of sacrificing Britain's minimum naval requirements merely to reach an agreement with the United States. He also emphasized that no stone should be left unturned in order to try to make better relations with Japan, and he agreed with Fisher that an eye had to be kept on the far more important developments that were occurring in Europe. The PUS was clear that it was not his view that Japan should be abandoned in favour of complete reliance upon the United States. But, the strategic reality and overall usefulness of Japan and the United States in the overall scheme of Britain's imperial policy was clear. It was important to

> maintain the present level of relations with the United States if possible and not forfeit the useful and marked advance in this respect achieved with much difficulty during the last decade. We have paid for what we have got, and neither you nor I would want to waste what we have already bought, such as it is, particularly having regard to all our other present and impending difficulties.

Vansittart's past experiences had shown how quickly Anglo-American relations could deteriorate into a series of mutual recriminations and hostile press propaganda, and this caused him to caution Fisher against turning a cold shoulder to the Americans, particularly at this delicate time. The PUS's final word on the matter was that, while presenting a united front at the Naval Conference with the Americans against Japan would certainly cause bad relations with the latter, it was more important to realize that the Japanese were more likely to behave themselves if there was no sign of any open deterioration in Anglo-American relations. He ended his lecture on international relations and British imperial defence to Fisher succinctly, telling the Secretary of the Treasury:

> If we wish to improve our relations with Japan, it may well be sound policy simultaneously to keep on good terms with the United States, provided

that these terms are neither too obtrusive nor of a kind to wound Japanese sensibilities ... But while fully recognising how little reliance can safely be placed on the United States in present circumstances it is well to remember that there are certain fundamental reasons why, in point of fact, no government here will really be allowed, or allow itself to treat Anglo-American relations with anything but considerable respect when it comes to a show-down. I will only mention two here: (1) Public opinion and the press here have invariably been critical of any British Government which has allowed a marked deterioration in Anglo-American relations to occur, almost irrespective of the merits of the case. The same is true of public opinion in the Dominions ... (2) Bad relations with the United States would greatly increase the difficulty of this country giving any form of security guarantee to France and so relieving the present tension in Europe, since the adequacy of any such guarantee and the safety with which it could be given are admittedly dependent on some degree of American co-operation – or at least benevolent neutrality. Hence the extent of the influence we exercise in Europe is to some extent dependent on the quality of the relations we maintain with the United States.[113]

Other strategic considerations were also present in Vansittart's thinking, but he declined the opportunity to lecture Fisher on the intricacies of Britain's imperial foreign policy and so removed them from the final version of the document. Those critical considerations were that, except for trade issues, the fundamental interests and objectives of Great Britain and the United States were more nearly identical than those of any two other powers. Also, the obvious need to have access to American resources if a major war broke out was a key to the Foreign Office's demand for friendly relations with the Americans.[114] Ultimately, in the question of Britain's imperial balance-of-power scheme in the Far East, the Foreign Office continued to support its 'no-bloc' policy that held that, 'The best hope for peace in the Pacific lies in the promotion of a steady improvement in the relations between the three Great Powers, Japan, the United States, and ourselves, and not in one country seeking to fish in the troubled waters lying between the other two.'[115] The Foreign Office's intention was to allow the Japanese to worry about American and British interests and actions coinciding, but never to admit to or act as if such an arrangement was the real desire of British policy. Ignorance of that relationship's true nature by the Japanese was seen as being one of the safest ways of protecting Britain's position in the region while rearmament took place. That position was one which was supported by the Prime Minister as well.[116]

The Americans were also in the midst of trying to work out their tactical position regarding the naval talks. State Department officials were keen on the idea of coming to some sort of understanding with the British, but were concerned about whether the US Navy was going to cooperate. Far Eastern considerations were so intimately bound up with the naval talks that it appeared to Hull and Davis that the two could not be discussed entirely separately.[117] Davis was given the go-ahead by the President, however, to have talks with the US Navy with a view to meeting bilaterally with the British some time in the summer or early autumn. As of the end of April, it was still not clear to the State Department what the exact response from the Navy would be, nor who would be the US Navy's voice at any talks.[118]

By 1 May various pressures had created a need for the British to issue an invitation to the Americans and Japanese to come to England and hold preliminary talks. Throughout the month of May, mutual suspicions concerning leaks to the press about the nature of these secret and very preliminary discussions threatened to poison the whole process. Both the State Department and the Foreign Office, as well as the US Navy and Royal Navy, put the need to establish a cooperative spirit ahead of the issue of who was to blame for any leaks.[119] However, the pressure created by the press in both countries helped fuel the expectation that something would happen soon. The Japanese Amau Declaration, the Manchukuo Oil Monopoly issue and other trade disputes between Japan and Great Britain had not allowed an atmosphere conducive to exploring the matter of Japan's attitude towards naval ratios to develop.[120] This instability in the Far East had created some doubt and concern on the part of the British policy-makers. These feelings were not lost on the American observers. The time had come to see whether Japanese actions would cause Britain either to appease the Asian power or cooperate with the United States and oppose Japanese naval expansion.

Ambassador Bingham met with King George in late April, and they discussed Anglo-American relations in the Pacific. His Majesty informed Bingham that Britain had given up the treaty with Japan as an act of good faith towards the United States. He also believed that the two Anglo-Saxon nations had similar if not identical interests in the Pacific, and it was his hope that the two nations would be able to cooperate in the maintenance of trade and peace in that region.[121] Bingham reported back to Roosevelt that, after talking to the King and having lunch with Vansittart (whom the Ambassador thought most able), it was now clear to him that the British had changed their mind as to how much they would cooperate with the Americans during the naval talks. Bingham did not suspect prior bad faith. He was satisfied that, until the Amau Declaration, MacDonald and Craigie had dealt honestly with the United States' representatives and that British policy had been to go along with the Americans as far as possible, so long as no offence was given to the Japanese. That position had changed. It was now British policy, he felt, ultimately to cooperate with the Americans, but there would be no willingness to adopt any Anglo-American policy that either could be interpreted in Japan as any form of coercion or would help solidify the control of the militaristic element in that country.[122]

Bingham emphasized Vansittart's preoccupation with Germany, and his fears of a growing threat in Europe. The PUS had made it clear that Britain now relied on the Soviet, Chinese and US attitudes in the Far East to deter the Japanese from taking any immediate action. While understanding that the Japanese had never really abandoned their Twenty-one Points of 1915, Vansittart felt that there was no immediate threat to the Empire from the Far Eastern situation and believed that there would be no such disturbance unless the Japanese were given the opportunity by a British preoccupation with Germany in a European war.[123] Bingham concluded that, 'The only deduction, in my opinion, to be drawn from his [Vansittart's] statement was that the British Government has made up its mind to run no risk, so far as the Far Eastern question is concerned, at this time, and to concentrate all of its efforts upon trying to keep peace in Europe.'[124] He recommended that the United States leave the British alone now to sort out their situation and arrive at a more exact policy position.

That recommendation was ignored by the State Department, and overridden by the action of the British Cabinet, who issued an invitation to the Americans and Japanese to send delegations to London for preliminary talks.[125] The State Department accepted the invitation on 24 May, and would send a delegation headed by both Davis and Bingham, and consisting of such technical experts as Rear Admiral Richard A.H. Leigh, Chairman of the General Board, Commander Theodore S. Wilkinson, Secretary of the General Board, and Noel H. Field of the State Department. The delegation was to assemble in London at some time around mid-June.[126] Concerns about Simon's real attitude towards the conference, and the United States in general, still plagued the American delegation, but a feeling that some sort of Anglo-American cooperation could be achieved predominated. During disarmament talks in Geneva in late May, Simon had told Davis that such cooperation was his desire. The Foreign Secretary expected the American and British delegations to clear up any questions between themselves before the Japanese arrived. As to the question of the Japanese demand for parity, when Davis pressed Simon to confirm that the statements of Sir Roger Keyes and other British naval officers advocating a closer cooperation between Great Britain and Japan were not the government's position, Simon told the American that the British government could not control the comments made by Keyes. However,

> he could not believe that any naval officer on the active list could take such a position because it was positively not the attitude of either the Government or the Admiralty: that Great Britain has more seas to cover than Japan and that parity with Japan would be absurd.[127]

Davis was guardedly optimistic that the British would not bow to Japanese pressures, but was also concerned that the British would try to manoeuvre the talks so that it appeared that they were the 'honest brokers' trying to bring the

Americans and Japanese together, when all along it was in Britain's interest not to support Japanese parity. Davis feared that the British would attempt to make it appear that it was American reluctance to accept parity that would be the reason for any failure.[128]

President Roosevelt was also growing weary of Sir John Simon and his slippery ways. The President told Henry Stimson at a long lunch on 17 May that he was very irritated by Simon turning down Bingham's unofficial initiatives to cooperate against Japanese advances and the Foreign Secretary's obvious shying away from the first, promising, position of cooperation put forward by Craigie in March. Roosevelt was now of the opinion that the only hope for generous cooperation with the British would come after a change of government in London, an event to which he looked forward.[129] Roosevelt also shared his personal views of the Far Eastern situation with the former Secretary of State – views which coincided closely with those held by Stimson himself.

Stimson told Roosevelt that he approved of the American recognition of Russia, the intention to increase the US fleet to its treaty strength, and the recent note to Japan disapproving its Amau declaration. All were important steps in a policy aimed at taking a firm line in the Pacific against Japan, but he regretted the movement of the fleet from the Pacific back to the Atlantic. Roosevelt then informed him of his future plans to strengthen greatly the fleet in the Pacific and his desire to take an even stronger tone with the Japanese, but said that the State Department, Mrs Roosevelt and the newspapers' strong negative reaction to a watered-down version of his reply to Japan had caused him to rethink how strongly he should push the Japanese.[130] Both men agreed that the American policies towards the Far East and Europe had to be different and were different, as the former was an area where the United States had interests and faced a real threat, while the later was not as yet an important US arena. In order to illustrate how and why he felt the way he did, the President told Stimson a story of his encounter in 1902 during his sophomore college days with a young Japanese he considered a friend. This story was also known to various British officials between 1933 and 1939 and reveals to some extent why Roosevelt's views of the situation in the Far East were what they were:

> This young Japanese boy had told him of the making in 1889 of the one hundred year Japanese plan for the Japanese dynasty, which involved the following steps in the following order: 1. An official war with China to show that they could fight and could beat China. 2. the absorbtion of Korea. 3. A defensive war against Russia. 4. The taking of Manchuria. 5. Taking of Jehol. 6. The establishment of a virtual protectorate over northern China from the Wall to the Yangtsze. 7. Encircling movement in Mongolia and the establishment of the Japanese influence through instructors as far as Tibet, thus establishing a precautionary threat against Russia on one side and India on the other. 8. The acquisition of all the

islands of the Pacific including Hawaii. 9. Eventually acquisition of Australia and New Zealand. 10. Establishment of Japanese (using word indicating a rather fatherly control, which the President said he could not quite remember) over all of the yellow races, including the Malays. In this way the young man said they would have [a] definite point of threat against Europe. When young Roosevelt asked him what they were going to do to the United States, he said that the United States need not have any fear; that all they would do in the new hemisphere would be to establish outposts, one probably in Mexico and another one perhaps in Peru; otherwise they would leave us alone. But we must remember that they were a temperate zone people and they must have Australia and New Zealand to expand in. The President commented in how many particulars this plan revealed to him by the young Jap, who was a high class member of the Samuri caste in Japan, had been confirmed by subsequent events ...

Therefore, Roosevelt was convinced that the United States' best bet for staying out of war in that region was 'to adopt a policy of firm statements as to our rights and of full preparedness for war. A policy of drift or timidity would be the surest way of getting into war.'[131] The need to find some sort of security in the Far East, and, at the same time, achieve a naval reduction for the American taxpayer were clearly at odds as the Americans prepared for naval talks.

In London, the Foreign Office began to prepare for the meetings with the Japanese and the Americans. Position papers on cruisers, ratios and agendas were prepared by Craigie and the Admiralty, in conjunction with guidance from the NCM, in order that the British position could be put to both nations in a vigorous and comprehensive manner.[132] Still, the key point was what would be the Japanese attitude towards parity. The latest reports from Japan and the Japanese Ambassador in London all pointed to the fact that the Japanese government would indeed demand parity. The Americans had similar unproductive communications with the Japanese.[133] Such a Japanese position was unacceptable to both the Americans and British.[134] Adding to the uncertainty, was the Foreign Office's lack of a clear understanding of what was the US long-term commitment in the Far East. Lindsay informed the Foreign Office, just before talks began with the US delegates, that if Japan obstinately refused to come to an agreement in 1935, then a naval understanding between the United States and Great Britain became the obvious solution for the Americans. There was growing public awareness in the United States of the fact that Washington lagged behind the Japanese and British in terms of naval strength. As well, the Japanese arguments as to why they needed a larger navy were unintelligible to the Americans, who saw the request as a simple mask for further aggression in Asia. While there was some concern that the Americans might be prepared to 'scuttle' out of the Far East by coming to some agreement with the Japanese,

Lindsay did not share it.[135] Orde, Wellesley and Simon thought it would be typically American, however, if such concessions as Lindsay had outlined were made in order to get a naval agreement. Still, the attitude remained that recommended by Craigie, one of wait-and-see.[136]

The US delegation had internal troubles of its own. Davis was not happy that he had to share the limelight of leadership for the mission with Ambassador Bingham, and petitioned Washington to be given supreme command.[137] Roosevelt and Hull rejected Davis' arguments on the grounds that those preliminary talks had to appear to be not really preliminary talks. If the discussions appeared to be directed by the Embassy, then they could be linked to the Disarmament Conference at Geneva. The State Department had stressed the informal nature of the upcoming naval conversations to the American press, and were most careful to give the impression that they were in no way a preliminary conference in themselves. Neither the President nor Hull expected much success in coming to grips on technical problems, and so wanted the exercise to have the appearance of being nothing more than a sounding-out process. A separate delegation at London, outside normal diplomatic channels, would ruin that psychological effect.[138] Davis, forever the professional negotiator, thought they were being too pessimistic and that some understanding, especially with the British, could be reached. Hull explained to Davis that Japanese pressure had put the Americans in a difficult position. Japanese suspicions of an Anglo-American united front had caused them to indicate that they would not discuss even technical matters and were not in favour of any preliminary conference, only informal conversation. In order to make sure that the Japanese did not continue to suspect that the Americans were organizing any concerted opposition, and to keep the American press from suspecting any Anglo-American collusion, the informal route was proposed. In the end, Roosevelt personally assured Davis that he, too, thought that success was possible with the British and that Davis would be the lead man when naval negotiations reached a critical stage. For now, however, Bingham and the embassy would be required as a cover for the talks.[139]

Hull himself was not hopeful that the talks would result in any joint or concerted naval action on the part of the two Western powers, but he was worried that the talks would turn into an attempt to find some sort of cooperative solution for Far Eastern problems in general.[140] The Secretary of State had kept Japanese advances to the United States about a non-aggression pact or some other sort of public utterance of understanding at arm's length that spring. Unwilling to incur the wrath of Great Britain or the American public, and continually warned of the pitfalls of such action by Hornbeck, Hull refused to entertain any idea of an agreement with Japan.[141] Those inclinations were reinforced by Phillips' view that there was enough anti-American sentiment in British circles to make the attempt at cooperation impossible.[142] Hull was much concerned about Japan's attitude at the talks and the British being ill-disposed to the Americans. But Phillips and Moffat convinced him to commit to the idea of the talks; otherwise the Americans would be exposed to 'incurring a charge of sharp practice ...' Moffat and Phillips soothed the worried brows in Washington with the suggestion that Davis be limited to a discussion of procedural questions and technical naval aspects of the problem, and not talk on political matters.[143] Hull and Roosevelt expected Davis certainly to be able to iron out any differences between the two views on technical matters so that a common viewpoint could be created before the Japanese delegation arrived. Davis' final orders gave him tactical latitude over how he went about achieving that goal, so long as he did not 'run any risk of losing control of the talks you are guiding and that what we envisaged was a system of informal talks some what analogous to that you and Bingham had worked out last spring'.[144]

Talks with the British were enjoined on 18 June, at Number 10 Downing Street, with the British being represented by MacDonald, Monsell, Admiral Little and Craigie; the Americans by Bingham, Davis, Admiral Leigh and Atherton. The American attitude was to wait and see what the British proposal and opening position were to be. When they were given, Davis found them penetrating, frank and sympathetic, even more so than the American position. MacDonald laid out the problems that had arisen in the Far East and Europe since the London Conference in 1930. Both groups agreed that the Washington Treaty system was worth saving and that they would work to discourage any denunciation of it. Officially, both sides also agreed that they did not understand Japan's request for parity, and if the Japanese demanded such parity, then a written explanation as to why Japan felt it needed such a naval presence would be asked for. The two parties also agreed that their 'joint policy should be respectively to refuse to accept even a minor modification in the Japanese ratio without previous Anglo-American consultation'.[145] This item was left out of the official minutes due to its sensitive nature. MacDonald had reacted to Davis' suggestion that the two nations should agree 'that in no circumstances would either country agree to any increase in the Japanese ratio of naval strength' with some trepidation.[146] MacDonald had proposed that neither side would end its opposition to the Japanese demands without first consulting the other. This method, he recalled, had been the basis for success at the 1930 London Naval Conference, where American and British delegates had conferred, consulted and cooperated without any written agreements being required.[147] Davis was reassured that both parties would work to keep Japan from gaining parity and that both also wished to avoid a naval race among the principal naval powers. Both the American and British delegations agreed that the substance of the meeting had to be kept utterly secret.[148]

Those initial agreements were followed up by a second series of conversations on 20 June. In the interim, Davis asked for and received confirmation of Roosevelt's desire for an agreement among the principal naval powers for a percentage reduction of possibly up to 20 per cent, in the total treaty tonnages of all categories (except we should keep the present tonnage in aircraft carriers) without modification of the treaty rations, or failing such reduction, a prolongation of the Washington and London Treaty limitations for as long a period as possible, say from 10 to 15 years.[149]

Certain technical issues concerning capital ship displacement and gun size were areas that had the potential to create problems, but in Davis' opinion it was the question of the Japanese ratio that needed to be agreed on. As it appeared there was agreement with the British on that matter, he was most confident that even if no other nations wished to join, the Americans and British could arrive at a treaty between themselves.[150]

At the meeting on 20 June, Davis put the question of what would happen if only the United States and Great Britain could agree on a programme of future naval construction.[151] MacDonald replied that it would be most unfortunate if a race in naval construction ensued between the two countries, and, therefore, their objective should be to reach a naval agreement that would 'regulate their respective naval construction, it being understood that the levels agreed upon would be liable to modification, either upwards or downwards, in accordance with the rate of building actually undertaken by other Powers'.[152] Once again, this admission was to be left out of the official record.

The Admiralty's technical and building plans did not sit well with the Americans. Proposals for 25,000-ton battleships with 12-inch guns were unacceptable to the General Board, and the British requirements concerning cruisers were also 'shocking' to Davis and his fellow representatives. However, Davis was willing to accept that British requirements were grounded in some strategic realities.[153] MacDonald was pleased with the result of the talks, believing that

> the United States may refuse to build to our parity as it would be a waste of their money but we might get an agreement that we should on full understanding of each other's needs agree upon a naval attitude to each other eliminating competition. Unless we get a well signed Treaty I should deliberately work for this, as it would have more promise for the future than a bargained and uneasy agreement on limitation.[154]

MacDonald believed that the United States could indeed be brought into some type of coalition. He explained to Simon the idea that the British and Americans could have agreement on general naval policy as follows: 'With America rather nervous about Japan we might secure an agreement as regards the Pacific which would be of great benefit to the maintenance of peace.'[155] Craigie agreed with that assessment, but cautioned that he believed it was the American plan to let the talks break down because of the uncompromising attitude of some other power, probably Japan or France, and then 'to work for an Anglo-American naval understanding under which both countries would adhere to the principle of parity but the United States would probably only build up to the level of parity in so far as she is forced by Japan to do so'.[156]

The American delegates were disappointed, however, in the British position. Davis himself had hoped for a solid anti-Japanese front and had not gotten it, although there was agreement that both Britain and the United States would oppose Japan's quest for parity.[157] Davis told Craigie that he felt a sense of betrayal, because it had been the Americans' understanding that the British had merely wanted to maintain the London Naval Treaty figures, not make increases in them. Those increases were in direct contrast to President Roosevelt's desire to see a reduction in numbers and tonnage. Craigie tried to sooth the delegates' sense of failure by expressing his belief that what had occurred was a beneficial and frank airing of each other's requirements in the light of the present world situation: 'It would now be for the two missions to endeavour to find some way by which, without endangering our security, any unnecessary building by the United States and Japan could be avoided. This I did not believe to be by any means a hopeless problem if there were good will on both sides.'[158] Davis agreed generally with Craigie's view, but told him confidentially and personally that Washington had been very upset by reports that Britain was going to curry favour with the Japanese at all costs and would sacrifice Anglo-American friendship if necessary in the process. That suspicion of British intentions, now coupled with this 'change of attitude' towards the naval building programme, would make it very difficult to induce the US government to take a generous view of Britain's naval proposals. Craigie pointed out that it was the British government's intention to arrive at some tripartite entente, rather than a bilateral understanding, that would improve relations with both the United States and Japan. He also highlighted some of the frustration that the British administration felt concerning such issues as America's true intentions in the Far East and the war debt matter, when it seemed that the executive's alleged desire for cooperative solutions were checkmated by the Senate. Davis assured Craigie that 'in all matters relating to the Pacific we could be quite sure that the President and Congress saw absolutely eye to eye and that any policy approved by the President would be warmly endorsed by Congress'.[159]

A good deal of discussion ensued on the British side after the talk between Craigie and Davis as to whether the Americans were really surprised or only feigning disappointment in order to help their position. After the talk with Davis, Craigie reported to the Prime Minister and the Admiralty that it was his opinion that the Americans were sincerely hurt by the Admiralty's demand for more cruisers and that this was not some sort of bargaining tactic.[160] Vansittart was not so sure, however, suspecting that the Americans had been fully aware of the British position but were now using this sense of betrayal as a manoeuvre to try to cast the blame for failure on Britain.[161] Admiral Little agreed with

Craigie that the Americans had expressed surprise and alarm at British cruiser demands, but noted that the Americans did not criticize Britain's desire for the maintenance of an increased fleet. In fact, it was his view that Davis had not only quite explicitly agreed with the proposed increases, but also had expressed his government's desire to see a 20 per cent reduction on the London Naval Treaty tonnages.[162] The mixed signals being put forward by the chief American negotiator were not lost on Little, who also had been told by Davis that the US Navy had no figures of their own and planned to mould their fleet after the British.[163] Little's advice, which was accepted by Chatfield, was that:

> There can be no doubt that the great surprise which the American representatives have shown at our increased cruiser requirements must be artificial. In the first place, a close study of the problem which undoubtedly must be made in the Navy Department at Washington shows that with the increased qualitative limit of cruisers there is an automatic and unavoidable increase in the London Naval Treaty tonnages from this reason alone ... We have been very frank with the Americans but in view of Mr Norman Davis's suggestion that we may be able to reduce our requirements after discussion with the other Powers it seems that he has not understood that the figures we have put forward for cruisers are a minimum based on an absolute requirement, in spite of the very full explanation of this problem given at the meeting with the technical experts.[164]

Little ended his analysis by wondering if it would not be best if he had a private, strictly unofficial, talk with Davis to try to explain the British cruiser position more clearly. This idea was not accepted. Monsell did not want to push the Americans on the matter as yet, and was in favour of waiting to see what kinds of option could be produced by discussions with the Japanese.[165] Both MacDonald and Simon agreed with the Admiralty's assessment of the situation, in particular with Monsell's proposal to let the Americans have time to sort themselves out. MacDonald's only suggestion was to try to get the US Navy to come up with some solid figures and numbers, especially on what their minimum requirements for capital ships would be.[166]

The US delegation was split on what options to follow, now that it looked as if the technical discussions with Britain had stalled. Bingham and Davis argued over when and what message to deliver to the President. The Ambassador recommended leaving the British alone, for it was his belief that, in the light of the new strategic realities of the world, the British would eventually have to come to the Americans for assistance. Davis, on the other hand, was reluctant to acknowledge that perhaps these preliminary talks had been a failure, or that he had misread British intentions regarding cruiser limits.[167] He argued that the Admiralty's attitude, supported by the Foreign Office, confirmed his view that the proper American strategy was to take a strong stand at the outset against any increases and face down the British demands. By threatening such an early break-down of the conference, Davis was sure that the American position could weather any public relations storm in the press, as well as leave the British with no choice but to come back to negotiate, after they had reconsidered their 'extreme' position.[168]

The President and the State Department agreed with Davis' point of view. Hull instructed him to take a strong stand against the British cruiser and capital ship proposals and to inform London that the President considered any increases to the existing tonnages to be absolutely unacceptable.[169] There was a tone of disappointment in Washington's reply, but the level of malice towards the British was negligible. Hull's telegram to Davis confirmed the American desire to see some Anglo-American working relationship agreed, for he instructed his key negotiator not to let the press create any ill-will or poisonous conditions around the talks:

> It is difficult to understand the subtle distinction made by MacDonald and Craigie between a 'statement of position' and a 'proposal' but this may well offer them a golden bridge for retreat and we for our part will facilitate it by indicating to the press, if necessary, that whatever increases the British technical experts may have indicated as their preference the British delegates have not committed themselves in any way, and that the conversations are still in an exploratory stage.[170]

Roosevelt lent his own weight to the effort to make sure relations with Great Britain did not rupture at this critical point by making a personal appeal to MacDonald.[171] He emphasised the need to control the desires of Admirals and navy departments and hoped that technical issues could be put aside and some 'big basic principles' arrived at. Desiring to keep as much of these naval conversations as quiet as possible, Roosevelt told MacDonald that the Prime Minister could let the Cabinet know what he had written but did not want the press to get hold of the news.[172] Indeed, the President refused to let himself admit that the conversations might fail and no limitation treaty would be produced.[173]

Roosevelt and the State Department were also making certain that US Navy objections and reactions were not allowed to put an end to the talks. The General Board was most annoyed with the British proposal and demanded that Leigh and Wilkinson be brought back to the United States immediately. Admiral Standley disagreed, and countered the Board's demand with a promise to issue instructions to the naval representatives putting limits on the conversations that they could have with the British delegates. The CNO's actions did not correspond with the political aspects of the issue. Moffat and other State Department officials lobbied Standley not to put any restrictions on the naval representatives.[174] The primary purpose of the talks was to see if an accord could be reached in 1935, argued Moffat, and, if technical discussions were not allowed at this stage, then the Americans would go blind into the actual conference itself next year. He also pointed out that Standley's suggested actions could effectively end the talks before the Japanese arrived, thereby shifting the blame to the American delegation. Finally, he believed that the British were already showing signs of making some accommodations. Standley and Admiral Taussig and Admiral Clark were swayed by Moffat's points and the powers of the naval personnel in London remained unchanged.[175]

MacDonald replied to Roosevelt that he, too, certainly wished for a reduction in the size and numbers of naval vessels, but that the strategic realities facing the British Empire made such concessions impossible to contemplate. Dangers in the Far East and Europe mitigated against any such action until the risk of conflict was reduced. He told Roosevelt that the British delegation had made their position as clear and open as possible. It was MacDonald's hope

> that mutual examination and understanding will lead to an agreement on how to face the situation, remembering that a thorough understanding between us will enable us within bounds of our separate possibilities to maintain complete co-operation, because I firmly believe that that is an essential condition of the maintenance of sanity and peace in the world.[176]

Craigie and Vansittart were less charitable about the President and his motivation for writing to MacDonald. Both condemned his views as being reflective of a need to assist domestic Congressional elections and desire to shut his eyes to international problems.[177] Neither man had much faith in a useful outcome to the talks if there was not a legitimate will on the part of the President to engage the real issues.

Davis and Bingham were now both convinced that Britain was determined to build a two-ocean navy, one which would allow it to deal with the Japanese in the Far East while at the same time providing the forces necessary for protecting European waters. The only thing that could arrest such a construction programme, Davis wrote, was a contractual agreement, passed by the US Senate, that gave Britain assurance in advance that it would not stand alone against Japan.[178] Both men also agreed that Japan was the main threat for both the Admiralty and the Cabinet. The movement to cooperate with the Americans and not to appease the Japanese was in the ascendant, said Davis, but the factional nature of the British policy-makers could not be ignored. Both the British and American delegations agreed that talks had reached a point where it was best not to go on to certain failure, but instead, to explore talks with the Japanese and French, in the hope that some solution might thereby materialize.[179] With no clear cooperative atmosphere created, the two sides agreed to disagree and to suspend any further official talks between themselves until October, when a Japanese delegation (which had been delayed) was expected to arrive.[180] Both parties cooperated in putting a positive face on the stalled talks to the press. Each side claimed that a recess was natural and did not indicate any unsolvable problems or unbridgeable positions, nor did it mean that the talks had broken down.[181] Neither side was willing to accuse the other in public, for each camp had too much to lose from a failed conference, and there was a strong sense that some agreement between the two nations could still be arrived at.[182]

Craigie was very worried that a disgruntled and disappointed Davis would return to the United States after 19 July in a foul mood, spreading anti-British sentiment in a Stimson-like fashion. Such actions could damage forever any hopes of Anglo-American cooperation at the naval conference. He was most concerned that the realities of Britain's strategic position, particularly in the Far East, had to be spelled out most carefully and fully for the President, whom Davis was scheduled to see and brief immediately after his return from England.[183] Vansittart doubted that the Americans could ever be expected to see such realities. He did not want Craigie to lead the Americans on to expect that the British would be willing to compromise their security needs and was reluctant to approach them at all.[184] However, with the Admiralty's approval and assistance, Craigie composed a seminal summary of the British naval and foreign policy position that was approved by both the Admiralty and Foreign Office for transmittal to the President.[185]

Craigie enlisted the assistance of Ray Atherton at the US Embassy in London to help ensure that the British message was properly constructed so it would be well received by the right people and not discounted by Davis or any other State Department officials with anti-British sentiments.[186] Both Craigie and Atherton were aware of the Congressional elections in November and the problems that these were creating for the President and his foreign and defence policies. However, the two also were confident that after those autumn elections much more progress would be made.[187]

The head of the American department knew that he could count on Atherton, because the two had worked very closely together to ensure that Foreign Office and State Department attitudes proceeded along closely parallel paths, especially in the stage-managing of the press's commentary surrounding the conference.[188] When Davis announced his decision to return to the United States, Craigie had approached Atherton about what could be done to make certain that the two sides did not leave the discussions under a dark cloud of negative public comment. Davis and his delegation could no longer take the initiative on the matter, so Atherton told Craigie that, for the sake of American public opinion, the next step had to 'appear' to come from the British, and should best be in the form of some declaration to the press that American and British objectives remained identical. Such a step would remove any impression that irreconcilable differences had arisen. An offer could then be made to the US delegation to join the British in issuing the statement to the press.[189] Craigie, privately and entirely off the record, took the unusual step of asking Atherton to draft just such a press release. Atherton obliged, asking that his actions in the matter be kept absolutely anonymous, and submitted a draft which was then altered by Vansittart and Chatfield. Simon presented the statement to Norman Davis and his delegation, who much appreciated the document, and, after a brief re-drafting, wished to make the joint announcement.[190] They believed that it would give them the leverage required to keep relations on a friendly footing while they presented the British case to the US Navy and State Department.[191] However, when Davis asked Hull if the statement could be issued as a joint communiqué, his request was denied on the grounds that it would create an impression of differences of opinion between the two nations, make the Japanese suspicious that a common front against them was being formed, lead the press to ask embarrassing questions because it contained glaring omissions, and commit the United States to continued negotiations regardless of future developments.[192] Nevertheless, the Secretary of State did use the statement as a general basis for his conversations with the American press. Hull told them he was not worried about the recess, that the talks would begin again in the autumn and that any lack of progress on that point was the fault of the Japanese, who had not yet managed to get an authoritative delegation to London. Craigie liked the Secretary's handling of the matter, and thought the British could take the same line, except for the part about the Japanese being at fault.[193]

Even though the joint communiqué itself was never issued, the process of cooperation had done much to improve the general tone of Anglo-American relations towards the talks. Atherton informed Craigie that such was the case, especially from the point of view of the State Department:

> In the last few days the atmosphere had been greatly improved by the following ... events: (1) the issue of the Anglo-American-Japanese communiqué stating that further discussions would be postponed until October, pending the arrival of Japanese representatives; (2) Mr Hull's statement to the press on the 16th instant which was to the effect that 'the suspension of the London discussions did not mean that there had been a breakdown in the talk; the conversations had gone as far as possible for the time being and Mr Davis would be prepared to return to London whenever the Japanese were ready to send delegates for the preliminary talks'; a report which the American journalists here had cabled over to Washington newspapers stating that Mr Bingham and Mr Norman Davis had had a very friendly final talk with the Secretary of State yesterday. The United States Government felt that the discussions had now been adjourned on such a 'friendly and harmonious note' that it would be a pity to take any step which might conceivably provoke a discord.[194]

Craigie was also assured that Davis and his delegation had gone home in a happy frame of mind, with each nation's position clarified. Stanley Baldwin, former Prime Minster, the Lord President of the Council, and soon to be Prime

Minister once more, who had often taken the place of the disliked Simon in critical talks with the Americans, rejoiced at the news.[195] Simon himself thought it had been Davis' intention to leave in a good atmosphere all along, and believed that the rescue effort was very good for all parties.[196] A rescue had indeed been performed, as both sides now regrouped on their respective sides of the Atlantic and prepared to take up the negotiations in the autumn.

## NOTES

1. Wellesley, *Diplomacy in Fetters*, 33.
2. On pre-Roosevelt relations and a sense of trust in Anglo-American relations over Far Eastern and naval matters see D.C. Watt, 'The Nature of the Foreign-Policy Making Elite in Britain', in Watt ed., *Personalities and Policies*, 1–15; F.C. Costigliola, 'Anglo-American Financial Rivalry in the 1920s', *JEH*, 37 (1977): 911–34; Greg Kennedy, 'The 1930 London Naval Conference and Anglo-American Maritime Strength, 1927–1930', 149–72; Kennedy, 'Depression and Security'.
3. Stimson's anger at Sir John Simon and the British Cabinet, and his ability to transform that anger (which in many cases was shared by the listener) into suspicion in other members of the Roosevelt administration, especially those in the State Department, is evident: see Stimson Diary entry, 17 May 1934, talk with FDR; ibid., Diary entry, 24 July 1934, talk with Stanley Baldwin. See also Norman H. Davis MSS (hereafter Davis MSS), Library of Congress, Washington, DC, Container 54, FO memo on Stimson–Simon debate, 30 Apr. 1935. See also, on microfilm at the National Archive, Washington, DC, CSDCF, 711.41/275, memo by Pierrepont Moffat (Division of Western European Affairs), 14 July 1934; Jay Pierrepont Moffat Diary (hereafter Moffat Diary) Harvard University, Cambridge, MA, Vol. 35 (1 Jan. to 1 July 1934), entry for 4 Apr. 1934. Also, William R. Castle Papers (hereafter Castle Papers or Castle Diary), Herbert Hoover Presidential Library, West Branch, Iowa, Box 4, Folder England 1931–33, private, personal and confidential letter from Ray Atherton (member of US Embassy in London) to Castle, 23 Feb. 1933; ibid., private, personal and confidential letter from Atherton to Castle, 7 Mar. 1933; Diary entry for 5 Dec. 1934.
4. For some of the literature on the failed World Economic Conference of 1933, see A.P.N. Erdmann, 'Mining for the Corporate Synthesis: Gold in American Foreign Economic Policy, 1931–1936', *DH*, 17 (1993): 171–200; A. Booth, *British Economic Policy, 1931–49* (London, 1989), 1–43; D. Kunz, *The Battle for Britain's Gold Standard in 1931* (London, 1987), 160–3; J. Nichols, 'Roosevelt's Monetary Diplomacy in 1933', *AHR*, 56 (1992): 295–317; K.A. Oye, 'The Sterling–Dollar–Franc Triangle: Monetary Diplomacy, 1929–1937', *WP*, 38 (1985): 173–99. The most useful contextual works on this topic are Patricia Clavin, '"The Fetishes of So-Called International Bankers": Central Bank Co-operation for the World Economic Conference, 1932–3', *CEH*, 3 (1992): 281–311; Clavin, 'The World Economic Conference 1933: The Failure of British Internationalism', *JEEH*, 20 (1991): 489–527; Clavin, *The Failure of Economic Diplomacy: Britain, Germany, France and the United States, 1931–36* (London, 1996); Kenneth Mouré, 'The Limits to Central Bank Co-operation, 1916–36', *CEH*, 3 (1992): 259–79.
5. Moffat Diary, Vol. 33, entry 4 May 1933. Also, Avon Paper, AP14/1/324A-356A, secret and personal letter from Orsmby-Gore to Eden, 11 May 1934.
6. SKH Papers, Box 453, Chronological Day File, memo by Hornbeck to Phillips and Hull, 31 Oct. 1933.

7. Davis MSS, Container 51, letter from Davis to FDR, 7 Apr. 1933; Moffat Diary, Vol. 35, entry 4 Apr. 1934; Dallek, *Franklin D. Roosevelt and American Foreign Policy*, 74.

8. For insights into those Anglo-American discussions on disarmament and their negative legacy, see Moffat Diary, Vol. 33, 1 Jan. to 30 June 1933, diary entries for 22, 23, 24, 25 Apr.; Phillips memo, 24 Apr. 1933, Vol. I, 68–9, in Edgar B. Nixon, *Franklin D. Roosevelt and Foreign Affairs*, 3 vols (Cambridge, MA, 1969) (hereafter known as *FDR&FA*); *FDR&FA*, 'Roosevelt to Heads of Nations Represented at the London and Geneva Conferences', 16 May 1933, Vol. I, 126–8; FO 800/291, Simon MSS (hereafter Simon Papers), PRO, letter from Vansittart to Simon, 23 May 1933; CSDCF 711.41/261, despatch from Atherton to Hull, 9 Mar. 1933.

9. FO 371/17581/A961/198/45, telegram from Lindsay to FO, telegram dated 1 Jan. 1934; ibid., Simon minute, 8 Feb. 1934.

10. FO 371/17581/A2700/198/45, letter from Lindsay to Vansittart, 22 Mar. 1934, and minutes by Vansittart, Craigie, Wellesley and Simon. In a pattern soon to become familiar, Anthony Eden stood out from these FO officials in his total support of Lindsay's warnings not to incite anti-British feeling in the United States through any propaganda war; Eden minute, 13 Apr.

11. For the pro-Japanese views of the Chancellor of the Exchequer, Neville Chamberlain, see CAB 2/6, Committee of Imperial Defence Minutes (hereafter CID minutes), PRO, Kew, London, 261st meeting, 9 Nov. 1933.

12. Despite various claims made that Sir Robert Vansittart was the catalyst and main constructor of British defence strategy from 1934 onwards, the evidence available shows clearly that Sir Warren Fisher and Vansittart did not control the DRC and the formulation of its eventual report. They were submerged and manipulated by Hankey and the Service Chiefs, and the resulting report was really about rearming to meet imperial defence needs in the Far East. Germany was for the future, not the immediate, which was what the DRC was all about. See Keith Neilson, '"Russia Herself is the Great Enigma": The Soviet Union in British Foreign and Defence Policy, 1930–1940', a paper given at the Canadian Historical Association meeting at Brock University, 2 June 1996; Neilson, 'The DRC and Imperial Defence', a paper given at the annual Society for Military History conference, 23–24 May 2001, Calgary, Alberta, Canada.

13. See, CAB 16/109, Minutes of the 3rd Meeting of the Defence Requirements Committee (hereafter DRC), 4 Dec. 1933; CAB 16/109, Minutes of 19th Meeting of DRC, 'Note by Sir Warren Fisher', 17 Feb. 1934; CAB 21/434, Cabinet Registered Files, letter from Fisher to Hankey, 17 Feb. 1934; CAB 21/434, Fisher to Hankey, 26 Jan. 1934.

14. CAB 16/109, DRC 12, 'Note by Sir Warren Fisher', 30 Jan. 1934.

15. Ibid.

16. Hankey Papers (HNKY), private and personal letter, Hankey to Baldwin, 23 Aug. 1934. Writing about the upcoming Naval Conference and the future of the Royal Navy, Hankey says, 'To speak frankly, I am apprehensive of Warren Fisher's influence in this question. I don't think he is a fit man or that his judgment is at its best. Moreover he has never been sound about the Navy or understood the defence question in the Pacific. I say this with the more regret that Warren is one of my greatest personal friends.'

17. Fisher and the Treasury feared being left out of the 1935 naval talks. His fears were, understandably, that the FO and Admiralty had traditionally treated such negotiations as their exclusive territory. If the Treasury's concerns about relations with the United States and their effect on Anglo-Japanese relations were not formally included in the DRC's report then they could be ignored during the naval negotiations because they would have no documentary basis. Fisher's fears were well founded. Vansittart and Chatfield both agreed with Fisher to some extent about the usefulness of the United States coming to Britain's aid in the Far East, but neither was willing to go the Treasury

route and cavalierly alienate the United States. See CAB 16/109, minutes of 11th DRC Meeting, 19 Feb. 1934; CHT/3/1, 4 June 1934.

18. See Greg Kennedy, '1935', 190–217; Roskill, *Naval Policy Between the Wars*, Vol. II, 164–93; Roskill, *Hankey: Man of Secrets*, Vol. III (London, 1974), 67–120; CAB 53/5, Chiefs of Staff Committee, minutes of meeting (hereafter COS), meeting 132, 24 July 1934; CAB 16/109, minutes of 5th and 6th DRC Meetings, 19 Jan. and 23 Jan. 1934.

19. Despite the claims by Morrisey and Ramsay, '"Giving the Lead in the Right Direction"'; Wark, *Ultimate Enemy*; Varey, 'Fraught with the Gravest Difficulties'; and McKercher, 'Old Diplomacy and New', which support the narrow continentalist views of Brian Bond, *British Military Policy between the Two World Wars* (Oxford, 1980); and Michael Howard, *The Continental Commitment* (London, 1972), that the service chiefs were timid in their demands for defence funds during the DRC process, evidence shows that this hesitation was a realistic desire to not alienate reluctant government officials by demanding unrealistic sums of money for defence. One of the most powerful of those political figures who was wary of excessive defence spending was Prime Minister Ramsay MacDonald himself, who held the view that 'The military are getting too much on top, but up till now defence is so neglected that the time for pulling in has not come. They are, however, getting up pace and may not be easy to pull up.' It was that sort of attitude which the service chiefs' cautious approach was designed to circumvent. MacDonald MSS PRO, 30/69/1753, MacDonald Diary (Large),(hereafter MacDonald Diary), diary entry, 27 Nov. 1934.

20. CAB 21/434, Hankey letter to Fisher, 17 Feb. 1934; Avon Papers, AP14/1/127-153, Cadogan to Eden, 6 Mar. 1933.

21. CAB 53/23, COS Papers, Paper No. 307, 20 May 1933. See also CAB 4/2, CID Papers, Paper No. 1112-B, 6 June 1933.

22. CAB 16/109, minutes of the 3rd meeting of DRC, 4 Dec. 1933.

23. Various other views of the usefulness or lack thereof of the Second London Naval Conference are found in: Meredith W. Berg, 'Protecting National Interests by Treaty: the Second London Naval Conference, 1934–1936', in McKercher, ed., *Arms Limitation and Disarmament*, 203–29; Robert G. Kaufman, *Arms Control During the Pre-Nuclear Era* (New York, 1990), 165–93; Stephen E. Pelz, *Race to Pearl Harbor: The Failure of the Second London Naval Conference and the Onset of World War II* (Cambridge, 1974); Trotter, *Britain and East Asia*, 88–114.

24. For the background to Vansittart's short-tempered attitude towards the United States, see Chapter 2.

25. CAB 16/109, minutes of 11th DRC Meeting, 19 Feb. 1934.

26. One example that serves as an instructive insight into Vansittart's over-zealous desire to teach the Americans a lesson and protect British *amour propre* is demonstrated in an incident concerning Sir H.G. Armstrong, an ex-Consul-General to New York. Armstrong wrote a letter to the *New York Times* arguing that the Americans subsidized their shipping in order to keep it competitive with the British. Vansittart was so outraged by and apoplectic over the incident that he began a campaign to see if Armstrong's government pension could be intercepted, reduced or cut off. After being informed that the ex-Consul-General was independently wealthy, and that his pension could not be interfered with in any case, Vansittart still insisted in bringing Armstrong in to his office for a thorough going-over, despite assurances from his friend, Ambassador Lindsay, that Armstrong's mistake had been one of excitement, rather than any attempt to subvert the British merchant shipping position *vis-à-vis* the United States. It was not until after the successful conclusion of the 1935 London Naval talks that Vansittart began to see the Americans in a better light. FO 371/18747/A297/282/45, despatch and article from Lindsay to FO, minutes by Craigie, Wellesley and

Vansittart, 31 Dec. 1934; FO 371/18747/A636/282/45, despatch and letters, from Lindsay to FO, 8 Jan. 1934; FO 371/18747/A1206/282/45, telegram from Lindsay to FO, and minutes by Gore-Booth, Broad and Craigie, 7 Feb. 1934.

27. While Vansittart may have been unfairly cast in the past as a man obsessed by the German threat to Great Britain and Anglo-French relations, recent attempts to paint him as more imperially minded have been unconvincing with regard to Vansittart's role in the formulation of British foreign policy towards the United States, the Far East and the Soviet Union.

28. FO 371/17593/A785/785/45, confidential letter from Admiralty to Under-Secretary of State, 24 Jan. 1934; Vansittart minutes, 5 Feb.

29. Ibid., Vansittart minute.

30. FO 371/17596/A2060/1938/45, FO minute, 9 Feb. 1934.

31. Ibid.

32. Craigie was not only the technical expert for the Foreign Office on naval matters, but during the course of the preliminary talks for the 1935 London Naval Conference he met with Prime Minister MacDonald in the mornings on a regular basis to inform the PM of events and to receive MacDonald's personal instructions on how to proceed on matters: MacDonald Diary, entry 29 Nov. 1934. For his supremacy over Chatfield and Treasury on conference matters, particularly the lead in working for closer Anglo-American relations see, CHT/3/2, secret draft of note from Fisher to Chamberlain, 12 Nov. 1934.

33. FO 371/17596/A1977/1938/45, letter from Vansittart to Chatfield, 19 Jan. 1934.

34. Until indicated, the following is based on, ibid., FO memo by Craigie, 9 Jan. 1934.

35. Ibid., Craigie minute, 9 Jan. 1934.

36. FO 371/17596/A1977/1938/45, Simon minute, 1 Feb. 1934.

37. These critics reflected the theorizing of Admiral Sir Herbert Richmond and his calls for smaller capital ships. See Barry Hunt, *Sailor-Scholar: Admiral Sir Herbert Richmond, 1871–1946* (Waterloo, Ontario, 1982), 189–208; Lord Chatfield, *It Might Happen Again*, Vol. II (London, 1947), 60. For views on the importance of Craigie and events leading up to the conference, see ibid., Vol. II, 64–76.

38. FO 371/17596/A1977/1938/45, Simon minute, 1 Feb. 1934.

39. Ibid., Vansittart minute, 5 Feb. and Simon minute, 5 Feb. 1934.

40. For a useful look at ADM and FO relations and British naval planning see, Orest Babij, 'The Royal Navy and the defence of the British Empire, 1928–1934', in Kennedy and Neilson, eds, *Far-Flung Lines*, 171–89.

41. FO 371/17596/A1978/1938/45, letter from Chatfield to Vansittart, 23 Jan. 1934.

42. Ibid., Craigie minute, 26 Jan. 1934.

43. Ibid., draft letter from Vansittart to Chatfield, 27 Jan. 1934.

44. Davis Papers, Container 41, letter from Pierrepont Moffat to Davis, 25 Sept. 1933.

45. Ibid.; Davis Papers, Container 41, letter from Moffat to Davis, 3 Oct. 1933.

46. Davis Papers, Container 41, letter from Davis to Moffat, 10 Oct. 1933.

47. For earlier evidence of Pratt and Hepburn's desire for closer Anglo-American cooperation on naval matters, see Davis Papers, Container 17, secret memo on USN naval disarmament plans, 21 Sept. 1932.

48. Moffat Diary, Vol. 33, entry for 16 Mar. 1933.

49. Ibid., entry for 18 Mar. 1933; RG 80, General Board, 1900–47, GB 420-2 (hereafter GB 420-2), National Archives, Washington, DC, memo from CNO Pratt 'The Navy's Needs', 20 July 1933. See also Gerald H. Wheeler, *Admiral William Veazie Pratt, US Navy* (Washington, DC, 1974), 359–75.

50. *FRUS*, Vol. I, 'General and British Commonwealth', telegram from Grew to Hull, 22 Jan. 1934, 217.

51. Moffat Diary, Vol. 35, entry for 31 Jan. 1934.
52. Robert W. Bingham Diary (hereafter Bingham Diary), Library of Congress, Washington, DC, entry 20 Feb. 1934.
53. Ibid.
54. Ibid., entry 1 Feb. 1934.
55. FO 371/17596/A1979/1938/45, official letter from the Admiralty to Under-Secretary of State for the FO, 10 Feb. 1934.
56. Ibid.
57. Ibid., Craigie minute, 15 Feb.
58. Ibid., Vansittart minute, 16 Feb.
59. Ibid., Craigie minute, 21 Feb.; CAB 29/147, NCM(35) Ministerial Committee for the 1935 Naval Conference, minutes of meetings.
60. For some insights into MacDonald's handling of foreign affairs and his mental state at the time, see David Marquand, *Ramsay MacDonald* (London, 1977), 704–5, 715, 736–7, 757–9.
61. Stanley Baldwin Papers (hereafter Baldwin Papers), University Library, Cambridge, 131, untitled memo by MacDonald of conversation with Norman Davis and Atherton, 5 Mar. 1934.
62. Bingham Diary, entry for 1 Mar. 1934; MacDonald Diary, entry 4 Mar. 1934; FO 371/17596/A1938/1938/45, record of a conversation, 5 Mar. 1934; *FRUS*, Vol. I, telegram from Bingham to Hull, 5 Mar. 1934, 222.
63. *FRUS*, Vol. I, memo from Davis to FDR, 6 Mar. 1934, 222–30. See also CSDCF, 741.94/32 despatch from Atherton to Hull, 16 Mar. 1934.
64. *FRUS*, Vol. I, memo from Davis to FDR, 6 Mar. 1934, 222–230.
65. Bingham Diary, 1 Mar. 1934; *FRUS*, Vol. I, telegram Bingham to Hull, 5 Mar. 1934, 222.
66. For views on Simon's role in armament and disarmament talks at this time, see David Dutton, *Simon: A Political Biography of Sir John Simon* (London, 1992), 181–210.
67. Bingham Diary, entry for 2 Mar. 1934.
68. Ibid. Bingham's beliefs on the desire of the British for cooperation was reinforced by Admiral Sir Roger Keyes, who told the Ambassador that the Americans and British should prepare themselves militarily to be able to 'take care of these nigger[s]', referring to the Japanese. See Bingham Diary, entry for 21 Mar. 1934. The personal relationship between Simon and Bingham only got worse as the year went on. Sniping by Mrs Simon about southerners lynching blacks provoked a strong reply from Bingham at a dinner party. This was followed up by remarks made by Simon at a luncheon at No. 10 Downing St, which the Ambassador heard, about how Mrs Simon was being forced to use antiseptics to ward off disease ever since attending a luncheon given at the Bingham's residence. The result of these incidents added dramatically to Bingham's negative view of Simon and his handling of British foreign policy. See Bingham Diary, entry for 30 Oct. and 1 Nov. 1934.
69. President's Private Secretary's Files (hereafter FDR–PSF), Franklin D. Roosevelt Presidential Library, Hyde Park, New York, Confidential Files, Box 142, Folder, London Naval Conference 1934, note by Phillips to FDR, 21 Mar. 1934.
70. For the particulars of that struggle and the final success of the Foreign Office in directing a policy which kept Britain from maintaining a formal alliance with any one nation against Japan – the 'No-Bloc' policy – see Kennedy, '1935'.
71. Treasury [T], PRO, 172/1815, 1933 World Economic Conference, memo for the Chancellor from R.V.N. Hopkins, 5 May 1933; T172/2110, Carbons of letters from the Chancellor of the Exchequer, 1932–34, letter from Chamberlain to Grigg, 26 Sept. 1934; T172/1831, Anglo-Japanese Relations, note and attached letter from F.R. Hoyer

Millar to J.D.B. Fergusson, 15 Nov., and Fisher minute, 17 Nov. 1934; ibid., memo from Fergusson to Chamberlain, 15 Jan. 1935.

72. See CAB 2/6, CID Minutes, 261 Meeting, 9 Nov. 1933; CAB 4/22, CID Paper No. 1112-B, 'Imperial Defence Policy', 6 June 1933 and CID Paper No. 1113-B, 'Imperial Defence Policy, Annual Review of the Chief of Staff', 12 Oct. 1933; CAB 53/23, COS Paper No. 304 (Joint Planning Committee, hereafter JP), 'The Situation in the Far East, Plans for Singapore and Hong-Kong', 7 Apr. 1933, COS Paper No. 305, 'Situation in the Far East', 31 Mar. 1933, COS Paper No. 306, 'Imperial Defence Policy', 8 Apr. 1933, COS Paper No. 307, 'Imperial Defence Policy and Memo by the Foreign Office', 20 May 1933, COS Paper No. 310, 'Imperial Defence Policy, Annual Review of the COS', 12 Oct. 1933; CAB 16/109, DRC 19, 'Memo by Sir Warren Fisher', 17 Feb. 1934; DRC 20, 'The Far Eastern Situation, letter and set of memorandum from Sir Robert Vansittart and the Foreign Office', 24 Feb. 1934.

73. CAB 23/78, Cabinet Minutes, PRO, minutes of meeting 9(34), 14 Mar. 1934.

74. Ibid.

75. Ibid.

76. See *Documents on British Foreign Policy, 1919–1939* (hereafter *DBFP*) (London, 1984), 2nd series, Vol. XX, *Far Eastern Affairs*, 20 May 1933–5 Nov. 1936, No. 77, 'Summary by Sir V. Wellesley of memorandum on the situation in the Far East', [F295/295/61], 18 Jan. 1934.

77. The centrality of Wellesley and the FED is shown in the negative comments of Cadogan, who wished Wellesley and the FED scrapped due to the way in which that group dominated Far Eastern issues in the FO. CAD, entry for 28 May 1935.

78. *DBFP*, Vol. XX, letter from Vansittart to the Permanent Secretary of the Admiralty [F295/295/61], 12 Mar. 1934. This letter was also sent to the War Office, Air Ministry, Colonial Office, Dominions Office, Board of Trade and India Office, with copies also going to Hankey and Cabinet Ministers.

79. CAB 24/248, Cabinet Papers (hereafter CP), PRO, 80(34), 'Memo by the Secretary of State for Foreign Affairs', 16 Mar. 1934.

80. FO 371/17596/A2176/1938/45, memo by the Chief of the Naval Staff in preparation for the 1935 London Naval Conference, 14 Mar. 1934.

81. Ibid. See also, Kennedy, '1935', 204–6.

82. FO 371/17596/A2176/1938/45, memo by CNS, 14 Mar. 1934.

83. Ibid., Simon minute, 19 Mar. 1934.

84. Ibid.

85. FO 371/17596/A2416/1938/45, record of meeting held at Admiralty on 20 Mar., 23 Mar. 1934.

86. Ibid. For Chatfield's view on Britain's naval position during these talks see Roskill, *Naval Policy Between the Wars*, Vol. II, 72–5; Chatfield, *It Might Happen Again*, Vol. II, 64–73; Eric J. Grove, 'Admiral Sir (later Baron) Ernle Chatfield (1933–1938)', in Malcolm H. Murfett, ed., *The First Sea Lords* (Westport, CT, 1995), 157–73. For Chatfield's earlier career see his autobiography, *The Navy and Defence* (London, 1942).

87. FO 371/17596/A2416/1938/45, record of meeting on 20 Mar., 23 Mar. 1934.

88. FO 371/17596/A2417/1938/45, memo from Director of Plans on 1935 Naval Conference, 23 Mar. 1934.

89. Ibid., Craigie minute, 28 Mar. 1934.

90. Ibid., covering note signed by Vansittart and Chatfield, 23 Mar. 1934.

91. CSDCF, 741.93/71, confidential memo of conversation, 10 Mar. 1934.

92. Moffat Diary, entry for 16 Mar. 1934; Bingham Diary, entry for 12 Apr. 1934.

93. Moffat Diary, entry for 16 Mar. and 1 Apr. 1934.

94. On the centrality of Hornbeck in the formulation of American Far Eastern policy, see:

Castle Diary, entries for 26 May 1933; 7 Nov. 1933, and 29 May 1934; Oral History of Eugene Dooman (hereafter Dooman interview) on occupation of Japan, by Columbia University, May 1962, on microform at the Herbert Hoover Presidential Library, West Branch, Iowa, 98; Richard D. Burns, 'Stanley K. Hornbeck: The Diplomacy of the Open Door', in Burns and Bennett, eds, *Diplomats in Crisis*, 90–117; Russell D. Buhite, 'The Open Door in Perspective: Stanley K. Hornbeck and American Far Eastern Policy', in Merli and Wilson, eds, *Makers of American Diplomacy*, 431–58.

95. Nelson T. Johnson MSS (NTJ), Library of Congress, Washington, DC, Container 23, folder G-M, personal and confidential letter from Hornbeck to Johnson, 14 Feb. 1934.

96. NTJ papers, strictly confidential letter from Hornbeck to Johnson, 9 July 1934.

97. NTJ papers, copy of a letter dated 5 June sent from Hornbeck to Ray Atherton in London, copy sent by Hornbeck to Johnson on 9 July 1934.

98. *FRUS*, Vol. I, memo from Hornbeck to Hull, 31 Mar. 1934, 230–1.

99. Ibid.

100. FO 371/17597/A2966/1938/45, Admiralty and Foreign Office memo, 'Report by Admiral Little to NCM(35) (Ministerial Committee on London Naval Conference for 1935–36) on preparations for the 1935 Naval Conference', 12 Apr. 1934. The cruiser question was an old song for the two nations. See Roskill, *Naval Policy*, Vol. II, 286–9, 290–5, 300–17; Pelz, *Race to Pearl Harbor*, 119–22; Berg, 'Second London Naval Conference', 213.

101. The General Board of the USN was not in favour of smaller battleships carrying guns of less than 16 inches because of the lack of US bases in the Pacific and the lack of destructive power in the 14-inch guns. The General Board's view was that, if and when war broke out, and given the limited bases for repairs available to the United States, the maximum damage had to be inflicted on the enemy whenever the opportunity to inflict damage occurred, thus the need for the 16-inch guns. See RG 80, Proceedings and Hearings of the General Board of the US Navy, 1900–1950 (hereafter Proceedings and Hearings), National Archives, Washington, DC, 'Reduction in Displacement and Armament of Capital Ships', 31 Mar. 1931, Reel 21; 'Capital Ships', 8 Oct. 1935, Reel 22; 'Capital Ships', 14 Oct. 1935, Reel 22; 'Capital Ships', 22 Oct. 1935, Reel 22; and 'Capital Ships', 13 Dec. 1935, Reel 22.

102. FO 371/17597/A2966/1938/45, report by Little, 12 Apr. 1934.

103. FO 371/17597/A2966/1938/45, report by Craigie, 12 Apr. 1934.

104. FO 371/17597/A2966/1938/45, private and secret letter from Craigie to Lindsay, 17 Apr. 1934.

105. FDR–PSF, Confidential Files, Box 142, Folder, London Naval Conference 1934, letter from Davis to FDR, 23 Apr. 1934.

106. For details on the Amau Declaration see Dutton, *Simon*, 191–3; Crowley, *Japan's Quest for Autonomy*, 195–8; P.A. Reynolds, *British Foreign Policy in the Inter-war Years* (London, 1954), 92; S. Endicott, *Diplomacy and Enterprise*, 45–50, 66; Akagi, *Japan's Foreign Relations, 1542–1932*, 138–9; Nish, 'Japan in Britain's View, 1919–37', in Ian Nish, ed., *Anglo-Japanese Alienation, 1919–1952*, 42–3; Nish, *Japanese Foreign Policy*, 210–13, 216.

107. FDR–PSF, Box 142, Folder – London Naval Conference, 1934, letter from Bingham to FDR, 23 Apr. 1934.

108. CAB 29/147, Minutes of NCM(35), First Meeting, 16 Apr. 1934.

109. Ibid.

110. FO 371/17597/A4114/1938/45, memo from Sir Warren Fisher, 16 May 1934.

111. Ibid., Craigie minutes, 18 and 25 May 1934.

112. Until indicated, the following is based on ibid., draft memo from Vansittart to Fisher, undated for May 1934.

113. Ibid. For Admiralty support of FO see CAB 29/148, NCM(35)10, memo by CNS, 18 May 1934.

114. FO 371/17597/A4114/1938/45, draft memo, undated for May 1934.

115. Ibid. That sentence was omitted from the final copy sent off to Fisher.

116. CAB 29/148, memos for NCM(35), NCM(35)4, memo by the PM, 25 Apr. 1934.

117. Moffat Diary, entry for 26 Apr. 1934.

118. Moffat Diary, entry for 27 Apr. 1934.

119. See FO 371/17597/A4132/1938/45, record of conversation between Craigie and Atherton, 25 May 1934; FO 371/17597/A4136/1938/45, report from DNI, Vice-Admiral Dickens, 26 May 1934; FO 371/17597/A4538/1938/45, record of conversation between Atherton and Craigie, 1 June 1934; Moffat Diary, entry for 2 May 1934.

120. FO 371/17597/A4517/1938/45, FO memo on 'Preparations for the 1935 Naval Conference', written by Craigie, 1 May 1934. On the context for the situation, the Amau Declaration and Oil Monopoly problem, see Louis, *British Strategy in the Far East*, 222–3; Trotter, *Britain and East Asia*, 115–31; Lowe, *Britain in the Far East*, 148; Kennedy, '1935', 193–6.

121. FDR–PSF, Britain 1933–36, letter from Bingham to FDR, 1 May 1934.

122. FDR–PSF, Great Britain 1933–36, letter from Bingham to FDR, 8 May 1934; Hull Papers, Container 37, letter from Bingham to Hull, 23 July 1934.

123. FDR–PSF, Great Britain 1933–36, letter from Bingham to FDR, 8 May 1934.

124. Ibid.

125. *FRUS*, Vol. I, 1934, telegram from Bingham to Hull, 18 May 1934, 235–6. The Prime Minister and the FO had been urging the Cabinet to make some sort of gesture before the Americans lost interest in attending such a meeting. See FO 371/17597/A4517/1938/45, FO memo by Craigie, 1 May 1934.

126. FO 371/17597/A4282/1938/45, FO Minute by Craigie, 30 May 1934; *FRUS*, Vol. I, telegram from Hull to Ambassador in France (Straus) for Norman Davis, 24 May 1934; FO 371/17598/A4777/1938/45, personal and confidential note from Atherton to Craigie, 8 June 1934.

127. *FRUS*, Vol. I, telegram from Davis to Hull, 29 May 1934, 241–2; ibid., telegram from Davis to Hull, 2 June 1934, 244–5.

128. *FRUS*, Vol. I, telegram from Davis to Hull, 2 June 1934, 245–6.

129. Stimson Diary, entry for 17 May 1934.

130. Ibid.

131. Ibid.

132. FO 371/17598/A4969/1938/45, FO memo by Craigie, 13 June 1934; FO 371/17598/A4970/1938/45, FO memo by Craigie, 14 June 1934. Basic British naval requirements were finalized to a large extent along Admiralty lines at the end of May, see CAB 29/147, NCM(35), Minutes of the 5th Meeting, 31 May 1934. The committee would not meet again until mid-October.

133. FO 371/17598/A4792/1938/45, notes from Naval Attaché in Japan from Capt. King (ADM) to Craigie, 8 June 1934; FO 371/17598/A5182/1938/45, secret telegram from C.-in-C. China to First Sea Lord, 9 June, and minutes by Craigie, 19 June and Orde, 20 June; FO 371/18184/F2109/591/23, Vansittart minute, 24 Apr. 1934; FO 371/1718184/F6050/591/23, report of conversation between Simon and Japanese Ambassador Matsudaira, 8 Oct. 1934; *FRUS*, Vol. I, 1934, telegram from Bingham to Hull, 31 May 1934, 243; *FRUS*, Vol. I, 1934, telegram from Davis to Hull, 2 June 1934, 244–5. See also Pelz, *Race to Pearl Harbor*, 45–63, 104–18; Berg, 'Second London Naval Conference', 212–13; Kaufman, *Arms Control During the Pre-Nuclear Era*, 165–9.

134. On 23 May Hull had Williams Phillips send a 38-page memo produced by Stanley Hornbeck, on the problems in US–Japanese relations, to the President. The thrust of

Hornbeck's argument was similar to that of the British FO: that American foreign policy in the Far East would best be served by making commitments to no one power and that any changes in that position were to be made quietly and without any great announcement. Certainly, he argued, the United States had to hold the line in the Pacific against the Japanese, and, therefore, could not agree to any changes in the naval ratios that would make the USN weaker than the IJN. See FDR–PSF, Japan 1933–34, covering note from Hull dated 23 May, memo dated 5 Apr. 1934.

135. FO 371/17597/4595/1938/45, despatch from Lindsay to FO, 31 May, covering report by Naval Attaché Capt. A.R. Dewar, 29 May 1934.

136. Ibid., minute by Orde, 15 June; Wellesley minute, 16 June; and Simon minute, 19 June, all 1934.

137. FRUS, Vol. I, telegram from Davis to Hull, 12 June 1934, 247–8; Moffat Diary, entry for 14 June 1934.

138. FRUS, Vol. I, telegram from Hull to Davis, 13 June 1934, 248–9; ibid., telegram from Davis to Hull, 14 June 1934, 249–50.

139. FRUS, Vol. I, memorandum of trans-Atlantic telephone conversation between Davis, Hull and Roosevelt, 14 June 1934, 250–4; ibid., telegram from Hull to Bingham, 14 June 1934, 254–5; ibid., telegram from Davis to Hull (and FDR), 14 June 1934, 255. Davis sulked after being brought up short of his goal by the President and Hull. Hull liked Davis, but the manner in which Davis had tried to capture the centre stage at the expense of greater concerns in the process had disappointed the Secretary of State. See Moffat Diary, entry for 15 June 1934.

140. FDR–PSF, Britain 1933–36, Memo from Hull to FDR, 26 Apr. 1934.

141. Castle Diary, entry for 31 May 1934.

142. Moffat Diary, entry for 21 May 1934.

143. Moffat Diary, entry for 23 May 1934.

144. FRUS, Vol. I, telegram from Hull to Davis, 15 June 1934, 258–9.

145. FRUS, Vol. I, telegram from Davis to Hull, 18 June 1934, 259–61.

146. FO 371/17598/A5183/1938/45, FO minute on present position of naval conversations, by Craigie, 21 June 1934.

147. Ibid.

148. FRUS, Vol. I, telegram from Davis to Hull, 19 June 1934, 261–2. Davis was also worried about the British being able to read the delegation's confidential cables back to Washington.

149. FRUS, Vol. I, telegram from Davis to Hull and FDR, 19 June 1934, 262–4.

150. Ibid. Davis' cautious optimism about a successful technical agreement with the British was shared by Admiral Standley and Hull, see FRUS, Vol. I, telegram from Hull to Davis, 19 June 1934, 266.

151. FO 371/17598/A5183/1938/45, FO minute by Craigie, 21 June 1934; FRUS, Vol. I, telegram from Davis to Hull, 21 June 1934, 266–7.

152. Ibid.

153. Ibid.; FRUS, Vol. I, telegram from Bingham to Hull, 22 June 1934, 267–8; MacDonald Diary, entry for 20 June 1934.

154. MacDonald Diary, entry for 20 June 1934.

155. FO 37117598/A5384/1938/45, letter from MacDonald to Simon, 28 June 1934.

156. Ibid., minute by Craigie, 2 July 1934.

157. Bingham Diary, entry for 22 June 1934; FO371/17598/A5184/1938/45, FO minute, record of conversation between Craigie and Davis, 23 June 1934; FRUS, Vol. I, telegram from Davis to Hull, 25 June 1934, 272–4.

158. FO 371/17598/A5184/1938/45, FO minute, record of conversation between Craigie and Davis, 23 June 1934.

159. Ibid.
160. Ibid., letter from Craigie to Little, and Craigie minute, both 25 June 1934.
161. Ibid., Vansittart minute, 26 June 1934.
162. FO 371/17598/A5314/1938/45, most secret memo by Admiral Little, 28 June 1934.
163. Ibid.
164. Ibid.
165. Ibid., most secret covering note from C.B. Coxwell, First Lord's secretary, to Craigie, 28 June 1934. Copies of this memo were also sent to the Prime Minister and Foreign Secretary, but not to the Chancellor of the Exchequer. On talks with the Japanese, see Berg, 'Second London Naval Conference', 214–17; Kaufman, *Arms Control During the Pre-Nuclear Era*, 166–72; Pelz, *Race to Pearl Harbor*, 118–51.
166. FO 371/17598/A5314/1938/45, letters from Neville Butler (MacDonald's Private Secretary) to Coxwell, 29 June, and from H.J. Seymour (Simon's Private Secretary) to Coxwell, 3 July 1934; Baldwin Papers, 131, secret letter from Simon to Baldwin, 27 June 1934.
167. Bingham Diary, entry for 29 June 1934; ibid., entry for 16 July 1934; Hull Papers, Container 37, letter from Bingham to Hull, 23 July 1934.
168. *FRUS*, Vol. I, telegram from Davis to Hull, 25 June 1934, 272–4; ibid., telegram from Davis to Hull, 25 June 1934, 274–5.
169. *FRUS*, Vol. I, telegram from Hull to Davis, 26 June 1934, 276–7.
170. Ibid. The State Department had learned its lesson on how to handle the press during the World Economic Conference and over war debt debates. During the entire Naval Conference process, the State Department and the Foreign Office manipulated and starved the press until they were certain of a favourable outcome.
171. *FRUS*, Vol. I, telegram from FDR to Davis, 26 June 1934, 277–8; FO 371/17598/A5315/1938/45, secret note and copy of message from Butler to Seymour, 29 June 1934.
172. Ibid.
173. Moffat Diary, entry for 26 June 1934.
174. Moffat Diary, entry for 25 June 1934.
175. Moffat Diary, entry for 26 June 1934.
176. FO 371/17598/A5315/1938/45, secret telegram from MacDonald to FDR, 28 June 1934; *FRUS*, Vol. I, telegram from Davis to Hull, 27 June 1934, 281–2.
177. FO 371/17598/A5315/1938/45, Craigie and Vansittart minutes, both 6 July 1934.
178. *FRUS*, Vol. I, telegram from Davis to FDR and Hull, 28 June 1934, 282–4.
179. FO 371/17598/A5428/1938/45, record of conversation and minutes between Craigie and Matsudaira, 28 June 1934; FO 371/17598/A5430/1938/45, FO minute, 2 July 1934; FO 371/17598/A5511/1938/45, FO minute by Craigie on talks with French delegation, 5 July 1934; FO 371/17598/A5556/1938/45, FO minute, 4 July 1934; FO 371/17598/A5564/1938/45, NC(F) minutes of 1st–5th meetings with French naval delegation, 9 July 1934.
180. Moffat diary, entries for 27 and 28 June 1934.
181. *FRUS*, Vol. I, telegram from Hull to Davis, 29 June 1934, 284; ibid., telegram from Davis to Hull, 3 July 1934, 285–6; ibid., telegram from Davis to Hull, 3 June 1934, 286–7; ibid., telegram from Acting Secretary of State (Carr) to Davis, 3 July 1934, 287; ibid., telegram from Davis to Hull, 5 July 1934, 287–9; ibid., telegram from Hull to Davis, 6 July 1934; FO 371/17598/A5167/1938/45, NCM(35) 14, private and secret memo by Craigie on direction of naval conversations to date, 20 July 1934; ibid., telegram from Davis to Hull, 17 July 1934, 295–6; ibid., telegram from Hull to Davis, 17 July 1934, 296–7; ibid., telegram from Davis to Hull, 18 July 1934, 297–8.
182. Suspicions on both sides ran high about leaks to the press. These suspicions threatened to create a strained atmosphere for further negotiation, but, eventually, the State

Department was shown that the British were not responsible for certain leaks to the American press. The end result was an improvement in Anglo-American relations during the remainder of the talks because the Americans now believed in the honesty of the British. Atherton and Craigie worked closely together on this incident, helping to ensure that the matter did not become a major stumbling block to Anglo-American relations. See FO 371/17599/A5850/1938/45, record of conversation between Norman Davis and Sir John Simon, 4 July 1934; FO 371/17599/A5851/1938/45, FO memo by Sir V. Wellesley, 7 July 1934; FO 371/17599/A5852/1938/45, secret letter from Commander Clarke (CID) to Craigie, 9 July 1934; FO 371/17599/A5853/1938/45, FO memo by Craigie, 9 July 1934.

183. FO 371/17598/A5606/1938/45, FO memo by Craigie, 10 July, minute by Craigie, 11 July 1934.

184. Ibid., Vansittart minute, 12 July 1934; FO 371/17598/A5607/1938/45, Vansittart minute, 13 July 1934. Simon had read and approved of the final copy of the memo as well, see ibid., Seymour minute, 13 July 1934.

185. FO 371/17598/A5606/1938/45, letter from Craigie to Admiral Little, 10 July, and letter from Little to Craigie, 13 July 1934; FO 371/17599/A6144/1938/45, FO memo by Craigie, 25 July 1934. Vansittart thought the final draft an excellent statement of the British position, as did Sir John Simon, who wanted a copy for his own files. See FO 371/17599/A6144/1938/45, Vansittart and Simon minutes, both 25 July 1934. The final copy sent to the Americans is also in *FRUS*, Vol. I, enclosure in despatch from Atherton to Hull (and was sent on to White House), 27 July 1934, 299–303.

186. FO 371/17598/A5606/1938/45, record of conversation between Atherton and Craigie, 10 July 1934.

187. Ibid.

188. See notes 172 and 184 above.

189. FO 371/17598/A5606/1938/45, record of conversation, 11 July 1934.

190. *FRUS*, Vol. I, telegram from Davis to Hull, 17 July 1934, 295–6; FO 371/17599/A5854/1938/45, draft communiqué and Craigie minute, 16 July 1934; FO 371/17599/A5855/1938/45, drafts from Capt. Danckwerts (Plans Division, ADM) to Craigie, 17 July 1934; FO 371/17599/A5856/1938/45, letter from Norman Davis to Sir John Simon, 17 July 1934.

191. FO 371/17598/A5607/1938/45, record of conversation, 13 July 1934.

192. *FRUS*, Vol. I, telegram from Hull to Davis, 17 July 1934, 296–7; Davis Papers, letter from Moffat to Davis, 20 July 1934.

193. FO 371/17598/A5740/1938/45, despatch from Osborne (Washington Embassy), 17 July 1934; ibid., Craigie and Wellesley minutes, both 18 July 1934. According to Capt. A.R. Dewar, the RN Naval Attaché in Washington, the stage-managing of the press releases in London and declaration of support were keeping the talks from becoming an issue which the American press could savage at home. See FO 371/17599/A5915/1938/45, despatch from Naval Attaché, 23 July 1934.

194. FO 371/17599/A5966/1938/45, record of conversation between Atherton and Craigie, 18 July 1934.

195. Ibid., Baldwin minute, 19 July 1934. Baldwin was much better liked than Simon, and the British delegation and NCM knew this. They strove to use Baldwin during the naval talks with the Americans as much as possible in order to avoid having to overcome the Americans' distrust of Simon. Stimson had told Baldwin very frankly in July that the Roosevelt administration was sour on Simon and blamed him for the lack of progress in creating Anglo-American cooperation. See Stimson Diary, entries for 24, 25, and 26 July 1934. See also, Baldwin Papers, 131, letter from Tom Jones to Baldwin, 8 July 1934.

196. FO 371/17599/A5966/1938/45, Simon minute, 18 July 1934.

# 5

# The Development of Anglo-American Trust and the 1935 London Naval Conference (II)

The return of the American delegation to the United States signalled the beginning of the final clash between the Admiralty and Foreign Office against the Treasury in preparation for the renewed naval talks scheduled for October. A position had to be taken, once and for all, as to whether Japan's demand for parity would be either accepted or refused; a refusal which would mean having to work much closer with the Americans.

On the very day that Davis and his colleagues left for home, Hugh Wilson, the American representative to the Disarmament Conference in Geneva, called on Anthony Eden. Wilson told Eden that the Americans had information from Geneva that showed clearly that the Japanese would not participate in any technical committee at the Disarmament Conference, which led the Americans to believe that Tokyo would not agree to a new naval treaty in 1935.[1] Wilson relayed to Eden a message from Davis, repeating the latter's belief that the Japanese, if they demanded parity, would have to be the ones blamed for the failure of the conference. In order to ensure that this was the case, the United States and Britain needed to take a similar position during the conference talks. The message ended with Wilson repeating that the British were faced with two choices: either to renew the Anglo-Japanese alliance and suffer the consequences, or to try to establish an Anglo-American relationship. He did not think the latter likely, in a formal, public sense, but re-emphasized the need to make a joint effort that maintained as far as possible a full measure of Anglo-American cooperation. It was the cruiser tonnage issue (a 60 per cent increase) which was the fly in the ointment for the Americans, said Wilson.[2]

This message, along with a public announcement by the US Secretary of the Navy, Claude L. Swanson, for cuts in the treaty tonnages of between 10 per cent and 30 per cent, provoked an angry and hostile reaction from the Foreign Office. Craigie called the American arguments disingenuous at best. His view was that,

So far the main result of these tactics has been to make agreement more difficult not only with Japan but also with this country. Unfortunately Mr Norman Davis fancies himself as a diplomatic tactician while Mr Swanson fancies himself as a naval die-hard and this is the difficult combination with which we have to deal.[3]

Vansittart, who had been informed by Atherton that such a message from Davis was simply an American tactic to try to get the British to move closer to the US position, was, as usual, even more scathing in his assessment of events:

Unfortunately the American idea of tactics, which is one always inspired by their own internal politics, is not one which could conceivably be adopted by our Admiralty. And even if it were, it would be completely disingenuous – and very dangerous – for *us* to be talking of reduction, in view of the Admiralty minima. As to Mr Wilson's panacea, no sane person dreams of renewing the Anglo-Japanese alliance. As to America there is no question of closer relations. These *may* become possible when America realises that she must have a policy. Hitherto she has thought it possible to dispense with the inconvenience – indeed with the inconvenience of all but the most nebulous and smug thinking. Events will force her out of that already waning illusion, – events, not we. We meanwhile can only wait and try to steer a middle course, as regards America and Japan. Personally I do not think that the American politician's idea of tactics is going to be very helpful to 'a full measure of Anglo-American agreement'.[4]

The Foreign Secretary did not object to these views. However, other voices were still to be heard from.

Neville Chamberlain and Warren Fisher were attempting to bring the Treasury point of view into play once more.[5] On 3 August Fisher telephoned Commander Clark of the Cabinet Office to inform him that the Treasury took a dim view of the naval talks to date. It appeared that there had been no approved policy for the British delegation to follow during the preliminary discussions, said Fisher, who then proceeded to launch into another tirade on the need not to work with the Americans. Fisher then suggested that talks with the other powers in the autumn be delayed until after the recess, so that ministers would have time to consider Britain's naval policy.[6] Clark responded by, first, pointing out the fallacies underlying Fisher's assumptions concerning the British delegation's instructions.[7] Fisher, however, was clearly determined to pursue his line. It was obvious to Clark that the Treasury would make attempts to force a ministerial meeting or meetings after the recess in the hope that they might pressure British negotiators into adopting a policy more in accord with Chamberlain's and Fisher's ideas. Clark passed the Treasury view on to the Admiralty and Foreign Office so that Monsell and Simon were informed of the Treasury's attitude. Both ministers refused to contemplate a postponement.[8]

Craigie and the Admiralty were at that moment discussing the possibility of sending an emissary to Washington to speak to Roosevelt personally about the naval talks. Both were desperately anxious to keep the Americans happy and working towards some sort of agreement, but their views on how to go about doing so were at odds.[9] Craigie wanted to go to Washington himself, for he feared that without someone actually present to explain the British position, there was a chance that no understanding would be reached that autumn:

The recent Anglo-American conversations proved unsatisfactory for four principal reasons: 1. Mr Roosevelt, having only the haziest knowledge of the question, has hitherto looked upon it largely in terms of domestic politics and has consequently laid it down that he will be content with nothing less than an all-round percentage reduction. 2. His principal advisor on naval matters, Mr Swanson, is a type of die-hard big-navalist who believes in bluster and the big stick, and who has had the misfortune to sit for a generation in the United States Senate. 3. Mr Norman Davis is a politician who draws his main support from peace societies and goodwill organisations in the United States, and, as he said to me in a moment of candour, he could not afford to sign an agreement which provided for increases over existing Treaty figures; thus our case for cruiser increases will certainly not have gained in its presentation by Mr Norman Davis … 4. Mr Hull is what Americans call a 'poor fish', and there is no reason to believe he is friendly to this country. Mr Roosevelt personally would like good relations with this country, but he is surrounded by men who try to narrow what would normally be a broad vision in foreign affairs. In his hands is the key to this naval problem and, unless he can be won over first, the resumed conversations in the autumn are likely to fare no better than the last.[10]

Further, Craigie was worried about the possible damage that could be done to the negotiations because of the Treasury view of Anglo-American relations:

It is held in some quarters here that if the United States continues to be uncompromising we might reach some kind of naval understanding with the Japanese. This hope is in my humble opinion quite illusory and, in any case, such a course would be politically dangerous. If matters cannot be improved between the United States and ourselves Japan will have an unrivalled opportunity to fish in troubled waters – a pastime in which she has always shown herself most proficient.[11]

Vansittart thought that the personal touch would be useful, but was reluctant to let that touch be Craigie's, given that the American press would immediately suspect some sort of deal on naval issues was being struck.[12] However, the whole matter was abandoned after Chatfield protested against such an approach. He and other Admiralty planners feared that such tactics would antagonize and infuriate the US Navy, and, in particular, the General Board. If the US Navy were provoked in such a fashion, this could only lessen the chances of persuading US naval officials of any merit in the British position. Chatfield was particularly concerned that, if the US Navy was pushed to that point, it would then try to manipulate the Japanese into an even more anti-British position.[13] In the face of such Admiralty opposition, Craigie and Vansittart were agreeable to letting the matter die on the vine. The Admiralty and Foreign Office were working well together in their traditional roles as chief constructors and negotiators of British naval policy. However, both recognized that, once and for all, before the crucial October talks began, the Treasury demands for some sort of agreement with Japan had to be discredited.

The Japanese suggestion that they would be interested in a non-aggression pact with the British was seen as a hollow promise by both the Admiralty and the Foreign Office. Both departments saw the United States as a more important participant in terms of possible future strategic problems involving Britain in the Far East, if Britain were to retain any of its imperial position in that region. Japan was seen as being clearly an aggressive and dangerous power, and one that was not expected to compromise during the naval talks in 1935. It would welcome some sort of arrangement with the British, but, any such agreement would not protect Britain's Far Eastern interests from eventually falling to Japan. So, even though there was much doubt about the Americans formally cooperating with the British against the Japanese during a crisis, there was no doubt that cooperation with the Japanese over Far Eastern matters was not an acceptable option.[14] Still, the Treasury remained to be convinced.

The matter was brought to a head in August and September when Chamberlain pushed forward his idea of a non-aggression pact with Japan to Vansittart and Simon.[15] The Foreign Office, while understanding the need to keep the Japanese calm, would not accept any proposal that required cutting the Americans out of the agreement. Vansittart pointed out to Sir John that there was no use expecting the Japanese to agree to anything less than parity with the British and the Americans. Reports from Sir Robert Clive, the British Ambassador in Tokyo, persuaded the PUS that no Japanese delegation, or government, would risk their very lives by agreeing to anything less. It was Vansittart's belief that, because of those great pressures being put on the Japanese government by militarists, the probability of Japan signing an extension of the 1930 London Naval agreement in 1935 was 'black in the extreme'.[16] Simon agreed. But, he hoped to find some sort of multiparty solution, or at least to extract a voluntary declaration by the Japanese not to build above the London Treaty limits. The Foreign Secretary asked Vansittart and Craigie what they thought of such a gentleman's agreement.[17] As for the non-aggression pact, Simon asked the Foreign Office to provide reasons for its rejection. If the recognition of Manchukuo or giving Japan a free hand in China was the price, then what were the consequences? Sir John wanted the Department's recommendations on paper quickly in order that a position could be taken, for he was sure that the pressures to revive some vestiges of the old Anglo-Japanese alliance would be great.[18]

Vansittart sought out the views of the American and Far Eastern Departments. His own opinion was that the Admiralty and the Americans would not be satisfied with any voluntary declaration by Japan. Neither was willing to see any increase in Japan's ratio, and any Japanese minister who failed to get a significant increase would be assassinated. Therefore, a vicious circle was sure to ensue and it was unlikely that a voluntary declaration could really mean anything.[19] As for the non-aggression pact, Vansittart pointed out that a similar offer had already been made to the Americans, who had unhesitatingly rejected it to a chorus of hostile press commentary as to whether the Japanese thought the Americans were fools. He felt:

> It would surely be rather difficult for us (quite apart from the merits of the case) to accept what the United States have refused without a very serious breach with the United States, who, moreover, I should say were entirely justified in their scepticism, for I do not see what kind of pact of non-aggression the Japanese Government could offer to us which would not be open to all the criticism directed at the idea from America. Surely a pact of non-aggression concluded merely between us and the Dominions on the one side, and the Japanese on the other, or even if it were so stretched as to make it tripartite, bringing in the United States as well, would merely give Japan a free hand for aggression in China, unless the case of China were very carefully and specifically covered; and would any Japanese Government allow us or the Americans so to cover the case of China? The Americans have clearly thought that the Japanese Government would not, and I should say that on the face of things they were clearly right.[20]

Craigie sided with Simon on the idea of a voluntary declaration. The former believed that such a declaration would allow the moderate elements in Japan to save face, thereby gaining the momentum necessary to overcome the military extremists who wanted no treaty at all. In his view, from the point of view of Anglo-Japanese relations, some agreement, even if it had no basis in reality, was better than no agreement. However, he doubted whether such camouflage was likely to deter Japan in its quest to attain parity with the United States. Craigie floated the idea of a naval agreement with Japan and France, leaving the Americans to build what they wished. He did not think that the Admiralty would support such a motion, and the risks to future Anglo-American relations were obvious. As for the non-aggression pact, Craigie considered any imaginable agreement to be nothing more than political camouflage, although he was unwilling to condemn the idea forcefully.[21]

The Far Eastern Department had no such qualms about pointing out the formidable price that would have to be paid to obtain an Anglo-Japanese non-aggression pact. Nor did Charles Orde shy away from commenting directly against the likelihood of Japan's honouring such an understanding in any fashion that would safeguard Britain's Far Eastern Empire in the long term.[22] He directed policy-makers to refer to the complete estimate of the situation in the Far East that had been presented to Cabinet the previous March, and how the objections to any bilateral agreement with Japan had outweighed the factors in its favour.[23] Orde emphasized that he now felt even more strongly that these views were correct. He agreed with Vansittart that the United States and its attitude towards such a pact were a most important consideration, and, given that the Americans had rejected the Japanese offer, any British acceptance would be a great shock to Anglo-American relations. There was no evidence of Japan's being willing to keep out of Chinese affairs. Any agreement with Japan would create resentment in China against the British, who were looked on as the primary brake against Japanese aggression. The Soviet Union would not approve of such a pact, for it would see the pact as being an encouragement to Japan to turn against Moscow. The Netherlands East Indies and their protection was a serious issue, said Orde, as was the opposition that was certain to arise in some Dominions. Overall, he considered that a tripartite pact between Japan, Britain and the United States might be something to consider, but even then, Britain's imperial and European security concerns would make such an agreement almost impossible. It was an idea not even worth considering if the Americans were not willing to participate. As for the voluntary declaration by Japan, the Far Eastern Department had the greatest doubts as to whether the Japanese civilians in government could sell such a plan to the navy and army.[24] In fact, neither department was overly confident that either option could be realized. Both also recognized that the American attitude towards such proposals was a key as to how they should respond.

Vansittart objected to Craigie's 'soft' analysis of the problem, arguing that the American Department did not have a full sense of the security issues at stake. Further, it was his own belief that no Japanese statesman could afford to tie his hands over the naval status quo, no matter how camouflaged.[25] Orde's views, and their recognition of the multifaceted danger involved, were fully supported by Vansittart and Sir George A. Mounsey, Assistant Under-Secretary of State and a key advisor on Far Eastern issues.[26] Orde's position and arguments were those which Vansittart presented to Simon. The PUS petitioned the Foreign Secretary to acknowledge the logical superiority of avoiding either a pact or a voluntary declaration and to reaffirm his conclusion that 'a bilateral pact is out of the question; that a tripartite one is not only superfluous but dangerous'. The PUS strongly recommended that Simon modify the position that he was developing for presentation to the Cabinet on Anglo-Japanese relations, and to express the Foreign Office's views to the Chancellor of the Exchequer, who had been lobbying Vansittart vigorously the whole time to adopt a pro-Japan stance. It was also time, he ventured, for the Admiralty to put forward their views on what they thought a voluntary declaration from Japan was worth.[27]

The Far Eastern Department's position gained momentum steadily through-out September. The Marquess of Lothian, Philip Kerr, an independent Liberal MP, planned to go to the United States in the near future. An avid supporter of closer Anglo-American relations, Lothian petitioned the Foreign Office for their opinion, as it was his intention to bring these matters up with the US government, indeed the President himself, when he was in the United States. Lothian argued that there were three choices open to the British as far as their Far Eastern policy and the upcoming naval talks were concerned. At the 1935 Conference, Britain could decide either to go it alone and build a navy to take on all comers, to rekindle the Anglo-Japanese alliance by acknowledging Japan's right to naval parity with the United States, or to present a common front against Japan's demands and move towards better cooperation and an understanding with them. Lothian left no doubt that it was his view that a common policy or closer relations with the Americans was the way to go.[28] His views on the need for closer Anglo-American relations against Japan at the next set of naval talks also sparked the Foreign Office into demanding that a solid policy towards those talks and Britain's attitude towards Japan and the United States be established.

Vansittart was sceptical of the ease with which Lothian thought the Americans could be brought into an agreement satisfactory to both the Admiralty and the US Navy and which also acknowledged each nation's over-all security needs.[29] His suspicions of Roosevelt and the Americans in general did not allow the PUS to expect much success in reaching a compromise with them. It was his view that Britain would have to go it alone in the Far East. Nevertheless, Vansittart approved of Lothian's talking to Roosevelt and doing some 'very plain speaking' to the Americans about what were Britain's global strategic concerns.[30]

Craigie was impressed by the clarity that Lothian's memorandum brought to the policy-making process at such a critical time. He agreed that it was absolutely essential that the government formulate some definite policy at once, before the American and Japanese delegations arrived.[31] To him, the choices were quite clear: was Britain going to attempt to achieve some form of Anglo-American cooperation, or was it going to align with Japan and 'throw up the sponge' in the Far East? He saw the political issues surrounding the upcoming talks as being:

> (a) even assuming that we shall not be prepared in the future to fight Japan either for the integrity of China or for the protection of our special rights

there (a large assumption), will it not encourage Japan to embark on further aggression in China if she detects a readiness in this country to compromise on the relative sizes of the British and Japanese navies? (b) since *l'appétit vient en mangeant,* is it not reasonable to suppose that Japan, if thus encouraged to feed on China, would eventually turn hungry eyes upon British possessions in the Pacific? If the answer to both questions is in the affirmative, then the forthcoming naval discussions are likely to be the turning point in our future policy in the Pacific; and immense difficulties in the future may be avoided by the adoption now – in cooperation with the United States – of a firm attitude towards a Japanese claim to change the existing relationship of the naval forces of the British Empire, the United States and Japan. If we fail to face firmly this beginning of overt naval aggression, Japan will be quick to read the omen.[32]

Craigie steadfastly demanded that the Treasury policy of aiding and abetting Japan against the United States be dealt with in Cabinet before the delegates arrived and the issue was brought to a head. If a pro-US cooperation position was agreed to, then the Admiralty would also have to decide as to whether it could reach some accommodation with the US Navy on quantitative and qualitative issues related to the cruiser and capital ships debates. To muddle between those two choices was unacceptable, as such a course held perils of its own.[33] A decision had to be made: either go with the United States or go against it.

Orde and the Far Eastern Department supported Craigie's demand for a decision, pointing out that Japan's word on protecting and maintaining the Open Door in China and Chinese integrity was worthless in the light of Japanese actions that had unashamedly torn up the Nine Power Treaty.[34] To bow to the Japanese meant not only having to deal with Japan a few years down the road again, but, 'If we show fear we shall have not only Japan but China attacking our interests and we shall be driven out of the Far East … She [Japan] is full of self-confidence at present, but she still has to settle with Russia … I feel sure that weakness towards her will lead to worse things than firmness …'[35] Mounsey and Vansittart agreed with Craigie, believing that a solid and definite policy was required.[36] Vansittart was determined, however, to get the Americans to allow the British a naval increase 'before we begin bearding the Japanese for or with them'.[37]

The PUS was deeply disillusioned by what he saw as a steady and rapid decline in Anglo-American relations. Information from Washington told Vansittart that many in the State Department, including William Phillips, thought Anglo-American relations were deteriorating and that Britain was responsible for this lack of cooperative spirit. Vansittart blamed a lack of plain speaking on the part of the British government for this turn of events. However, although he professed to being as friendly as ever towards the United States, he also believed that the American public and Congress on the whole were too stupid and self-righteous to take direct criticism and objections well.[38] Vansittart's views were held in response to the reported attitude of Phillips, who was said to have lamented the fact that 'there was no longer that automatic consultation and co-operation between the two governments which had existed in the past ...' and gone on to describe the ideal situation as one in which the United States and Great Britain kept 'the peace hand in hand and so firmly and formidably that there would be none to say them nay. And it was a lack of that cooperation that allowed chaos.'[39] Vansittart agreed with Phillips' sentiment, but firmly rejected any responsibility for the lack of that cooperative spirit. Consideration of past Anglo-American difficulties – during the First World War; over the formation and abandonment of the League of Nations; Britain's abandonment of the Anglo-Japanese Alliance for the Americans; the war debt; the Irish issue; naval disarmament; the failed Economic Conference; liquor smuggling – resulted, in Vansittart's mind, to a net debt owed by the Americans, who had consistently been treated with lenience and tolerance by the British. Vansittart was adamant that it was time for the Americans 'to undertake initiatives and gestures ...' if any progress was to be made. Worried about the worsening situation in Europe and the gloomy conditions facing the empire in the Far East, Vansittart told Lindsay that he was most concerned about the feeling of disillusionment with the United States that was permeating the world. This sense of disillusionment was brought on by the American tendency to cut and run from their responsibilities in the world: Cuba, the Philippines, Haiti, and most important, the Far East. The PUS drew the analogy that, 'the United States would not be a safe companion for "tiger-shooting"; and I for one should like a higher howdah if not a "bigger and better elephant"'. Returning to his favourite obsession (Germany), Vansittart felt that this was a most unfortunate condition for Britain to find itself in. With Britain unable to face a war with Germany and Japan, it was this American reluctance to assume a larger world role that was causing a cry in some British quarters for a return to the Anglo-Japanese Alliance. If the United States stepped forward at the naval talks, then something could be done, but Vansittart doubted whether that was likely to occur. Sharing his darkest fears of the strategic situation facing the British Empire, Vansittart told Lindsay that Britain was not nearly as strong as it had been in 1914, largely due to the possibility of having to fight a two-front war separated by such great distances. He then asked Lindsay for his help and guidance to deal with the pressures being brought to bear on the Foreign Office by the Treasury:

> Many influential people here are beginning to ask insistently whether, in circumstances which America does not share, we can afford to neglect any opportunity of reinsuring in the Far East till the muttering German storm

has burst or blown over. (We *can* make it blow over if we are wise and determined enough.) Can we, they ask and are difficult to answer, run this great risk for the American will o' the wisp that has given, and is giving, equally plain intimations of leaving us in the lurch in case of need. But the difficulty, as I see it, will be that if the answer is to be that we cannot run the risk, then this answer however translated must involve some damage, unreasonably perhaps but none the less certainly, to Anglo-American relations. Of course there would be another answer in a different world; namely that we could afford the risk if we could count on the United States. But we must take the world as we find it, and that answer just does not seem to be practical politics.

While Vansittart waited for Lindsay's help, Sir John Simon took up the battle with the Treasury in Cabinet. Afraid to challenge the powerful Chancellor of the Exchequer too forcefully, Simon agreed that looking into the matter of finding some sort of non-aggression agreement with the Japanese was useful. He cautioned repeatedly, however, that the likelihood of being able to find the political and strategic grounds for making such a bilateral agreement was not promising.[40] Thus, a compromise was struck between the Foreign Office and Treasury in the form of a joint position paper on relations with Japan, to be prepared for Cabinet by Chamberlain and Simon. The final victory of Foreign Office opposition to the Treasury desire for closer Anglo-Japanese relations over naval matters was reflected in that joint memorandum, which clearly stated the long-term need for better relations with the United States, rather than with Japan, if Britain's Far Eastern position was to have any hope of being maintained.[41] The net result of the deadlock between the two departments was two-fold. First, there was the eventual formation of a Cabinet Committee on Political and Economic Relations with Japan (on 13 February 1935), a body then used to explore the validity of the Treasury and industrialists' views of creating closer economic ties with Japan.[42] Second, no absolute recommendation for or against moving closer to either the Japanese or Americans was issued from Cabinet or the Ministerial Committee on the London Naval Conference (NCM) before the autumn session began. The Foreign Office had gained more time to fend off any further serious Treasury interference and to allow the Foreign Office and Admiralty to continue to make naval policy for the upcoming talks.[43]

By the first week of October, just before the naval talks were to resume, Vansittart received Lindsay's views on the state of Anglo-American relations and where his reading of the diplomatic tea leaves indicated they were heading. First, the Ambassador told his friend that William Phillips' comments were not petulant, but lachrymose. Phillips and others in the State Department were saddened by the deterioration of relations between the two countries. It was a regrettable circumstance that most in the department wished to remedy. But, it was a delicate situation, balancing public opinion and executive desires. Phillips was concerned not so much with the formal idea of cooperation, reported Lindsay, but more with a desire to ensure that an intimacy of relations, an informal understanding of each nation's needs and points of view, remained a viable part of the Anglo-American diplomatic relationship. He recognized, as did Lindsay, that cooperation could not exist between England and the United States as it did between England and France, but that some sort of relationship was possible.[44]

Lindsay then moved to his assessment of Anglo-American relations. In that analysis he revealed a masterful understanding of the American nation and its government. These views are worth looking at in depth, as they formed the foundation for the Foreign Office's views of the United States during this critical period, and, indeed, well after:

> it is over sanguine to expect the United States ever to commit itself to any engagement with another Power, and perhaps even to cooperate in any important field, until its vital interests are affected; and that moment will never come till the eleventh hour has struck. For this there are a whole series of inexorable reasons – first geographical and political remoteness. Even in the Far East she can truly point out that our interests are greater than hers; in Europe she is normally not directly interested at all, and only becomes interested, indirectly, when war breaks out, i.e. in the fact of war rather than in its causes. Next, she is a vast country that moves only with almost incredible slowness … And finally, of course her policy is selfish, narrowly selfish, perhaps even more so than ours. And yet we must not reproach her too much for her stand-off attitude and her refusal to commit herself. Don't we do the same by Europe? Is it not freely said that if we had been able before 1914 to take a definite line, the last war would never have come about? And are not the statesmen of Europe at this very moment saying that by a definite commitment England may yet prevent the next war? Of course we can't do it, even if we didn't think it inadvisable; nor can America, a fortiori. Lay this maxim to heart; that in any war, in which America is destined not to remain neutral, she will be the last to come in; and the cause which she espouses will win the victory. The above maxim is almost susceptible of definite proof – let me lay down another which is more based on faith; 50 per cent of the population and 90 per cent of the governing class of America are of British stock, and are proud of it, and this fact, if ever America ceases to be neutral in a war, will ensure that, though she may postpone her decision till the eleventh hour and the fifty-fifth minute, she will in the end flop down on the English side. Is it not also a historic fact that owing to some deep immanent compulsion of public opinion, England has never been able long to pursue a policy antagonistic to America? Therefore I say, foam at the mouth and furiously

rage (as I myself frequently do) as much as you like, but you will be wiser to pull yourself together and be patient once again. This Japanese flirtation, or reassurance, which you are about to embark on, I find it difficult to believe that you or anyone in the Foreign Office can really desire it, but I suppose it must come, because there is so much mere rotten logic to support it. I'm afraid it's too much to hope that the Japanese in their arrogance will decline the overture. Rather we must expect that they will respond, but mainly to split us off from America. This is not basis for a pleasant flirtation and it must inevitably come to grief. We shall have a very stormy time with America, possibly amounting to great danger; and we shall finally try to crawl back. It will be up to you to see that we don't go too far with Japan, and that we don't postpone our crawl back till it is too late.[45]

Lindsay's message was insightful and clear: siding with the Japanese at the naval talks would imperil the future of the British Empire. It remained to be seen how such advice would be received.

American policy-makers also used the summer respite to assess the overall strategic situation facing them in the Far East and tried to decide whether they could trust the British against the Japanese. Davis reassured Roosevelt, that, in spite of rumours circulating that there was the possibility of the British making a deal with the Japanese, such was not the case.[46] Faith in the British was also being pronounced in the State Department, where there was a growing sense of confidence that the British were most unlikely to return to the Anglo-Japanese Alliance. If such a deal were struck, then Britain would be seen in American eyes as having performed an act of double-dealing 'unequalled for a very long time'.[47] Reports from Atherton in London confirmed those beliefs. Atherton, citing a number of well-connected sources in the government and in British society, reported that the British government was not happy with the way it had handled the talks with the Americans that spring. The British were coming to the realization that it would not be practical to do a deal with the Japanese and thus would be more willing to work with the Americans later in the autumn.[48] Bingham gave a similar view to Cordell Hull:

The present British attitude is the result of several factors: Lack of real leadership in the government itself; pressure from the Admiralty; narrow-mindedness among some of the old Conservatives; determination by some of the younger Conservatives to run the show themselves in their own way. In addition (1) they base their calculations on the assurance that they are in no danger of armed aggression from us, and (2) that they do not want to irritate Japan until their Singapore base is finished; and there is a better outlook in Europe; and (3) that their chief danger is in Europe itself ... They would, of course, jump at an armed alliance with us, but, knowing that is wholly impracticable, they have concluded that they must have a military establishment large enough to enable them to handle the situation alone, either in Europe or in the Far East … In the end they will need us worse than we shall ever need them. In the end they will come to us in a frame of mind that will enable us to deal with them on a basis safe and satisfactory to ourselves, and which will make for peace.[49]

As well, talks between Lindsay and members of the State Department all pointed towards the British moving towards the American camp.[50] Expectations that Great Britain would agree to form a united front against Japan at the talks were increasing as State Department and US Navy officials met to make final preparations for the American delegation's move back across the Atlantic. The personalities on that mission would be critical for the outcome of the talks.

Davis' petitioning for Admiral Standley to go to London in October had been rewarded. The CNO would be the chief naval advisor to the American team, able to speak with great authority on building programmes and questions concerning the strategic vision and direction of the US Navy.[51] His lack of anti-British sentiment was also sure to be a helpful factor in negotiations over capital ship qualities and cruiser quantities.[52] At a high-level meeting of Hull, Phillips, Hornbeck, Standley, Moffat and others, called to decide the American position going into the next round of naval talks, the CNO and Stanley Hornbeck led the others in a tour of the United States' strategic realities in the Far East. Standley, in response to questions about how the United States' proposed withdrawal from the Philippines was weakening its Far Eastern position in the eyes of other powers, such as Britain, told the gathering that

> our Philippine policy had greater effects diplomatically than strategically. Diplomatically, it was causing Powers in the Far East to realign their policies and re-examine their situations. Strategically, however, he felt that the force of our fleet would not be affected. In the last analysis, the strength of our fleet depended on our policy in the Orient. If we desire to give adequate support to the policies which we have been following in the past, such as the Open Door, the 9-Power Treaty, the Kellogg Pact, et cetera, then we must possess adequate naval force. If we were going to back down, throw over the rights of trade, et cetera, then we might as well do so now when we were not challenged than at some later date when we might be challenged.[53]

He reminded the meeting that talks with the British had been kept at a general level and thus there was still hope of having some sort of compromise struck. In fact, the US Navy appeared to see the British desire for a naval increase as a useful precedent for their own forces, and, thus, one that could be, if not supported, at least not disparaged too forcefully. The Assistant Secretary of the

185

Navy, Henry L. Roosevelt, reminded everyone that the President's instructions were clear: no agreement that did not involve an actual reduction in armaments could be agreed to, and all the British proposals to date meant an increase. The naval officers, however, countered by arguing that it was their position that an agreement with the British could be found that would not involve an actual increase in tonnage. As no one at the table was willing to give the Japanese a higher ratio, Standley pushed home the US Navy argument that it could not allow Japan to catch up in size: 'The utmost that we could do would be to make it difficult for the average man to compute but the present difference of strength between our fleet and the Japanese fleet must be maintained at all cost.'[54] Without such strength, the United States would not be able to exercise any influence in the Far East.

Hornbeck supported Standley fully, repeating his calls for a tough stance against Japan, backed up by naval expansion. He also acknowledged the political realities that faced the British in the Far East and the fact that such a circumstance could lead them to have to make a deal with the Japanese over the recognition of Manchuria in exchange for promises from Japan not to advance any further into the Southern Pacific. He did not believe, however, that the British would do so. This was based on broad strategic analysis. An Anglo-Japanese agreement might allow a Soviet–Japanese collision to occur, the result of which, if there were a Japanese victory, would be that an even more powerful Japan could then turn on Britain without having to worry about any Anglo-Soviet alignment. On the other hand, a Soviet victory would allow Moscow to have even greater influence in China, another risk the British were unwilling to take.[55] Overall, the consensus of opinion that emerged from the meeting was that the United States, and particularly its navy,

> could in no sense give up such policies and that a definite indication that we had abandoned any intention of using force for their maintenance would be viewed by all Oriental countries as the removal of an obstacle to further aggression in the Far East on the part of those so disposed. It was further the consensus that Japan's policy was definitely to continue its aims at dominating Eastern Asia. In these plans she is being held up at present by the United States and similarly by Great Britain. It was not felt, however, that she would give up her long-term ambitions and would seek every occasion to press them further.[56]

Clearly, US naval policy needed a helping hand from the outside, to allow it to solve the dilemma in which it found itself. On the one side, were the President's demands for a reduction; on the other, the desires of the Navy and State Department for a strong navy to block Japanese expansion. Only if the British presented some sort of face-saving compromise, or if the full weight of any new construction could be blamed squarely on the Japanese, could a solution be found that satisfied both groups.

Lothian arrived in Washington in early October, just as the American and Japanese delegations were leaving for London.[57] He discussed the British Far Eastern situation with President Roosevelt and members of the State Department. In his meeting with the President, on 10 October, Lothian outlined the strategic options available to the British in the Far East. He pointed out the changed circumstances that now existed because of an imperialistic Japan, a resurgent Germany and a possibly hostile Italy, and told Roosevelt that Britain could not now denude its home oceans to send a fleet to the Far East. That strategic reality meant that Britain had a limited number of options concerning how to safeguard the Far Eastern regions of its empire. Those alternatives (Lothian's 'frontline views') were to build a Far Eastern fleet and base it in Singapore; to have a definite understanding with the United States on a common approach to the region; or, to come to terms with the Japanese in a replay of the 1902 Anglo-Japanese Alliance.[58]

Roosevelt responded, telling Lothian that anything in the nature of a definite commitment on the part of the United States was impossible. He added that,

> even if an individual President like himself entered into an informal understanding which might be effective during his tenure of power, no one could guarantee that the successor would take the same view. The cooperation between the United States and Great Britain would have to rest on the fundamental identity of their interests and ideals.

As for Lothian's points about the uncertainty of the situation in the Far East and Britain's fear that it might find the Empire alone and at war in that region, Roosevelt stated:

> in no circumstances would he agree to Japanese parity; that if Japan insisted on parity and denounced the Treaties he would ask Congress for 500 million dollars for naval purposes, and he added that he would have no difficulty in getting it. He said that Norman Davis had instructions not to use threats but to make this clear to the British Government in London. The President spent some time in setting forth his view of Japanese policy. He had no illusions about it. They were pursuing a very long-distance programme of imperialist expansion in Asia and would use with vigour but discretion the ordinary tactics of power diplomacy. He agreed with me that the immediate object of their diplomacy was to attain such a strategic position in the Pacific, either by means of parity or by means of new bases in the islands or China, or both, as to make it impossible for the United States or Great Britain to interfere with their Asiatic designs. He said that much the best way of dealing with the situation would be for Great Britain and the United States to take firmly the same line. If this were so the Japanese would face the facts and agreement might

be possible, possibly under a formula which was based on 'security' rather than ratios … He evidently did not think that in practice it would be possible for Great Britain to come to terms with Japan in her present temper.

When questioned as to whether the United States would abandon the Philippines and the naval bases there, and what the United States' Far Eastern attitude was, Roosevelt told Lothian:

He said not for ten years but that at the end of ten years it was possible and even probable. So far as the relations between the United States and Great Britain were concerned he did not see why each side should not build the types of ships which suited themselves in friendly consultation. The essence of Anglo-American cooperation was agreement on political objectives rather than on technical questions. He ended the interview by saying emphatically that we ought to stand by the principle of sanctity of treaties, that the war of 1914 had been largely fought on that issue …

The President's message appeared to give a lead in the direction of allowing Britain to build the navy it felt necessary to fulfill its security commitments. And, while it did not give a formal promise of alliance with Britain over Far Eastern matters, Roosevelt was committed to keeping American interests in the region and not scuttling immediately.

While on his tour of the United States, Lothian also met and talked to important State Department people, such as Henry Stimson, who had returned from his European excursion, and William Phillips. Stimson agreed that it was vital for the United States and Great Britain to work together on Far Eastern matters and especially on naval issues. Talks with Lothian had convinced Stimson and Davis that many in the British Cabinet, particularly Stanley Baldwin and Anthony Eden, were behind the idea of a firm commitment from Britain to cooperate with the United States in Far Eastern matters and that that school of thought was winning ascendancy within Cabinet.[59] With Phillips, Lothian was also direct. He told the Under-Secretary that the British needed American help in the Far East because Britain could not exert any effective military power against Japan. The United States could take on that area with its navy and allow Britain to continue to carry the bulk of the responsibility for European and Middle Eastern security. As for the ability and foreign policy vision of Neville Chamberlain, Lothian classified the Chancellor of the Exchequer as representing 'a purely local point of view; he was not internationally minded and, although a brilliant man, could not be counted upon to favor cooperation with the United States'.[60]

The net result of Lothian's mission was to obtain a clearer statement by the President on the United States' Far Eastern policy, a signal from Roosevelt that Britain's naval expansion would not be fought with any great conviction so long as Britain did not make a deal with Japan; and, to give reassurance to the State Department that the move towards an Anglo-Japanese agreement was not gaining support in the British policy-making elite. The timing of the visit was fortunate, for now, with these new insights and information, the British and American camps could engage in the final stages of deciding whether a naval agreement between the two would be possible. A naval agreement in 1935 would signal the beginning of an informal programme of cooperation between the United States and Great Britain to try to limit Japan's expansion.

Preparations for such talks were at full speed in London. Craigie was not hopeful that the Japanese delegation to the talks would prove able to provide the material necessary to create a tripartite agreement. The appointment of Admiral Yamamoto as the head of the delegation was seen as 'a very remarkable choice', given the Admiral's personality and attitude towards Great Britain. However, to Craigie's mind there had probably been very little competition for such an unattractive appointment.[61] Still, the British and Japanese representatives, often Simon and Matsudaira, went through the motions of civilized discourse, meeting in mid-October to see if a common ground could be found.[62] British concerns centred around the question of whether the Americans would be willing to cooperate in the setting up of a tripartite or a simultaneous bilateral agreement between the two Western powers and Japan, possibly also with China involved. Craigie saw the possibility of getting American assent for such action as being a formidable task, but a tripartite arrangement was the only one which could satisfy all of Britain's strategic need.[63] The Far Eastern Department's experts on China, Sir John Pratt, Orde and Victor Wellesley, all voiced their doubts as to the practicability of expecting the Americans to go so far. To do so would be an act which would signal the end of the Open Door policy in China, as well as amount to the recognition of Manchukuo.[64] Neither was thought acceptable, either to the United States, or to China. Pratt further argued that making any deal with Japan would weaken Britain in the Far East, and emphasized the disastrous effect such a pact would have on Sino-British relations:

> As regards our prestige we should to some extent be covered if America joined us in accepting this undertaking from Japan, but if, as seems more likely, America were to refuse and we alone accepted it, the shock to our prestige and to our whole position in the Far East would be more immediate and greater. The Chinese would not look for any real help from America, whose stake in China is comparatively small and they would still think that their only course was to placate Japan. They would however feel with great bitterness that it was we who had delivered them into the hands of the enemy; and they would believe that any necessary placating of Japan might justly and with impunity be effected at our expense ... I do not myself see any way out of this difficulty.[65]

189

So, while the British policy-makers struggled over their choice, Norman Davis and the US delegation waited and watched in the wings to see whether the British would indeed try to reach some agreement with the Japanese.

Simon summoned Davis to his office on 18 October to discuss the Japanese position. The Secretary of State reported that there was still no sign that the Japanese were willing to compromise on the ratio question. Davis told Simon that it was his hope that trilateral, rather than bilateral, talks could begin soon. Davis' request for three-way discussions was a reflection of his suspicion that the British would try to further their position with the Japanese by painting the Americans as the reason why approval for a change in ratios could not be obtained.[66] By the 25th of that month, the two Western powers were once again sharing information on Japanese proposals and attempting to coordinate their response to their demands. When MacDonald and Simon met with Davis and Atherton that morning, both parties agreed that neither could accept the Japanese position. The Prime Minister would not allow Japan to hold Britain by the throat while it increased its forces.[67] Simon hoped that, when the Japanese ran into a solid opposition of American and British disapproval, they would soften their stand and try to find some 'gentleman's agreement' or agree to some meaningless general statement. MacDonald suggested that the Japanese delegation be questioned closely on technical proposals and allowed to try to develop their ideas further before Britain and the United States made a formal refusal. In the meantime, while the Japanese were kept talking in committees, Simon inquired whether, after another meeting with the Japanese, the Americans would be willing to have a meeting of the full British and American delegations, at which time the two would resume the discussions begun in the summer. Davis agreed, and was supported in his action by the State Department. Both he and the Department were anxious to ensure a solid opposition to the Japanese. However, both were also aware that such a cooperative gesture would have to be made carefully, so as to not evoke a return to discussions over the technical differences existing between the two navies' positions.[68] Davis planned to deal with that potential stumbling block by telling MacDonald that the United States still favoured a net reduction in total tonnage and would not agree willingly to an increase in total tonnage. He recognized, however, 'in agreement with Standley, that if we could agree upon a common position with regards to the issues raised by Japan there was a possibility of reaching an agreement, within the limits imposed upon us, for an increase in cruiser tonnage provided any such increase could be offset by an equal if not greater decrease in other categories'.[69] The need for the United States and the British Empire to find common ground was becoming increasingly important, as Japan grew less and less concerned with observing the Washington Treaty system.

On the 29th, the American delegation met with MacDonald, Simon, Monsell and Chatfield to begin working out an acceptable understanding regarding

Anglo-American naval relations and the Far East. Davis told MacDonald that there now seemed very little to gain worrying over the technical details of a treaty which the Japanese were not going to sign. Both sides then shared the information gained from their experiences with the Japanese delegation, in an attempt to ensure that both parties were working from the same page.[70] Both MacDonald and Davis desired the exploration of all possible alternatives with the Japanese, within reason. Davis was sure of the anxiety the British felt over the Japanese position. MacDonald told him that he had come to the conclusion, however, that Britain had only two options: to build a fleet of a size sufficient to defend the empire's far-flung responsibilities and the home islands, or to seek some political agreement covering the Pacific that would give the United Kingdom the security it needed.[71] The Prime Minister was not hopeful, however, that any such agreement could be reached with the Japanese and that they would also refuse to retreat from their demand for parity. Therefore, he felt it was necessary for the Americans and British to 'sit down together and discuss how we should deal with the resultant situation, particularly with regard to our own navies. He thought it, however, inadvisable for the United States and Great Britain to attempt to do this until all hope of a tripartite agreement is exhausted.'[72] Davis reassured the Prime Minister that the United States had no desire to impose a treaty on Britain incompatible with its national security. If Japan left the treaty system, then the onus for that failure would have to rest with it, and Britain and the United States would have to work out a new arrangement.[73] Agreement between the two Anglo-Saxon powers seemed imminent. However, British efforts to make a last-ditch appeal to Japan not to denounce the treaty system almost destroyed this tentative beginning to a new understanding with the Americans about the Far East situation.

On 13 November, Simon sent Clive a secret telegram outlining the result of British and American talks with Japan. As well, instructions were provided for the Ambassador about the idea of Japan's agreeing to a 'gentleman's agreement' not to build a navy larger than the Royal Navy. The difficulty, wrote Simon, was how to get the Japanese to agree to such a plan while at the same time keeping the Americans from finding out and thinking that Britain was attempting to betray their interests in exchange for Japanese assistance. Fear of making a repeat of the Manchurian fiasco was uppermost in the Foreign Office's mind.[74] Sir John, therefore, informed Clive that the closest possible communication had been ongoing between the American and British delegations, and therefore,

> It is obviously undesirable that you should appear to be going behind the backs of the American representatives here but at the same time it would be unfortunate if the United States Government were really to gain the impression from American press reports that: (i) we have made our suggestion to the Japanese without the courtesy of first informing the

United States representatives; (ii) that the suggestion involved any change in our views on the question of the relative defensive needs of the British and Japanese navies; or (iii) that we were seeking to make a deal with Japan in the matter of our respective naval strengths as a means of furthering some economic deal which we are alleged by the American press, quite falsely, to be negotiating with Japan.[75]

Those instructions concerning the 'gentleman's agreement' were accidentally passed on by the British embassy in Tokyo to the Japanese Vice Minister of Foreign Affairs. Panic swept through the Foreign Office as the Japanese now had the written evidence needed to paint the British as being false to the Americans. Craigie, in particular, who had all along argued that the Americans be kept fully informed of all British dealings with the Japanese, fired off a round of telegrams to try to prevent any great damage being done.[76] The document was eventually returned by the Japanese Foreign Office without further incident. However, while not causing an Anglo-American rupture, the mistake had revealed the Japanese Ambassador to his foreign office as being too cooperative with the British.[77] Still, the duplicity of the British position – the need to try to keep both Japan and America in play – had created panic because of the fear of ruining Anglo-American relations at a critical moment.[78]

The attitude of Foreign Office members and other British policy-makers towards the United States and its Far Eastern policy was improving steadily.[79] In fact, Sir John Simon reported to Lindsay that, 'There is, in fact, the closest co-operation between us all and all reports to the contrary should be scouted as preposterous.'[80] Craigie, too, was optimistic about the Americans developing a lasting relationship with the British over Far Eastern matters, but knew that it would never be a formal entente. Referring to Roosevelt's talks with Lothian, Craigie adroitly summarized the British situation:

> The President is quite right when he says that co-operation between the United States and Great Britain must rest on the fundamental identity of interests and ideals. His remark is useful for us as a reminder of the reality and what must long if not always remain the reality. It is obvious that now, as always hitherto, it is quite futile to expect United States co-operation with the United Kingdom on specific points, in specific ways, and in specific places. If we do not realize this but on the contrary think that we can safely let any of our calculations depend on United States co-operation in any specific situation we are deceiving ourselves, and laying up trouble between ourselves and the United States through disappointment with them at the pinch. If we expect nothing definite we are not disappointed and therefore not irritated. This does not mean that we must not on our side aim at co-operation in a large way or at a harmony of general aims. This we must do, always remembering at the same time that

the benefits we can get from this are likely to be negative rather than positive. It would be quite unsafe at this moment to try to say whether the United States of America are likely to be a *really* powerful political or economic unit in this generation.[81]

At the same time, Craigie was also pressing for the British government, if the Japanese refused to negotiate, to move towards the United States and away from the Japanese during the remainder of the talks. He believed that earlier signals sent to the Japanese, emanating primarily from the Treasury and other economic sources, had created a belief among the Japanese naval authorities that all they needed to do to get the British to capitulate was sit tight and remain firm in their resolve to achieve parity.[82] The time had come to bring the Japanese back to reality, said Craigie, and he recommended that, at the upcoming meeting between Simon and Matsudaira, the opportunity should be taken to 'mettre les choses au point', and that the Japanese Ambassador should be informed in no uncertain terms that 'we regard Japan's claim to eventual parity with the British Empire as unjustifiable on any ground of strategy or logic. Accordingly, there is no prospect at all of Japan's being able to secure any modification in the present relative strengths either by process of negotiation or of building.'[83] Britain's chief negotiator was also sure that, if the Japanese left the treaty system and went off on their own building programme, then the United States and Great Britain would move closer and work together to counter that threat. The Prime Minister agreed with Craigie's views, and supported the idea that it was now time for some frank talk with the Japanese. MacDonald wanted the Foreign Office to remain in control of passing that message to the Japanese delegation and to avoid giving the impression an Anglo-American bloc was forming.[84]

As the American and British delegations met to discuss their final approach to the Japanese, Sir John Simon told Davis that it was his belief that the Japanese would probably leave the treaty system.[85] That being the case, Simon needed to know what the American position would be regarding the British desire to retain its overaged cruiser tonnage, even if there was a 'gentleman's agreement' with Japan that it would not build beyond its allotted tonnage limits. Simon avoided Davis' attempts to get a firm commitment from the British that the initiative meant that there was to be an exclusive Anglo-American solution. The Foreign Secretary insisted that various formulae would continue to be presented to the Japanese, in an effort to get them involved in the process once more. But, when pushed hard, Simon could not avoid admitting that it was indeed looking as if an agreement between Britain and the United States would be the final outcome of any naval conference in 1935. Davis replied that the United States was still not willing to sign a deal which permitted a tonnage increase, but also admitted that Admiral Standley and the US Navy were moving towards a position that understood Britain's cruiser needs. It was his view that if the treaty system broke down then qualitative issues between the two powers would become academic.

The Prime Minister also pressed Davis hard on the cruiser issue, telling him that since 1922 the British had hoped to get more out of cooperating with the Americans, but things had now changed drastically in the Pacific. MacDonald told Davis that he desired to establish a form of cooperation with the United States during his tenure as Prime Minister that would last after he had left the post. He wanted the Americans to realize that, 'we have got a minimum requirement, a minimum requirement of the number of ships and a minimum requirement of capacity to carry out their job. If we can get an agreement to permit us to carry out those requirements, we are in the game.' Davis answered that he believed that the two powers would be able to work out an agreement that would satisfy both parties. But, he also stressed that the United States was not ready to consider a middle ground with Japan, one which would see either an end to the Open Door or a threat to American interests in the Far East due to Japanese naval building. This suited the Prime Minister. MacDonald's view of the Pacific situation was that, if there were going to be trouble in that region with Japan, both the United States and Great Britain would be involved. His position remained:

> Our eyes are primarily on the Pacific. What we want primarily is that we should both understand what is in our minds, that we are not for aggression, but for defense, and then quietly continue to bring pressure on Japan as to what she purposes to do, making it plain to them that both of us regard this as a very serious thing. This pressure should be separate, of course, and not give the impression of concerted action. But let us understand each other's minds.

MacDonald wanted the two delegations to begin meeting more frequently now, in order to iron out any remaining difficulties and to build confidence in each other's position. Davis agreed with those sentiments. The British government had come to the critical point in their strategic planning process: a choice now had to be made between the United States and Japan.

By now, the Admiralty were also convinced that no deal could be reached with the Japanese. But, they were still unsure whether the Americans would agree to their cruiser and capital ship position. Chatfield and the Admiralty were worried about the Japanese building fast battlecruisers for raiding across the Pacific.[86] The Royal Navy was not interested in getting into an arms race in new types and desired some sort of limitation on them. Standley replied that there was no disagreement between the two services as to the dangers posed by unrestricted design and construction. Each service was moving towards a better understanding of the other, but serious technical discussions would have to take place some time in 1935 before assurances about qualitative matters could be given.[87] At the same time, continued Japanese actions against British interests, especially British oil companies in Manchukuo, added to a growing sense of a common Anglo-American anti-Japanese vision.[88] That growing sense of empathy with the United States did not go unnoticed by the American delegation and State Department.

Norman Davis told President Roosevelt that, although a strong pro-Japanese faction did exist in the British government, such sentiment had faded with the continued Japanese violations of British rights to trade in the Far East.[89] He was certain that the most influential group in Cabinet was

> definitely opposed to any deal with Japan that could be misinterpreted by the United States and that, after all, might not be lived up to by Japan. This hostility in Parliament towards the United States is one of soreness, which began during the Economic Conference and which has reached full expression as a result of the Johnson Resolution ... While the British still wish to be as conciliatory as possible with Japan, and avoid an absolute impasse, it is still my belief that, whenever they feel the situation demands the choice between standing with us on basic principles or of trying to conciliate Japan in such a way as to alienate us, they will choose the former.[90]

After his talks with the British delegation on 14 November, Davis elaborated on his views of the split in the British Cabinet. It was still his contention that the pro-Japanese group were not in control of the naval negotiations, but merely that the realities of Britain's imperial defence needs caused great concern about offending the Japanese in the Far East while fears of a possible European war grew.[91] It was his recommendation that the United States follow along with the British in trying to find some sort of 'middle course' that would still include the Japanese in some form of agreement, even if it was a voluntary agreement not to build over established limits. Davis, still suspicious of British attempts to make some last-ditch effort to appease the Japanese, felt, however, that the American delegation could agree to talk to the Japanese with the British, for thus 'the British take the primary responsibility and we safeguard our position by preventing them from acting as mediator and later proposing something that would be embarrassing to us'.[92] Assured by such high-ranking officials as Stanley Baldwin that he and others were willing to let Japan go rather than embarrass the British position by appeasing Tokyo, Davis was certain that informal, but solid, Anglo-American cooperation was under way.[93] That belief seemed to be confirmed on 21 November when the chief American negotiator reported that:

> Neville Chamberlain, head of the group which has been in favor of a conciliatory policy towards Japan, has come to the conclusion that Great

> Britain should make no agreement with Japan to which the United States is not a party, that Anglo-American cooperation is a vital necessity to world peace and stability, that the Japanese are bluffing and that if and when it is necessary to call that bluff the United States and England should unhesitatingly do so together … I am informed that in a secret meeting of High Commissioners of Australia, Canada, and New Zealand with Simon, attended by Smuts a week ago the unanimous opinion was that cooperation with the United States … must be the cardinal policy of the British Empire.[94]

The direction and pace of negotiations towards the end of 1934 seemed to indicate that matters were moving in the United States' favour.

Roosevelt, not willing to let the British stray too far towards the Japanese, had reinforced his own position earlier in the month. The President had instructed Davis to let the British know that if they leaned towards the Japanese, Roosevelt would see to it that the United States would place great pressure on the Dominions, particularly Canada, to reject such action.[95] Now it appeared that the Dominions were themselves pressuring the British to commit to an Anglo-American bloc. Hull and the State Department were warmed by Davis' evaluation of the movement towards a common viewpoint now forming between the British and American delegations. These high-level talks with the British policy-makers caused them to believe that

> a definite and obvious common alignment of British and American viewpoints as a symbol of coincidence of view between them on the subject of naval limitation – which is the subject for consideration in these conversations – and of future cooperation between them offers greater promise of eventual success than any current search for a formula to salvage portions of the existing naval treaties.[96]

The State Department did not favour discussing any 'middle course' with the British. If the British were to do so, then it would only lead to increased suspicion and resentment on the part of isolationists and other groups already hostile to any cooperation with Britain. Furthermore, if such Anglo-Japanese talks did lead to a bilateral agreement, Japan would then move forward even more aggressively in the belief that any potential Anglo-American front had been split. Therefore, the State Department recommended that the talks in London be brought to a swift and open conclusion.[97]

Any thoughts on the part of the Americans that a simple Anglo-American open alliance against Japan would be the result of the deterioration in Anglo-Japanese relations were misguided. British strategic planners would not allow any such action to take place because of the risk of provoking a greater Japanese assault on British interests in the Far East, and because a real commitment to finding some workable solution to Anglo-Japanese tensions still existed, even among some of those who were inclined to want close Anglo-American co-operation. That cooperation could be close, but it could not be either overt or insulting to the Japanese. MacDonald had himself ordered Craigie to make sure that the Japanese government would not enter 1935 mistaken or misinformed about Britain's intention to defend its Far Eastern empire. The Prime Minister was moved to such action, in part, by a sense of hope that if the Japanese had an absolutely crystal-clear idea of what denouncing the Washington Treaty would mean to Anglo-Japanese relations, they would re-examine their position. But another part of him, the pragmatist, wanted to make sure that the Americans knew that the British government was not trying to make a deal with the Japanese, and, as they had argued to the Americans at the November series of meetings, were forcing the ball into the Japanese court.[98] He was very sure that the Americans were moving further and further towards the British view of naval arms limitation, and 'the more they understand it the less able are they to refuse to agree to it'.[99] The Prime Minister and Craigie would not allow British interests to be submerged merely for the sake of an Anglo-American agreement. And they were not yet well enough assured of American determination to remain a Pacific power to follow the American lead blindly. Allowing an overall increase in the size of the Royal Navy, working towards bringing Japan into some sort of agreement, and, if that were impossible, establishing a solid, yet informal working understanding with the Americans were the British goals.[100]

Shortly after Davis' extensive Anglo-American conversations with the British, Secretary Hull replied to statements made by MacDonald and Simon in the House of Commons concerning how well the American and British delegations were working together during the talks. Hull's statement in the American press reassured the British government that he, too, held such sentiments and was happy to see the greater degree of cooperation.[101] Lindsay assured the Foreign Office that Hull had made a point of making such a statement both to express his genuine desire for closer Anglo-American cooperation and to arrest the vicious US press reports and attacks which had plagued the talks and created unnecessary tension and anxiety on both sides of the Atlantic.[102] Now a final attempt to include Japan in some agreement was to be made, and, if that failed, then a conference that cemented American and British cooperation, while at the same time putting full blame on the Japanese for the failure, was to be prepared.

Initial State Department wishes for the talks in London to be seen to be at a complete and utter end once Japan abrogated the Washington Treaty were not supported by Davis or Roosevelt.[103] In meetings with MacDonald, Craigie and Simon, Davis had pressed for a formal end to all talks and an open joint denunciation of the Japanese destruction of the naval arms limitation system, as instructed by the Department.[104] But he was aware of the different public needs of the two governments over how the end of the process should be interpreted. The British delegation, not wanting to be blamed by the public for having either pushed Japan into a corner or forced it to leave the talks, wanted to give Japan all the rope it required to hang itself in denouncing the Treaty. As well, there was the complicated question of, if the talks were allowed to die, who would be obliged to re-start them a few months later. MacDonald was certain that he would not be the one to allow the Japanese to walk away only to invite them back to try once more, for this would give an impression of weakness and appeasement.[105] Other pressures affected the Americans. Davis and his delegation, as well as the State Department, were under increasing pressure from the American press to come home and not to associate with any 'deal' brokered by the British.[106] Each delegation once more reassured the other that neither wanted anything other than solid mutual cooperation, even though it would not be either formal or open. Davis told the British members that he, and the administration, were convinced that neither MacDonald, Baldwin nor Simon would ever willingly or unwisely do anything to rupture Anglo-American cooperation. Davis also implied that future British demands for more tonnage to meet Far Eastern and European strategic needs would not be seriously challenged, as the 'United States was in a very reasonable frame of mind'. Impressed with the British attitude towards the American position and their rationale for allowing the talks to adjourn and not simply to end, Davis asked the State Department to abandon their policy in favour of a recess.[107]

Davis was now convinced that Anglo-American cooperation on the naval limitation issue was a viable reality. Calling off the talks in a manner not palatable to the British would only make matters worse in 1935. He believed that the British, even with their imperial defence problems and contending views on how to deal with the Far Eastern question, had no choice but to continue to rank Anglo-American cooperation higher than cooperation with Japan:

> Their [British] policy is, first and foremost, to cooperate with us in any event, but, second, to induce Japan as far as possible to co-operate with us both, which they are hopeful of achieving by making Japan realize that, there is not today a common Anglo-American front, there is a common point of view on fundamentals from which we will not depart.[108]

He wrote to the President personally, telling Roosevelt that the British hesitation over how to end the talks was not related to any sort of duplicity. Mounting pressure was coming from the Dominions, all of it aimed at pressuring Whitehall to move towards some sort of Anglo-American arrangement. As for the important Cabinet members, such as MacDonald, Baldwin and Simon, he reported that they, and not the pro-Japanese forces, still held the upper hand in questions concerning Britain's strategic preparations. It was now only a matter of ironing out the tactics for dealing with the Japanese.[109] Simon, still considered in Washington as insincere and lacking in conviction, was credited by Davis as having worked faithfully and fully with the Americans during the naval talks:

> While he [Simon] undoubtedly wants to maintain if possible the most friendly relations with Japan, he thinks we could both restrain Japan and deal more effectively with her through a tri-partite agreement. However, if the choice has to be made between alienating Japan or the United States, his choice I feel sure will be to go with us. He has I am sure dealt as frankly with me as is possible for him in his official position to do and he has assured me that they now have no agreement whatever with Japan and under no circumstances will they make one to which we are not a party or to which we can object.[110]

Davis also relayed information as to how Simon had worked to persuade Neville Chamberlain, the leader of the pro-Japanese British Cabinet Ministers, that cooperation with the United States was of more value to the British Empire than a pact with Japan. Even though Chamberlain was not enthusiastic about an Anglo-American front, he had admitted that Japan's naval 'bluff' would have to be called by the cooperative efforts of the United States and Great Britain. The Chancellor of the Exchequer had reservations, however, that a rupture with Japan at that moment would lead it to seek any sort of possible assistance, even an understanding with Germany. Davis reassured Roosevelt that, in the face of such efforts and with personal assurances by MacDonald and Simon that Britain would never do anything to jeopardize the growing sense of trust between the two great Western powers, Britain could be trusted to talk to the Japanese without any danger of selling out the Americans.[111] Roosevelt, swayed by the argument put forward by the British and Davis, wrote to Hull on 7 December, informing him that he was willing to allow the talks to continue.[112] Finally, the State Department agreed to an adjournment, after the expected Japanese denunciation was issued, with the British government taking the responsibility for deciding when the talks would resume.[113] Both American and British policy-makers now retired to consider how the next stage of the process would continue, once Japan had formally denounced the idea of naval limitation. The nature of the Anglo-American understanding that was being forged now had to be given texture.

The Foreign Office and Admiralty were still not as generous, in their praise for the American attitude towards the naval limitation issue and the Japanese, as Davis had been of the British position. Vansittart and the American Department as a whole were still irritated by what they saw as a lack of effort on the part of Secretary Hull to foster better relations.[114] They believed that American questioning of the sincerity of the Foreign Office's desire for closer cooperation was insulting, as such a desire was axiomatic in the American Department.[115] Further, the need to protect Britain's global position could not be sacrificed to American interests any more than to those of Japan. For that reason, Vansittart still insisted that, in any future talks with the Americans over naval issues, both sides would have to make the running.[116] Officially, however, the Admiralty and Foreign Office claimed to be happy with how the talks in London had gone. It was their view that the Americans had indeed come a long way towards recognizing the reasons why Britain required an increase in certain tonnages, especially in cruisers. A quantitative settlement between the United States and Great Britain was thought assured, as were such qualitative measures as a limit on gun calibres for capital ships, a reduction in their size, the size of aircraft carriers and some changes in the cruiser classes.[117] It was the United States, however, that would change most from its original position in order to make Anglo-American relations closer.

Upon his return to the United States, Davis moved swiftly to push the administration to continue working towards finding common ground with Great Britain for the upcoming Conference. At a high-level meeting with Hull, Standley, Phillips, Moffat, Hornbeck, Eugene Dooman and various naval officers, Davis summed up his perceptions of the results of the last few months of talks with the British and Japanese. He repeated what he had told Roosevelt: that Britain would not throw Japan aside without a clear promise of an alliance from the United States to assist in the Far East. Without such a promise, the British would try to protect their interests by working to bring all three powers together into some face-saving arrangement. One of the principal benefits of the talks had been to force the pro-Japanese group in the British Cabinet into the open, he said, and thereby to make those who favoured an Anglo-American approach work to crystallize their thoughts on how the two powers could come to a naval agreement.[118] He and the rest of the delegates reported that:

> As a result the group favoring going along with the United States had been tremendously strengthened and Mr Davis was satisfied that it would, in the long run, control British policy, although the small but powerful pro-Japanese group would still have to be reckoned with.[119]

That feeling of cautious optimism was present throughout the State Department as well, from Secretary Hull down through the various departments, but particularly in the Far Eastern Division and the Western European Division.[120] Certainly, faith in Stanley Baldwin and in his belief in strong Anglo-American relations was seen as a pillar of and testament to the growing strength of the bond between the two nations. Moreover, confidence in Baldwin and MacDonald compensated for the lingering doubts about the good faith of such other British leaders as Simon and Chamberlain.[121] Eugene Dooman, another

State Department official with a long history of dealing with the British on naval arms limitation, also spread the good word around the Department and Washington about the changed face of the British and, in particular, Sir John Simon. The Far Eastern expert answered critics of the talks insightfully, pointing out that, while there may have been no great accomplishments to publish to the world, the level of understanding that had been established between the three parties was most beneficial. He defended the British need for flexibility in their foreign policy, because of their imperial interests, and was not shocked or dismayed that no permanent or formal agreement between the United States and Great Britain had been reached. That was the nature of the British game, he said, and American policy-makers would be wise to accept that fact.[122]

Once the American delegation had left London, Craigie and Atherton resumed their management of the situation, massaging departments and egos on both sides of the Atlantic, all in an effort to ensure that the two sides reached a naval agreement in 1935. Despite continued worries about Anglo-Japanese relations, the new involvement of Italy, France and eventually the Soviet Union in the process, Anglo-Italian tensions, and the signing of the Anglo-German Naval Treaty in June of 1935, Anglo-American relations concerning how they would regard each another's navies remained fairly constant.[123] The change of Prime Minister from MacDonald to Baldwin, and from Simon to Samuel Hoare (and then to Anthony Eden in December 1935) as Foreign Secretary also helped to ensure that better personal relations with the Americans continued.[124] These new British leaders continued to build on an already solid Anglo-American foundation in the belief that such a relationship was vital.

Over the summer and into the early autumn of 1935, changes in the global strategic situation and in the British policy-making elite itself solidified Anglo-American trust over naval issues. Sir Ronald Lindsay told former Under-Secretary of State William Castle that, even though there had been a chance some months previously of a renewal of the Anglo-Japanese Alliance, that time had passed, and now Britain would not dare go that route.[125] Castle passed along this information to a relieved Secretary Hull, who had been somewhat worried that just such an event might still take place.[126] By mid-September, President Roosevelt was so comfortable with the British position and so confident of being able to work with them during the actual conference that he had no reservations about showing London the American 'hand' as far as future naval building programmes went. He was not happy to have to accommodate British desires on both capital ships and cruisers, and was still concerned with having the 20 per cent cut in tonnage that had been such an obstacle before, but opposition to the British needs was feeble at best.[127] Admiral Standley was also happy to have been able to reach such an understanding with the British. He recognized the importance of close collaboration with Great Britain and the elimination of the naval rivalry that had plagued the two nations for almost nine years. To end such animosity and establish a new, more trusting relationship would be worth much to both nations and both navies in this troubling time.[128] Now that Great Britain had finally decided not to pursue a formal Anglo-Japanese pact, the Americans were happy to work on an informal, yet close and coordinated Anglo-American programme of naval development with regard to the Far East. Britain would continue to try to create better relations with the Japanese, but Roosevelt and his administration were confident it would not be at their expense.

In fact, the net result of events from January 1935 until the calling of the Second London Naval Conference on 9 December of that same year produced few surprises.[129] American and British officials remained unmoved by Japan's continued demands for parity. As the talks went on, until 26 March 1936, the two Western powers worked out an agreement that closely mirrored earlier British demands, with the resulting treaty preserving modified qualitative limitations.[130] Chatfield and the Admiralty became much more familiar with and understanding of their American counterparts, with firm, close ties growing out of the information which was shared about each navy's strategic planning and future programmes, even if for safety's sake the Royal Navy had to keep its distance from the US Navy.[131] All hope of quantitative limitations left with the Japanese. Without those quantitative issues to create tension and conflict, the two rival services could turn to re-establishing the close ties forged during the First World War.[132] However, the real value of the entire two-year process lay in the creation of a new sense of openness and trust between the two countries' strategic foreign-policy-making elite.

This was evident to many of those individuals. In late January 1936, Craigie harkened back to the early commitment Davis had made in 1934, and repeated in October 1935 that the United States was prepared to proceed with a qualitative arrangement only if Japan did not participate. If such a reply had not been forthcoming, he doubted whether his government would have called the conference at all. That promise had held true, and his, as well as Norman Davis' and Ray Atherton's, belief that the two powers could find an agreement that would let each nation 'live and let live' to the benefit of all, had been made a reality. Now both nations were rewarded with praise from their respective populations for having tried to implement naval limitation. Even though the idea of a comprehensive naval agreement had been destroyed, because of the narrow and aggressive policies of Japan, no blame could be placed on either administration. Both Britain and the United States had created the best solution for their own national security interests out of a crumbling and decaying naval arms limitation system. Each of the Western powers had also obtained a renewed sense of common purpose and common ground with respect to the naval and Far Eastern aspects of the Anglo-American relationship, a sense that had not been evident since the Washington Conference itself.[133] As 1936 wore on, sceptics on both sides of the Atlantic began to see that a new era in

Anglo-American relations had been forged in the fires of the naval disarmament process.

Sir Robert Vansittart and the First Lord of the Admiralty in 1936, Viscount Monsell, provided examples of the changes in attitude that had taken place in those British policy-makers who did not really support the pro-Japanese tactics of Chamberlain and Fisher, but were still often incapable of seeing any good coming from fostering better relations with the United States. In the wake of the success of the Anglo-American naval talks, they had continued to predict that the US Navy and the Roosevelt administration would resist Britain's request to keep the overaged cruiser tonnage required to meet Japan's naval expansion. When the expected American indignation and resistance did not materialize, Vansittart and Monsell began to understand that relations with the United States over Far Eastern matters were now cast in a different light, and Victor Wellesley was another convert.[134] On the American side, Pierrepont Moffat, a man well connected in the State Department hierarchy, who was often reluctant to be generous towards the British position, had to admit in August 1936, that 'In matters of Pacific politics the British and ourselves are viewing matters more eye to eye ...'[135] These were the successes of the London Naval Conference process. There was a renewed sense of trust and cooperation between the United States and Great Britain over naval issues, and thus, over how each was approaching the troubles brewing in the Far East.

The improvement in Anglo-American naval relations caused a major shift in relations between the two nations that would have a profound effect on the balance of power in the Far East. That change in the balance of power had been achieved without fundamentally changing the existing policies of either state, therefore, without creating the appearance of a formal anti-Japanese coalition. On the British side, the 'no-bloc' policy of the Foreign Office remained intact.[136] Its attempt to balance the various Pacific powers in a system which would protect the Far Eastern parts of the empire remained. The State Department's need to avoid any formal entangling alliances had been met and a new basis for American naval power established. And, there is no doubt that by the summer of 1936 more policy-makers on both sides of the Atlantic were favourably disposed to view the other with a sense of trust than had previously been the case. Each understood the other's strategic needs, even if they did not agree. A mutual belief that Japan, through its pursuit of increased naval arms building, was a violator of international peace had also been reached. How to solve the Japanese problem permanently, if such a thing could be done, had not. Both sides acknowledged that it was not yet possible to make a formal alliance to counter Japan. But each also now knew that informal consultation and cooperation, along parallel but not joint lines, was a useful strategic reality. It was along that path that British and American foreign-policy-makers now began to search further, in hopes of finding a solution for the problems in the Far East.

NOTES

1. FO 371/17599/A6404/1938/45, FO memo by Eden, 19 July 1934.
2. Ibid.
3. Ibid., Craigie minute, 2 Aug. 1934.
4. Ibid., Vansittart minute, 10 Aug. 1934. See also FO 371/17599/A6233/1938/45, telegram from Washington Embassy with report of press conference, 1 Aug. 1934, and Vansittart minute, 4 Aug. 1934.
5. Baldwin Papers, 131, secret letter from Fisher to Chatfield, 11 July 1934; CHT/3/2, Naval Conference, 1935, letter from Fisher to Chatfield, 1 Nov. 1934; ibid., secret draft of note from Fisher to Chamberlain, 12 Nov. 1934.
6. FO 371/17599/A6474/1938/45, secret letter from Clark to Craigie, 8 Aug. 1934.
7. Ibid.
8. Ibid.
9. FO 371/17599/A6484/1938/45, FO minute by Craigie, 7 Aug. 1934.
10. Ibid.
11. Ibid.
12. Ibid., Vansittart minute, 8 Aug. 1934.
13. FO 371/17599/A6485/1938/45, record of telephone conversation between Craigie and Chatfield, 9 Aug. 1934; FO 371/17599/A6501/1938/45, letter from Capt. Danckwerts to Gore-Booth, 9 Aug. and Gore-Booth minute, 16 Aug. 1934.
14. FO 371/18169/F5943/57/23, very confidential letter from Clive to Wellesley, 23 Aug. 1934; FO 371/18177/F5809/316/23, FO memo by Richard Allen (clerk in Far Eastern Dept.), letter from Commander Shelley, Naval Staff, Intelligence Division, 22 Oct. 1934; FO 371/18181/F4798/373/34, confidential despatch from Clive to FO, 5 July, 1934; CAB 53/5, Minutes of COS meetings, No. 132, 24 July 1934; CAB 29/147, NCM (35), Minutes of 5th Meeting, 31 May 1934; Kennedy, '1935', 204–6.
15. Neville Chamberlain Papers [NC], University Library, Birmingham, 8/17/24–8/21/7, memo by Chamberlain 'The Naval Conference and our Relations with Japan', Sept. 1934.
16. FO 371/17599/A7695/1938/45, note from Vansittart to Simon, 14 Aug., and accompanying despatch from Clive to FO, dated 5 July 1934.
17. Ibid., letter from Simon to Vansittart, 20 Aug. 1934.
18. Ibid.
19. Ibid., instructions to American and Far Eastern departments, 22 Aug. 1934.
20. Ibid.
21. Ibid., minutes by Craigie, 23 Aug. 1934; on the question of whether there were really any moderates in Japanese policy-making circles see Kennedy, '1935', 191–7.
22. FO 371/17599/A7695/1938/45, minutes by Orde, 28 Aug. 1934.
23. CAB 24/248, CP 77 (34) 'Situation in the Far East, 1933–34', by Simon, 15 Mar. 1934; ibid., CP 80 (34), 'Imperial Defence Policy', by Simon, 16 Mar. 1934.
24. Ibid., CAB 24/248, CP 77 (34).
25. FO 371/17599/A7695/1938/45, Vansittart minute, 25 Aug. 1934.
26. Ibid., Vansittart minute, 29 Aug. and Mounsey minute, 28 Aug. 1934.
27. Ibid., Vansittart minute to Secretary of State, 29 Aug. 1934; see also Anthony Eden minute of 2 Sept. which tries to find some sort of common ground, but Eden was not willing to let Japan have a free hand in China. Nor was he willing to let Japan's naval construction to go on unchecked. Thus, in the end, Eden was in agreement with Orde's views, except concerning the worth of Soviet Russia as a counter against Germany.
28. FO 371/17599/A7185/1938/45, Lothian memo, received on 10 Sept. 1934; Templewood Papers, University Library, Cambridge, Box 8, part VIII, File 1, letter from Lothian to

Hoare, 26 Aug, 1935.

29. FO 371/17599/A7185/1938/45, Vansittart minutes undated throughout.

30. FO 371/17599/A7186/1938/45, Vansittart minute, 13 Sept. 1934.

31. Ibid., Craigie minute, 7 Sept. 1934.

32. Ibid.

33. Ibid.

34. Ibid., Orde minute, 11 Sept.

35. Ibid.

36. Ibid., Mounsey minute, 12 Sept. Vansittart minute, 13 Sept. 1934.

37. Ibid., Vansittart minute, 13 Sept.

38. Baldwin Papers,124, D'Arcy (British Embassy, Washington) to Vansittart, 24 Aug. 1934; FO 371/17603/A9942/1938/45, letter from Vansittart to Lindsay, 24 Sept. 1934.

39. Until indicated, the following is based on, FO 371/17603/A9942/1938/45, letter from Vansittart to Lindsay, 24 Sept. 1934.

40. CAB 23/79, Minutes 32 (34), 25 Sept. 1934.

41. CAB 24/250, CP 223 (34), 'The Future of Anglo-Japanese Relations', by Chamberlain and Simon, 16 Oct. 1934; CAB 23/80, Minutes of 36th Meeting, 24 Oct. 1934.

42. Trotter, *Britain and East Asia, 1933–1937*, 115–47; Endicott, *Diplomacy and Enterprise*, 73–101.

43. FO 371/17599/A7695/1938/45, Craigie minute, 27 Sept. 1934; FO 371/17600/A8313/ 1938/45, memo by Admiral Dickens (DNI), 15 Oct. 1934.

44. FO 371/17600/A8313/1938/45, letter from Lindsay to Vansittart, 8 Oct. 1934; ibid., letter from Lindsay to Vansittart, 18 Oct. 1934.

45. Ibid., letter from Lindsay to Vansittart, 8 Oct. 1934.

46. President's Personal File (hereafter FDR–PPF), Franklin D. Roosevelt Presidential Library, Hyde Park, New York, PPF 33, 33, folder – Norman H. Davis, letter from Davis to FDR, 30 Aug. 1934; Pelz, *Race to Pearl Harbor*, 126–36.

47. Davis MSS, Container 41, confidential letter from Moffat to Davis, 22 Aug. 1934.

48. Davis MSS, container 2, letter from Atherton to Davis, 29 Aug. 1934.

49. Hull MSS, Container 37, letter from Bingham to Hull, 23 July 1934. Bingham sent this same message to FDR on 8 May, see FDR–PSF, Britain 1933–36, letter and enclosed telegram from Bingham to FDR, 8 May 1934.

50. Davis MSS, Container 2, letter from Davis to Atherton, 12 Sept. 1934.

51. The Foreign Office and Admiralty were happy with the appointment of Standley to the delegation, as both departments believed that he was well respected by the USN, and therefore would be able to carry the day against any opposition on that front. Also, he was thought to be friendly towards Great Britain, although he was a big navy advocate, which could mean trouble as far as quantitative agreements were concerned. See FO 371/17599/A7965/1938/45, Gore-Booth minute, 9 Oct. 1934.

52. William D. Leahy Diary (hereafter Leahy Diary), Library of Congress, entry for 9 Oct. 1934; Moffat Diary, entries for 5 and 9 Mar. and 26 June 1934.

53. FDR–PSF, Japan, record of meeting between Hull, Phillips, Dunn, Hornbeck, Moffat, Standley, Assistant Secretary of the Navy Roosevelt and Admiral Greenslade, 26 Sept. 1934.

54. Ibid. On 5 Oct. Rear Admiral Frank H. Schofield, now retired from the USN, prepared a memo for Admiral Standley on the limitation of armaments in relation to the upcoming naval talks. Schofield's memo vigorously rejected the theories of British naval planner Admiral Sir Herbert Richmond, who published an article on the topic in the October edition of *Foreign Affairs*. Schofield thought the only explanation for such ideas was that Richmond was either 'dumb or dishonest'. See FDR–PSF, Box 142, Folder – London Naval Conference, 1934, memo from Schofield to Standley,

'Limitation of Armaments', 5 Oct. 1934.

55. FDR–PSF, Japan, record of meeting between Hull, Phillips, Dunn, Hornbeck, Moffat, Standley, Assistant Secretary of the Navy Roosevelt, and Admiral Greenslade, 26 Sept. 1934.

56. Ibid.

57. The British Cabinet did not want Davis to arrive in London before the Japanese because Chamberlain had insinuated that talks with the Japanese would go better without Davis present. Craigie countered Chamberlain's suggestions to Simon, by pointing out that Davis did not want to attend British talks with the Japanese delegation, but merely wanted to be in London slightly before or at the same time as the Japanese arrived so as to be ready to begin tripartite talks immediately. Simon then reassured Ambassador Matsudaira that the British and Japanese delegations would meet without a third party being present for the first stage of talks. See FO 371/17599/A7708/1938/45, Craigie minutes, 10 Oct. and Simon minutes, 9 Oct. 1934; CAB 23/79, Minutes of 32nd meeting, 25 Sept. 1934. Davis and his delegation did, however, finally arrive before the Japanese. The delegation consisted of Norman H. Davis, Chairman of the American Delegation to the General Disarmament Conference; Adm. William H. Standley, CNO, Principal Naval Advisor; Ray Atherton, advisor; Eugene H. Dooman, Foreign Service Officer and advisor; Commander Roscoe Schuirmann USN, Technical Advisor; Lt. Com. J.H. Duncan, USN, Aide to Adm. Standley, Technical Advisor; Noel H. Field (Dept of State), Secretary of the Mission; Samuel Reber, Foreign Service Officer; and Robert Pell (public relations). The addition of Pell to the delegation caused some concern, as he was thought to be a source of leaks to the press. This was a danger because, due to his belief that the British were flirting with the Japanese, he would compromise the sensitive talks. See FO 371/17599/A7965/1938/45, Gore-Booth minute, 9 Oct. 1934.

58. Until indicated, the following is based on, FO 371/18184/F6784/591/23, letter and attached record of conversation from Lindsay to Vansittart, 12 Oct. 1934.

59. Stimson Diary, entry for 8 Oct. 1934.

60. CSDCF, 711.41/280, record of conversation between Lothian and Phillips, 15 Oct. 1934.

61. FO 371/17600/A6006/1938/45, Craigie minute, 12 Oct. 1934.

62. FO 371/17600/A8641/1938/45, record of conversation between Secretary of State and Japanese Ambassador, 30 Oct. 1934; ibid., FO 371/17600/A8410/1938/45, record of meeting, 23 Oct. 1934.

63. FO 371/17602/A9844/1938/45, secret FO minute, by Craigie, 29 Oct. 1934.

64. Ibid., Orde minute, 30 Oct.; ibid., Wellesley minute, 1 Nov.; ibid., Pratt minute, 31 Oct., all 1934.

65. Ibid., Pratt minute, 31 Oct. 1934.

66. FRUS, Vol. I, telegram from Davis to Hull, 19 Oct. 1934, 311–12.

67. For Japanese proposals, see CAB 24/251, CP 238, 'Report on the Preliminary Naval Discussions which have taken place with the Japanese Representatives', 30 Oct 1934.

68. FRUS, Vol. I, telegram from Davis to Hull, 25 Oct.1934, 312; ibid., telegram from Phillips (Acting Secretary of State) to Davis, 26 Oct. 1934, 315–14; ibid., telegram from Davis to Phillips, 26 Oct. 1934, 216–317.

69. FRUS, Vol. I, telegram from Davis to Phillips, 27 Oct. 1934, 317.

70. FRUS, Vol. I, telegram from Davis to Phillips, 29 Oct. 1934, 318–21.

71. Ibid. See also CAB 24/251, CP 247 'Statement of the British position vis-à-vis the Japanese Proposals', 7 Nov. 1934.

72. FRUS, Vol. I, telegram from Davis to Phillips, 29 Oct. 1934, 318–21.

73. Ibid.

74. FO 371/17600/A9035/1938/45, secret telegram from Simon to Clive, 13 Nov. 1934.
75. Ibid. For the informing on Davis and the British plans see *FRUS*, Vol. I, telegram from Davis to Hull, 9 Nov. 1934, 326; ibid., telegram from Hull to Davis, 13 Nov. 1934, 327–8.
76. FO 371/17600/A9052/1938/45, secret Craigie minute, 9 Nov. 1934; FO 371/17601/ A9191/1938/45, private and secret telegram from Craigie to Clive, 20 Nov. 1934.
77. FO 371/17601/A9262/45, telegram from Clive to FO, 21 Nov. 1934.
78. *FRUS*, Vol. I, telegram from Hull to Davis, 13 Nov. 1934, 327–8.
79. Relations between Simon and Davis remained strained, with neither man trusting the other to really give a full or fair hearing to the other's position. Simon in particular refused to talk to Davis without Atherton being present, to act as a witness to the discussion and be an accurate reporter. The Foreign Office staff at all levels, except for Vansittart, had a great deal of faith in the ability of Atherton to give a complete and accurate rendition of any exchange. Atherton also kept Bingham in the 'loop', therefore ensuring that the US Embassy remained a vital part of Anglo-American negotiations. See FO 371/17601/A9264/1938/45, Craigie minutes, with Simon minutes, 17 Nov. and separate Simon minutes, 18 Nov. 1934; FO 371/17601/A9379/1938/45, secret FO minute by Craigie, 19 Nov. 1934.
80. Ibid., draft telegram from Simon to Lindsay, 19 Nov. 1934. See also FO 800/291, Simon Papers, PRO, Kew, London, note from Simon to MacDonald, 3 Oct. 1934.
81. FO 371/18184/F6784/591/23, Craigie minute, 19 Nov. 1934.
82. FO 371/17601/A9379/1938/45, secret minute by Craigie, 19 Nov. 1934.
83. Ibid.
84. FO 371/17601/A9379/1938/45, Craigie minute, 19 Nov. 1934.
85. Until indicated, the following is based on, *FRUS*, Vol. I, Minutes of meeting between British and American delegations, 14 Nov. 1934, 334–50.
86. FO 371/17602/A9712/1938/45, FO minute and NC (D), minutes of first meeting, 13 Nov. 1934.
87. *FRUS*, Vol. I, Minutes of meeting between British and American delegations, 14 Nov. 1934, 334–50.
88. FO 371/18191/F7024/1659/23, FO minutes by Pratt, Orde, Wellesley and Craigie done at Simon's request, 27 Nov. 1934.
89. Hull Papers, Container 37, letter from Davis to FDR, 6 Nov. 1934.
90. Ibid.
91. *FRUS*, Vol. I, telegram from Davis to Hull, 16 Nov. 1934, 351–3.
92. Ibid.
93. *FRUS*, Vol. I, telegram from Davis to Hull, 21 Nov. 1934, 356–8.
94. *FRUS*, Vol. I, telegram from Davis to Hull, 21 Nov. 1934, 358–9.
95. FDR–PSF, Box 142, Folder – London Naval Conference, 1934, letter from FDR to Davis, 9 Nov. 1934. Ambassador Bingham helped spread this message in the right circles, telling the influential Lady Astor that if the British did not choose the Americans over the Japanese, then they were putting their money on the wrong horse. It was Bingham's intention to ensure that the British government was given a clear signal of the importance that the United States were attaching to their future actions. Bingham Diary, entry for 7 Nov. 1934.
96. *FRUS*, Vol. I, telegram from Hull to Davis, 17 Nov. 1934, 353–4.
97. Ibid. See also, *FRUS*, Vol. I, telegram from Hull to Davis, 17 Nov. 1934, 355.
98. MacDonald Diary, entry for 23 Nov. 1934.
99. Ibid.
100. Last-ditch efforts before the American delegation left for Washington to get a joint Anglo-American front established in the open against the Japanese were rebuffed by MacDonald in a meeting with Davis on 13 Dec. Davis was annoyed and disgruntled

at his failure to get such a formal position statement, but the Prime Minister informed him in no uncertain terms that, 'Once again, I asked him whether he would think we were anything but incompetent if we went into a dangerous situation in the Pacific knowing that the Americans would be likely to leave us to do the fighting and nearly added, and the paying. He knows quite well that I am right and asks us to trust them. They have let us down too often in recent negotiations.' MacDonald Diary, entries for 13 Dec. and 19 Dec. 1934. See also *FRUS*, Vol. I, memo of conversation in the Prime Minister's Office at the House of Commons on 23 Nov. 1934, 368–74.

101. FO 371/17601/A9358/1938/45, telegram from Lindsay to FO, 24 Nov. 1934.
102. Special efforts were made by Hull, Phillips and other high-ranking officials to ensure that no great public outcry or antagonism was allowed to be created in isolationist newspapers. See 371/17601/A9360/1938/45, telegram from Lindsay to FO, 24 Nov. 1934; *FRUS*, Vol. I, record of teletype conversation between Davis and Hull, 22 Nov. 1934, 361–3; ibid., telegram from Hull to Davis, 22 Nov. 1934, 363. No research into the actual influence of the press and reporters on these talks has been done to date, which is a pity as there is much to be done.
103. *FRUS*, Vol. I, telegram from Hull to Davis, 22 Nov. 1934, 364–5.The Department's attitude reflected the influence of Hornbeck and his desire to send a clear message to the Japanese that any further acts of aggression would be met with equal resolve by the United States. See *FRUS*, Vol. I, telegram from Hull to Davis, 8 Dec. 1934, 391, which has all the markings and phrases to indicate that Hornbeck was most influential in its drafting. Standley wanted a clear statement on the American position, followed by an immediate departure. See Bingham Diary, entry for 16 Nov. 1934.
104. *FRUS*, Vol. I, Memo of conversation in PM's office at House of Commons, 23 Nov. 1934.
105. Ibid. See also *FRUS*, Vol. I, memo of conversation between the American and British delegations at the House of Commons, 4 Dec. 1934, 381–8.
106. *FRUS*, record of conversation in PM's office at the House of Commons, 23 Nov. 1934.
107. *FRUS*, Vol. I, telegram from Davis to Hull, 3 Dec. 1934, 378–9; ibid., telegram from Davis to Hull, 7 Dec. 1934, 388–90.
108. Davis Papers, Container 51, strictly personal letter from Davis to FDR, 14 Dec. 1934.
109. Davis Papers, Container 51, personal and confidential letter from Davis to FDR, 27 Nov. 1934.
110. Ibid.
111. Ibid. See also Hull Papers, Container 37, personal and confidential letter from Davis to Hull and copy of strictly personal letter from Davis to FDR, both dated14 Dec. 1934.
112. *FRUS*, Vol. I, note from FDR to Hull, 7 Dec. 1934, 390–1.
113. For interpretations on the adjournment process, see Pelz, *Race to Pearl Harbor*, 141–3; Kaufman, *Arms Control During the Pre-Nuclear Era*, 172–4; Berg, 'Second London Naval Conference', 216–20.
114. FO 371/18731/A343/22/45, telegram from Lindsay to FO, 11 Jan. 1935. In October 1935, Vansittart was still annoyed with the Americans and their Far Eastern policy, which he incorrectly appraised as moving towards a withdrawal from that region. See CAB 16/112, DRC Meeting No. 17, 10 Oct. 1935.
115. FO 371/18760/A531/531/45, Craigie minute, 31 Jan. 1935.
116. Ibid., Vansittart minute, 14 Jan. 1934.
117. FO 371/18731/A901/22/45, NCM (35) 46, 'Survey of the Present Position of Naval Conversations and Recommendations as to Future Procedure', 17 Jan. 1935.
118. *FRUS*, Vol. I, 'General', memo of meeting in the office of the Secretary of State with returned members of the US naval delegation, 8 Jan. 1935, 64–6.
119. Ibid.

120. SKH Papers, Box 454, memo 'Relations Between the United States and Countries of the Far East – Especially Japan – in 1935', 3 Jan. 1935.
121. Castle Diary, entry for 5 Dec. 1934.
122. Castle Diary, entry for 25 Feb. 1935.
123. On the Anglo-German naval agreement and the inclusion of other countries into the naval negotiation process, see Charles Bloch, 'Great Britain, German Rearmament, and the Naval Agreement of 1935', in Hans W. Gatke, ed., *European Diplomacy between Two Wars, 1919–1939* (Chicago, IL, 1972), 125–51; D.C. Watt, 'The Anglo-German Naval Agreement of 1935: An Interim Judgment', *JMH*, 28 (1956): 155–75; H.H. Hall III, 'The Foreign Policy Decision-Making Process in Britain, 1934–1935, and the Origins of the Anglo-German Naval Agreement', *HR*, 19 (1976): 477–99; Joseph A. Maiolo, *The Royal Navy and Nazi Germany, 1933–39: A Study in Appeasement and the Origins of the Second World War* (London, 1998); R.A. Best, 'The Anglo-German Naval Agreement of 1935: An Aspect of Appeasement', *NWCR*, 34 (1981): 68–85. On Anglo-Italian relations in the interwar years, see Robert Mallett, *The Italian Navy and Fascist Expansionism, 1935–1940* (London, 1940); R.A.C. Parker, 'Great Britain, France and the Ethiopian Crisis', *EHR*, 89 (1974): 293–332; J.C. Robertson, 'The Hoare–Laval Plan', *JCH*, 10 (1975): 433–65; M. Roi, '"A Completely Immoral and Cowardly Attitude": The British Foreign Office, American Neutrality, and the Hoare–Laval Plan', *CJH*, 29 (1994): 331–51; Reynolds M. Salerno, 'Multilateral Strategy and Diplomacy: The Anglo-German Naval Agreement and the Mediterranean Crisis, 1935–36', *JSS*, 17 (1994): 39–78.

    For primary evidence of the oil-on-troubled-waters workings of Atherton and Craigie, see FO 371/18733/A4531/22/45, letter from Atherton to Craigie, 10 May 1935; FO 371/18736/A6077/22/45, despatch from Hoare to Lindsay, 9 July 1935; FO 371/18738/A7073/22/45, despatch from Lindsay to FO and minutes, 30 July 1935; FO 371/18738/A7125/22/45, Vansittart minute, 9 Aug. 1935; FO 371/18738/A7286/22/45, aide-mémoire from Atherton to FO, 18 Aug. 1935; FO 371/18738/A7377/22/45, FO minute by Craigie, 18 Aug. 1935; FO 371/18738/A7416/22/45, letter from Lindsay to Craigie, 7 Aug. 1935; FO 371/18738/A7442/22/45, record of conversation between Craigie and Atherton, 23 Aug. 1935; FO 371/18739/A7690/22/45, letter from Captain Phillips, ADM Plans Division to Holman, 31 Aug. 1935; FO 371/18739/A7885/22/45, draft memo, minutes and letters, 1–11 Sept. 1935; FO 371/18739/A8031/22/45, NCM (35) 66 and minutes, 12 Sept. 1935; FO 371/18739/A8361/22/45, record of meeting at FO between Craigie and Captain Danckwerts (RN) and Atherton and Captain Anderson (USN), 27 Sept. 1935; FO 371/18739/A8599/22/45, record of conversation between Craigie and Atherton, 12 Sept. 1935; FO 371/18740/A8850/22/45, record of conversation between Craigie and Atherton, 10 Oct. 1935; FO 371/18740/A8892/22/45, record of conversation between Craigie and Atherton, 17 Oct. 1935; FO 371/18740/A9213/22/45, FO minute by Craigie, 28 Oct. 1935; CAB 24/257, CP201 (35), Report of Ministerial Committee on 1935 Naval Conference and NCM, 35(75), 22 Oct. 1935; CAB 24/260, CP62 (36), Defence Requirements, 3 Mar. 1936; *FRUS*, Vol. I, telegram from Bingham to Hull, 25 July 1935, 81–2; ibid., telegram from Bingham to Hull, 29 July 1935, 82–5; ibid., memo on meeting of State Department and USN officials to discuss American position for conference, 7 Aug. 1935, 85–7; ibid., telegram from Hull to Atherton, Aug. 14, 1935, 91–2; ibid., telegram from Atherton to Hull, Aug. 21, 1935, 97–8; ibid., telegram from Hull to Atherton, 26 Aug. 1935, 100–1; ibid., telegram from Atherton to Hull, 12 Sept. 1935, 107–8; ibid., telegram from Atherton to Hull, 12 Sept. 1935, 109–10; ibid., telegram from Bingham to Hull, 27 Sept. 1935, 116–18; ibid., telegram from Bingham to Hull, 1 Oct. 1935, 120–2; ibid., telegram from Bingham to Hull, 10 Oct. 1935, 123–5.

124. CAB 23/82, Cabinet Minutes, meeting 54 (35), 11 Dec. 1935; FO 371/19804/A243/4/45, LNC (London Naval Conference) (35) (UK) 9, record of discussion between Eden and Davis, 9 Jan. 1936; CAB 23/83, meeting 11 (36), 26 Feb. 1936; Anthony Eden, *Facing the Dictators*, 2 Vols (London, 1960–65): Vol. II, 315–27.

125. Castle Diary, entry for 27 July 1935. See also FO 371/18769/A7224/3169/45, letter from Lindsay to Vansittart, 8 Aug. 1935.

126. Castle Diary, entry for 28 July 1935.

127. *FRUS*, Vol. I, memo by Noel H. Field, 17 Sept. 1935, 112–13; ibid., memo by Noel H. Field of the Division of Western European Affairs of a meeting held at the executive office of the White House, 19 Nov. 1935, 144–9.

128. Hugh R. Wilson Papers, Herbert Hoover Library, West Branch, Iowa, Container 1, Folder – Norman Davis, letter from Wilson to Davis, 29 Feb. 1936. Also, FO 371/19805/A773/4/45, LNC (35) (UK) 21, 23 Jan. 1936; ibid., LNC (35) (UK) 26, 29 Jan. 1936; ibid., LNC (35) (UK) 28, 3 Feb. 1936; Chatfield, *It Might Happen Again*, 70–2.

129. *FRUS*, Vol. I, memo of conversation of State Department and USN officials, 14 Sept. 1935, 110–12; FO 371/18740/A8758/22/45, NCM (35) 72 and minutes, 11 Oct. 1935; FO 371/18740/A9070/22/45, Craigie minute, 18 Oct. 1935.

130. Eden MSS, FO 954/6, PRO, Kew, London, 'The Far East', FE 36/1, memo by Eden of conversation with Davis, 10 Jan. 1936; ibid., FE 36/4, memo by Eden of conversation with Davis, 18 Jan. 1936; FO 371/19804/A234/4/45, LNC (35) (UK) 9, record of discussion between Eden and Davis, 9 Jan. 1936.

131. FO 371/19809/A2020/4/45, LNC (35) (UK) 92, 10 Mar. 1936; FO 371/19813/A3416/4/45, letter from Capt. Phillips to Craigie, 9 Apr. 1936; CAB 23/83, meeting 20 (36), 16 Mar. 1936; ibid., meeting 21 (36), 18 Mar. 1936; CAB 24/261, CP103 (36), 'Programme of New Construction for 1936', 7 Apr. 1936.

132. Berg, 'Second London Naval Conference', 220. Also FO 371/19804/A243/4/45, LNC (35) (UK) 12, 13 Jan. 1936; FO 371/19804/A234/4/45, LNC (35) (UK) 13, 14 Jan. 1936; FO 371/19804/A234/4/45, LNC (35) (UK) 19, 17 Jan. 1936.

133. FO 371/19805/A773/4/45, LNC (35) (UK) 26, 29 Jan. 1936.

134. See FO 371/19819/A7766/4/45, Vansittart minute, 25 Sept. 1936; FO 371/19820/A8791/4/45, FO minute by Craigie, 30 Oct. 1936; CAB 2/6, CID Minutes, Meeting 278, 12 May 1936. Fisher was so frustrated by the FO's dominance of things Far Eastern that by this point he was asking Chamberlain to move him to the FO in place of Vansittart and instead of Cadogan, even though such a move would result in a loss of rank and pay; NC/7/11/28/43–7/11/29/23, Fisher to Chamberlain, 15 Sept. 1936.

135. See Hugh Wilson Papers, Container 1, Folder – Pierrepont Moffat, letter from Moffat to Wilson, 21 Aug. 1936.

136. CHT/3/1, most secret 'Notes by the First Sea Lord on Sir Robert Vansittart's Memorandum on The World Situation and Rearmament, and on the Comments Thereon by Sir Maurice Hankey', 5 Jan. 1937. Chatfield continued to see the Far East as the most important theatre, before Europe, but was willing to consider an agreement with Japan in order to buy time for rearmament to occur.

# 6

# The Foreign Office and the State Department, 1937–39

American neutrality must be accepted by his Majesty's Government as something that it is useless to call in question. It and the native suspiciousness of foreign effort to influence it must dictate the action of His Majesty's Government in their desire to make the best of the situation. – Sir Ronald Lindsay, 22 March 1937 [1]

It will be seen then that in the Far East co-operation is not ruled out, though the desire to reduce commitments is evident; towards Europe, on the other hand, and towards the League as being in the United States view a mainly European institution, the ancient tradition of no entanglements has full sway. [2]

Between 1935 and 1939, the administration of President Franklin D. Roosevelt, and in particular the State Department and Under-Secretary of State Cordell Hull, developed close, informal relations with Great Britain in order to work in a coordinated fashion against Japanese aggression in the Far East. [3] On the British side, the main forces pushing for the continued recognition of the centrality of Anglo-American relations for the safeguarding of British interests in the Far East were the Secretary of State for Foreign Affairs, Anthony Eden; the British Ambassador in Washington, Sir Ronald C. Lindsay; the US and Far Eastern Departments of the Foreign Office; the Permanent Under-Secretary (PUS), Sir Robert Vansittart; the Secretary of the CID, Maurice Hankey; and the British Ambassador to China, Sir Alexander Cadogan (who later succeeded Vansittart as PUS in 1938). The Treasury and its Chancellor, Neville Chamberlain (later Prime Minister), did not control the conduct and formulation of Britain's Far Eastern foreign policy, although they were a nuisance to those responsible for that policy. [4] Anglo-American relations regarding the Far East during this period were a convoluted mix of departmental communication, public education and informal strategic planning. Was this situation an improvement on the way the two countries had viewed Far Eastern matters before 1935? The short answer is, yes. But, the continuing reality was that the United States and Great Britain each had many self-interests and restraints, both international and domestic, which, even by mid-1937, continued to prevent the two from working openly and quickly against Japanese expansion.[5]

As the two institutional bodies responsible for the ongoing development of Anglo-American relations, the Foreign Office (in particular, Far Eastern (FED) and American (AD) Departments) and the State Department (in particular the Division of Far Eastern Affairs (DFEA)) were the key organizational links between the two nations. How these two groups viewed one another on a personal level, how they viewed Japan and the Far Eastern situation in general, and how they viewed the direction in which Anglo-American relations should develop determined whether there was any 'special relationship' between these two countries with regard to things oriental. Between 1935 and September 1939, their mental maps, those images of the issues, were solidified by the close cooperation of the State Department and Foreign Office. The result was an informal understanding between the two that allowed strategic planners on both sides of the Atlantic to assume with some confidence that Japan ran a great risk of starting a general war in the Pacific if it attacked either the United States' or Great Britain's interests in that region.

The man most responsible for the formulation of American Far Eastern policy, the Chief of the State Department's Far Eastern Division, Stanley K. Hornbeck, had a very good understanding of the British view of the Far Eastern situation.[6] Because the United States was not able to commit to a formal alliance, Britain would not be able to give public support to any American initiatives for fear of provoking Japan. However, Hornbeck was assured by the US Embassy in London that the Foreign Office was most favourably inclined to working quietly with the Americans to counter further Japanese aggression.[7] He agreed with that assessment, and thought that the US Chargé d'affaires, a nine-year veteran of the London embassy, Ray Atherton, was one of the most important sources of information about and insight into Great Britain's Far Eastern policy. Hornbeck also agreed with Atherton that Britain's Far Eastern policy, as also US policy, was based on self-interests, which were roughly similar to those of Washington. But, each nation could appreciate the reasons, largely political ones, that sometimes made a joint approach to the region impractical.[8]

By the end of 1935, Hornbeck was telling his Secretary of State, Cordell Hull, some truths about US foreign policy in the Far East. First, the United States had to ensure that Great Britain did not become frustrated because no formal agreement and joint relationship was forthcoming. The Chief of the Far Eastern Division advised Hull to be certain that American expressions of sympathy for the British position in the Far East were made often and to as many different policy-making groups as possible, including the press. Second, the reality of the strategic situation facing both the United States and Great Britain had to be recognized. It was Hornbeck's opinion that neither power was prepared, at that moment, to use force to defend China. China may indeed have had an intention to use force to defend itself, but would not unless it could get the support of either of the Western powers. In matters relating to China, it was imperative to Hornbeck that the United States be seen as acting on its own, without following any British lead. To be seen as a puppet for British interests would make the isolationists only stronger and the American public suspicious of any relations with Great Britain. Even if parallel action with Great Britain were decided upon, the United States policy had to be seen as protecting American self-interests.[9] He told Hull that:

> There remains among the possibilities ... one course of action which might be advantageous: that is, to make a statement to the British Government. At all times in deciding upon courses of action with regard to Far Eastern matters, we should keep in mind the fact that where common interests are involved cooperative or parallel action on the part of the American and British Governments offers possibility of advantage. Experience has shown that it is difficult to have this cooperation. Both countries should, however, strive for it when and where possible.[10]

Those views were also shared with the US Ambassadors in China and Japan, respectively Nelson T. Johnson and Joseph Grew. Hornbeck informed both men that he wanted close cooperation and harmony with Britain, advocating that such American agencies and institutions as the embassies were to go out of their way to keep their British opposite numbers informed as to what was American policy and what was the thinking in Washington on any issue.[11] This was significant, for both Johnson and Grew were vital sources of information and reflection for Hornbeck. And, although governed by his own experiences and beliefs, the Chief of the Far Eastern Division saw both ambassadors as his trusted eyes and ears and could think of no better men to have in those positions.[12]

Both ambassadors agreed with Hornbeck's attitude towards Great Britain. In correspondence with the former Secretary of State Henry L. Stimson, Johnson concurred with Stimson that, in light of the talks about naval issues and the Far East that had occurred over the last year and a half, Britain was beginning to come alive to the fact that it needed to rearm. Still, while generally well disposed to the British Empire and its position in the world, Johnson was concerned that, faced with German, Italian and Japanese aggression, which could present a concerted and possibly coordinated threat, Great Britain would need to look to a collective security arrangement for safety.[13] In that regard, Johnson was not opposed to the United States working in an informal and parallel manner with Great Britain against Japan, although Great Britain would of course have to take the lead.[14]

Grew was also happy with the way the Anglo-American naval talks had gone over the past two years. It was his opinion that:

> So far as we can evaluate here the proceedings of the recent preliminary naval conversations in London, I am of the opinion that the most important and the most valuable result issuing therefrom has been the apparent tendency towards closer Anglo-American cooperation in the Far East. If we can count in future – again as a direct result of Japan's 'bungling diplomacy' – on a solid and united front between the United States and Great Britain in meeting Japan's flaunting of treaty rights and her unrestrained ambitions to control East Asia, the future may well assume a brighter aspect for all of us.[15]

Grew and the British Ambassador at Tokyo, Sir Robert Henry Clive, had worked steadily and closely together on Sino-Japanese issues during 1935, sharing sensitive information, as well as opinions on what the other's government was likely to do or be able to do in any given circumstance involving Japanese aggression.[16] Johnson had a similar relationship with Sir Alexander Cadogan, the British Minister (soon to be Ambassador) in China.[17]

Both Grew and Johnson, like the members of the Far Eastern and American Departments of the Foreign Office, were also sceptical about the growth, or possibility of growth, of any meaningful liberal movement in the Japanese government.[18] Grew summed up the views of all four observing bodies when he told Hull that:

> It would seem unwise to predicate American policy in the Far East on the hope of democratic developments in this country. The military should be kept in mind as still the strongest single element in Japanese affairs. But the fact that the leaders are persons of military training is incidental only they are not primarily soldiers but are strong nationalists who, in a country in which the army is a popular institution which offers a career to talent, happen to have been trained as soldiers.[19]

Such goodwill and cooperation between the British and US embassies in the Far East was repeated in London and Washington. The State Department's relations with Lindsay were at their apogee, with the former looking almost solely to the Ambassador to provide the British position and its interpretation.[20] As well, Lindsay had powerful allies, in the shape of former Under-Secretary of State, William R. Castle Jr, working hard to persuade Cordell Hull that Great Britain was an ally that could be trusted and relied upon in the Far East.[21] Such efforts, the Secretary believed by August 1935, were necessary, because 'if a misunderstanding arose between England and America there would be no hope left of saving even a semblance of democracy anywhere'.[22] Similarly, in London,

Ray Atherton continued to be given access to the Foreign Office's inner sanctum in order to be able to transmit to Washington, clearly and confidently, the real British position on any Far Eastern matter, and to obtain sensitive material about Britain's Far Eastern policy.[23] Atherton, along with Ambassador Robert W. Bingham and the latter's successor, Joseph Kennedy, kept intact the hard-won trust of the Foreign Office. The mechanisms for creating better Anglo-American relations at the foreign-policy level were in place.[24] Thus, as 1935 drew to a end, the views and relationships between the American and British organs seemed to be moving along parallel, but not joint, lines.

On 22 December 1935, Anthony Eden took over as Secretary of State, succeeding Sir Samuel Hoare. His move to that office was taken by the US Embassy as a clear signal that continued improvement in Anglo-American relations could be expected. Bingham reported to Hull that Eden had informed him that 'at the basis of his [Eden's] policy was his purpose to cooperate in every possible way with the United States Government'.[25] And for Eden, the primary immediate threat to Great Britain's security came from the Far East. To meet that threat, in the face of a more aggressive Italy and a resurgent Germany, the United States had to be brought into a closer, cooperative relationship.[26] Therefore, following up the success of the Anglo-American naval talks was an important part of Eden's Far Eastern policy. Norman Davis, the chief US naval negotiator, saw immediately that Eden was desirous of making better Anglo-American naval relations blossom into something more. Davis invited Eden to come to the United States to visit the President at Hyde Park and to help educate the American public about the realities of the circum-stances of international relations. The newly appointed Foreign Secretary reacted cautiously, and showed good sense in eliciting the opinion of the most able Foreign Office observer of the United States, Lindsay, as to whether to pursue the matter. Lindsay told Eden that it was hard to believe that Davis would have made such an advance without it being on Roosevelt's behalf. The Ambassador assured the Foreign Secretary that the President was 'funda-mentally friendly to Great Britain, though of course he is not going to give anything away for less than its value ...'[27] The American Department was anxious that not too much cold water be poured on the idea, for fear that future talks with the Americans about trade agreements and economic cooperation be discouraged.[28] However, the head of the American Department, Robert Craigie, cautioned against any such visit occurring until after the fall presi-dential elections took place. If Roosevelt won, then his administration would be stronger, and a more productive and aggressive attitude towards the Far East could result in any such talks.[29] Vansittart, still fearful of being left in the lurch by the Americans, pushed Eden not to 'run after' the United States because of its unreliability.[30] Eden, not wanting to overstep his own position within the Cabinet, and fearing his visit would be used by American isolationists as an example of British propaganda aimed at drawing the United States into a war, politely declined the offer, assuring Vansittart that there was no question of British policy 'running after' the US.[31] Moreover, Eden first had other fights to wage within his own government before he could move in such a bold fashion.

Many of these involved the other departments that wished to influence foreign policy. The new Foreign Secretary supported the Far Eastern Department's efforts to thwart the Treasury's.[32] As well, he understood the need not to embarrass the United States on the world stage through 'overt invitation or undue publicity', but instead to let them assist British interests in their own way and at their own speed.[33] Eden's predecessor, Sam Hoare, had been doubtful of Japan's willingness to work cooperatively with Great Britain in the future, and had sought to come to a better understanding with the Americans on Far Eastern plans. In a conversation with Ambassador Bingham, Hoare had confided that

> it was his policy as far as possible to strengthen the liberal element in Japan, if there was any such element left; but that he thought there was grave danger of further action by Japan which would flagrantly violate the Kellogg-Briand Pact, and because he thought this was probable, he thought that we should try in advance to clear our minds as to what action, if any, could be taken in the face of the situation which would arise, and which probably would arise in the comparatively near future, and that meanwhile he was trying, as he had said, to strengthen the liberal element in Japan if there was any liberal element left.[34]

Fed a steady diet of pro-Japanese intelligence and viewpoints by Major General F.S.G. Piggot, the British Military Attaché in Tokyo and a confirmed Japanophile and Foreign Office irritant, the War Office and the Chief of the Imperial General Staff (CIGS), Field Marshal Sir Archibald A. Montgomery-Massingberd, also promoted the view that, considering the global strategic situation facing the empire, it would be better to give Japan what it wanted than risk a conflict.[35] When pressed by the CIGS in Cabinet to move towards a more accommodating approach to Japan, Eden responded that he, too, would like to be able to improve relations with Japan. However, desiring such a circumstance and facing the reality were two different things. Eden, aware of the need to avoid giving the United States the impression that Britain was willing to 'cut a deal' with the Japanese over China, politely rebuffed the idea of any sort of Anglo-Japanese understanding being possible in the foreseeable future.[36] The hard-won gains in Anglo-American relations would not be squandered so quickly for such an unlikely cause.

His rejection of the War Office–Treasury proposal was based partly on such information as given to him by Charles Orde, the head of the Far Eastern Department. Aside from considerations of the animosity that such an agreement would create with China, Orde's approach was influenced prominently by thought of the United States. Although sceptical of the exact usefulness of the United States and its willingness to stay engaged in the Pacific, and more concerned about how such an agreement would endanger the vital Anglo-Soviet relationship, Orde believed that 'The United States of America would look on us as selfish opportunists who had left the path of rectitude, and League circles, official and unofficial, would regard us in the same light and as traitors to the cause of international morality.'[37] Vansittart and Sir Victor Wellesley and Lord Stanhope (both Deputy Under-Secretaries of State with remits for the Far Eastern Department), all agreed with Orde's analysis.[38] As a result of the naval talks and the other movements towards closer Anglo-American relations which were occurring simultaneously, Eden was certain to consult and coordinate any major move in Britain's Far Eastern policy with the United States.

Eden utilized the skills of an important ally in his fight against the Treasury and War Office when the transfer of Sir Alexander Cadogan took the future PUS from China to London, where he became Deputy Under-Secretary. Cadogan brought with him to London some useful first-hand experiences of the Far East, as well as the benefit of having had a close and productive relationship with Ambassador Johnson. As he prepared to leave China, Cadogan held some final talks with Johnson on British and American commitments in China. The British Ambassador had tried to discourage the Chinese from expecting open military support against Japan. While Johnson pointed out that, given British support for Ethiopia, the Chinese perhaps had some grounds for thinking that Britain would do the same for them, Cadogan replied that:

> the Chinese ought to be able to see that the two situations are entirely different; in Europe it was possible for Great Britain to enlist the joint support of other nations, whereas in the Far East there would be no nation to join Great Britain in opposing Japan's encroachments on China. He pointed out that it would be impossible for Great Britain to exert any military strength of its own in the Far East. I [Johnson] assented to his general view and admitted that the nearest Great Power, the United States, would be extremely unlikely to take any part in the matter, since American participation in any way is enormously more expensive than participation by any other nations, and there were no American interests in China which would seem to warrant the colossal expenditure that past experience indicated would probably be necessary.[39]

The US Ambassador was also very appreciative of Cadogan's knowledge of the Far East, telling him that he believed he possessed a 'thorough comprehension of the psychological factors which mould political events in the Far East and the details were more or less inconsequential'.[40] On his return to Great Britain, Cadogan shared his views on Britain's Far Eastern policy with Atherton, who was about to go home on leave. The Deputy Under-Secretary's views were the same as those he had expressed to Ambassador Johnson. He repeated that Britain would not fight for China and neither would the United States. As well, Cadogan did not support making a deal with Japan for the exploitation of China; nor was he willing to provoke Japan by any unnecessary efforts at alliance building against its actions in China. Finally, the former Ambassador to China impressed Atherton with the idea that neither he nor the British government desired to create a thoroughgoing Anglo-American front. Such a formal and open bloc would only make the Japanese harder to work with. Atherton agreed with those views, telling Cadogan that a fear of possible Anglo-American cooperation was likely to make the Japanese more willing to accommodate both Western nations.[41] With Cadogan in London to assist him, Eden would be able both to counter opposition to the Foreign Office's hardline approach to Japan and, at the same time, to conduct an insightful and comprehensive campaign to solidify Anglo-American trust on Far Eastern matters. Both men believed in the need to safeguard Britain's imperial needs first, but both were also willing to acknowledge the need for American support in the Far East to protect them.

By May 1936, the evidence of the effect of that 'parallel but not joint' union of US and British interests on a number of issues was beginning to be seen in Japanese reactions. On 29 May, Grew reported that Japan was terrified at the prospect of Anglo-American cooperation in the Far East. He supported the idea of continuing the policy of issuing similar if not joint representations, as he saw the great advantage being produced by such actions.[42] Clive shared Grew's assessment, and reported thus to the Foreign Office. When charged by the Japanese that Anglo-American pressure was being brought to bear, Clive denied the existence of any such pressure. He rebutted the allegations by stating that there had been no joint action or combined pressure (a blatant stretching of the truth) and that each government had acted in defence of its own interests.[43] This creation of uncertainty in Japan's ability to judge the Anglo-American relationship in the Far East accurately was beneficial to both Western powers, as it acted as a brake on the Japanese when there was little militarily that either nation could do to influence matters. The Japanese, faced with an uncertainty on one hand and a certainty – the animosity of the Soviet Union – on the other, were forced to take stock of their strategic position. Meanwhile, the Foreign Office and State Department continued to work at strengthening Anglo-American ties, for each office had certain lingering suspicions and uncertainties about the other's Far Eastern policy that needed clarification and explication.[44]

In London, Vansittart, now more impressed with the need for maintaining better Anglo-American relations, began a public relations campaign aimed at educating the American Mid-West about Britain's strategic position in the Far East. When Ronald Tree, an MP for Harborough, returned from a visit to the American Mid-West he gave the American Department a briefing on the views towards Great Britain that he found there.[45] The PUS was suitably impressed, both with Tree's opinion that the Mid-West had been too long ignored by foreign representatives and with the idea that Lindsay should arrange for a tour through that region.[46] Lindsay's reply revealed one of the major problems facing British attempts to 'educate' the American public from 1936 to 1941: a fear that such actions would be seen as propaganda aimed at 'trapping' the United States in a compromising position. Lindsay argued that, along with the physical effort required for such a trip, the State Department was emphatic that anything remotely resembling propaganda be absolutely avoided.[47] Craigie and the American Department argued that Lindsay was overstating the case and should be ordered to conduct the tour, but, as usual, the Ambassador's views on American attitudes won the day.[48] Lindsay continued to warn off Foreign Office attempts to recreate the propaganda campaign of the First World War, knowing full well the deep resentment felt in certain areas of the American mentality towards that episode in Anglo-American relations. Furthermore, nothing along such lines could really be considered until the results of the autumn presidential election were known.

Throughout the late summer and autumn, British Far Eastern policy-makers had had to deal with proposals put forward by the new Japanese Ambassador to Great Britain, Shigeru Yoshida, about the possibility of a renewed Anglo-Japanese understanding. The talks had created some embarrassment and discomfort for the Foreign Office, as no one there really believed that Yoshida had either the authority or the political power to make the agreement he was proposing a reality. Furthermore, in seeking to circumvent the Far Eastern experts available in the Foreign Office, the Ambassador had sought to bypass the normal channels of communication and had approached directly the pro-Japanese Chancellor of the Exchequer, Neville Chamberlain, with his proposals.[49] By the end of the year, however, the Foreign Office had disproved Yoshida's ability and disabused the Cabinet of any idea that his initiatives would create better Anglo-American relations.[50] Similarly, by the end of 1936, the Japanese Ambassador in the United States was also seen as being weak and ineffective.[51] Part of the reason for the decreased credibility of the Japanese Embassies was the signing of the Anti-Comintern Pact between Germany and Japan, and the Keelung Incident (where British sailors and an officer were assaulted in the Japanese-controlled port of Keelung), both coming late in 1936. The incidents seemed to prove what those who argued against being able to trust Japan had proclaimed.

Furthermore, both episodes had strengthened Anglo-American cooperation. US and British diplomatic organs had worked closely and shared sensitive information about both events, finding that their views on the Anti-Comintern Pact were almost identical. This working together helped to augment a growing sense of confidence and trust in Anglo-American Far Eastern relations, while at the same time discrediting the Japanese.[52] In the Keelung matter, the rapid and forceful British response and the subsequent Japanese apology and reaction enhanced Britain's prestige in the Far East.[53] The Commander-in-Chief of the China Squadron, Admiral Sir Charles J.C. Little, had shared the Royal Navy's anger over the incident with his counter-part, Admiral Harry E. Yarnell, the C.-in-C. of the US Asiatic Fleet, and had found a sympathetic ear. Ambassador Grew had also advised the State Department strongly to support the British position and to deprecate any visits of the US C.-in-C. to Japan. The State Department agreed with Grew.[54] Certainly, American sympathy for the injustices being suffered by the British at the hands of the Japanese military was increasing.

The year 1936 came to a close on another high note for Anglo-American naval relations. When asked by Vansittart and Eden for comment on an article dealing with Britain's seapower and the Pacific that Winston Churchill was preparing for publication, Craigie replied to Churchill's theory that Britain did not care anymore what size fleet the United States built with an illuminating and absolutely accurate four-point summation of the state of Anglo-American naval relations:

> 1. If America were to increase her building programme beyond the point of parity with us and Japan were to follow (As she certainly would), this could not be immaterial to us, because we should have to follow in our turn. Whether we like it or not, the building of the three countries is therefore hopelessly interconnected. 2. Even if we do not mind much what America builds, the same is not true of the United States, which watches our building with the greatest care and regards parity not as an abstract theory but as a real necessity. 3. If the purpose of the article is to appeal to Japanese opinion, then it is perhaps a mistake to say that, so much do we trust America that we do not mind what she builds, but that we shall be most careful to watch and match every ship which you, Japan, build. This may be true, but there are certain facts which are better not insisted upon too much. 4. The chances of our bringing Japan into the new Naval Treaty will be diminished in proportion as she regards this as a frame-up between the Americans and ourselves.[55]

Cadogan agreed fully with Craigie's analysis, believing that, while the idea of Anglo-American relations being closely coordinated and full of trust was indeed the reality, it was also a fact that neither nation desired to fling in Japan's face. He did not object strenuously, however, to Churchill's tough tone towards Japan and its foreign policy of the last five years.[56]

Stanley Hornbeck echoed many of the sentiments expressed by Craigie as to the usefulness of the recent naval agreement. He, like Craigie, believed that the only way to ensure Japanese cooperation in international relations was to show a strong front. Hornbeck and Craigie also held similar views on the probability of Japan returning to the bargaining table once it became obvious that Great

Britain and the United States would not allow it to win any naval race. The Chief of the Far Eastern Division was a strong supporter of naval preparedness, assuming that a reasonable Japan would see the futility in trying to out-produce the United States in armaments. Carefully watched, and faced with a united front, Japan would be forced by outside pressure to make an approach to the western nations, a path which would be more beneficial to the United States.[57]

This close approximation of views led to an unusual occurrence. Gradually, the State Department and the Foreign Office began to place more emphasis on what each other thought about Japan than they did on what was being reported to them through their own official diplomatic channels. This parallel shutting down of part of the traditional information-passing system occurred in both Western powers simultaneously, making them both more reliant on and receptive to the other's views on Japan. This phenomenon also reflected the more direct control both Washington and London had begun to exercise in the guidance of Far Eastern affairs due to the increasing strategic importance of the region. The shared information passing back and forth between the Foreign Office and the US Embassy in London, and the material shared between the two Embassies in Tokyo, became the key foundations upon which British and American assessments of Japan were created. During a conversation about the recently completed naval talks, Ambassador Bingham and Robert Craigie displayed how that process worked when the topic shifted to the Far East and what each nation could do there. Bingham relayed the sentiments of President Roosevelt and Secretary Hull to Craigie, telling the latter that, owing to the success of the naval talks, the opportunity to create closer Anglo-American relations in general had now arrived. Public opinion was moving along with Roosevelt and Hull's view, said Bingham, and that view was certainly the one held by many Americans who held responsible positions. While the chances of an actual military alliance being created were non-existent, barring an emergency, there was now 'ample scope for the closest consultation and co-operation'.[58] For his part, Craigie told the Ambassador that his government felt the same, but that there were of course differences as to the method of dealing with the Japanese question. Increasing pressures in Europe were making it more difficult for the British to act in the Far East, said Craigie, and there was the added question of whether the United States was going to stay engaged in the Philippines or abandon that responsibility. If these realities of the British strategic position could be accepted more by American policy-makers, then, thought Craigie, any serious difference between the two nations over Far Eastern policy would be avoided. Craigie told Bingham that the constant exchange of full and frank views and information on that region had to be maintained, as that openness and trust was vital to the maintenance of the Anglo-American relationship. Bingham agreed entirely, assuring Craigie that the United States administration fully recognized how the situation had changed over the previous two years.[59] For their part, both Cadogan and

Vansittart were anxious to play on that American desire for full and closer cooperation. A trade agreement was thought a logical next step in the process of eliminating areas of contention with the United States, with both men also agreeing such a trade agreement would have strategic benefits for Britain's imperial defence problems.[60] This change of attitude towards Britain's global situation on the part of the United States coincided with an initiative by President Roosevelt to hold a world peace conference.

Stronger on foreign-policy matters after his re-election, Roosevelt began floating the idea of summoning such a conference in order to force the 'gangster powers', Italy, Germany and Japan, out into the open. If those powers refused to participate or give way to the peaceful demands of the rest of the world, then the peace-loving nations would come together in a close agreement on how to proceed further against the outlaws.[61] Roosevelt's plan received mixed reviews from the British government, with Eden and Neville Chamberlain, who would become Prime Minster in May 1937, wanting the idea kept in play, while Vansittart and Craigie both objected to such a scheme. Because of their lack of faith in the American diplomatic machinery, the latter pair felt Roosevelt's idea was dangerous. Their professional bias against American diplomats and negotiators caused them to believe that such a proposal was impulsive, displaying improper and insufficient preparation. Remembering the problems caused in the past by the failure of 'The Big' conference, both Craigie and Vansittart feared that if Roosevelt's conference failed it would drive the United States into a deeper isolationist mood. However, if pre-conference cooperation, similar to that which had occurred with the naval limitation talks, was in evidence between the United States and Great Britain, then a safe environment for such an event could be arranged.[62] Eden and Chamberlain rebuffed the idea that such a call by Roosevelt was 'dangerous'. Instead, both men were emphatic that the British response to Roosevelt's initiative should avoid discouraging the President. In their minds, the President's move would allow a greater education of the American people to the dangers in the world. That could only help inspire sympathy for the British position in the Far East.[63]

Faced with strong political direction, Vansittart and Craigie quickly changed gears, with the former taking the matter up with Lindsay. The PUS agreed, after being instructed by his ambassador, that to squash the American project was not the proper course to take. To do so would endanger the goodwill found in current Anglo-American relations and undo all the good achieved over the preceding three years. Instead, Lindsay should continue to point out the need for proper preparation and what the potential difficulties of calling such a conference would be. The attitude to be taken was one of concerned instruction, not outright disdain and rejection (Vansittart's natural reaction). Lindsay was both to ensure that he stayed in close contact with Hull on any future matters related to Roosevelt's proposal and to avoid giving the appearance of discouraging the idea.[64] Despite this, Roosevelt's initiative eventually ran its course without any concrete result. The President was not willing to undertake any future action without first having a complete and full consultation with the British. He did, however, assure Eden that it was his desire to cooperate with Great Britain on foreign affairs and that he was 'not only ready but eager to help, that he would be ready to take an initiative if and when we thought the moment right, and that he would take none unless we were in accord as to its appropriateness'.[65] The need to ensure close Anglo-American efforts at all levels on strategic issues was now beginning to dominate American and British policy-makers in their formulation of a Far Eastern policy.

Not surprisingly, given the commonality of material available to the State Department and the Foreign Office, their attitudes, while not identical, certainly became similar. However, in 1937, changes in the strategic balance of power in the Far East and to the Tokyo Embassy would disturb the peace of that region and, for a time, the coordination of that Anglo-American information sharing. This occurred when Sir Robert Craigie became Britain's Ambassador to Japan. His appointment and his ensuing handling of Anglo-Japanese relations created a resurgence of Grew's suspicion about what Britain's intentions towards Japan were.[66] Those suspicions were overridden, however, by the continued close workings of the Foreign Office and the State Department through the London and Washington embassies, as well as by a growing amount of direct contact.

The year 1937 began on a high note for Great Britain, as Ambassador Bingham issued a glowing report to President Roosevelt on that nation's relations with the United States. Bingham believed that the empire was rearming in order to take a leading role in the maintenance of peace in the world, and was in the midst of a drive to establish closer relations with the United States.[67] In particular, Bingham believed that the policies of the two nations, in international affairs, were certainly moving along similar lines. Members of the British government, prominent public and private figures, various private and government committees, all were involved in trying to improve Anglo-American relations. Further, 'Official orders have been given in the British Army and Navy that good relations with their American opposite numbers at home and abroad must be established and maintained.'[68] Relations between the US Embassy and the Foreign Office had a marked friendliness that could not go unnoticed, and the British press were working hard to make the American public more aware of the dangers being presented to Britain.[69]

At the same time, Norman Davis continued to add his voice to those advising Roosevelt to make Britain's path to better Anglo-American relations an easier one. Faced with the need to find a solution to the naval building programmes of Germany, Italy, France and Japan, the United States could try to broker some sort of new plan to limit naval arms. However, as the likelihood of such an agreement was slim, in reality there was a need for the US Navy to increase its own building. Above all else, argued Davis, if such a buildup were to take place, then the Royal Navy was the standard to be matched. That did not mean, however, that Britain was to be the target of the building programme. In fact, Davis was insistent that Britain not be held responsible in any respect for the American need to build a bigger fleet. He lobbied Hull that 'I think we should avoid even the appearance that it [increased American naval building] is because of the British but should make it clear that it is the world situation which impels the British to increase and for us to do likewise in order to maintain our nation's position and safeguard our interests.'[70] Davis had been confirmed in his views by the actions of the ex-Secretary of State for Foreign Affairs, Sir Samuel Hoare, now the First Lord of the Admiralty. Hoare was grateful that the United States had been willing and able to talk openly and honestly about naval matters in such trying times. Because of the close understanding between the two nations

> he [Hoare] said that they were prepared to give us any information which we may seek. Our naval attaché was delighted that I was able to get the information I did about the British plans because our navy had been most eager to get it and he had been unable to do so from any of the more subordinate officials.[71]

Hoare also promised to let the Americans know anything about Japanese naval plans or building as soon as the British found out any details. In such fertile conditions, the pro-Britain lobby in the Roosevelt administration grew quickly.

On the other side of the globe, intimate discussions with Clive had led Joseph Grew to report that Britain was improving its diplomatic leverage over Japan because of Japan's worsening relations with the Soviet Union and Great Britain's improved relations with the Russians. Both men agreed that, in such conditions the natural course of action for Japan would be to try to improve its relations with the United States in order to alleviate Tokyo's isolation. Neither was convinced that Japan could be trusted, however, to make substantial changes in its aggressive foreign policy. Any changes would be cosmetic only, and based on the 'all take and no give' formulae of negotiations.[72] It was Grew's belief, as well as that of Ambassador Johnson in China, however, that Japan's new Minister for Foreign Affairs, Naotake Sato, would be far more accommodating than his predecessor, General Hayashi Senjuro Arita.[73] Still, both British and American expectations of any significant change in Japan's foreign policy were low.[74] As a result of these limited expectations of Japan, US and British officials continued to share their views and plans for the Far East with one another in case an emergency arose in that region. Direct contact between British Cabinet members and high-ranking State Department officials was utilized in that information-sharing scheme.

Early in 1937, the President of the Board of Trade, Walter Runciman, travelled to the United States as a precursor to serious Anglo-American trade negotiations. From there, he informed the Prime Minister, Stanley Baldwin, that the US administration was very much desirous of exchanging 'information even of very secret nature' between various departments, most importantly of all, the foreign affairs departments, the two Treasuries, and the air forces.[75] Runciman was impressed by the genuine desire of Roosevelt to cooperate with the British on these matters, and urged Baldwin and Eden to do all they could to ensure swift and full cooperation.[76] On 23 January, the President of the Board of Trade had a private talk with the President at the White House. The two men talked a great deal about the international situation facing the democracies. When discussion turned to the Far East, Roosevelt told Runciman that 'The Japanese situation ... was causing him anxiety and he would welcome any joint action which we could undertake. After describing the Far East as he saw it, he asked whether it was not possible to have [a] closer examination of the situation by our two Governments so that if and when action is called for we could act in accordance with a consistent policy.'[77] Craigie and Vansittart were sceptical of the President's sincerity, but Eden could not help but be impressed by the open discussion of the Far East that Roosevelt had initiated.[78] Besides such high-level, secret advances, aimed at creating a common strategic vision, more open but no less vital talks were taking place between the State Department and the Foreign Office over what action to take towards Japan.

At the urging of Stanley Hornbeck, who desired some clarification on certain aspects of the British vision of the Far Eastern situation, Ray Atherton met with Cadogan. Cadogan had sent Hornbeck an outline of his views of the Far Eastern situation and asked Hornbeck to reply with his own opinions.[79] In addition to expressing his and Hornbeck's appreciation of the closeness of the cooperation and information sharing that had been occurring between the two organs, Atherton's visit signalled a beginning of an even greater move towards openness in that relationship. Atherton began by reading the text of Hornbeck's telegram on the world's international situation. As far as the Anti-Comintern Pact was concerned, Hornbeck thought that it had done Japan more harm than good and had earned that nation the undying distrust of the Soviet Union. The embassy official also told Cadogan that Hornbeck understood Britain's need to be aware of any reasonable opportunity to make better relations with Japan. That being said, however, the State Department official wanted to know if the British had in mind any definite advantage that could be gained from better relations with Japan, and, if so, what was the Foreign Office's objective?[80] Cadogan replied first by re-stating that the British government was not getting ready to make any sort of deal with Ambassador Yoshida.[81] He continued by saying that Britain's policy towards Japan was aimed at trying to maintain good terms, but at the same time trying to get that country to change its aggressive tactics towards China. The British were willing to work with the Japanese to help China develop itself, because the development of the China market was in the interests of everyone concerned. When Atherton pressed him to put a priority on those objectives, and in particular asked if Britain would ever throw China over in order to improve relations with Japan, Cadogan gave an emphatic no. The Deputy Under-Secretary told Atherton that to treat China in such a fashion would retard the development of China and taint Great Britain with the same odium that was at present attached solely to Japan. Such a policy would benefit no one and could not be contemplated. He assured Atherton that, 'Really our whole aim was to try and influence Japan to drop her present tactics and join with us and the United States Government and other Governments interested in helping develop China …' Cadogan also reiterated that Britain would undertake no new initiative with the Japanese without first conducting close and thorough consultations with the United States. Atherton was pleased with that response, as was Eden, who congratulated Cadogan for having disabused the State Department of any baseless suspicions of Britain's unwillingness either to assist China or to punish an aggressive Japan.

The Foreign Secretary was also adamant that, on the Far Eastern issue, 'We must continue to keep the US government informed of any subsequent developments.'[82] To reinforce this, he sent his own message to Secretary Hull and President Roosevelt through Ambassador Bingham on 20 March. During a luncheon meeting, the Foreign Secretary returned to items that he had discussed on 11 March with the Ambassador, particularly the issues of neutrality and the Far East. Eden told Bingham that he did in fact speak for the Cabinet, and even Neville Chamberlain, when he said that Britain desired good, close Anglo-American relations in the Far East. Bingham had other sources of information that confirmed that Eden was indeed speaking for the entire British Cabinet, and reported the full details of his exchange with Eden to Hull and Roosevelt.[83] Eden was not going to allow the Far East to be the area of tension which would again create friction in Anglo-American relations. He was sure, that if any nation was certain to be ready to place odium on Great Britain for a betrayal of China, it was the United States. To go back now, or to give the United Nations any reason to suspect that Britain was becoming 'soft' on the issue of Japan's treatment of China would spell disaster for the entirety of imperial foreign policy, not just in the Far East. To be certain that he did not commit a critical error in his efforts to move Anglo-American relations closer, Eden turned to the man most trusted to gauge accurately the temperament and thinking processes of the Roosevelt administration, Sir Ronald Lindsay.[84]

Thus, Eden requested Lindsay to prepare a special report on American attitudes towards a wide range of items: politics, foreign policy, economics, propaganda, exchanges of information and so on, in order that the Foreign Secretary would have a comprehensive mental map of how the Roosevelt Administration was thinking and to what pressures it would be responding in any given circumstance. Eden also wanted Lindsay's recommendations on what attitude His Majesty's government should take towards the United States on these issues and what pitfalls to avoid. The Foreign Secretary saw the

Ambassador as the most important bell-wether on American behaviour and trusted his recommendations as to what courses of action to take.[85]

Lindsay's report became a classic within the foreign-policy-making elite, winning high praise from the American Department as well as from other departments and officials like Vansittart.[86] The Ambassador stressed that Anglo-American relations had been progressing extraordinarily well since around 1933 and commented on the myriad reasons why that was so.

> This happy state of affairs is due in the first place to the elimination of sources of friction – to the disappearance of the Irish question, to the cessation of naval rivalry ... The next point of sympathy is democracy which in many countries of Europe has crashed to the ground, in some is tottering, but in England as in America continues to be the solid rock on which the structure of the State is raised. Can it be that in this country there is a lurking subconscious fear that if all Europe were to become totalitarian, the foundations of democratic liberty in America too might be menaced? Be that as it may the totalitarian philosophy rouses the most violent animosities in America, and Mr Roosevelt himself has publicly and outspokenly expressed himself on the subject on more than one important occasion. Lastly it happens that on the broadest issue of foreign politics the desires of the United States and of the United Kingdom completely coincide. Neither has any acquisitive ambitions, or aggressive inclinations, neither wants anything but that the various countries of the world shall settle down to peaceful trade with each other. England is placed on a plane apart from that of other countries; she is regarded as the one country in Europe that has preserved its sanity, and her efforts as the only hope of peace.

As for US isolationism, Lindsay had no doubt that the American public were not interested at all in becoming involved in European affairs, and that there was really no blandishment that Britain could offer to draw the Americans onto such a path: 'American neutrality must be accepted by his Majesty's Government as something that it is useless to call in question. It and the native suspiciousness of foreign effort to influence it must dictate the action of His Majesty's Government in their desire to make the best of the situation.' If war came, however, especially in the Far East, Roosevelt's approach to neutrality would favour Great Britain. American intervention was not likely, immediately, and even when it intervened it might not be to Britain's benefit, but only to save the entire world from destruction.

Lindsay advised that the British government would be wise not to launch any initiative on a major political issue, because to attempt to do so would excite the suspicions of groups who believed Britain to be trying to entangle the United States in war. This left the economic approach open. Owing to the

Democratic Party's traditions of low tariffs and a desire on the part of the Roosevelt administration to resume international trade, progress in Anglo-American relations was certainly possible provided always that no political implications were involved.

On the issue of working closer with the Americans on foreign policy matters, especially in the Far East, Lindsay considered it vital not to turn down any American overtures for cooperation, as that would be considered a snub reminiscent of the 1932 Stimson–Simon exchange. The Ambassador acknowledged the need to be wary of the Americans' leading Great Britain on and then deserting it in the face of further aggression, but he also believed that such a situation could be avoided:

> When I advocate grasping the proffered hand when it is proffered, I do not recommend obsequious acquiescence. Officious assiduity is only less bad than the British standoffishness which offends every American instinct. I advocate a cordial response with a patent and earnest desire to do mutually satisfactory business.

He also wisely and insightfully identified how and where British efforts to create closer relations would do the most good. Cooperation was easier, he argued, with the administration than with the Congress. The whole diplomatic machine was controlled by Roosevelt, and this gave him great authority over everything short of a treaty:

> Let it be understood that the Administration, from the President downwards is well disposed towards us. The divisions of the State Department, except perhaps Latin America, are all friendly, and I think the same may be said of other Ministries including the Army and Navy. I consider that it would be politic to assume American friendliness, and to welcome or invite cooperation over departmental questions, always remembering that even in the Departments on this side politics and 'interests' may intervene and obstruct, and postulating that as both we and the Americans will wish to hold up our own ends, we may have a certain number of failures. But I believe that where business is conducted away from the glare of publicity, the present cordiality is strong enough to stand a percentage of failures.

As for exchanging secret information with the Americans, he repeated his view that, as there was no fear of Britain going to war with the United States, there was, therefore, nothing to fear from such exchanges. It was the Embassy's opinion that the Army and Navy could be trusted to keep secrets. Exchanges would certainly foster goodwill and that was the most important element to keep in mind: the creation of more goodwill. As for suggestions as to how to approach the Americans on that issue, Lindsay was not definitive. His recommendation was that

> action is far the most difficult point on which to make recommendations, for America is the despair of the diplomat. In her remoteness, both physical and political, she resembles a prize fighter with a very long reach. He stands with his left arm stretched far out, and the opponent may dance round and round in the ring and never come to close quarters.

He did, however, make two suggestions as to possible courses of action open to Eden. The first was for the British government to spend a great deal of money and make a spectacular showing at the world fair in 1939. But, more important, was the idea that some sort of trade agreement be concluded.

Lindsay's response fell on fertile ground generally in the Foreign Office. The need for Great Britain to obtain American goodwill in order to be able to plan effectively for the defence of the Empire was a theme which resonated well, in the American Department especially.[87] Further proof of the United States' desire to work closely with the British on Far Eastern matters came from Lindsay in early June, when he reported Cordell Hull's views on the situation in that region. Responding to statements made by the new Prime Minister, Neville Chamberlain, Hull concurred with the British opinion that orderly stability was desirable, and he believed that measures which might be expected to contribute towards ensuring harmony of purpose and action should be investigated by the United States with other powers, especially Great Britain.[88] Hull did not, however, move beyond the idea of closer consultation and parallel representation whenever the two governments held similar views. He preferred the idea of similar action as opposed to the reality of such action. It was clear to the Foreign Office that the United States still intended to preserve its independence of action and would not assume any new defence obligations in that region. Cadogan and Vansittart were not surprised by Hull's limited response, knowing that, given the mood of American public opinion, the Secretary of State was unlikely to move too far ahead of Britain in Far Eastern matters.[89] Secretary Hull was pleased, however, with the manner by which the British were conducting their own Far Eastern policy. He informed Ambassador Grew that Cadogan had told Yoshida frankly and firmly that Great Britain would not be a partner to any Anglo-Japanese rehabilitation or protection programme for China. The Deputy Under-Secretary had emphasized Britain's desire to work with the United States, China and Japan on the matter, but would not consider working solely with Japan.[90] While the Foreign Office were mildly frustrated at the American inability to move faster on developing a solid Far Eastern policy, the State Department was secure in its understanding of the British position.

Lindsay's brilliant dissection of the state of Anglo-American relations and

Hull's affirmation of the Roosevelt administration's desire to keep working on a more coordinated Far Eastern policy had barely worked their way through the Foreign Office, Admiralty, War Office and other government offices when matters took a severe turn for the worse in the Far East. On 7 July 1937, an undeclared war began as Japanese troops invaded mainland China.[91] New pressures began to work on driving the foreign policies of the United States and Great Britain closer together.

On 13 July, Lindsay delivered a memorandum to Stanley Hornbeck outlining the British view of events in China. One of the items in that document was the question of whether the United States would consider the idea of a joint representation to the Japanese.[92] The British request created a stir within the administration, a stir which reached from Hornbeck to the President himself. Roosevelt approved a State Department reply, drafted primarily by Hornbeck and Hull, with contributions from Under-Secretary Sumner Welles and Norman Davis. This document was given to Lindsay that same night. The US reply stated that they were 'heartily in accord with the idea of there being made by British representatives in Japan and China representations such as outlined by Mr Eden. It seems to us that this would be action parallel with though not identical with that which we have already taken here and which we intend to repeat.'[93] When he came to the State Department to receive the American reply, Lindsay, after carefully reading the document asked Hornbeck if it meant that the US government was not prepared to join in representations at Tokyo and Nanking. Already prepared with instructions as to how to answer such an enquiry, Hornbeck replied that

> it was fully the desire of this Government to cooperate with the British Government in the effort to discourage entry by the Japanese and Chinese upon serious hostilities, that is, effort to preserve peace; that this Government had already urged upon both the Japanese and the Chinese the importance of maintaining peace; that we hoped that the British Government would do likewise; that we intended to continue our efforts; and that we felt that cooperation on parallel but independent lines would be more effective and less likely to have an effect the opposite of that desired than would joint or identical representations through our representatives in Japan and China along with representatives of Great Britain and other powers.[94]

Hornbeck emphasized to Lindsay that, during the conference at which the reply was created, there had been unanimity in the view that cooperation between British and US governments towards the maintenance of peace was most desirable. Lindsay was reported to have smiled knowingly at Hornbeck's answer and seemed pleased as he left the meeting.[95] Eden responded gratefully to Hull the next day, and provided information on how the British Ambassadors in

China and Japan were going to deliver their representations to their respective governments.[96] The Foreign Secretary was not satisfied, however, that the State Department was going far enough, and, so, a week later returned to the question of a joint proposal being put forward to the Japanese.[97] More vigorous attacks by the Japanese Army against the Chinese led the Americans to move closer to the British on the idea of a joint petition, and, through to the end of 1937, Anglo-American cooperation grew closer.

On 27 July, Vansittart told Ambassador Bingham that British intelligence sources were predicting a Japanese attack on Peiping. The PUS also informed the Ambassador of the proposed British plan to press the Japanese for moderation. He pointedly expressed to Bingham his hope that the United States government would do the same.[98] The State Department did not take long to reply. That same day, Hull instructed Bingham to let Vansittart know that he had directed Johnson and Grew 'to confer immediately with the British Embassies and in their discretion to take action on lines parallel with the British action towards dissuading the Japanese authorities from proceeding with any plan for military operations which would be likely to endanger the lives of American nationals'.[99] The British were happy to receive this symbolic gesture from Hull. However, coordinated diplomatic pressure was one thing, a coordinated military plan or consensus on any actions to be taken against Japan was an entirely different issue.

Stanley Hornbeck once again summed up the strategic position of both the United States and Great Britain in the Far East as both nations watched Japan grow bolder in its designs every week.

> The issue so far as the powers, especially the United States and Great Britain, are concerned is whether pursuit of national policy by force, in contravention of treaty obligations and with complete indifference to the question of peace, is or is not to be objected to by those powers to whom it seems objectionable, and, if the answer is in the affirmative, then by what process ... Nothing short of a definite indication on the part of one or more of the great foreign powers that it would be prepared to throw some type of force into the equation would appreciably affect the play of force (forces) which is now taking place on the Chinese–Japanese diplomatic and military battlefield. As neither Great Britain nor this country is prepared to throw in any kind of force (other than that of moral suasion), we need not expect that action on our part (use of words) is going to be in any way decisive ... We should take full account of the fact that once a stage of real and serious hostilities is embarked upon all sorts of interests of ours may, from time to time and increasingly, become involved. In what ever we say, we should take great care to say only those things which may tend to pacify and to avoid saying those things which may tend to inflame the parties directly in conflict. This Division shares

> the view expressed by Ambassador Grew ... that 'cooperative action by the United States and Great Britain along lines more vigorous than had hitherto been attempted' would not favourably affect developments (at this stage) – unless such action can carry some implication of a sanction.[100]

The idea of sanctions against Japan and how effectively to implement them became a topic for discussion between the State Department and the Foreign Office.

Chamberlain, responding to Roosevelt's correspondence concerning the need to prepare the diplomatic aspects of any Far Eastern policy properly, was of similar mind to Hornbeck, and had to admit that there was no need or opportunity for high-level conversations to take place:

> Perhaps the community of sentiment between our two countries as to the events in the Far East and the developments in the European situation may be doing something to create a favourable atmosphere and the conclusion of an Anglo[-]American commercial agreement when we have found ways of overcoming its obvious difficulties will undoubtedly be an important step in the right direction.[101]

With neither nation possessing either the will or the military power to return the Far East to its pre-July status quo, working out a trade agreement in order to present Japan with a unified front seemed a logical next step. Chamberlain, like Hull, expected to obtain more leverage against Japan from an Anglo-American trade agreement than from a show of force. This view was reinforced by naval considerations. Great Britain, and in particular the Royal Navy, was not enthusiastic about any ideas concerning sanctions. To make a sanction effective, vast amounts of seapower would be required, and, given the numerous threats to British sea lines of communication at that moment, the Royal Navy was unlikely to have the vessels necessary. Furthermore, any effective sanction would have to ensure that the United States cut off the supply at source. To make sanctions or an embargo system effective, American and British cooperation would have to come into the open and act as a clear challenge to Japan. Economic coordination between the two Western powers would have to be improved as well.[102]

In China and Japan, the two sets of embassies kept up a constant and close exchange of information aimed at ensuring that each was fully apprised of the other's next move. However, both Grew and Johnson were reluctant to join openly with Britain in a formal protest or in a set of actions aimed at Japan, and Hornbeck was cautious about how much the British might expect of the United States in these new circumstances.[103] But, some of that reluctance came from a professional distrust of British tactics, which both Americans felt had unnecessarily antagonized the Japanese in the past year.[104] Some of the renewed suspicion on the part of the Americans came also from the statements made by the new British Ambassador to Japan, Sir Robert Craigie, who had stopped in Ottawa on his way to Japan for a chat with State Department officials. In Ottawa, Craigie had created confusion and concern for the Americans by elaborating on the various views on the Far East held in the Foreign Office and the varying views of the degree of cooperation with the United States that was desirable. He wanted the State Department to know that he had not stopped in Washington itself because he feared that such an exhibition would cause the Japanese to suspect an Anglo-American plot, and he had not wanted that to occur. His belief in liberal moderates being a useful force in the Japanese government, as well as his reserved attitude towards open Anglo-American cooperation were in marked contrast to the signals being sent by Eden, Cadogan and the American Department.[105] Craigie's early mis-steps created immediate problems with the State Department, and he also quickly became the object of much criticism from both the American and Far Eastern Departments at the Foreign Office. By the end of his first year as Ambassador, his views were being all but ignored by those important information brokers.[106]

The reluctance displayed by Grew and Johnson to create a greater sense of cooperation was overruled by Hull. Meeting twice a day to discuss the Far Eastern crisis with Under-Secretary Judge R. Walton Moore and the chief of the Division of European Affairs, Jay Pierrepont Moffat – both coached by Hornbeck[107] – Hull instructed his Ambassadors:

> I share your view that among our fundamental objectives there should be (1) to avoid involvement and (2) to protect the lives, property and rights of American citizens. I doubt whether we can pursue those objectives and at the same time expect to pursue the third of the objectives which you suggest. I therefore do not feel that we should make it a definite objective to solidify our relations with either of the combatant nations. We are opposed to the courses which they are pursuing, especially the course which Japan is pursuing. We have no desire to injure either country, we wish to be a good neighbor to both, but we should not permit ourselves to be hampered in the making of our decisions by being especially solicitous that what we do shall not be displeasing to one or the other or both of the combatant countries. We do not desire that the Japanese shall entertain any impression that this Government looks with less dis-approval or less of apprehension upon the course which Japan is pursuing than does the British Government or that we condone Japan's course in any sense whatever.[108]

The Secretary of State was now using the British reaction as his benchmark for Far Eastern policy formulation. Hull informed the Ambassadors how public opinion in the United States had been outraged by the Japanese actions and was becoming increasingly critical of Japan. The Chinese were getting some opprobrium, too, for their bombing of the US passenger ship, *President Hoover*, but not to the same degree. And, while not anxious to act as a mediator, Hull did expect his Ambassadors to let the Japanese government know at every opportunity that the United States looked upon their actions with great disapproval.[109]

Both Johnson and Grew agreed with Hull that an Anglo-American united or concerted front should be presented diplomatically. Beyond that, however, both Ambassadors feared that Britain's lack of military power in the region would not allow that nation to take the lead against Japan, and, therefore, that Great Britain would try to get the United States to assume that role.[110] Grew prepared another response to Hull and Hornbeck's corrective to him in early November, a reply which was a forceful condemnation of both the administration's attitude towards Japan and of the US Far Eastern policy in general. However, realizing the futility of trying to woo Hull away from Hornbeck's influence and opinions, and the dangers that such a condemnation could pose to his own career, Grew did not send it.[111] In reality, the only formal attempt to form a unified, formal, public position on the crisis came in the first week in November 1937, at the Brussels Conference. The Conference was mostly an exercise in public relations, where neither the US nor the British delegation expected much to change in their positions. Nor was either at all offended by the other's performance at the conference or the outcome of that gathering.[112]

Before the conference was convened, President Roosevelt took several steps on the international stage, which, while not aimed specifically at creating closer Anglo-American relations, actually did help to do so. His first act was his famous 'quarantine' speech in Chicago, on 5 October. While not mentioning any nations by name, he called on all civilized nations to respond and make a concerted effort to oppose the aggressive powers of Italy, Germany and Japan. Specifically, he called on Americans to acknowledge that perhaps isolation would not be the safest route for the nation to take.[113] In addition, the President made a veiled allusion to the idea of utilizing some sort of sanction against aggressor nations, but he was careful to send a message along to Anthony Eden that there were certain limits to his power to move the American masses.[114] The British embassy reported that Roosevelt had indeed tried to point out the dangers of the world to his people, and had also agreed with the British view that neutrality and peace were not compatible. However, there were three things that he required of Britain's foreign policy regarding the United States if he were to be successful in positioning himself to be able to support Great Britain in the future. Those points were:

(1) It should not speak or think or act as though it were possible for me [Roosevelt] to be in any way an exponent of British Foreign Office policy.

234

(2) It should never forget I cannot march ahead of our very difficult and restive American public opinion; and

(3) It must not try to push me in any way to the front or to thrust leadership upon me ...[115]

The President was supportive of the British cause, but he had to be allowed to play his own game in his own way on their behalf.

Prior to his public statement, Roosevelt had avoided implementing the neutrality laws available to the administration during the crisis by arguing that there was no declared state of war between China and Japan.[116] Roosevelt had done so in order that China might continue to have access to US supplies, an act of which the British government thoroughly approved. British Far Eastern experts were less enthusiastic about the idea of sanctions being promoted in public, but, on 15 October, Chamberlain responded to Roosevelt's first steps with the assurance that 'the United States Government could be assured of the "whole-hearted cooperation of the British Government at all times" in approaching a solution of the difficulties which had arisen in the Orient'.[117] The Brussels Conference and the preparations for it afforded the Americans and the British a chance to exchange their views on the situation and what each nation's position would be.[118]

Knowing Roosevelt's refusal to allow himself to be forced to take the lead in any Far Eastern exercise made preparing for the Brussels Conference a very simple procedure for Anthony Eden. In late October the Foreign Secretary had a long chat with Ambassador Bingham to determine what exactly the President wanted to come out of the conference.[119] Although he was annoyed at the British press, which was trying to get him to clarify just what his Chicago speech had meant for US foreign policy, Roosevelt knew that this was not an attempt on the part of the Foreign Office to trap him into a definitive statement.[120] Roosevelt's objectives for the conference were to repeat the successes of the Buenos Aires conference of 1936:

> The United States had not played any role publicly greater than that of the smallest State present, and yet by her presence and by the atmosphere of cooperation, something in the nature of a common front had been created ... And so at the Brussels Conference he hoped that we should not 'rush ahead' for this would prove embarrassing for the United States, where the Administration was frequently accused of being dragged along at Britain's tail. At the same time the United States Government did not intend to take the lead. They hoped that some smaller Powers would begin discussions and that ultimately, as the result of Anglo-American cooperation, an important degree of unity would emerge.[121]

Eden was concerned that there was a great risk that, if neither the United States nor Britain was willing to take the lead, then the smaller powers would certainly shy away from doing so. The result would be a failed conference, at which no nation was willing to state its true sentiments about the Far Eastern crisis. Bingham, however, ignored this problem, and proposed that careful management would solve that problem. Eden managed to extract from the Ambassador a statement that Roosevelt's main hope 'in this Conference was that it would familiarise the people of the United States with the idea of cooperating with HM government in international affairs. This had never been possible for them at Geneva, since the League had many enemies in the United States. It would be easier for them at Brussels.'[122] Eden was even given the impression that the President thought 'it possible that out of the beginnings of this cooperation at Brussels might grow some larger organisation of world Powers'. Happy with the assurance of close American cooperation, Eden told Bingham that the British government was ready and anxious to cooperate with the United States. He also intimated to him that the Chicago speech had been well received in Britain, but Eden wanted to know just what quarantine actually meant. Did it mean that Roosevelt was willing to impose sanctions against Japan? Bingham replied that the administration was not that far along yet, but he was sure that the speech was intended to lay the foundation for future Anglo-American cooperation.[123] The American public's interest in the Far East was increasing, but there were definite limits of action for Roosevelt's administration. Eden and the Foreign Office respected those limits, but were intent on ensuring that the Americans did all they possibly could in the Far East. A cooperative and sympathetic manner was a good start, but solid support on a plan of action was what the British really desired.[124]

Concrete action would not arise out of the efforts to bring peace to the Far East at Brussels.[125] Roosevelt instructed Norman Davis, the head of the US delegation to the conference, above all else, to ensure that the United States was not pushed into a leadership role in the Far East. His orders to Davis paralleled the views that he had passed to Eden through Ambassador Bingham: the United States would not participate in a joint action with the League; the United States would not suggest or take an initiative that would be seen by Japan as creating a bloc against it; and, at the same time the President did not want the British to create circumstances where isolationists could accuse American Far Eastern policy being a tail to the British kite.[126] The President was very cautious about and wary of any British attempt to trap the US delegation into making too bold a commitment, and, therefore, emphasized to Davis that the British had to be made to understand the American situation. He qualified his point by adding that:

> We naturally, because we have got a decent community of interest in the preservation of peace in the Far East and adherence to law, want to cooperate wholeheartedly with the British, but it must be an independent cooperation, neither one trying to force the other into something. This

means that final resulting action can perfectly well be identical, though not necessarily joint.[127]

Once more, the parallel but not joint nature of the balance of power in the Far East made its presence felt.

Ambassadors Craigie and Grew had been in close contact, trying to collaborate on a set of proposals upon which the US and British positions at the conference could be based. One of the most important of these was that Japan might accept a mediation by either the United States or Great Britain but not both.[128] Each was trying to get his own government to move away from the cooperative and towards the individual approach in order to safeguard national interests. Both ambassadors had failed to realize that American and British Far Eastern policy was no longer really about Japan, so much as it was about ensuring that their Far Eastern policies did not prevent the other from being a potential ally in any possible conflict with Japan. Further, and besides the fact that it flew in the face of the efforts being made in London and Washington, Norman Davis had his own personal experiences and reasons for pouring cold water on the advice from Tokyo. His prior knowledge of Sir Robert Craigie, and the tactics he had used as Britain's foremost naval negotiator, caused Davis to reject Grew and Craigie's proposal. He contended:

> I suggest that the opinion expressed to the effect that Japan would not accept mediation if offered jointly by Great Britain and the United States, but would be more likely to do so if it were offered by one or the other is something that Craigie would like to have us assume. I worked closely with Craigie and I know not only his strong pro-Japanese bias but how his mind functions; and his optimism with regard to the moderate element in Japan was clearly shown in the statements which Ottawa reported as having been made by him when there. Craigie probably calculates that the United States would not wish to undertake mediation alone, which I feel strongly we should never do, but that we might agree to have the British undertake it with the backing of the United States and other powers which I also feel would be a dangerous procedure for us to be connected with.[129]

Given the trust President Roosevelt placed in Davis' opinion, it is likely that Craigie was becoming a hindrance to the construction of a common Anglo-American mental map of the Far East.

Eden and Davis did nothing to embarrass each other's position during the actual conference. Each man told the other why, for strategic and political reasons, it was impossible for his nation to take a more active leadership in the Far East.[130] Both were also convinced that if Japan overstepped itself and began an actual war in the region, then Britain and the United States would join in a common front against Japan. When Davis argued that, if the conference provoked a Japanese retaliation, then it would be primarily the United States that would have to use force against Tokyo, Eden responded quickly. The Foreign Secretary denied that such would be the case, and assured Davis that even though the Royal Navy was pre-occupied with the Mediterranean and Europe, Great Britain could and would send a fleet to the Far East to operate out of the recently completed base at Singapore.[131] Eden summed up his views by promising Davis not only that he would not push the United States into a leadership position, but 'that he could make us a promise that he would not only second any initiative of the United States during the Conference but that British policy would be based upon American policy during the present crisis'.[132] Clearly, the need to maintain the balance of power in the Far East now dictated that British Far Eastern policy be a willing participant to that of the United States. Equally, while still hesitant to take an active role to save China, the United States was now committed to presenting a much stronger face to the Japanese in the Pacific.

The conference ended with neither the Americans nor the British offending one another over the crisis: a feat of diplomatic trust, full of hope for future cooperation.[133] After conferring with Sumner Welles and other State Department officials, Lindsay called the conference a great success for Anglo-American relations.[134] He also acknowledged that the conference was a set-back for those who believed in the orderly conduct of international affairs and the system of collective security. However, because of the close coordination between the two Western powers during the conference, the prospect of further, stronger and more tangible Anglo-American cooperation in the future was certain: 'As international co-operation declined Anglo-American cooperation would arise.' This was especially so now that the two powers were beginning to work, with great expectations of success, on an Anglo-American trade agreement.[135] Such optimism also was apparent on the American side. Norman Davis assured Hull and Roosevelt that he, too, was convinced that Eden and the British government had acted fairly and honestly during the conference. He was especially impressed by the fact that, given the great public pressure being put on the British delegates to find a solution to the crisis, as compared to the United States' relatively low-key approach, the Foreign Office personnel and other British officials had respected that difference and would not attempt to exploit the US 'soft' approach in their own policy formulations.[136]

That spirit of cooperation and intimacy which Lindsay observed was certainly evident, as 1937 drew to a close, in the actions of the State Department and the Foreign Office. However, others did not like this trend. Prolonged protests from Grew that American Far Eastern policy was getting too close to that of Britain and that the Japanese were equating one policy with the other continued in the wake of the Brussels conference. He and his Chargé d'affaires, Eugene Dooman, another earlier antagonist of Craigie, blamed the United

States' move towards Britain for the hardening of Japanese attitudes towards the United States. As well, neither US officer trusted the style and method of British diplomacy in Japan. Both men allowed their professional pride and territoriality to override the global considerations and strategic realities that their government now faced.[137] The eventual result was that Cordell Hull and the State Department began to put less and less emphasis on the analyses being received from Tokyo. Instead, as the year came to a close, the Foreign Office, the US Embassy in London, and the British embassy in Washington became the focus of Anglo-American Far Eastern relations and policy creation. Through those channels, more and more information was shared, both on possible Japanese intentions and on the Soviet Union and its role in the Far East. Such analysis was passed, often at the request of high-ranking officials such as Secretary Hull himself, freely from US sources to the British and vice versa.[138] The Foreign Office, although reluctant, was willing to do so, even at the risk of exposing some of their intelligence sources and revealing which foreign codes they could read.[139] For the Foreign Office, educating the State Department and ensuring that the mental maps on both sides of the Atlantic remained parallel, if not identical, was of primary importance.[140]

However, the anti-American sentiments and ill-conceived foreign policy of Neville Chamberlain reared its head in early 1938, threatening the very fabric of the newly established Anglo-American relationship.[141] Chamberlain's disregard for the importance of the United States in Great Britain's foreign and defence policies eventually ended with the resignation of Anthony Eden and his replacement by Lord Halifax. The catalyst of this crisis among the British foreign policy elite was the aftermath of the Abyssinian Crisis. Chamberlain's actions, Eden's reaction to Italy and the idea of appeasing Mussolini by offering *de jure* recognition of the Italian conquest of Abyssinia, are well chronicled elsewhere.[142] However, the important issue for our purpose here is that the final straw that led to Eden's resignation was Chamberlain's refusal to appreciate the nature of the balance of power that had become the pillar of Britain's imperial defence policy. This led the two men down different paths. Eden agreed that appeasement was a legitimate foreign policy tactic, but was not certain that the ends would justify the means in the Italian case. On the other hand, if Roosevelt were snubbed by Chamberlain, if the Americans were made to believe that they could not trust the British on any issue, even if that issue were not directly involved with the Far Eastern situation, then the sense of trust and cooperation that had been established on Far Eastern issues would be destroyed immediately. If cooperation concerning, and coordination on, Far Eastern matters were destroyed, then there would be little hope of drawing the Americans into any closer cooperation in the European theatre.[143]

When commenting on a meeting held on 18 December 1937, at All Souls College, Oxford, to debate Great Britain's foreign policy choices, Eden had stated his belief that Anglo-American cooperation in the Far East was a vital part of Britain's foreign policy. His views were reflective of the consensus reached by that gathering. The latter came to the conclusion that, while the United States could not be counted on for immediate assistance in any conflict, when it did weigh into the fray, that action, just as in 1917, would be decisive. Overall, their advice to Britain's foreign-policy-makers was that, if Britain led, the United States would follow in the Far East, but that the Americans would promise nothing in advance. Furthermore,

> It was felt that this risk was worth taking because: (a) It would settle the Japanese question. (b) More importantly, it would provide us with an affirmation of strength as regards Germany and the Berlin–Tokyo Axis. (c) It might encourage Germany to exchange Japanese friendship for Russian friendship. (d) It would be comparatively acceptable to our own opinion since London would not be bombed. (e) It would unite us with America.[144]

Eden took that message to Chamberlain at the end of 1937, telling the Prime Minister that although 1938 was going to be a difficult year for British diplomacy, one bright spot was cooperation with the United States. The Foreign Secretary was certain that real progress was being made, even if it was at times slow and difficult. His approach to the Americans in the new year would be to 'do everything we can privately to encourage the Americans'.[145] The Foreign Secretary had also implied to the new US Ambassador to Berlin, Hugh Wilson, a future tougher stance against the Japanese, knowing that such a posture would impress Roosevelt.[146] Eden's optimism appeared to be rubbing off on Chamberlain, who, in light of the American gunboat *Panay* being sunk by the Japanese on the Yangtze River, thought that the Americans might indeed now be willing to do something more substantial than just talk.[147] By January 1938, Chamberlain was considering asking the Americans to use their Navy in conjunction with the Royal Navy to provide a show of force against the Japanese.[148] With critical trade negotiations under way, and this being a large part of the final steps required to obtain even more American goodwill, Eden felt betrayed when Chamberlain ignored Roosevelt's warning not to make a deal with the Italians over Abyssinia lest that alienate American public opinion towards Britain.[149] For Eden, if that coordination of Anglo-American policy and sentiment were erased, if the American mental map of British foreign policy were torn apart, then Britain would one day find itself facing Japan, Italy and, quite possibly Germany, alone.[150] That had been the situation which every British Foreign Secretary from 1932 onwards had desperately tried to avoid. Eden was unwilling to allow such steps as Chamberlain proposed to go ahead without consequence, and, so, on 20 February, he resigned.[151] As a result of that sacrifice, strategic foreign policy relations between the State Department and the Foreign Office continued to build on common Anglo-American perceptions of events in the Far East.

Eden's successor was Lord Halifax. He, like Eden and Cadogan, was resigned to the fact that concrete action from the United States in the Far East was not going to take place in the near future. As well, as long as Japan remained embroiled with China and fearful of the Soviet Union, the chances remained good that Tokyo would not move southward against British and American interests there.[152] Not enthusiastic about foreign policy formulation or being Foreign Secretary under such trying conditions, Halifax was willing to allow the Foreign Office professionals to present their cases to him. He listened with an open and unbiased mind. It was not long before he, too, realized the need to keep the United States happy in the Far East, especially after the Munich agreement that autumn.

Overall, 1938 was a year of stalemate and the maintenance of the status quo for Anglo-American Far Eastern relations, as each side drew back, rearmed, considered whether to apply sanctions to Japan, and continued to look for some signs of change in the balance of power in that region.[153] As had been the case for the past two years, the two departments were largely in accord. However, overcoming those last remaining differences, which still included a reluctant American public, would not come about before the end of the year.[154] In the meantime, the efforts of the State Department and the Foreign Office in the first half of the year reinforced for the British the impracticality of expecting the Americans to use force in the Far East. In May, after a frank and open exchange of information about, and plans for, the region, Cadogan advised Hornbeck that it was clear that the powers were seeing the situation in the Far East from very different viewpoints. He described Great Britain's consideration of using armed intervention to protect their interests as being something that the more detached US position would not allow.[155] Nonetheless, Cadogan was interested in the idea, brought up by the State Department, of taking commercial reprisals against those who interfered with American interests in the Far East.

> Hitherto our consideration of this question has been with a view to cooperation with other Powers in applying economic sanctions against Japan with the object of forcing her to cease hostilities. Like you, however, we are now turning our attention to the possibility of economic retaliation against the many insults and injuries to which our nationals and interests are being subjected and for which we have failed so far to obtain any reasonable satisfaction. As soon as we have come to any definite conclusions on the subject we shall be glad to inform you of them. Needless to say, we should be extremely interested to learn on what lines you have been working and what conclusions seem to be indicated by your enquiry so far; and we shall be happy to exchange information on Japan's economic position if that would be considered helpful.[156]

The two departments were committed to maintaining and increasing the Anglo-American informal relationship with respect to information and planning, even though there was no firm commitment from either side that one would be able to support the other. Still, the Foreign Office remained convinced that the United States' new-found goodwill was a vital component in the Far Eastern balance of power that protected Britain's interests.

Sir John Brenan, a notable Far Eastern expert in the Foreign Office, put that dynamic into words nicely in late July, summing up how the various nations involved in the Far East were linked in a complicated balancing act. Because Great Britain could not trust Japan's future motives and actions, and as the new Japanese government had yet to perform any act of compromise or goodwill that would signal to British policy-makers that there was indeed any point listening to Japanese pleas for trust and cooperation, British interests would be protected by the 'stalemate' policy. That policy, consisting of China and the Soviet Union, proved to be too large a bite for Japan to be able to swallow comfortably. After exhausting itself on the Chinese mainland, Japan would be obliged to deal more amicably with its neighbours. The United States was important here because of its stiffening attitude towards Japan and the US decision to stay engaged in Pacific affairs.[157] Under those circumstances, Cadogan and the Foreign Office instructed Craigie to continue to cooperate totally with Grew in gathering, assimilating and transmitting information about Japan to the State Department.[158] Not coincidentally, Ambassador Johnson, when asked for his assessment of Japan's future in China, recommended the same approach to Cordell Hull as Brenan had to the Foreign Office. Johnson also believed that Japan was now committed to a war it could not win and, thus, would founder in China.[159]

Such cooperation served its purpose. The longstanding attempt to get Japanese observers and foreign-policy-makers to consider US and British actions and attitudes towards Japan as one had finally paid off. Not everyone was happy about this 'identity crisis'. Ambassador Grew, chagrined, continued to warn the State Department of the resultant dangers to the United States. Nonetheless, he reported to Secretary Hull that

> the predominant view in the [Japanese] Foreign Office is that the United States and Great Britain must be considered for all practical purposes in connection with the Far Eastern situation as one unit and that Japan cannot take aggressive measures against the interests of either nation without eventually becoming involved with the other.[160]

This development was exactly the result that the British Far Eastern foreign-policy-makers had been working towards for the last four years. Now it seemed, despite Grew's misgivings, as if the State Department was not concerned about Japan developing that perception.[161] This reflected the advantage that such a perception had for Washington. In those circumstances, the balance of power in the Far East could easily contain Japan until rearmament was achieved, so long as all the powers remained in play and Japan remained uncertain of their exact intentions and alliances.[162]

Such behind-the-scenes support from the United States became one of the main pillars of Britain's Far Eastern policy, especially as problems with Japan began to develop over the decision by officials in the British Concession at Tientsin to protect suspected Chinese assassins in the late autumn of 1938.[163] Even Craigie acknowledged that, at Tientsin, the Japanese were pushing too far. It was due only to parallel US pressure that Japan hesitated to become more domineering over the matter.[164] Grew confirmed that the two Western powers were working on more than parallel lines on the issue. In fact, Craigie believed:

> The recent stiff United States Note, to which the Japanese Government have not yet replied, has raised hopes that we shall be able to count upon the support of the United States Government, if we are ultimately provoked to take some economic retaliatory or perhaps, we should say, persuasive action against this country. Such joint or parallel action – or the threat of such action – represents the only certain way open to us of ensuring not only respect for existing foreign rights and interests in China but also the maintenance of the 'open door' for the future. But, although opinion in the United States appears to be slowly evolving, it would be unwise to count on any resolute action from that quarter; the next best policy is to continue the present method of playing for time, protesting against infringements of our rights, withholding credits and hoping that a continued resistance by General Chiang Kai-shek, despite the fall of Hankow and Canton, may induce a more reasonable frame of mind among the Japanese.[165]

The Foreign Office, and especially the Far Eastern Department, were happy that Craigie had finally begun to get in step with the views and policy promoted by them for so long.[166] Now, perhaps, a more concerted effort could be made to keep the pressure on the Japanese government. Indeed, the two Ambassadors to Japan, under instruction from home, became the model of cooperative energy in the last month of 1938.

Despite his continued suspicions that the United States was not willing to stick it out in the Far East, and his desire that some rapprochement be tried with the Japanese, Craigie now believed that Anglo-American cooperation in the Far East was the key to any successful opposition to Japan's expansion.[167] However, neither he nor Grew was genuine in his desire to form a united front between the two Western powers.[168] The Foreign Office and State Departments, however, were not reluctant to explore the question. Believing that the United States and its parallel approach was becoming more useful in the Far East, Cadogan and other members of the Foreign Office, including Halifax, once more prepared to sound out the State Department on what action the United

States might be prepared to take in the region. Through the channels of Craigie and Grew, the State Department was asked for its opinion on possible courses of action.[169] As for Great Britain's probable policy, the Permanent Under-Secretary summed up Britain's situation best. With growing troubles around the world, the Far East was the only certain region where the United States was at all engaged in helping to contain an aggressor power, even if only in an informal and parallel manner. Still, even without a formal alliance or a guarantee to 'absolutely' come to Britain's aid in the event of a war in the Far East, the potential of the United States to do more, and the lack of faith in Japan and its word, meant that, for British policy for the region, 'the overriding consideration is the danger of alienating the US'.[170] The United States, along with the Soviet Union, remained the two powers which, in conjunction with Great Britain, could halt any further Japanese expansion. Britain's Far Eastern policy now had to remain centred on the creation of an active and open, not just informal and secretive, Anglo-American cooperation in that region.[171]

One of the possible avenues for open cooperation was to impose sanctions on Japan, a method favoured by British strategic planners.[172] In early January 1939, Craigie was instructed to pass along to Grew secret British documents concerning the 'Possibility of Economic Counter Measures' for his and the State Department's consideration.[173] The Foreign Office hoped to educate the State Department about the benefits of and the limited retaliation which such action would engender if it were applied to Japan. Grew objected once more. He reminded Hull that, if such measures were to be taken, then the United States was obliged to do so in the knowledge that the use of force might well be involved.[174] Grew's view was countered by Hornbeck, who painted a stronger case in favour of supporting the British idea of sanctions. Hornbeck's argument swayed the Secretary of State to approve of the use of sanctions against Japan. By early February, Sumner Welles was able to inform the Washington Embassy that, while sanctions were not going to be imposed immediately, Hull had reached the conclusion that the State Department's attitude towards the idea was more or less the same as that of the Foreign Office.[175] Henry Morgenthau Jr, the US Secretary of the Treasury, was also in favour of working with Britain in applying sanctions against Japan, not only to apply a brake to Japan's aggression, however, but also as 'a test of English sincerity as to whether or not they meant business in regard to Germany and Italy'.[176] In fact, the episode was viewed many in the US administration as another litmus test of the Chamberlain government, in the aftermath of Eden's resignation and Britain's appeasement of Italy. The newly forged bonds of Anglo-American cooperation were being tested in the Far East.

The goodwill and closeness of spirit surrounding Anglo-American cooperation were openly discussed and accepted within the halls of the Foreign Office as 1939 dawned, but were still not sentiments that could be voiced in public. For example, in February a parliamentary question was put to

Chamberlain about whether the government consulted the United States on all matters concerning Britain's relations with totalitarian states, in order to ensure that no difference of opinion threatened to damage Anglo-American relations. In this question, the Far East was singled out for special attention.[177] The answers reflected both the delicacy of the situation and an awareness that all replies would be carefully scrutinized in the United States. William Strang, the head of the Foreign Office's Central Department, suggested the following answer to this potentially embarrassing query:

> So far as Central Department are concerned, the US Government are kept <u>informed</u>, on the same general lines as the Dominion Prime Ministers, about all our major acts of foreign policy. They are not, as a general rule, <u>consulted</u>. [emphases in original] The question might be answered by saying that we naturally maintain close contact with the Government of the United States on matters of interest to the two Governments, unless this would be too much for the Middle West to stomach.[178]

E.M.B. Ingram, head of the Southern Department, insisted that his department did not 'consult the US Govt. about Italian policy but keep them informed of any major issues which we think may interest them or require a little preparation of the ground from the point of view of American opinion'.[179] It was only in the Far East that anything approaching consultation took place. Indeed, R.G. Howe, the new head of the Far Eastern Department, reported that, in fact, 'We <u>do</u> consult the US Govt. on certain aspects of Far Eastern policy but I do not think it would be advisable to say so in Parliament. I agree with the last para of Mr Strang's minute.'[180] Overall, the Foreign Office, and particularly the American Department, were convinced by April 1939 that if Japan moved to take advantage of a European war then the United States would do more than consult with the British: it would side with the British in a Far Eastern war.[181] Even in the face of calls in the summer of 1939, by the new US Ambassador to Britain, Joseph Kennedy, who took over from Bingham in late 1937, for the United States not to help the empire if it were attacked by Japan, Foreign Office opinion remained solid that the Americans would arrive at the eleventh hour.[182] That belief was also held at the highest strategic planning levels. In the Strategic Appreciation sub-committee, the multi-service and departmental body with the remit to assess Britain's overall strategic position, the same themes prevailed. In the case of Europe, there was probably not much to be expected from the United States. At best a helpful neutrality and supplier of material was the role the United States would play, unless the action of European totalitarian powers created a direct challenge to the United States and its strategic position. In the Far East, however, in the event of Britain facing a three-front war:

The foregoing negative conclusions as to the likelihood of early United States intervention in a European war are somewhat less applicable to the contingency of Japan ranging herself as a belligerent with Germany and Italy. In that event the United States might well feel themselves compelled in the opening phases of hostilities to resort to common naval action with Great Britain and France. In particular, any Japanese threat to Australia and New Zealand, whether by way of direct descent upon them or indirectly in the form of an expedition against Singapore, would be a matter to which the United States could hardly remain for long indifferent.[183]

Much of that confidence had evolved from observations and discussions with the Americans during the ongoing Tientsin Crisis, which had continued from late 1938 onwards. Britain's firm stand had not always been an easy position to maintain, nor was it accepted by everyone. Craigie disapproved of the Foreign Office's choice of battleground for drawing a line in the sand with the Japanese.[184] Equally, the Royal Navy's inability to provide sufficient force to support Britain's position left very little choice for the Foreign Office in its selection of tactics. Without the ability to show force, negotiation was required, and that meant the reluctant use of Craigie in handling the matter. However, London remained firm. Halifax made it clear to Ambassador Kennedy that Great Britain had no intention of creating another 'Munich' by which the United States could judge its resolve, but if President Roosevelt and his administration could assist in any way, it would help to ensure Britain was not embarrassed in the Far East.[185] In Washington, Lindsay, in one of his final triumphs in his office of ambassador, equally demanded that the Foreign Office not allow the Japanese to create another Munich. His disgust at the Chamberlain government's handling of the Far Eastern situation over the previous year boiled over during discussions with Sumner Welles over Tientsin. Forgoing his usual calm and professional demeanour, and fearing that there was a good possibility that a mishandling of this matter could cause irreparable damage to Anglo-American relations in the Far East, Lindsay exploded:

> For the first time the Ambassador spoke with ill-concealed impatience and even indignation of the foreign policy pursued by his own government. Until recent months in his conversations with me he had always supported very enthusiastically Mr Chamberlain's foreign policy. During the last two or three months he has made no reference to it other than to carry out his instructions as they were given to him. Today he spoke with considerable vehemence of the situation in which England found herself and said that there came a time in the affairs of any country when, if it had any self-respect, it had to fight even if it had to fight alone. He said this with immediate reference to the Far Eastern situation.[186]

Lindsay's views echoed throughout the British foreign policy-making machine, and every effort was made to avoid an 'agreement' with Japan that would insult the Americans, even if some thought the United States had not been overly helpful during the crisis.[187] A choice had to be made and made at that moment: was Britain's destiny tied to Japanese or to American goodwill? If a deal were struck with the Japanese, all the gains made in the last four years in Anglo-American relations would be lost. And, would such an agreement relieve Britain's hard-pressed global position? That was the choice facing Great Britain's Far Eastern policy in the summer of 1939.

Without American assistance, however, Britain's prestige in the region would have suffered another serious blow. Cooperation from the State Department and President Roosevelt allowed Great Britain to save face in the nasty exchange with Japan over Tientsin. This support was not only of British making. Morgenthau also pressured Roosevelt to take a firmer line and to cooperate with the Chinese, British and French in a united front against Japanese aggression.[188] On 1 July, Cordell Hull informed the Tokyo embassy that the United States was preparing a strong note, one which would leave little doubt that the United States would not take lightly the embarrassment of Great Britain.[189] Worried about the Japanese response to such a move, and that the British would now take this as *carte blanche* to expect further US protection in the Far East, Grew and Dooman warned Hull and the State Department against any formal or regular method of delivering such a statement. Instead, they advocated that, while Hull made public noises about the United States being concerned about Japan's attitude towards American interests in the Far East, interests which seemed much like Britain's interests, Dooman would utilize his extensive network of important Japanese contacts to spread the word informally and unofficially that the United States would not tolerate any abuse of Great Britain in the Tientsin case. Such a campaign was certain to catch the ear of the Japanese Foreign Minister, Arita, and have the desired effect of working its way through Japan's military.[190] Roosevelt, Hull and the rest of the State Department apparatus agreed. They instructed Dooman to be certain to impress upon the Japanese that, because of Tientsin, the United States would not condone giving Japan a free hand in China. By 23 July, Dooman reported that his efforts had reached the ears of Prince Konoye, Baron Harada Saeto, Prince Saionji and Mr Fujii, personal advisor to the Prime Minister. It was his opinion that the Roosevelt administration's message had been effective in achieving its purpose.[191] When asked by the Japanese Foreign Minister whether the United States would intervene in Tientsin, Dooman replied:

> that the American Government is concerned over the difficulties which have arisen between the British and the Japanese over questions arising within the British concession and hopes that they can be speedily solved, but that I could not indicate what its attitude would be if there arose that

more serious situation which the Foreign Minister envisaged [Arita feared that military extremists would seek to eliminate the British Concession as a refuge for national currency, the continued circulation of which in North China offered an effective obstacle to the success of the Japanese currency scheme]. I added that I assumed he did not expect that the American Government would assist the Japanese military in establishing their currency in North China to the prejudice of the interests of all except the Japanese.[192]

Confident that the Japanese were now wary that the United States, if pushed too far, would assist the British, the State Department reinforced the message, instructing Dooman to inform the Japanese Foreign Office orally that the State Department was becoming very tired of the anti-foreigner agitation being instigated at Tientsin.[193]

With that informal, yet vital, support, the British Foreign Office continued its firm stand against Japan.[194] This position was strengthened in July by the US denunciation of the 1911 Treaty of Commerce and Navigation between the United States and Japan. The Japanese were thrown completely off balance by that action, a situation that caused Lord Halifax and Cadogan great glee. Worried as to whether this signalled the beginning of the dreaded Anglo-American bloc moving against it, Japan now had to stop and take stock of the situation. This application of a brake to Japan was seen as another parallel but not joint act of support from the Roosevelt administration, and it was much appreciated by the Foreign Office heads.[195] Even Craigie read the American termination in a similar light, informing London that Dooman had intimated to him that

> he [Dooman] had himself been unable so far to penetrate the 'smoke screen' which surrounded the recent American action. He believed that it was intended as a support to us in our present difficult negotiations and by no means as a mark of disapproval such as some American newspapers implied. He gave private and confidential reasons for this view which seemed to me valid. In general he felt that while it was impossible for the United States Government to co-operate with us openly in these matters at present, they were constantly seeking means by which our joint interests could be served without the appearance of collaboration or even prior consultation. Speaking very privately he said that he was unable yet to make out whether this step implied an intention to adopt any form of retaliatory action ... My own view is that this is a clever move designed to put pressure on Japan without involving United States in any serious risk of trouble with this country, such risk as there is being minimized by excellent feeling prevailing in Japan towards United States.[196]

The Far Eastern Department thought Dooman's assessment a shrewd guess, and believed that the Japanese good feeling towards the United States was simply an attempt by the Japanese to split the Americans away from the British, by showing preferential treatment. But, as usual, London found Craigie's views too critical of the Americans and not worth considering in any fashion that would deter Great Britain from falling into line with the Americans.[197] Slowly but surely, American and British Far Eastern strategies were being drawn together. Now it was up to Halifax and the British government to see if they would follow the new American lead.

Fears of the 'failure' to support Stimson's lead in 1932 still haunted the minds of Foreign Office officials as the options were weighed.[198] Frank Ashton-Gwatkin, an economics and Far Eastern expert, met with the Secretary of the US Embassy to inquire as to what the US government now would like Great Britain to do. Opinion was split amongst the Foreign Office officials, with men like Ashton-Gwatkin and Nigel Ronald from the Far Eastern Department recommending close, immediate consultation with the Americans. Others, like Sir George A. Mounsey, recommended consultation, but opposed inquiring of the Americans as to what Britain was to do next.[199] The Foreign Office's deliberations were all being made within the context of knowing also that Roosevelt and his administration would react more favourably to evidence of a strong British stance and commitment towards China.[200] A firm opinion on how to appease the American expectations was prepared, however, before the war intervened in September and changed the entire system. As war broke out, the Foreign Office was committed to following the US lead in the Far East because of its strengthened belief in the United States' commitment to act in that theatre in the event of a major Japanese attack. As well, Japan had no allies at the Foreign Office, nor in other areas, who could effectively argue why it should be trusted or be allowed any further leniency.[201] A new plan would now have to be constructed taking into account the new strategic realities created by a general war in Europe. There was no doubt, however, that in the summer of 1939 the actions of the United States had ushered in a new age of Anglo-American relations in the Far East. That new age held out the promise of an even closer and more productive Anglo-American policy of cooperation in the region.

Evidence for this appeared on the eve of the European war when the new British Ambassador to the United States, Lord Lothian, informed the Foreign Office that the President now felt so strongly about the Far East because

> he thought government and public opinion here were profoundly shocked by Russo-German agreement. He thought it would probably lead to fundamental realignment of Japanese policy to the direction of coming to terms with China with the assistance of Britain and the United States. He thought our attitude should be friendly but that we should display no eagerness. If Japan became hostile again he had two more methods of

pressure 'in the locker'. First was to send aircraft carriers and bombers to the Aleutian Islands about 700 miles from Japanese northern islands. Second was to move American fleet to Hawaii.[202]

Those words, as well as the apparent American preparations for a more vigorous development of their Far Eastern naval strength and bases, buoyed the Foreign Office's hopes to the point that the head of the American Department now believed that, 'The President can be relied upon to give the right lead to US public opinion and he is also ready, if need be, to assist in holding the ring in the Far East.'[203] With the President of the United States in the possession of a mental map that was almost identical to that held in the Foreign Office, with his impulsive act of terminating the 1911 Treaty, thereby initiating a growing economic pressure through embargo, a clear demonstration of US resolve to act in the Far East had been made.[204] British foreign-policy-makers had good reason to believe that strong Anglo-American relations regarding that region had been formed.[205] With the new pressures caused by events during the summer of 1939, only time would tell if such confidence in the United States' parallel interests and goodwill towards Britain's dilemma in the Far East would be justified in an actual crisis.[206]

## NOTES

1. FO 371/20651/38/45, confidential despatch from Lindsay to Eden, 22 Mar. 1937.
2. FO 371/20661/A4808/228/45, draft copy of Secretary of State Anthony Eden's address to the Imperial Conference, as amended by Sir Robert Vansittart, 8 July 1937.
3. Cordell Hull, *The Memoirs of Cordell Hull*, 2 Vols (New York, 1948); Joseph C. Grew, *Ten Years in Japan* (New York, 1944); Benjamin D. Rhodes, 'Sir Ronald Lindsay and the British view from Washington, 1930–1939', in Clifford L. Egar and Alexander W. Knott, eds, *Essays in Twentieth Century American Diplomatic History dedicated to Professor Daniel H. Smith* (Washington, DC, 1982); Sir Robert Craigie, *Behind the Japanese Mask* (London, 1946); Antony Best, '"That Loyal British Subject"?: Arthur Edwardes and Anglo-Japanese Relations, 1932–41', in J.E. Hoare, ed., *Britain and Japan: Biographical Portraits*, Vol. III (Richmond, Japan Library, 1999).
4. On Eden and Vansittart, see Eden, *Facing the Dictators*; Ian Colvin, *The Chamberlain Cabinet* (London, 1971); Ritchie Ovendale, *'Appeasement' and the English Speaking World: Britain, the United States, the Dominions, and the Policy of Appeasement, 1937–1939* (Cardiff, 1975); Sidney Aster, *Anthony Eden* (New York, 1976); V.H. Rothwell, *Anthony Eden: A Political Biography* (Manchester, 1992); David Dutton, 'Simon and Eden at the Foreign Office, 1931–1935', *RIS*, 20 (1994): 35–52; R.R. James, *Anthony Eden* (London, 1986); N. Rose, 'The Resignation of Anthony Eden', *HJ*, 25 (1982): 911–31.

   For the Treasury, and/or Neville Chamberlain, and relations with the Foreign Office see: G. Peden, *British Rearmament and the Treasury, 1932–1939* (Edinburgh, 1979); R. Shay, *British Rearmament in the Thirties: Politics and Profits* (Princeton, NJ, 1979); R.A.C. Parker, 'Economics, Rearmament and Foreign Policy: The United Kingdom before 1939 – A Preliminary Study', *JCH*, 10 (1975); Davenport-Hines and Jones,

*British Business in Asia since 1860.*

5. J. Connell, *The 'Office': A Study of British Foreign Policy and its Makers, 1919–1951* (London, 1958); David French, '"Perfidious Albion" Faces the Powers', *CJH*, 28 (1993): 177–88; Gordon Martel, 'The Meaning of Power: Rethinking the Decline and Fall of Great Britain', *IHR*, 13 (1991): 662–94.

6. SKH Papers, Box 455, memo by Hornbeck, 'Great Britain, Japan, China, Leith-Ross, and U.S. Relations in and with the Far East', 8 Aug. 1935; ibid., strictly confidential record of conversation between Hornbeck and Lindsay, 12 Aug. 1935.

7. *FRUS*, Vol. III, 'The Far East', letter from Ray Atherton (counsellor at US Embassy in London) to Hornbeck, 29 Jan. 1935, 28–9.

8. *FRUS*, Vol. III, letter from Hornbeck to Atherton, 19 Feb. 1935, 59–60; ibid., memo by Hornbeck, 8 Aug. 1935, 328–30.

9. *FRUS*, Vol. III, memo by Hornbeck, 2 Dec. 1935, 462–7; Nelson T. Johnson Papers (hereafter NTJ), Library of Congress, Washington, DC, container 27, folder L-Z, copy of a policy statement from the Far Eastern Division of the State Department, 'Far East: United States Policy: Desiderata', 17 Nov. 1935.

10. *FRUS*, Vol. III, memo by Hornbeck, 2 Dec. 1935, 463–7.

11. *FRUS*, Vol. III, memo by Hornbeck, 3 Jan. 1935, 829–8.

12. William R. Castle Jr Diary (hereafter Castle Diary), Herbert Hoover Presidential Library, West Branch, Iowa, entry for 7 Oct. 1935; NTJ Papers, container 17, Folder A-L, letter from Hornbeck to Grew, 2 June 1933.

13. NTJ Papers, Container 27, Folder L-Z, letter from Stimson to Johnson, 23 Oct. 1935; NTJ Papers, container 27, folder L-Z, letter from Johnson to Stimson, 9 Dec. 1935.

14. NTJ Papers, Container 27, Folder L-Z, report from Johnson to Hull, 9 Oct. 1935.

15. *FRUS*, Vol. III, despatch from Grew to Hull, 27 Dec. 1935, 821–9.

16. *FRUS*, Vol. III, telegram from Grew to Hull, 15 June 1935, 48; ibid., telegram from Grew to Hull, 18 June 1935, 262–3; Hugh R. Wilson Papers (hereafter Wilson Papers), Herbert Hoover Presidential Library, West Branch, Iowa, Container 1, Folder–Joseph Grew, section of Grew Diary, 22 Feb. 1933, shows that Grew liked and worked closely with Clive's predecessor, Sir Francis O. Lindley; Kennedy, '1935', 190–216.

17. *FRUS*, Vol. III, memo by Johnson, 24 Oct. 1935, 376–8. Cadogan came to the Far East with a favourable view towards US diplomats after his working with Hugh Wilson in Geneva. See CAD, entry for 27 Apr. 1933.

18. For the FO's view see Kennedy, '1935'.

19. *FRUS*, Vol. III, despatch from Grew to Hull, 3 May 1935, 148–51.

20. *FRUS*, Vol. III, memo by Phillips of conversation with Lindsay, 17 June 1935, 256–7; ibid., memo by Phillips, 1 July 1935, 283–4.

21. Castle Diary, entries for 29 May, 23 and 27 July, all 1935.

22. Castle Diary, entry for 2 Aug. 1935.

23. Confidential State Department Central Files (hereafter CSDCF), on microfilm, Library of Congress, Washington, DC, 711.41/306, despatch from Bingham to Hull, 28 May 1935.

24. Within the State Department itself, a number of the experts on Far Eastern matters kept in touch with one another's thinking through an exchange of diaries. Grew sent copies of his diary to his son-in-law, Jay Pierrepont Moffat, as well as to Hornbeck, Johnson, Castle and the Minister to the League of Nations, Hugh R. Wilson. Those men in turn responded to the diaries or sent copies of their own journals to one another, creating a very thorough and informal network serving to discuss Far Eastern matters and to present possible solutions for Hull and FDR to consider. In many cases, American Far Eastern policy evolved from this process and not from the formal organization in the State Department.

25. CSDCF, 711.41/325, telegram from Bingham to Hull, 6 Jan. 1936.
26. This can be inferred from Anthony Eden MSS (hereafter Eden MSS), FO 954/7, PRO, Kew, London, memo from Hankey to Eden, 11 Aug. 1936. Hankey felt that Eden would probably disagree with this memo on imperial defence because Hankey had rated Germany as the first priority as far as potential enemies went, and called for a reliance on a balance of power between Japan and Russia to safeguard British interests in the Far East.
27. FO 371/19829/A2130/180/45, private letter from Lindsay to Eden, 3 Mar. 1936.
28. Ibid., J.M. Troutbeck minute (Troutbeck would become acting head of the American Dept. when Craigie left to become Ambassador to Japan in late 1937), 14 Mar. 1936.
29. Ibid., Craigie minute, 24 Mar. 1936.
30. Ibid., Vansittart minute, 27 Mar. 1936.
31. FO 371/19807/A1355/4/36, despatch from FO to Lindsay, 14 Feb. 1936; FO 371/19829/A2130/180/45, Eden minute, 27 Mar. 1936.
32. War Office views and their relationship to FO views are found in WO 106/5509.
33. Avon Papers, AP14/1/273B-278A, Cecil to Eden, 11 July 1934; ibid., Eden to Cecil, 18 July 1934; AP14/1/583-610A, Eden to Roger Lumley, 13 June 1936.
34. Robert W. Bingham Diary (hereafter Bingham Diary), Library of Congress, Washington, DC, entry for 9 July 1935.
35. The full story of how Piggott, with good reasons, was marginalized by the FO has yet to be told. Some works which are sympathetic to the man and his views are, Carmen Blacker, 'Two Piggotts: Sir Frances Taylor Piggott (1852–1925) and Major-General F.S.G. Piggott (1883–1966)', in Sir Hugh Cortazzi and Gordon Daniels, eds, *Britain and Japan, 1859–1991: Themes and Personalities* (London, 1991), 118–28; Best, *Britain, Japan and Pearl Harbor*, 50–1; Watt, 'Chamberlain's Ambassadors', 166; F.S.G. Piggott, *Broken Thread: An Autobiography* (Aldershot, 1950). For the War Office's official view, see CAB 24/259, Cabinet Papers, PRO, CP 12 (36), 'The Importance of Anglo-Japanese Friendship', submitted by the Secretary of State for War, A. Duff Cooper, 17 Jan. 1936. See also the entire WO 106/5513.
36. CAB 23/83, Minutes of Cabinet Meetings (hereafter CAB 23/), PRO, meeting no. 3, 29 Jan. 1936.
37. FO 371/20279/F701/89/23, Orde minute, 22 Jan. 1936.
38. Ibid., Wellesley minute, 22 Jan.; Stanhope minute, 23 Jan.; and Vansittart minute, 25 Jan. all 1936.
39. *FRUS*, Vol. IV, 'The Far East', despatch from Johnson to Hull, 1 Apr., 1936, 95–8.
40. Ibid.
41. *FRUS*, Vol. IV, memo by Atherton, 13 July 1936, 241–3; SKH Papers, Box 456, Hornbeck to Atherton, 25 Feb. 1937; ibid., Hornbeck to Atherton, 24 Feb. and 2 Mar. 1937.
42. *FRUS*, Vol. IV, despatch from Grew to Hull, 29 May 1936, 177–80. The Hungarian Ambassador to the United States had been suspicious of an Anglo-American *rapprochement* as well: see Castle Diary, entry for 25 Jan. 1936.
43. FO 371/20279/F3476/89/23, despatch from Clive to FO, 21 May 1936.
44. *FRUS*, Vol. IV, despatch from Grew to Hull, 6 Aug. 1936, 261–4; ibid., despatch from Johnson to Hull, 11 Sept. 1936, 288–91; ibid., memo by Assistant Chief of the Division of Far Eastern Affairs, Maxwell Hamilton, 30 Sept. 1936, 319–20; ibid., telegram from Hull to Dickover (Chargé d'Affaires, Tokyo), 20 Sept. 1936, 321–2; FO 371/20279/F6511/89/23, Cadogan minute, 29 Oct.; Eden minute, 30 Oct.; Vansittart minute, 29 Oct. all 1936.
45. FO 371/19829/A9241/180/45, Troutbeck minute, 11 Nov. 1936.
46. Ibid., draft telegram from Vansittart to Lindsay, 23 Nov. 1936.
47. FO 371/20651/A842/38/45, letter from Lindsay to Vansittart, 19 Dec. 1936.

48. Ibid., Craigie minute, 9 Jan.; Troutbeck minute, 8 Jan. both 1937.

49. FO 371/20279/F6826/89/23, record of conversation between Eden and Yoshida, 6 Nov. 1936; FO371/20279/F6861/89/23, Cadogan minute, 11 Nov. 1936; FO 371/20279/ F6511/89/23, Treasury memo and all minutes, 29 Oct. 1936; FO 371/20279/F6724/ 89/23, telegram from Clive to FO, 4 Nov. 1936; FO 371/20279/F7302/89/23, Treasury memo and all minutes, 27 Nov. 1936.

50. FO 371/20279/F7660/89/23, record of conversation between Yoshida and Craigie, 4 Dec. 1936; FO 371/20287/F7427/553/23, Cadogan minute, 9 Dec. 1936; *FRUS*, Vol. III, 'The Far East', memo by Norman Davis of conversation with Cadogan, 27 Apr. 1937, 975–8; CAD, entries for 14 and 15 Jan. 1937. See also S. Olu Agbi, 'The Foreign Office and Yoshida's Bid for Rapprochement with Britain in 1936–37: A Critical Reconsideration of the Anglo-Japanese Conversations', *HJ*, 21 (1978): 173–9.

51. Castle Diary, entry for 26 Nov. 1937; CSDCF, 741.94/78, telegram from Hull to Bingham, 20 Nov. 1936.

52. CAB 23/86, minutes of meeting 66 (36), 18 Nov. 1936; FO 371/20279/F7661/89/23, FO minute by Craigie, 25 Nov. 1936; FO 371/20279/F7818/89/23, Cadogan minute and Orde minute, both 21 Dec. 1936; FO 371/20279/F7928/89/23, record of conversation between Eden and Yoshida and minutes, 22 Dec. 1936; FO 371/20286/F7504/303/45, Secret FO memo by N.B. Ronald and minutes, 4 Dec. 1936; FO 371/20286/F7926/ 303/23, record of conversation between Atherton and Cadogan, 17 Dec. 1936; CAB 24/267, Cabinet Papers, CP 45, 'The Keelung Incident', memo by Eden, 1 Feb. 1937; *FRUS*, Vol. IV, telegram from Bingham to Hull, 25 Nov. 1936, 389; ibid., despatch from Dickover to Hull, 26 Nov. 1936, 394–6; ibid., despatch from Grew to Hull, 16 Dec. 1936, 426–9; CSDCF, 741.94/69, memo from Johnson to Hull and covering notes by the Far Eastern Division, 11 Sept. 1936.

53. *FRUS*, Vol. III, 'The Far East', despatch from Grew to Hull, 16 Apr. 1937, 64–6. For another incident which reveals more about Anglo-Japanese tensions, see Brian Bridges, 'Britain and Japanese Espionage in Pre-War Malaya: The Shinozaki Case', *JCH* (21 1986): 23–36.

54. FO 371/21035/F455/1417/23, confidential telegram from Clive to FO, N.B. Ronald minute, Cadogan minute, all 25 Jan. 1937. When Ronald suggested that the American Dept. send along a few words of appreciation for the support through the US Naval Attaché in London, Orde rejected the idea, illustrating the unofficial nature of true Anglo-American Far Eastern relations when he wrote: 'I think I would *not*. Too much appearance of influence is not desirable.' Cadogan and Vansittart concurred with that approach, but were grateful to the Americans for the help. Ibid., Orde minute, Cadogan minute, Vansittart minute, all 26 Mar. 1937.

55. FO 371/20287/F6829/553/23, Craigie minute, 30 Oct. 1936.

56. Ibid., Cadogan minute, 2 Nov. 1936.

57. NTJ Papers, letter from Hornbeck to Johnson, Container 31, Folder A-K, 31 Dec. 1936.

58. FO 371/19829/A9447/180/45, confidential despatch from Eden to Lindsay, 1 Dec. 1936.

59. Ibid.

60. FO 371/19829/A9447/180/45, Cadogan minute, 24 Nov., Vansittart minute, 25 Nov. both 1936; Board of Trade (BT), PRO, BT11/790, USA–UK, Imperial Conference, 1937, letter from Lindsay to Vansittart, 25 June 1937. D.F. Drummond, 'Cordell Hull', in Norman Graebner, ed., *An Uncertain Tradition: American Secretaries of State in the Twentieth Century* (New York, 1961); I. Drummond and Norman Hillmer, *Negotiating Freer Trade: The United Kingdom, The United States, Canada and the Trade Agreement of 1938* (Waterloo, Ontario, 1989); A.W. Schatz, "The Anglo-American Trade Agreement and Cordell Hull's Search for Peace, 1936–1938", *JAH* 57 (1970): 85–103;

R.A. Harrison, 'The Runciman Visit to Washington in January 1937: Presidential Diplomacy and the Non-Commercial Implications of Anglo-American Trade Negotiations', *CJH*, 19 (1984): 217–39.

61. FO 371/19827/A8860/103/45, confidential telegram from Sir E. Phipps (British Ambassador in Berlin) to FO, 6 Nov. 1936.
62. FO 371/19827/A8860/103/45, Craigie and Vansittart minutes, 13 Nov. 1936.
63. FO 371/19827/A8860/103/45, Eden minute, 12 Nov. and Chamberlain minute, 1 Dec. 1936.
64. Ibid., Vansittart minute, 14 Nov. 1936.
65. FO 371/20651/A2197/38/45, confidential draft telegram from Eden to Lindsay, 20 Mar. 1937.
66. See S. Olu Agbi, 'The Strategic Factor in British Far Eastern Diplomacy, 1937–41', *Nigerian Journal of International Studies*, 2 (1978): 41–54; Agbi, 'The Pacific War Controversy in Britain: Sir Robert Craigie Versus the Foreign Office', *MAS*, 17 (1983): 489–517; Antony Best, 'Sir Robert Craigie as Ambassador to Japan 1937–1941', in Ian Nish, ed., *Britain and Japan: Biographical Portraits*, Kent, 1994), 238–51.
67. Hull MSS, Library of Congress, Washington, DC, container 40, letter from Bingham to FDR, 5 Jan. 1937.
68. Ibid.
69. Bingham's attitude had changed quickly on this matter: see President's Private Secretary Files (hereafter FDR–PSF), Franklin D. Roosevelt Presidential Library, Hyde Park Library, New York, Bingham Correspondence, letter from Bingham to FDR, 18 Dec. 1936.
70. Hull MSS, Container 40, letter from Davis to Hull, 22 Feb. 1937.
71. Hull MSS, Container 41, letter Davis to Hull, 22 Apr. 1937.
72. *FRUS*, Vol. III, despatch from Grew to Hull, 1 Jan. 1937, 1–11.
73. NTJ Papers, Container 31, folder A-K, letter Grew to Johnson, 17 May 1937; ibid., letter from Johnson to Grew, 4 June 1937; FO 371/21028/F1428/28/23, despatch from Clive to FO, 9 Mar. 1937; FO 371/21038/F1310/233/23, letter from Cadogan to Sir George Clerk, 23 Mar. 1937; Nish, *Japanese Foreign Policy*, 215–17.
74. FO 371/21040/F2117/414/23, despatch from Clive to FO, 12 Apr. 1937; FO 371/21040/ F2388/414/23, confidential letter from Clive to Orde, 22 Mar. 1937.
75. FO 371/20651/A665/38/45, secret telegram from Runciman to Prime Minister, 26 Jan. 1937.
76. Avon Papers, AP14/1/637A-666A, 11 June 1937; T188/175, Trade Policy Committee, 1937, Ashton-Gwatkin memo and comments, 24 Feb. 1937; NC 18/1/993, Chamberlain to Ida, 8 Feb. 1937.
77. FO 371/20656/A1059/93/45, secret letter from Runciman to Eden, 8 Feb. 1937; Harrison, 'The Runciman Visit to Washington', 229–35.
78. Ibid., Craigie and Vansittart minutes, both 15 Feb. 1937.
79. CSDCF, 741.94/88, report of conversation between Atherton and Cadogan for Hull, 25 Mar. 1937.
80. FO 371/21029/F1633/28/23, FO minute by Cadogan, 12 Mar. 1937.
81. Until indicated, the following is based on CSDCF, 741.94/88, Atherton's record of conversation, 25 Mar. 1937
82. FO 371/21029/F1633/28/23, Eden minute, 29 Mar. 1937.
83. Hull MSS, Container 40, letter from Bingham to FDR, 24 Mar. 1937. Davis was also reporting Chamberlain's shift in attitude towards Anglo-American cooperation as a check to Japan. 'Chamberlain insisted, however, that Japan would cause no trouble if she believed that the United States and Great Britain were standing together. The more Japan could see that our two countries were collaborating the more she would wish to

cooperate in promoting economic recovery and peace in China and the Pacific.' CSDCF, 711.41/350, covering note on telegram from Davis to Hull, 29 Apr. 1937.

84. See FO 371/20651/A1925/38/45, telegram from Eden to Lindsay, 10 Mar. 1937.

85. Ibid. Also, Eden Papers, AP13/1/51, confidential minute by Oliver Harvey on Britain's European foreign policy, 7 Mar. 1937.

86. Until indicated, the following is based on FO 371/20651/A2378/38/45, W.D. Allen (AD clerk) minute, 1 Apr. and Vansittart minute, 4 Apr. both 1937.

87. FO 371/20659/A2847/228/45, FO minute by Allen and various minutes, 15 Mar. 1937; FO 371/20659/A2970/228/45, FO minute by Troutbeck and various minutes, 5 Apr. 1937.

88. FO 371/20660/A4165/228/45, secret memo from Lindsay to FO, 1 June 1937.

89. FO 371/20660/A4165/228/45, Troutbeck minute, 17 June; Orde minute, 19 June; Cadogan and Vansittart minutes, 23 June all 1937.

90. *FRUS*, Vol. III, telegram from Hull to Grew, 24 June 1937, 117.

91. Lee, *Britain and the Sino-Japanese War*, 23–49; Lowe, *Great Britain and the Origins of the Pacific War*, 14–32.

92. *FRUS*, Vol. III, note from Hornbeck to Hull, 13 July 1937, 159.

93. *FRUS*, Vol. III, memo by Chief of Division of Far Eastern Affairs, 14 July 1937, 159–60.

94. Ibid.

95. Ibid.

96. *FRUS*, memo by Maxwell Hamilton of Conversation with Broadmead (First Secretary of British Embassy in Washington), 14 July 1937, 164.

97. *FRUS*, Vol. III, note from British Embassy to the State Department, 20 July 1937, 226.

98. *FRUS*, Vol. III, telegram from Bingham to Hull, 27 July 1937, 271–2.

99. *FRUS*, Vol. III, telegram from Hull to Bingham, 27 July 1937, 272.

100. *FRUS*, memo by Hornbeck, 27 July 1937, 278–80; SKH Papers, Box 455, Hornbeck to Hull, 28 Sept. 1935.

101. FDR–PSF, Britain, letter Roosevelt to Chamberlain, 28 July; letter from Chamberlain to Roosevelt, 28 Sept., both 1937.

102. CAB 2/7, minutes of meetings of CID, meeting no. 301, 18 Nov. 1937; CAB 2/7, CID meeting no. 303, 2 Dec. 1937; CAB 53/7, minutes of meeting of COS, meeting no. 209, 1 June 1937; CAB 53/32, COS Papers, no. 596, 'Appreciation of the Situation in the Far East', 14 June 1937; CAB 4/26, CID Papers, no. 1365-B, 'Economic Sanctions Against Japan', 5 Nov. 1937; *FRUS*, Vol. III, note from the British Embassy to the Department of State, and aide-mémoire, 1 Oct. 1937, 560–1.

103. SKH Papers, Box 538 Miscellany, strictly confidential memo from Hornbeck to Welles and Hull, 31 July 1937.

104. *FRUS*, Vol. III, despatch from Grew to Hull, 6 Aug. 1937, 340–1; ibid., telegram from Grew to Hull, 27 Aug. 1937, 485–8; NTJ Papers, Container 33, Folder D-G, letter from Johnson to Grew, 10 Nov. 1937.

105. *FRUS*, Vol. III, memo of conversation by the Second Secretary of Legation in Canada (Mr Key), 13 Aug. 1937, 401–4; Avon Papers, AP13/1/42–44, letter from Eden to Chamberlain, 9 Sept. 1937.

106. FO 371/21040/F8754/414/23, Vansittart and Cadogan minutes, both 1 Nov. 1937; FO 371/21030/F10443/28/23, letter from Craigie to Cadogan, 3 Dec. 1937; *FRUS*, Vol. III, despatch from Grew to Hull, 8 Oct. 1937, 590–3. Grew's initial impression of Craigie was that he thought the new British Ambassador was willing to cooperate to the limit. Both Grew and Craigie were of a mind that separate lines of advance for their nations would be of the greatest benefit when dealing with Japan, and so were somewhat at odds with their departments at home because of those attitudes. Wilson Papers,

Container 1, Folder Joseph Grew, letter from Grew to Wilson, 30 Sept. 1937.

107. Wilson Papers, Container 1, Folder Joseph Grew, letter from Wilson to Grew, 28 Aug. 1937.

108. *FRUS*, Vol. III, telegram from Hull to Grew, 2 Sept. 1937, 505–8; ibid., Vol. III, telegram from Hull to Grew, 2 Oct. 1937, 572–3.

109. Ibid.

110. NTJ Papers, Container 33, Folder D-G, letter from Grew to Hull, 15 Sept. 1937; *FRUS*, Vol. III, letter from Grew to Hull, 15 Sept. 1937, 525–30.

111. Wilson Papers, Container 1, Folder Joseph Grew, personal and private letter from Wilson to Grew, 16 Nov. 1937.

112. For varying views see Lee, *Britain and the Sino-Japanese War*, 70–78; Lowe, *Great Britain and the Origins of the Pacific War*, 30–1; Borg, *The United States and the Far Eastern Crisis of 1933–1938*, 399–441.

113. Borg, *The United States and the Far Eastern Crisis of 1933–1938*, 389; Borg, 'Notes on Roosevelt's Quarantine Speech', *Presidential Studies Quarterly*, 72 (1957): 405–33; Edgar B. Nixon ed., *FDR&FA*, Vol. II, 10–21.

114. FO 371/20663/A7441/228/45, letter from Wickham Steed (from British Embassy) to Vansittart, 13 Oct. 1937.

115. Ibid.

116. Dallek, *Franklin D. Roosevelt and American Foreign Policy*, 146–7.

117. *FRUS*, Vol. III, memo by Sumner Welles, 14 Oct. 1937, 608–9.

118. Previous to this, Eden had tried to get some idea of what FDR had meant by the 'quarantine' speech from the State Department and to know whether it meant that the United States was ready to sanction Japan. Eden also wanted to know if the Americans realized that if sanctions were imposed there was a very good chance that the Japanese would react violently and probably against British interests, as Japan was tending not to see any difference between American and British policy. The British were informed that there was no desire to put on sanctions at that time. See *FRUS*, Vol. III, memo by Sumner Welles, 12 Oct. 1937, 600–2; ibid., despatch from Grew to Hull, 2 Oct. 1937, 574–7.

119. *FRUS*, Vol. III, telegram from Bingham to Hull, 28 Oct. 1937, 114–16; Avon Papers, AP14/1/666B-689, Hugh Wilson to Eden, 4 Nov. 1937.

120. FO 371/20663/A7748/228/45, record of conversation between Eden and Bingham, 28 Oct. 1937.

121. Ibid.

122. Ibid.

123. Ibid., *FRUS*, Vol. III, memo by Assistant Secretary of State (Wilson) of conversation with British Chargé d'Affaires (Mallet), 5 Oct. 1937, 582–3.

124. Avon Papers, AP13/1/42–44, Eden to de la Warr, 18 Sept. 1937.

125. For particulars of the conference, which also included representatives from France, Italy, the Soviet Union and China, see Nancy H. Hooker, ed., *The Moffat Papers* Cambridge, 1956), 152–88.

126. *FRUS*, Vol. III, undated memo from file of President's Private Secretary, 1937, 85–6.

127. Ibid.

128. *FRUS*, Vol. III, telegram from Grew to Hull, 30 Oct. 1937, 124–5; Hooker, *The Moffat Papers*, 159–61.

129. *FRUS*, Vol. III, telegram from Davis to Hull, 1 Nov. 1937, 131–2.

130. *FRUS*, Vol. III, telegram from Davis to Hull, 2 Nov. 1937, 145–7; Hooker, *The Moffat Papers*, 162–5.

131. Ibid.

132. Ibid.

133. Hooker, *The Moffat Papers*, 181–3. Such a feat was indeed commendable given the dislike of such key participants as Hornbeck and Cadogan for one another personally: CAD, entries for 2, 4, and 30 Nov. 1937; NC 18/1/1029, Chamberlain to Hilda, 21 Nov. 1937; SKH Papers, Box 457, memo of conversation between Hornbeck and Cadogan, 14 Dec. 1937; ibid., letters from Hornbeck to Grew, 20 and 28 Dec. 1937; ibid., Hornbeck to Phillips, 3 Jan. 1938.

134. *FRUS*, Vol. III, memo by Welles of conversation with Lindsay, 13 Nov. 1937, 152–5.

135. FO 371/20664/A8259/288/45, telegram from Lindsay to FO, 16 Nov. 1937.

136. *FRUS*, telegram from Davis to Hull, 21 Nov. 1937, 221–4.

137. *FRUS*, Vol. III, telegram from Grew to Hull, 16 Nov. 1937, 189–93; ibid., telegram from Grew to Hull, 17 Nov. 1937, 202; Oral History of Eugene Dooman (hereafter Dooman Oral History), Herbert Hoover Presidential Library, West Branch, Iowa, 51, 66, 67, and 98.

138. FO 371/21028/F9655/26/23, very secret telegram from Lindsay to FO, 16 Nov. 1937; ibid., most secret telegram from FO to Lindsay, 24 Nov. 1937; FO 371/21028/10616/26/23, most secret telegram from Lindsay to FO, 30 Nov. 1937; ibid., most secret telegram, Lindsay to FO, 30 Nov. 1937; ibid., secret letter from Lindsay to Vansittart, 30 Nov. 1937; ibid., draft of most secret telegram from FO to Lindsay, 4 Dec. 1937; FO 371/21525/A651/64/45, secret despatch from Lindsay to FO, 26 Jan. 1938.

139. FO 371/21028/F10616/26/23, Nigel B. Ronald minutes, 2 Dec.; Orde minute, 2 Dec.; and Cadogan minute, 2 Dec. all 1937.

140. FO 371/21041/F11265/615/23, Frank Ashton-Gwatkin (FO financial and FED expert) minute, 4 Jan.; J. Balfour (now head of the American Dept.) minute, 8 Jan.; Nigel B. Ronald (FED) minute, 12 Jan.; Cadogan (now PUS) minute, 16 Jan., all 1938; CAD, entries for 17, 23 Sept. and 19 Oct. 1937; SKH Papers, Box 523 Miscellany, 1920–66, Folder: 1936–39, record of conversation between Hull and Lindsay, 17 Jan. 1938.

141. NC 18/1/1023, Chamberlain to Hilda, 9 Oct. 1937; NC 18/1/1034, Chamberlain to Hilda, 9 Jan. 1938.

142. Ovendale, *'Appeasement' and the English Speaking World*, 66–116; Rose, 'The Resignation of Anthony Eden'; Dallek, *FDR and American Foreign Policy*, 157.

143. Eden MSS, FO 954/6, 'The Far East', letter from Eden to the King, undated Nov. 1937.

144. Eden MSS, FO 954/7, record of meeting at All Souls College, 18 Dec. 1937.

145. Eden MSS, 954/7, letter from Eden to Chamberlain, 31 Dec. 1937; FO 371/20672/A8784/5016/45, draft of memo from to Colonial Office, Air, Dominions Office, and Admiralty, 2 Dec. 1937.

146. *FRUS*, *The Far East*, Vol. III, telegram from Johnson (Chargé d'Affaires in London) to Hull, 4 Feb. 1938, 69.

147. Reynolds, *The Creation of the Anglo-American Alliance*, 297, note 29.

148. Eden MSS, FO 954/6, letter from Cadogan to Eden, 12 Jan. 1938; Avon Papers, AP13/1/45–46, letter from Lindsay to Eden, 7 Feb. 1938.

149. *FRUS*, *General*, Vol. I, letter from FDR to Chamberlain, 17 Jan. 1938, 120–2; FO 371/21490/A556/1/45, FO minute by Ashton-Gwatkin, 21 Jan. 1938; ibid., J. Balfour minute, 31 Jan. 1938; *FRUS*, *The Far East*, Vol. III, memo of conversation between Hull and Lindsay, 20 Jan. 1938; Avon Papers, AP13/1/45–46, letter from Cadogan to Eden, 13 Jan. 1938; ibid., letter from Eden to Lindsay, 25 Jan. 1938.

150. Dilks, ed., *The Diaries of Sir Alexander Cadogan,* 35–55; Avon Papers, AP20/5/27–AP20/6/23A, Eden to Chamberlain, 9 Jan. and 17 Jan. 1938; Avon Papers, AP20/6/24–29B, minutes of Foreign Policy Committee meetings, Nos 17, 18, 19, 20 on 19, 20, and 21 Jan. 1938.

151. A full account of the American influences on Eden and his resignation are found in the extensive file, FO 371/21526/A2127/64/45, FO memo, 24 Mar. 1938. See also, FO

371/21547/A1409/1409, despatch from FO to Lindsay, 22 Feb. 1938.

152. FO 371/22180/F4462/71/23, draft telegram from FO to Craigie, 7 May 1938; P. Haggie, *Britannia at Bay: The Defence of the British Empire Against Japan 1931–1941* (Oxford, 1981), 130–2; A. Howard, *RAB: The Life of R.A. Butler* (London, 1987), 70–87; Andrew Roberts, *'The Holy Fox': A Biography of Lord Halifax* (London, 1991), 82–139; The Earl of Birkenhead, *Halifax: The Life of Lord Halifax* (London, 1965), 375–426; Paul Stafford, 'Political Autobiography and the Art of the Plausible: R.A. Butler at the Foreign Office, 1938–1939', *HJ*, 28 (1985): 901–22.

153. *FRUS*, Vol. III, letter and attached memo from Cadogan to Hornbeck, 14 Feb. 1938, 89–93; ibid., letter from Hornbeck to Cadogan, 13 Apr. 1938, 141–53.

154. FO 371/21527/A7504/64/45, most secret and important telegram from Lindsay to FO, 19 Sept. 1938. Lindsay had been invited to talk privately with FDR, a situation that not even the State Department was made aware of. The President had informed Lindsay of his views on the situation in Europe, and proposed to look at blockade issues and perhaps to summon a conference. Roosevelt recognized the dangers for the Far East if Germany threatened England, for Japan might feel that it could move unhindered. When Lindsay asked FDR whether the United States would do anything if Hong Kong were attacked, the President was unsure whether the nation would be ready for that sort of act, and, even if it were, noted that such action would take a good deal of time to implement given the state of the USN.

155. *FRUS*, Vol. III, letter from Cadogan to Hornbeck, 23 May 1937, 172–3.

156. Ibid.

157. FO 371/22181/F8961/71/23, Brenan minute, 8 Aug. 1938; ibid., secret letter from Cadogan to Craigie, 15 Sept. 1938; *FRUS*, Vol. III, telegram from Grew to Hull, 27 July 1938, 239–41.

158. FO 371/22181/F10611/71/23, Nigel B. Ronald minute, 12 Oct.; R.G. Howe (new head of the Far Eastern Department) minute, 12 Oct.; telegram from FO to Craigie, 13 Oct. all 1938; *FRUS*, Vol. III, telegram from Grew to Hull, 18 Aug. 1938, 265–6. See also Inverchapel Papers, General Correspondence and Papers, 1937–38, personal and confidential paper from Hall-Patch to Inverchapel, 18 Nov. 1938.

159. Hull Papers, Container 42, letter from Johnson to Hull, 17 Feb. 1938; ibid., letter from Johnson to Hull, 27 May 1938.

160. *FRUS*, Vol. III, telegram from Grew to Hull, 9 Sept. 1938, 282; ibid., despatch from Grew to Hull, 1 Nov. 1938, 354–6.

161. NTJ Papers, Container 34, Folder H-I, letter from Maxwell Hamilton to Johnson, 15 Sept. 1938.

162. *FRUS*, Vol. III, telegram from Grew to Hull, 20 Sept. 1938, 296–7; ibid., telegram from Grew to Hull, 27 Sept. 1938, 298–9.

163. Best, *Britain, Japan and Pearl Harbor*, 71–112; SKH Papers, Box 523 Miscellany, Folder: 1936–39, memo from Hornbeck and Division of Far Eastern Affairs, 18 May 1939.

164. FO 371/22181/F12972/71/23, confidential despatch from Craigie, 4 Nov. 1938; SKH Papers, Box 459, memo by Hornbeck 'American Landed Forces at Peiping and Tientsin', 18 May 1939.

165. FO 371/22181/F12972/71/23, confidential despatch from Craigie, 4 Nov. 1938.

166. For Chamberlain's misguided and uninformed views of Craigie and Tientsin see NC 18/1/1107, Chamberlain to Hilda, 15 July 1939.

167. FO 371/22181/F13894/71/23, very confidential despatch from Craigie to FO, 2 Dec. 1938.

168. *FRUS*, Vol. IV, *The Far East*, telegram from Grew to Hull, 15 Oct. 1938, 67–72.

169. FO 371/22186/F11672/152/23, Cadogan minute, 10 Nov. 1938; Halifax minute, 10 Nov. 1938; *FRUS*, Vol. III, telegram from Grew to Hull, 2 Nov. 1938, 357–8; ibid.,

telegram from Grew to Hull, 1 Dec. 1938, 400–2.

170. FO 371/22181/F13894/71/23, Cadogan minute, 16 Jan. 1939; Halifax agreed with Cadogan and the FO's assessment of the issue as did the Admiralty, see FO 371/23555/F2134/176/23, letter from Captain T.S.V. Phillips (Director of Plans), 2 Mar. 1939.

171. FO 371/23555/F779/176/23, telegram from Sir A. Clark Kerr (British Ambassador to China) to FO, 23 Jan. 1939; ibid., Nigel B. Ronald minute, 25 Jan.; R.G. Howe minute, 31 Jan.; Brenan minute, 25 Jan.; Cadogan minute, 31 Jan. all 1939.

172. FO 371/23560/F3478/456/23, FO minute by N.B. Ronald and all minutes, 28 Feb. 1939; CAB 24/284, CP 76 (39), 'Situation in the Far East', Halifax, 30 Mar. 1939.

173. *FRUS*, Vol. III, *The Far East*, despatch from Grew to Hull, 7 Jan. 1939, 478–81.

174. Ibid.

175. *FRUS*, Vol. III, memo by John Carter Vincent of Division of Far Eastern Affairs, 20 Jan. 1939, 483–5; ibid., memo by Hornbeck, 25 Jan. 1939, 489–90; ibid., aide-mémoire from the British Embassy to the State Dept., 25 Jan. 1939, 490–3; ibid., telegram from Grew to Hull, 31 Jan. 1939, 497–500; ibid., memo of conversation by Welles, 3 Feb. 1939, 501; ibid., memo by Grew, 13 Mar. 1939, 516–19; ibid., despatch from Grew to Hull, 15 Mar. 1939, 519–21.

176. Morgenthau Presidential Diaries (hereafter Morgenthau Diaries), Franklin D. Roosevelt Presidential Library, Hyde Park, New York, entry for 11 Apr. 1939.

177. FO 371/22812/A1274/98/45, Parliamentary question, 16 Feb. 1939.

178. Ibid., Strang minute, 9 Feb. 1939.

179. Ibid., Ingram minute, 9 Feb. 1939.

180. Ibid., Howe minute, 10 Feb. 1939.

181. FO 371/22829/A2856/1292/45, FO memo by J. Balfour, 14 Apr. 1939.

182. FO 371/22815/A4991/98/45, FO minute by the Earl of Perth, 12 July 1939. In many instances the Foreign Office's faith in Roosevelt was confirmed, as in the instance when he accelerated the Congressional process so that Britain would not be embargoed from purchasing material in the US after the war broke out. See, FDR–PSF, Great Britain, letter from FDR to Chamberlain, 11 Sept. 1939.

183. CAB16/209, Strategic Appreciation sub-committee, SAC (39), minutes of 1st meeting, 1 Mar.; 2nd meeting, 13 Mar.; 3rd meeting, 17 Mar.; 4th meeting, 6 Apr.; 5th meeting, 11 Apr., all 1939. Quote from 6th meeting, 17 Apr. 1939.

184. *FRUS*, Vol. IV, *The Far East*, telegram from Dooman to Hull, 15 June 1939, 181–2.

185. *FRUS*, Vol. IV, telegram from Kennedy to Hull, 19 June 1939, 185–6; ibid., telegram from Kennedy to Hull, 27 June 1939, 205–6; ibid., telegram from Dooman to Hull, 30 June 1939, 208–9.

186. *FRUS*, Vol. IV, memo by Welles of conversation with Lindsay, 23 June 1939, 194–5.

187. CAB 23/99, meeting 31 (39), 7 June 1939; ibid., meeting 32 (39), 14 June 1939; CAB 23/100, meeting 33 (39), 21 June 1939; ibid., meeting 34 (39), 28 June 1939; ibid., meeting 37 (39), 12 July 1939; ibid., meeting 36 (39), 19 July 1939; ibid., meeting 39 (39) 26 July 1939; ibid., meeting 40 (39), 2 Aug. 1939.

188. Morgenthau Diary, entry for 17 Oct. 1938.

189. *FRUS*, Vol. IV, telegram from Hull to Dooman, 1 July 1939, 213–15.

190. *FRUS*, Vol. IV, telegram from Dooman to Hull, 3 July 1939, 215–17; ibid., letter from Maxwell Hamilton to Grew, 4 July 1939, 217–18; ibid., telegram from Dooman to Hull, 5 July 1939, 219; ibid., memo by Grew, 6 July 1939, 220–1.

191. *FRUS*, Vol. IV, telegram from Dooman to Hull, 23 July 1939, 227.

192. Ibid.

193. *FRUS*, Vol. IV, telegram from Hull to Dooman, 25 July 1939, 356.

194. *FRUS*, Vol. IV, telegram from Dooman to Hull, 25 Aug. 1939, 238–9.

195. *FRUS*, Vol. III, telegram from Chargé (Johnson) in London to Hull, 17 Aug. 1939, 570–3.
196. FO 371/23569/F8388/1236/23, very confidential telegram from Craigie to FO, 5 Aug. 1939.
197. Ibid., Ashley Clarke minute, 5 Aug. 1939; Inverchapel Papers, Box 1939 and undated 1930s papers, Inverchapel to Craigie, 9 Sept. 1939.
198. Sir John Pratt Papers [Pratt], SOAS Library, University College London, Box 1, File 3, Pratt to Hudspeth, 26 Nov. 1939; ibid., Lothian to White, 6 Apr. 1939; ibid., Pratt to Lothian, 7 Jan. 1939.
199. FO 371/23569/F8284/1236/23, FO memo, 2 Aug. 1939; CAB 23/100, meeting 40 (39), 2 Aug. 1939; FO 371/13569/F8392/1236/23, FO minute by Ashton-Gwatkin, 2 Aug. 1939; ibid., Ronald and Mounsey minutes, both 8 Aug. 1939.
200. FDR's view of British attitudes was, 'I wish the British would stop this "We who are about to die, salute thee" attitude. Lord Lothian was here the other day, started the conversation by saying he had completely abandoned his former belief that Hitler could be dealt with as a semi-reasonable human being, and went on to say that the British for a thousand years had been the guardians of Anglo-Saxon civilization – that the sceptre or the sword or something like that had dropped from their palsied fingers – that the USA must snatch it up – that FDR alone could save the world – etc., etc. I got mad clear through and told him that just so long as he or Britishers like him took that attitude of complete despair, the British would not be worth saving anyway. What the British need today is a good stiff grog, inducing not only the desire to save civilization but the continued belief that they can do it. In such an event they will have a lot more support from their American cousins ... ' See FDR–PSF, Great Britain, letter from FDR to Merriman, 15 Feb. 1939; Reynolds, *The Creation of the Anglo-American Alliance*, 37; FO 371/23568/F4981/1236/23, M.E. Dening (Far Eastern Dept.), 26 May; Nigel B. Ronald minute, 26 May; R.G. Howe minute, 27 May; George Mounsey minute, 30 May, all 1939.
201. The British Ambassador in China, now Sir Archibald Clark-Kerr, was a strong opponent of Craigie's plan to deal with Japan's moderates, but did agree that Anglo-American cooperation in the Far East was vital. His views on Anglo-American relations in the Far East, made through close consultation with Ambassador Johnson, carried the day in the Foreign Office. His advice was 'Sir Robert Craigie ... say[s] that it has long been clear that the United States will not proceed beyond protests. ... Indeed it seems to us here that the Americans are now taking the lead and that we are failing to keep pace with them. It is impossible to say how far it is representative of the views of Washington, but, for what it is worth, local American opinion suggests that, if we could convince the United States of our determination not only to uphold but to support China also, we would find them more than ready to go with us.' FO 371/23555/F1402/176/23, confidential despatch from Clark Kerr to FO, 13 Feb. 1939; FO 371/23555/F1534/176/23, despatch from V.A. Mallet (Chargé in Washington) to FO, 16 Feb. 1939; FO 371/23568/F5037/1236/23, Brenan minute, 31 May; Mounsey minute, 2 June; Cadogan minute, 2 June, Vansittart minute, 2 June and Halifax minute, 3 June, all 1939; FO 371/23555/F4419/176/23, see all minutes, especially those of Cadogan, Vansittart, and Halifax, 20 May 1939.
202. FO 371/22815/A5899/98/45, record of conversation between Lothian and FDR, 30 Aug. 1939. Lothian had been involved in the creation of Anglo-American relations prior to this. At Ambassador Kennedy's request, Lothian had commissioned Maurice Hankey to compose an extensive memo on the impact of the loss of the British Empire on the United States. Kennedy took this document with him on his Christmas 1938 visit to Washington in order to brief Roosevelt, and Lothian retained it for his continued use

when he became Ambassador to the United States. See HNKY 4/30, 'What would be the effect on the United States of America of a collapse of the British Empire', sent to Lothian, 12 Dec. 1938, PHPP 3/3, secret letter from Hankey to Phipps, 13 Feb. 1939.

203. FO 371/22815/A5899/98/45, Balfour minute, 1 Sept. 1939.

204. FO 371/23568/F8077/1236/23, telegram from Lindsay to FO, 29 July 1939.

205. *FRUS*, Vol. III, telegram from Chargé in London (Johnson) to Hull, 17 Aug. 1939, 570–3; ibid., telegram from Welles to Chargé in London, 22 Aug. 1939, 557; FO 371/22799/A7345/26/45, FO memo by Graham Hutton (American Dept.), 18 Oct. 1939.

206. The literature on Anglo-American relations between 1939 and 1945 is far too extensive to list here. A brief outline of some of the issues is found in Peter Boyle, 'Reversion to Isolationism? The British Foreign Office View of American Attitudes to Isolationism and Internationalism during World War II', *D&S*, 8 (1997): 168–83; David Reynolds, 'Roosevelt, Churchill and the Wartime Anglo-American Alliance, 1939–45', in William Roger Louis and Hedley Bull, eds, *The 'Special Relationship': Anglo-American Relations since 1945* (Oxford, 1986), 17–44; Thorne, *Allies of a Kind*. See CHT/6/2, secret, private and personal letter, Lothian to Chatfield, 15 Sept. 1939; Pratt Papers, Box 1, File 3, Pratt to Hudspeth, 26 Nov. 1939; ibid., Pratt to Lothian, 29 Aug. 1939.

# 7

# Conclusion

When war broke out in Europe in September 1939, informal Anglo-American cooperation with respect to strategic foreign policy was already a reality. This did not occur solely because of concerns over European issues. In fact, the Far East had been the venue where American and British strategic interests intersected to create parallel but not joint policies. Far Eastern concerns had forged a close Anglo-American relationship modelled on the principles of competitive cooperation well before a formal alliance was declared after 7 December 1941.

The two nations had, over six long years, overcome the feelings of suspicion, abandonment and dishonesty that had plagued those relations from 1922 to 1933. Mutual trust and confidence in Anglo-American relations were achieved in the Far East, despite differences caused by events in Europe. In spite of the continued distrust and hostility of key British officials, such as Chatfield, Fisher and Chamberlain, out of the Far Eastern situation a belief in each nation's honesty, commitment, integrity and openness created an informal yet no less valuable and vital form of Anglo-American cooperation between the two policy-making elites. Throughout that period, Anglo-American relations in the two theatres were analogous to a set of train tracks. When viewed from one angle the two tracks could be seen to be running as two separate, distinct lines, but if that perspective were shifted – say to the view as seen from Tokyo – those same tracks merged into what appeared to be one solid, single line, not two separate paths. Anglo-American strategic foreign-policy relations were that sort of relationship: it depended on the perspective, or mental map, that each nation possessed of the other.

It was in Far Eastern matters and through the close observation of British conduct regarding foreign and naval policies towards that region that US policy-makers looked for answers to a number of questions. Was Albion perfidious? Would London make a deal with the Japanese to protect the British Empire at the expense of Chinese and US interests? Would the British commit military forces to the region in any sizeable number in a conflict? And could the British be trusted not to deceive the Americans into pulling their chestnuts out of the fire, with Washington gaining no visible return for its efforts? Many of the answers were provided from 1933 to 1939. On maritime and naval issues, on questions of diplomacy and attitudes towards Japan, and even on how each nation viewed the balance of power with respect to the Soviet Union, common ground, common values and common ties were established from 1933 to 1939, so as to make Britain and the United States into what Christopher Thorne later termed 'Allies of a Kind'. The basis of that alliance was built, however, before the Japanese attack on Pearl Harbor.

After the war in Europe began, a new set of strategic imperatives came into play. The appreciations and assumptions made from 1933 to 1939 were now subject to change. After 1 September 1939, the prewar beliefs blurred, as new actors (Lothian, Churchill, Stimson and Knox, to name just a few) claimed the spotlight on the stage of Anglo-American relations. Those earlier evaluations, while still useful, at times seemed nonsensical when extended into a period where much had changed. Without the same fundamentals – political, strategic and economic – to consider, Anglo-American relations in the Far East naturally had to evolve. And, while the basis for Anglo-American strategic foreign relations had been created in the Far Eastern context, that theatre now took on a less important status as the realities of the European war unfolded. The Pact of Steel, the Soviet–German Pact, the Soviet–Japanese Pact, the fall of France, the entry of Italy into the war, British naval losses and new strategic commitments, and, finally, the German attack on the Soviet Union, all changed the strategic givens. So, too, did the increase in British and American armaments productions and this latter, combined with the mobilization of both nations, had implications for Japan. Faced with the rapid growth of Britain's and the United States' war readiness, the Japanese could not afford to delay in its use of its own limited military power, as soon both Western powers would out-strip Tokyo's ability to wage war. After September 1939, Japan had only a limited window of opportunity in which to utilize its finite force to best purpose before its impact was rendered nugatory. And that limitation was reinforced by the success of the Foreign Office's 'no bloc' policy. Fearing that the two Western powers were in fact allied, Japanese policy-makers were forced to hesitate.[1] Within this context, then, the Japanese decision to attack the more powerful United States first, rather than pick apart the pieces of Great Britain's Far Eastern Empire only, in December 1941, becomes much more comprehensible. Japan attacked the United States first, because by the middle of 1941 the Japanese believed that the Americans would defend British interests in the region.[2]

A consideration of Anglo-American relations in the Far East also has some implications for any wider judgment of British foreign policy. The role of Neville Chamberlain and the interference of the British Treasury in the conduct of Great Britain's strategic foreign policy was more disruptive than constructive.[3] Chamberlain and his circle were uninformed amateurs in foreign policy, who distracted the Foreign Office from conducting a sensible and pragmatic foreign policy – based on realpolitik and the balance of power – in the Far East. Lord Lothian summed up Chamberlain's capabilities best, when he told the US Under-Secretary of State, William Phillips, that 'Chamberlain represented a purely local point of view; he was not internationally minded and, although a brilliant man, could not be counted upon to favour cooperation with the United States.'[4] Chamberlain's distrust of the United States, forged through the decades over continued clashes with the Americans over monetary and economic policies, blinded him to the realities of the balance-of-power structure that was vital to Britain's survival, not only in the Far East, but in the world. Forced to waste valuable time and resources, as well as to suffer interminable delays over policy decisions while the Treasury was educated in the reality of Britain's imperial interests and needs, the Foreign Office, with the support of the Admiralty, nonetheless stayed in command of the formulation of Great Britain's strategic foreign policy in the Far East from 1933 until the outbreak of war in 1939. The superiority of the Foreign Office's vision was particularly evident in the Far East. Unlike Europe, where Chamberlain's influence on foreign policy was paramount, there was no Far Eastern Munich.

The Foreign Office was the only decision-making body capable of gathering, processing and successfully utilizing the overwhelming amount of data required to create a comprehensive imperial strategic policy. People, finances, domestic affairs, defence matters and economics were all grist to the mill of the Foreign Office. Staffed by a number of clever, insightful and experienced observers of the Far East and the United States the Foreign Office and diplomatic service created an intricate mental map of Japan, the United States and Soviet Russia. This mental map enabled them to formulate and coordinate a British Far Eastern policy that worked masterfully within the context of the balance of power in the Far East. The Foreign Office also was able to project this mental map to the Americans for their consideration, in a confidence-building exercise designed to create support for the British position in the Far East. It is important to note that the Foreign Office did not make decisions on the basis of racial or national stereotypes; decisions and policies were driven by the strategic realities in the Far East.

How did both nations see the balance-of-power scheme which was created for the Far East? Given the vast literature which exists on Anglo-Japanese, US–Japanese, Anglo-Chinese and Sino-US relations in this period, very little space has been given over here to the question of whether the Americans and the British had the same mental map of China and Japan.[5] There is, however, certainly a sub-text developed in this study which elaborates how certain British and American policy-making groups came to have similar views of Japan. However, despite the similarity of the Anglo-American view of Japan, it is important to remember that neither country could control either Japanese foreign or military policy. Only the Japanese could do that. Both Western powers could rattle sabres, offer compromises, threaten sanctions or ignore Japanese actions and go about their own business in the Far East. Nonetheless, Japan would do what Japan would do.

The Soviet Union and its military capacity were central to both American and British evaluations of the balance of power in the Far East. This fact had several implications. First, the timing of such Japanese strategic movements as the attack on China in the summer of 1937 and the launching of the attack on Pearl Harbor can be understood only if the role of the Soviets in the Far Eastern balance of power is appreciated. Second, Anglo-American assessments of the Far Eastern situation were influenced by considerations of Soviet power and the policy of both nations was made accordingly.[6] Finally, and tangentially, the need to consider the Soviet bear before the creation of the bi-polar world in 1945 should suggest that studies of Soviet post-war involvement in the Far East must look back at least to 1933 if it is to be placed in its rightful context.

The Far East, where American interests came into direct contact with British imperial interests, presented an opportunity for the British to bring the United States into a strategic foreign-policy system; a relationship, not an alliance. The Foreign Office did not fail to exploit that situation, to the everlasting benefit of Great Britain and its empire. Neither administration, in Great Britain and the United States, desired a formal alliance aimed at the containment of a rogue Japan. The British, because of their extensive imperial interests and military vulnerability to a Japanese attack, did not wish to give any formal or public expression to a policy that was aimed at encircling or containing Japanese expansion for fear of provoking an attack. Yet, London worked to create in the mind of the Japanese an appearance of unity between American and British interests.[7] For, if the Japanese thought that the Americans (or even the Russians) would assist the British against a Japanese attack, then Japanese aggression could perhaps be deterred.

On the other side of the Atlantic, Roosevelt, the State Department and the US Navy had no desire to appear before the American public as defenders of British imperial interests in the Far East. Thus, Washington also wanted no formal alliance. Such an alliance would have caused enormous problems in Congress for Roosevelt, with respect to both his domestic and foreign policies, to say nothing of the reaction that would have resulted among the general public. On the other hand, if the relationship could be kept at the informal level, and left to the professional diplomats, assistant secretaries, ambassadors, counsellors and military personnel, out of sight of the public, then all would be well. It should come as no surprise, then, that it was only after the re-election of Roosevelt, in the autumn of 1936, that the US administration began to move, slowly, but more boldly, in this informal manner, towards the creation of an Anglo-American cooperative relationship. Here, the Roosevelt administration proved itself to be well ahead of the general public in its desire to participate on the world's stage, in cooperation with Great Britain, as the policemen of the world. The education of the American public to that reality, and to an acceptance of a level of Anglo-American cooperation, was a principal goal for the President and his government from 1936 to 1939.

Much of the British policy in the Far East flowed from the fact that Britain was the centre of an empire, with global interests. Here, David French's use of the term 'The British Way in Warfare' explains much about how Anglo-American relations worked in the Far East. As Britain's resources were stretched, it needed to co-opt as much of the United States' power as possible into a shadowy and undeclared alliance, to maintain a balance of power. This was no different, as French points out, from what Britain had done in the eighteenth and nineteenth centuries to preserve its primacy in the European great-powers system.[8]

Empire had yet another effect on Britain's policy. This was in the realm of administration and bureaucracy. The machinery for the maintenance of ties between parts of the empire had an obvious role in the creation of a defence plan that utilized the entire resource base of that empire. These bodies, both civilian and military, had close ties to all policy-making that was concerned with strategic planning. In this capacity, the Committee of Imperial Defence, in conjunction with the Treasury and the Colonial Office, all coordinated through the Foreign Office, played a vital role. These bodies assessed the attitude of friendly and not so friendly nations towards British foreign policy and created an appropriate and effective imperial response. This unique system explains why a wide range of topics must be investigated in order to understand what Anglo-American relations in the Far East really portended for the 'British Way in Warfare' generally. When that system is understood in detail, the picture of informal, yet confident, cooperation between Britain and the United States also becomes clearer and more important.

Geography was fundamental to the development of the Anglo-American relationship. This resulted from the fact that it was only in the Far East where US and British policy-makers had either conflicting or comparable interests that a need or basis for cooperation arose. This led to a relationship based on specific issues, not on generalities, and one which, in most cases, was not transferable from the Far Eastern to the European context until well after 1936.[9] Even so, much of that relationship was informal or institutional, in that it took place at levels below that of President, Prime Minister or even Secretary of State. Both nations were joined by Realpolitik because only that could deal with the strategic problems created in the Far East. But realpolitik took on differing British and American shapes. The concerns of an empire ran headlong into those of a relatively insular power whose governing body and public could be enticed only slowly out of their isolationist shell. The Far East was the crossroads where these two national systems met. The result, after a lengthy process of confidence-building, was that British and US Far Eastern policy travelled along the same path, forming a solid and unified Anglo-American relationship. The basis of the 'special relationship' of the Grand Alliance had been formed in the Far East by the events between 1933 and 1939.

NOTES

1. WO 208/859, most secret, DO 12/M.I.2a to AHQ. India, 'Japanese–Italian–German Anti-Comintern Pact', 2 Feb. 1939; WO 208/856, most secret, Far East Combined Bureau, Singapore, 'Japan Quo Vadis?', 6 Nov. 1939; CHT/6/2, secret and personal letter, Chatfield to Lothian, 26 Sept. 1939; ibid., private and confidential letter, Lothian to Chatfield, 3 Nov. 1939; ibid., Chatfield to Lothian, 27 Nov. 1939.
2. Captain A.H. McCollum, the head of the Far Eastern Section of the Division of Naval Intelligence in 1941, wrote to Admiral H.E. Kimmel that six days before the Japanese attack on Pearl Harbor he had prepared a memo for the CNO which pointed out that Japan was likely to attack soon, given the state of readiness of its fleet. Interestingly, his first choice of target for such an attack was Singapore, although he qualified it with the statement 'and possibly in other directions as well ...' McCollum's first instinct, however, was to assume that the Japanese would indeed start a war in the Pacific with an attack on the British. This attack was seen by him as being an act which would cause the USN to begin combat operations. See John F. Shafroth Papers, Herbert Hoover Presidential Library, West Branch, Iowa, Container 1, letter from McCollum to Kimmel, 21 May 1944. See also the opinion of Vice Admiral Charles A. Pownall, who was the commander of the USS *Enterprise* when war broke out in Europe. Pownall was sure that he and his ships were going to be sent to Singapore to counter any Japanese movements. See Reminiscences of Vice Admiral Charles A. Pownall, Nimitz Library, United States Naval Academy, Oral History Collection, 97–9.
3. This is in direct contrast to the unlikely arguments put forth by John Charmley, *Chamberlain and the Lost Peace* (London 1989). For a further dissection of Charmley, see David Reynolds, 'Churchill the Appeaser? Between Hitler, Roosevelt and Stalin in World War Two', in Dockrill and McKercher, eds, *Diplomacy and World Power*, 197–220.
4. Confidential US State Dept. Central Files, Great Britain 1933–39, confidential letter and memo from Phillips to Robert W. Bingham (US Ambassador to Britain), 17 Oct. 1934. Reel 22.
5. In addition to the literature on Japan already mentioned in the various chapters above, see W.G. Beasley, *Japanese Imperialism 1894–1945* (Oxford, 1987); Germaine A. Hoston, *Marxism and the Crisis of Development in Pre-War Japan* (Princeton, NJ, 1986); Gordon M. Berger, *Parties Out of Power in Japan: 1931–1941* (Princeton, NJ, 1977); Kaoru Sugihara, 'The Economic Motivations behind Japanese Aggression in the late 1930s: Perspectives of Freda Utley and Naewa Toichi', *JCH*, 32 (1997): 259–80; Yale C. Maxon, *Control of Japanese Foreign Policy: A Study of Civil–Military Rivalry, 1930–1945* (Berkeley, CA, 1957); Alvin D. Coox and Hilary Conroy, *China and Japan: Search for Balance Since World War I* (Santa Barbara, CA, 1978); John Toland, *The Rising Sun: The Decline and Fall of the Japanese Empire, 1936–1945* (New York, 1970); Bridges, 'Yoshizawa Kenkichi and the Soviet–Japanese Non-aggression Pact Proposal', *MAS*, 14 (1980): 111–27; Laura E. Hein, 'Free-Floating Anxieties on the Pacific: Japan and the West Revisited', *DH*, 20 (1996): 411–37; Shin'ichi Kitaoka, 'The Army as a Bureaucracy: Japanese Militarism Revisited', *JMH*, 57, Special Issue (1993): 67–86; Kyozo Sato, 'Japan's Position before the Outbreak of the European War in September 1939', *MAS*, 14 (1980): 129–43.

On China, see Arthur Waldon, 'War and the Rise of Nationalism in Twentieth-Century China', *JMH*, 57, Special Issue (1993): 87–104; Paul A. Varg, 'Sino-American Relations

Past and Present', *DH*, 4 (1980): 101–12.

6. WO 208/847, MI2 memo, 11 Oct. 1940.

7. DRAX, 2/19, War Plans, 'Notes on Foreign Office Letter of 12th January', 20 Jan. 1939.

8. For further insights into French's definition of the 'British Way in Warfare', and its applicability to the defence of the realm, see his *British Way in Warfare, 1688–2000* (London, 1990), 175–201; Keith Neilson, *Strategy and Supply: Anglo-Russian Relations, 1914–1917* (London, 1984). For the best discussion of the term strategic foreign policy, see J.R. Ferris, *Men, Money, and Diplomacy: The Evolution of British Strategic Policy, 1919–1926* (Ithica, NY, 1989), 32–52.

9. For a discussion of this idea of issue-specific policies and Anglo-American relations in the period 1914–33, see Priscilla Roberts, 'The Anglo-American Theme: American Visions of an Atlantic Alliance, 1914–1933', *DH*, 21 (1997): 333–64.

# Bibliography

PRIMARY SOURCES

*North America:*

*Franklin D. Roosevelt Presidential Library, Hyde Park, New York*

President's Official File
President's Personal File
President's Secretary's File
William C. Bullitt Manuscripts
Henry Morgenthau Jr Manuscripts
Henry Morgenthau Jr Presidential Diary
R. Walton Moore Manuscripts

*Herbert Hoover Presidential Library, West Branch, Iowa*

Herbert Hoover Presidential Manuscripts
William R. Castle Jr Manuscripts and Diary
Hugh R. Wilson Manuscripts
Eugene Dooman Manuscripts and Oral History
John F. Shafroth Manuscripts

*Harvard University, Cambridge, Massachusetts*

J. Pierrepont Moffat Diary

*Library of Congress*

Robert W. Bingham Diary
Claude C. Bloch Manuscripts
Norman Davis Manuscripts
Cordell Hull Manuscripts
Nelson T. Johnson Manuscripts
Hillary P. Jones Manuscripts

Ernest J. King Manuscripts
Dudley W. Knox Manuscripts
William K. Leahy Diary
William H. Standley Manuscripts
Montgomery M. Taylor Manuscripts
Harry E. Yarnell Manuscripts

*Hoover Institute, Stanford University*

Maxwell Hamilton Papers
Stanley K. Hornbeck Papers

*Memorial University, St. John's Newfoundland*

Strategic Planning in the US Navy: Its Evolution and Execution, 1891–1945
(Microfilm)

*National Archives, Washington, DC*

Confidential US State Department Files, Great Britain, Foreign Affairs, 1933–39
Records of the Department of State Relating to Political Relations Between the
United States and Great Britain, 1930–1939.
RG 32 Records of the United States Shipping Board
RG 38 Correspondence of London Naval Attaché, 1927–40
RG 38 Security Classified Records of the London Naval Attaché, 1927–53
RG 38 US Naval Attaché Reports on Estimate of Potential Military Strength
RG 38 US Naval Attaché Reports on Probability of Outbreak of War
RG 38 Division of Naval Intelligence, General Correspondence, 1929–42
RG 38 Record of the Deputy Chief of Naval Operations, 1882–1954, Office of
Naval Intelligence, 1882–1954
RG 38 Records Relating to United States Navy Fleet Problems 1 to 22, 1923–41
RG 80 General Board 1900–47
RG 80 Proceedings and Hearings of the General Board
RG 80 Office of the Secretary, General Correspondence
RG 80 Office of the Secretary of the Navy, Formerly Confidential Correspon-
dence, 1927–39
RG 287 Publications of the Federal Government committees of Congress,
House and Senate

*National Archive of Canada, Ottawa*

RG 25 Monthly Intelligence Summaries Issued by the General Staff, the War
Office

*Naval Historical Center, Washington Navy Yard, Washington, DC*

Records of the Strategic Plans Division of the Office of the Chief of Naval
Operations

Reports of the US Naval Technical Mission to Japan, 1945–46, Operational Archives, US Naval History Division, Washington, DC (On microfilm, Massey Library, Royal Military College of Canada)
Thomas C. Hart manuscripts

*Nimitz Library, United States Naval Academy, Annapolis*
Wilson Brown Manuscripts
William A. Moffett Manuscripts
Charles A. Pownall Oral History
Frederic S. Withington Oral History
Vice Admiral Charles Wellborn Oral History
Rear Admiral Kemp Tolley Oral History
John C. Niedermair Oral History
Felix L. Johnson Oral History
George C. Dyer Oral History
Alter C.W. Ansel Oral History

*US Army Military History Research Collection, Carlisle Barracks, Pennsylvania*

*Yale University, New Haven, Connecticut*
Henry L. Stimson Diary

*British*

*Public Record Office, Kew, London*
Admiralty
  ADM 116 Admiralty and Secretariat Case Books
Board of Trade
  BT
Cabinet Office
  CAB 2   CID Minutes
  CAB 4   Miscellaneous Memoranda (CID)
  CAB 5   Colonial Defence Memoranda (CID)
  CAB 16  CID Ad Hoc Subcommittees of Enquiry: Proceedings and Memoranda
  CAB 21  Registered Files
  CAB 23  Minutes to 1939
  CAB 24  Memoranda to 1939
  CAB 27  Committees: General Series to 1939
  CAB 29  London Naval Conference
  CAB 50  The Oil Board

CAB 53  Chiefs of Staff Committee
CAB 54  Deputy Chiefs of Staff Committee
CAB 55  Joint Planning Committee
CAB 56  Joint Intelligence Committee
Foreign Office
FO 371 General Correspondence: Political, for Japan, Soviet Union, and the
United States, 1933–40
FO 800/397/398 Private Office Papers
War Office
WO 106 Directorate of Military Operations and Intelligence
Treasury
T 172 Chancellor of the Exchequer's Office Miscellaneous Papers

*Private Papers*

Earl Baldwin of Bewdley
University Library, University of Cambridge
Vice Admiral Harold A. Brown
National Maritime Museum, Greenwich
Sir Alexander Cadogan
Diaries, Roskill Archives, Churchill College, Cambridge
FO 800 Series, PRO
Sir Neville Chamberlain
NC Series, University Library, University of Birmingham
Admiral Baron Chatfield
(CHT) National Maritime Museum, Greenwich
Admiral Cunningham
British Library, London
Admiral Sir Ernle Drax
(DRAX) Roskill Archives, Churchill College, Cambridge
Admiral Sir Frederick Dreyer
(DRYR) Roskill Archives, Churchill College, Cambridge
Sir Anthony Eden
FO 800 Series, PRO
FO 954 Series, PRO
1st Earl of Avon Papers – AP Series, University Library, University of
Birmingham
Sir Warren Fisher
T 172 Series, PRO
Vice Admiral Harold Tom Baillie Grohman
National Maritime Museum, Greenwich
Halifax FO 800/309, 314 and 324
Baron Hankey (HNKY)
Roskill Archives, Churchill College, Cambridge

Sir Samuel Hoare (Viscount Templewood)
  FO 800 Series, PRO
  Templewood MSS, University Library, University of Cambridge
Admiral Sir John Kelly
  National Maritime Museum, Greenwich
Sir Richard Hopkins
  T 175 Series, PRO
Sir Hughe Knatchbull-Huggesson (KNAT)
  Roskill Archives, Churchill College, Cambridge
Inverchapel Papers
  Bodleian Library, Oxford
Sir Miles Lampson
  Middle East Studies Centre, St Antony's College, Oxford
Sir Frederick Leith Ross
  T 188 Series, PRO
J. Ramsay MacDonald
  FO 30/69, PRO
Sir Frederick Phillips
  T 177 Series, PRO
Sir Eric Phipps
  (PHPP) Roskill Archives, Churchill College, Cambridge
Sir John Pratt
  SOAS Library, University College London
Sir Orme Sargent
  FO 800 Series, PRO
Sir John Simon
  FO 800 Series, PRO
Baron Vansittart
  (VNST) Roskill Archives, Churchill College, Cambridge

## PUBLISHED DOCUMENTS AND MEMOIRS

### American

*Foreign Relations of the United States Diplomatic Papers*, all volumes for 1933, 1934, 1935, 1936, 1937, 1938, 1939.

United States Department of Commerce. *Historical Statistics of the United States. Colonial Times to 1970* (Washington, DC, 1975).

Bullitt, O.H. (ed.), *For the President. Personal and Secret Correspondence Between Franklin D. Roosevelt and William C. Bullitt* (Boston, MA, 1972).

Hooker, Nancy H. (ed.), *The Moffat Papers* (Cambridge, 1956).

Grew, Joseph, *Ten Years in Japan* (New York, 1944).

Grew, Joseph, *Turbulent Era: A Diplomatic Record of Forty Years, 1904-1945*, Vol. II (Boston, MA, 1952).

Hull, Cordell, *The Memoirs of Cordell Hull*, Vol. I (New York, 1948).

Nixon, Edgar B. (ed.), *Franklin D. Roosevelt and Foreign Affairs*, 3 Vols (Cambridge, 1969).

Roosevelt, F.D., *Roosevelt's Foreign Policy, 1933–1941. Franklin D. Roosevelt's Unedited Speeches and Messages* (New York, 1942).


*British*

Avon, 1st Earl of (Robert Anthony Eden), *Facing the Dictators*, Vol. II (London, 1960–65).

Bond, B. (ed.), *Chief of Staff. The Diaries of Lieutenant-General Sir Henry Pownall, 1933–1940*, Vol. I (London, 1972).

Butler, Lord, *The Art of the Possible: The Memoirs of Lord Butler* (London, 1971).

Chatfield, Lord, *The Navy and Defence: The Autobiography of Admiral of the Fleet Lord Chatfield* (London, 1942).

Chatfield, Lord, *It Might Happen Again*, Vol. II, *The Navy and Defence* (London, 1947).

Cooper, D., *Old Men Forget* (London, 1954).

Craigie, Sir Robert, *Behind the Japanese Mask* (London, 1946).

Dalton, H., *Memoirs*, Vol. I (London, 1953).

Dilks, David (ed.), *Diaries of Sir Alexander Cadogan, 1938–1945* (London, 1971).

*Documents on British Foreign Policy, 1919–1939*, Second Series, Vol. XX, 1933–1936.

Domville, B., *By and Large* (London, 1936).

Gladwyn, Lord, *The Memoirs of Lord Gladwyn* (London, 1972).

Gore-Booth, Baron (Sir Paul Henry Gore-Booth), *With Great Truth and Respect* (London, 1974).

Halifax, Earl of, *Fulness of Days* (London, 1957).

Marquess of Londonderry, *Wings of Destiny* (London, 1943).

Medlicott, W.N. and Dakin, D. (eds), *Documents on British Foreign Policy 1919–1939* (London, 1970).

Piggott, S.G., *Broken Thread: An Autobiography* (Aldershot, 1950).

Selby, W., *Diplomatic Twilight* (London, 1953).

Simon, Viscount, *Retrospect: The Memoirs of the Rt. Hon. Viscount Simon* (London, 1952).

Snowden, Philip, Viscount, *An Autobiography* (London, 1934).

Temperley, A.C., *The Whispering Gallery of Europe* (London, 1938).

Vansittart, R.G., *Bones of Contention* (London, 1945).

Vansittart, R.G., *Lessons of My Life* (New York, 1943).

Vansittart, R.G., *The Mist Procession: The Autobiography of Lord Vansittart* (London, 1958).

Wellesley, Sir Victor, *Diplomacy in Fetters* (London, 1944).

SECONDARY LITERATURE

*Books*

Adams, Frederick C., *Economic Diplomacy: The Export-Import Bank and American Foreign Policy 1934–1939* (Columbia, 1976).

Adams, H.H., *Witness to Power: The Life of Fleet Admiral William D. Leahy* (Annapolis, MD, 1985).

Adams, R.J.Q., *British Politics and Foreign Policy in the Age of Appeasement, 1935–39* (London, 1993).

Addler, S., *The Uncertain Giant 1921–1941: American Foreign Policy Between the Wars* (New York, 1965).

Agaki, R.H., *Japan's Foreign Relations 1542–1932: A Short History* (Tokyo, 1936; reprint Washington, DC, 1979).

Albion, R.G. (Reed, R., ed.), *Makers of Naval Policy 1798–1947* (Annapolis, MD, 1980).

Aldcroft, D.H., *The Interwar Economy: Britain, 1919–1939* (London, 1970).

Aldcroft, D.H., *The British Economy, Vol I: The Years of Turmoil 1920–1951* (Brighton, 1986).

Aldrich, R.J., *The Key to the South: Britain, the United States, and Thailand During the Approach of the Pacific War, 1929–1942* (Oxford, 1993).

Ambrosius, L.E., *Woodrow Wilson and the American Diplomatic Tradition: The Treaty Fight in Perspective* (New York, 1987).

Anderson, I.H., *The Standard-Vacuum Oil Company and United States East Asian Policy, 1931–41* (Princeton, NJ, 1975).

Andrew, C., *Her Majesty's Secret Service: The Making of the British Intelligence Community* (London, 1986).

Aster, S., *Anthony Eden* (New York, 1976).

Auld, G.P., *The Dawes Plan and the New Economics* (New York, 1927).

Baer, G.W., *The Coming of the Italian-Ethiopian War* (Cambridge, 1967).

Baer, G.W., *One Hundred Years of Sea Power: The United States Navy, 1890–1990* (Stanford, CA, 1994).

Bailey, J.A., *A Diplomatic History of the American People* (New York, 1940).

Ball, S., *Baldwin and the Conservative Party. The Crisis of 1929–1931* (New Haven, CT, 1988).

Barnes, H.E. (ed.), *Perpetual War for Perpetual Peace: A Critical Examination of the Foreign Policy of Franklin D. Roosevelt and its Aftermath* (New York, 1953).

Barnett, C., *The Collapse of British Power* (London, 1972).

Barnett, C., *The Audit of War: The Illusion and Reality of Britain as a Great Nation* (London, 1986).

Beard, C.A., *American Foreign Policy in the Making, 1932–1940: A Study in Responsibilities* (New Haven, CT, 1946).

Beard, C.A., *President Roosevelt and the Coming of the War, 1941* (New Haven, CT, 1948).

Beasley, W.G., *Japanese Imperialism, 1894–1945* (Oxford, 1987).

Beloff, M., *Britain, America and Arms Control, 1921–37* (London, 1987).

Bemis, S.F., *A Diplomatic History of the United States* (New York, 1963).

Bennett, E.M., *Recognition of Russia* (Waltham, MA, 1970).

Bennett, E.M., *Franklin D. Roosevelt and the Search for Victory: American–Soviet Relations, 1933–1939* (Wilmington, IL, 1990).

Bergamini, D., *Japan's Imperial Conspiracy*, 2 Vols (New York, 1971).

Berger, G.M., *Parties Out of Power in Japan, 1931–1941* (Princeton, NJ, 1977).

Berstein, B.J. (ed.), *Towards a New Past: Dissenting Essays in American History* (New York, 1968).

Best, A., *Britain, Japan and Pearl Harbor: Avoiding War in East Asia, 1936–41* (London, 1995).

Birkenhead, Earl of, *Halifax: The Life of Lord Halifax* (London, 1965).

Birn, D., *The League of Nations Union, 1918–1945* (London, 1981).

Blake, R. and Louis, W.R. (eds), *Churchill* (New York, 1993).

Blum, John Morton, *From the Morgenthau Diaries, II: The Years of Urgency, 1938–1941* (Boston, MA, 1965).

Bond, B., *British Military Policy Between the Two World Wars* (Oxford, 1980).

Booth, A., *British Economic Policy, 1931–49* (London, 1989).

Borg, D., *The United States and the Far Eastern Crisis of 1933–1938* (Cambridge, 1964).

Borg, D. and Okamoto, S. (eds), *Pearl Harbor as History: Japanese–American Relations, 1931–1941* (New York, 1973).

Braemen, J., Bremner, R. and Brody, D., *Twentieth Century American Foreign Policy* (Columbus, 1971).

Braisted, W.E., *The United States Navy in the Pacific, 1909–1922* (Austin, 1971).

Brandes, J., *Herbert Hoover and Economic Diplomacy: Department of Commerce Policy, 1921–1928* (Pittsburgh, PA, 1962).

Browder, Robert Paul, *The Origins of Soviet American Diplomacy* (Princeton, NJ, 1953).

Buckley, T., *The United States and the Washington Conference, 1921–1922* (Knoxville, TN, 1970).

Buell, T.B., *Master of Sea Power: A Biography of Fleet Admiral Ernest J. King* (Boston, MA, 1980).

Bullen, R. (ed.), *The Foreign Office 1782–1982* (Frederick, MD, 1984).

Burns, Richard Dean and Bennett, Edward M. (eds), *Diplomats in Crisis* (Oxford, 1974).

Cain, P.J. and Hopkins, A.G., *British Imperialism: Crisis and Deconstruction 1914–1990* (London, 1993).

Cain, P.J. and Hopkins, A.G., *British Imperialism: Innovation and Expansion 1688–1914* (London, 1993).

Carley, M.J., *1939: The Alliance That Never Was and the Coming of World War II* (Chicago, IL, 1999).

Carlton, D., *MacDonald Versus Henderson. The Foreign Policy of the Second Labour Government* (New York, 1970).

Carlton D., *Anthony Eden* (London, 1981).

Carrison, D.J., *The United States Navy* (New York, 1968).

Catterall, P. and Morris, C.J. (eds), *Britain and the Threat to Stability in Europe, 1918–45* (London, 1993).

Ceadel, M., *Pacifism in Britain, 1914–1945: The Defining of a Faith* (London, 1980).

Challener, R.D. (ed.), *From Isolation to Containment, 1921–1952* (London, 1970).

Charmley, John, *Chamberlain and the Lost Peace* (London, 1989).

Charmley, John, *Churchill: The End of Glory, A Political Biography* (London, 1993).

Chida, T. and Davies, P.N., *The Japanese Shipping and Shipbuilding Industries: A History of Their Modern Growth* (London, 1990).

Chukumba, S.U. *The Big Powers Against Ethiopia: Anglo-French-American Maneuvers during the Italo-Ethiopian Dispute, 1934–1938* (Washington, DC, 1977).

Chung, O.C., *Operation Matador: Britain's War Plans against the Japanese 1918–1941* (Singapore, 1997).

Clarke, S.V.O., *Central Bank Cooperation, 1924–1931* (New York, 1967).

Clavin, P., *The Failure of Economic Diplomacy: Britain, Germany, France and the United States, 1931–36* (London, 1996).

Clifford, N.R., *Retreat from China: British Policy in the Far East 1937–1941* (London, 1967).

Coates, P.D., *The China Consuls: British Consular Officers, 1843–1943* (Oxford, 1988).

Cohen, W., *The American Revisionists: The Lessons of Intervention in World War I* (Chicago, IL, 1967).

Cohen, W. (ed.), *Pacific Passage: The Study of American–East Asian Relations on the Eve of the Twenty-First Century* (New York, 1996).

Cole, W., *America First: The Debate Against Intervention, 1940–1941* (New York, 1971).

Cole, W., *Roosevelt and the Isolationist, 1932–45* (Lincoln, NE, 1983).

Cole, W., *Determinism and American Foreign Relations During the Franklin D. Roosevelt Era* (Lanham, MD, 1995).

Coletta, P.E., *Patrick N.L. Bellinger and US Naval Aviation* (New York, 1987).

Colvin, I., *Vansittart In Office* (London, 1965).

Colvin, I., *The Chamberlain Cabinet* (London, 1971).

Combs, J.A., *The History of American Foreign Policy*, Vol. II (New York, 1986).

Connell, J., *The 'Office': A Study of British Foreign Policy and its Makers, 1919–1951* (London, 1958).

Conrad, P., *Imagining America* (New York, 1980).

Coox, A.D., *Nomahan: Japan Against Russia, 1939*, 2 Vols (Stanford, CA, 1985).

Coox, A. and Conroy, H., *China and Japan: Search for Balance Since World War I* (Santa Barbara, CA, 1978).

Corbett, J.S., *Some Principles of Maritime Strategy*, reprint edn (Annapolis, MD, 1988).

Cortazzi, H. and Daniels, G. (ed.), *Britain and Japan 1859–1991: Themes and Personalities* (London, 1991).

Costigliola, F., *Awkward Dominion: American Political, Economic, and Cultural Relations with Europe, 1919–1933* (Ithaca, NY, 1984).

Craig, G.A. and Gilbert, F. (eds), *The Diplomats, 1919–1939*, Vol. II (New York, 1977).

Crowley, James B., *Japan's Quest for Autonomy: National Security and Foreign Policy, 1930–1939* (Princeton, NJ, 1966).

Cull, N., *Selling War: The British Propaganda Campaign Against American Neutrality* (Oxford, 1995).

Current, R.N., *Secretary Stimson: A Study in Statecraft* (New Brunswick, NJ, 1954).

Dallek, R., *Franklin D. Roosevelt and American Foreign Policy, 1932–1945* (New York, 1979).

Dalton, H., *Towards the Peace of Nations: A Study in International Politics* (New York, 1928).

Davenport-Hines, R.P.T. and Jones, G. (eds), *British Business in Asia since 1860* (Cambridge, 1989).

Davis, G.T., *A Navy Second to None* (New York, 1940).

Day, David, *The Great Betrayal: Britain, Australia, and the Onset of the Pacific War* (Sydney, 1988).

Dayer, R.A., *Finance and Empire: Sir Charles Addis, 1861–1945* (New York, 1988).

Dilks, David (ed.), *Retreat From Power: Studies in Britain's Foreign Policy of the Twentieth Century, Vol. I, 1906–1939* (London, 1981).

Dingman, R., *Power in the Pacific: The Origins of Naval Arms Limitation* (Chicago, IL, 1976).

Divine, R.A., *The Illusion of Neutrality* (Chicago, IL, 1962).

Dixon, J.C. (ed.), *The American Military and the Far East* (Washington, DC, 1980).

Dobson, A., *United States Wartime Aid to Britain, 1940–1946* (London, 1986).

Dockrill, M.L. and Goold, J.D., *Peace Without Promise. Britain and the Peace Conferences 1919–23* (London, 1981).

Dockrill, M.L. and McKercher, B.J.C. (eds), *Diplomacy and World Power: Studies in British Foreign Policy, 1890–1950* (Cambridge, 1996).

Doenecke, J.D. and Witz, J.E., *From Isolationism to War, 1931–1941* (Arlington Heights, VA, 1991).

Doughty, M., *Merchant Shipping and War: A Study in Defence Planning in Twentieth-Century Britain* (London, 1982).

Dowart, J.M., *Conflict of Duty: The US Navy's Intelligence Dilemma, 1919–1945* (Annapolis, MD, 1983).

Dower, J., *War Without Mercy: Race and Power in the Pacific War* (New York, 1986).

Drea, E.J., *Nomonhan: Japanese–Soviet Tactical Combat, 1939* (Fort Leavenworth, KS, 1981).

Dreifort, J.E., *Myopic Grandeur: The Ambivalence of French Foreign Policy Toward the Far East, 1919–1945* (New York, 1991).

Drummond, D.F., *The Passing of American Neutrality, 1937–1941* (Ann Arbor, MI, 1955).

Drummond, I.M., *British Economic Policy and the Empire, 1919–1939* (London, 1972).

Drummond, I.M., *Imperial Economic Policy 1917–1939* (Toronto, 1974).

Drummond, I.M., *The Floating Pound and the Sterling Area, 1931–1939* (Cambridge, 1981).

Drummond, I.M. and Hillmer, N., *Negotiating Freer Trade: The United Kingdom, the United States, Canada and the Trade Agreements of 1938* (Waterloo, Ontario, 1989).

Dudden, A.P., *The American Pacific: From the Old China Trade to the Present* (New York, 1992).

Dutton, David, *Simon: A Political Biography of Sir John Simon* (London, 1992).

Eden, A., *Facing the Dictators* (London, 1960)

Edwards, P.G., *Prime Ministers and Diplomats: The Making of Australian Foreign Policy 1901–1949* (Melbourne, 1983).

Egar, C.L. and Knott, A.W. (eds), *Essays in Twentieth Century American Diplomatic History Dedicated to Professor Daniel H. Smith* (Washington, DC, 1982).

Egerton, G.W., *Great Britain and the Creation of the League of Nations: Strategy, Politics and International Organization, 1914–1919* (Chapel Hill, NC, 1978).

Eichengreen, B. (ed.), *The Gold Standard in Theory and History* (New York, 1985).

Ellis, L.E., *Frank B. Kellogg and American Foreign Relations, 1925–1929* (New Brunswick, NJ, 1961).

Elphick, P., *Singapore: The Pregnable Fortress, a Study in Deception, Discord and Desertion* (London, 1995).

Elphick, P., *Far Eastern File: The Intelligence War in the Far East, 1930–1945* (London, 1997).

Endicott, S.L., *Diplomacy and Enterprise: British China Policy, 1933–1937* (Vancouver, 1975).

Farley, M.S., *The Problem of Japanese Trade Expansion in the Post-War Situation* (New York, 1939).

Ferrell, R.H., *American Diplomacy in the Great Depression: Hoover–Stimson Foreign Policy, 1929–1933* (New Haven, CT, 1957).

Ferris, J.R., *Men, Money, and Diplomacy: The Evolution of British Strategic Policy, 1919–1926* (Ithaca, NY, 1989).

Fowler, W.B., *American Diplomatic History Since 1890* (Chicago, IL, 1975).

Fox, J.P., *Germany and the Far Eastern Crisis, 1931–1938* (Oxford, 1982).

Frame, T.R., Goldrick, J.V.P. and Jones, P.D., *Reflections on the RAN* (Kenthurst, 1991).

Fraser, H.F., *Great Britain and the Gold Standard* (New York, 1933).

Freedman, L., Hayes, P. and O'Neill, R. (eds), *War, Strategy, and International Politics: Essays in Honour of Sir Michael Howard* (Oxford, 1992).

Freidel, F., *Franklin D. Roosevelt. Launching the New Deal* (Boston, MA, 1973).

French, D., *The British Way in Warfare, 1688–2000* (London, 1990).

Friedberg, A.L., *The Weary Titan* (Princeton, NJ, 1988).

Friedman, I.S., *British Relations with China: 1931–1939* (New York, 1940).

Fry, M.G., *Illusions of Security. North Atlantic Diplomacy 1918–22* (Toronto, 1972).

Fry, M.G. (ed.), *Power, Personalities and Policies: Essays in Honour of Donald Cameron Watt* (London, 1992).

Gaddis, J.L., *Russia, the Soviet Union, and the United States* (New York, 1978).

Gardner, L.C., *Economic Aspects of the New Deal Diplomacy* (Madison, WI, 1964).

Gibbs, N.H., *Grand Strategy*, 2 Vols (London, 1976).

Goldman, E.O., *Sunken Treaties* (Pennsylvania, PA, 1994).

Goldrick, J. and Hattendorf, J.B., *Mahan is Not Enough: The Proceedings of a Conference of the Works of Sir Julian Corbett and Admiral Sir Herbert Richmond* (Newport, RI, 1993).

Gordon, G.A.H., *British Seapower and Procurement Between the Wars: A Reappraisal of Rearmament* (London, 1988).

Graebner, N.A., *Ideas and Diplomacy* (New York, 1964).

Graebner, N. (ed.), *An Uncertain Tradition: American Secretaries of State in the Twentieth Century* (New York, 1961).

Graham, G., *Empire of the North Atlantic: The Maritime Struggle for North America* (Toronto, 1950).

Graham, G., *The Politics of Naval Supremacy. Studies in British Maritime Ascendance* (Cambridge, 1965).

Griffin, W.V., *Sir Evelyn Wrench and His Continuing Vision of International Relations During 40 Years* (New York, 1950).

Griswold, A.W., *The Far Eastern Policy of the United States* (New Haven, CT, 1938).

Hagan, K.J. (ed.), *In Peace and War* (Westport, CT, 1984).

Hagan, K.J., *This People's Navy* (New York, 1991).

Haggie, P., *Britannia at Bay: The Defence of the British Empire Against Japan 1931–1941* (Oxford, 1981).

Hall, C., *Britain, America, and Arms Control, 1921–37* (London, 1987).

Halle, L., *Dream and Reality: Aspects of American Foreign Policy* (New York, 1959).

Harle, V. and Sivenon, P. (eds), *Europe in Transition* (London, 1989).

Haslam, J., *The Soviet Union and the Struggle for Collective Security in Europe, 1933–1939* (London, 1984).

Haslam, J., *The Soviet Union and the Threat From the Far East, 1933–1941* (London, 1992).

Hattendorf, J.B., *Ubi Sumus: The State of Naval and Maritime History* (Newport, RI, 1994).

Hattendorf, J.B., *Doing Naval History: Essays Toward Improvement* (Newport, RI, 1995).

Hattendorf, J.B. and Jordan, R.S. (eds), *Maritime Strategy and the Balance of Power* (London, 1989).

Heinrichs, Waldo H., *American Ambassador: Joseph Grew and the Development of the United States Diplomatic Tradition* (Boston, MA, 1966).

Hoare, J.E. (ed.), *Britain and Japan: Biographical Portraits*, Vol. III (Richmond, Japan Library, 1999).

Hogan, M.J., *Informal Entente: The Private Structure of Cooperation of Anglo-American Economic Diplomacy 1918–1928* (Columbia, MO, 1978).

Hoover, C.B. (ed.), *Economic Systems of the Commonwealth* (Durham, NC, 1962).

Hoston, G.A., *Marxism and the Crisis of Development in Pre-War Japan* (Princeton, NJ, 1986).

Hou, Chi-ming, *Foreign Investment and Economic Development in China 1840–1937* (Cambridge, 1965).

Howard, A., *RAB: The Life of R.A. Butler* (London, 1987).

Howard, C., *Splendid Isolation* (London, 1967).

Howard, M., *The Continental Commitment* (London, 1972).

Howarth, S., *To Shining Sea: A History of the United States Navy* (New York, 1991).

Hsu, I.C.Y., *The Rise of Modern China* (New York, 1975).

Hu, S., *Stanley K. Hornbeck and the Open Door Policy, 1919–1937* (Westport, CT, 1995).

Hubbard, G.E., *British Far Eastern Policy* (New York, 1943).

Hunt, B.D., *Sailor-Scholar: Admiral Sir Herbert Richmond, 1871–1946* (Waterloo, Ontario, 1982).

Hyde, H.M., *Neville Chamberlain* (London, 1976).

Ion, A.H. and Hunt, B.D. (eds), *War and Diplomacy Across the Pacific, 1919–1950* (Waterloo, Ontario, 1988).

Iriye, A., *After Imperialism: The Search for a New Order in the Far East, 1921–1931* (New York, 1965).

Iriye, A., *Across the Pacific: An Inner History of American–East Asian Relations* (New York, 1967).

Iriye, A., *Power and Culture: The Japanese–American War, 1941–1945* (Cambridge, 1981).

Iriye, A. (ed.), *The Chinese and the Japanese: Essays in Political and Cultural Interaction* (Princeton, NJ, 1980).

James, H., Lindgren, H. and Teichova, A. (eds), *The Role of Banks in the Interwar Economy* (Cambridge, 1991).

Jonas, M., *Isolationism in America, 1935–1941* (Chicago, IL, 1990).

Jones, R.R. and Seligmann, G.L., *The Sweep of American History*, Vol. I (New York, 1969).

Jordan, G. (ed.), *Naval Warfare in the Twentieth Century* (London, 1977).

Kaiser, D.E., *Economic Diplomacy and the Origins of the Second World War: Germany, Britain, France, and Eastern Europe, 1930–1939* (Princeton, NJ, 1980).

Kammen, M. (ed.), *The Past Before Us: Contemporary Historical Writing in the United States* (Ithaca, NY, 1980).

Kaufman, R.G., *Arms Control During the Pre-Nuclear Era* (New York, 1990).

Kennan, G.F., *American Diplomacy, 1900–1950* (Chicago, IL, 1951).

Kennedy, G. (ed.), *The Merchant Marine in International Affairs, 1850–1950* (London, 2000).

Kennedy, M.D., *The Estrangement of Great Britain and Japan 1917–35* (Manchester, 1969).

Kennedy, P.M., *The Rise and Fall of British Naval Mastery* (New York, 1976).

Kennedy, P.M., *The Realities Behind Diplomacy: Background Influences on British External Policy, 1856–1980* (London, 1981).

Kennedy, P.M., *The Rise and Fall of the Great Powers: Economic Change and Military Conflict from 1500 to 2000* (London, 1988).

Kimball, W., *The Juggler: Franklin Roosevelt as Wartime Statesman* (Princeton, NJ, 1991).

Kindleberger, C.P., *The World in Depression, 1929–1939* (New York, 1973).

King, F.H.H., *The Hongkong Bank Between the Wars and the Bank Interned 1919–1945: Return From Grandeur* (New York, 1988).

Kirkendall, N.S., *The United States, 1929–1945: Years of Crisis and Change* (New York, 1974).

Klatchko, M. and Trask, D.F., *Admiral William Shepherd Benson. First Chief of Naval Operations* (Annapolis, MD, 1987).

Knox, D., *A History of the United States Navy* (London, 1936).

Kottman, Richard N., *Reciprocity and the North Atlantic Triangle, 1932–1938* (Ithaca, NJ, 1968).

Kunz, D.B., *The Battle for Britain's Gold Standard in 1931* (London, 1987).

Langer, W.L. and Gleason, S.E., *The Challenge to Isolation*, Vol. I (Gloucester, 1970).

Lee, B.A., *Britain and the Sino-Japanese War, 1937–1939: A Study in the Dilemmas of British Decline* (London, 1973).

Leigh, M., *Mobilizing Consent: Public Opinion and American Foreign Policy, 1937–1945* (Westport, CT, 1976).

Lensen, George A., *The Damned Inheritance: The Soviet Union and the Manchurian Crises, 1924–1935* (Tallahassee, FL, 1974).

Leuchtenburg, W.E., *Franklin D. Roosevelt and the New Deal, 1932–1940* (New York, 1963).

Leutze, J.R., *Bargaining for Supremacy: Anglo-American Naval Relations, 1937–1941* (Chapel Hill, NC, 1977).

Link, A.S., *President Wilson and His English Critics* (Oxford, 1959).

Linz, J.J. and Stepan, A. (eds), *The Breakdown of Democratic Regimes* (London, 1978).

Lippman, W., *US Foreign Policy: Shield of the Republic* (Boston, MA, 1943).

Lippman, W., *US War Aims* (Boston, MA, 1944).

Livingston, W.S. and Louis, W.R. (eds), *Australia, New Zealand, and the Pacific Islands Since the First World War* (Austin, TX, 1979).

Lochheim, K., *The Making of the New Deal* (Cambridge, 1983).

Louis, W.R., *British Strategy in the Far East 1919–1939* (Oxford, 1971).

Louis, W.R., *Imperialism at Bay: The United States and the Decolonization of the British Empire, 1941–1945* (Oxford, 1978).

Louis, W.R. and Bull, Hedley (eds), *The 'Special Relationship': Anglo-American Relations Since 1945* (Oxford, 1986).

Love, R.W. (ed.), *The Chiefs of Naval Operations* (Annapolis, MD, 1980).

Love, R.W., *Pearl Harbor Revisited* (New York, 1995).

Lowe, P., *Great Britain and the Origins of the Pacific War: A Study of British Policy in East Asia, 1937–1941* (Oxford, 1977).

Lowe, P., *Britain in the Far East* (London, 1981).

Lynn, J.A. (ed.), *Feeding Mars: Logistics in Western Warfare from the Middle Ages to the Present* (Boulder, CO, 1993).

MacDonald, C.A., *The United States, Britain and Appeasement* (New York, 1981).

Maddox, R.J., *William E. Borah and American Foreign Policy* (Baton Rouge, LA, 1969).

Maddux, Thomas R., *Years of Estrangement: American Relations with the Soviet Union, 1933–1941* (Tallahassee, FL, 1980).

Maiolo, J.A., *The Royal Navy and Nazi Germany, 1933–39: A Study in Appeasement and the Origins of the Second World War* (London, 1998).

Manchester, William, *The Caged Lion: Winston Spencer Churchill, 1932–1940* (London, 1989).

Manseargh, N. (ed.), *Commonwealth Perspectives* (Durham, NC, 1958).

Marder, A.J., *Old Friends, New Enemies: The Royal Navy and the Imperial Japanese Navy* (Oxford, 1981).

Marks III, F.W., *Wind Over Sand: The Diplomacy of Franklin Roosevelt* (Athens, OH, 1987).

Marquand, D., *Ramsay MacDonald* (London, 1977).

Martel, G. (ed.), *The Origins of the Second World War Reconsidered* (Boston, MA, 1986).

Maxon, Y.C., *Control of Japanese Foreign Policy: A Study of Civil–Military Rivalry, 1930–1945* (Berkeley, CA, 1957).

May, E.R., *American Imperialism: A Speculative Essay* (New York, 1968).

May E.R. (ed.), *Knowing One's Enemies: Intelligence Assessment Before the Two World Wars* (Princeton, NJ, 1984).

May, E.R. and Thomson, J.C. (eds), *American–East Asian Relations: A Survey* (Cambridge, 1972).

McCarthy, J.M., *Australia and Imperial Defence, 1918–1939: A Study in Air and Sea Power* (St. Lucia, 1976).

McFarland, Keith D., *Harry H. Woodring: a Political Biography of FDR's Controversial Secretary of War* (Lawrence, KS, 1975).

McIntyre, D.W., *The Rise and Fall of the Singapore Naval Base, 1919–1942* (London, 1979).

McKercher, B.J.C., *The Second Baldwin Government and the United States: Attitudes and Diplomacy* (Cambridge, 1984).

McKercher, B.J.C., *Esme Howard. A Diplomatic Biography* (Cambridge, 1989).

McKercher, B.J.C., *Transition of Power: Britain's Loss of Global Pre-eminence to the United States, 1930–1945* (Cambridge, 1999).

McKercher, B.J.C. (ed.), *Anglo-American Relations in the 1920s: The Struggle for Supremacy* (London, 1991).

McKercher, B.J.C. (ed.), *Arms Limitation and Disarmament* (New York, 1992).

McKercher, B.J.C. and Aronsen, L. (eds), *The North Atlantic Triangle in a Changing World: Anglo-American–Canadian Relations, 1902–1956* (Toronto, 1996).

McKercher, B.J.C. and Moss, D.J. (eds), *Shadow and Substance in British Foreign Policy, 1895–1939: Memorial Essays Honouring C.J. Lowe* (Edmonton, Alberta, 1984).

McLellan, D.S., *Dean Acheson. The State Department Years* (New York, 1976).

Menzies, R.G., *The Measure of the Years* (London, 1970).

Merli, F.J. and Wilson, T.A. (eds), *Makers of American Diplomacy* (New York, 1974).

Meyer, R.H., *Bankers' Diplomacy: Monetary Stabilization in the Twenties* (New York, 1970).

Middlemas, K. (ed.), *Thomas Jones: Whitehall Diary*, 2 Vols (London, 1969).

Middlemas K. and Barnes, J., *Baldwin. A Biography* (London, 1969).

Middleton, R., *Towards a Managed Economy: Keynes, the Treasury and the Fiscal Debate of the 1930s* (London, 1985).

Miller, E.H., *Strategy at Singapore* (New York, 1942).

Millar, E.S., *War Plan Orange: The US Strategy to Defeat Japan, 1897–1945* (Annapolis, MD, 1991).

Millar, T.B., *Australia's Defence* (London, 1965).

Millar, T.B., *Australia's Foreign Policy* (Sydney, 1968).

Millar, T.B., *Australia in Peace and War: External Relations 1788–1977* (London, 1978).

Millett, A.R. and Murray, W. (eds), *Military Effectiveness*, Vol. II: *The Interwar Period* (Boston, MA, 1988).

Mitchell, B.R., *European Historical Statistics 1750–1970* (Cambridge, 1975).

Mitchell, B.R., *British Historical Statistics* (Cambridge, 1990).

Moggridge, D.E., *British Monetary Policy 1924–1931: The Norman Conquest of $4.86* (Cambridge, 1972).

Monger, G., *The End of Isolation: British Foreign Policy, 1900–1907* (Boston, MA, 1963).

Morgenthau, H.J., *Politics among Nations: The Struggle for Power and Peace* (New York, 1948).

Morison, E.E., *Turmoil and Tradition: A Study of the Life and Times of Henry L. Stimson* (Boston, MA, 1960).

Morley, J.W. (ed.), *Deterrent Diplomacy: Japan, Germany, and the USSR 1935–1940* (New York, 1976).

Moulton, H.G. and Paslovsky, Leo, *War Debts and World Prosperity* (Washington, DC, 1932).

Mouré, K., *Managing the Franc: Poincaré* (New York, 1991).

Murfett, M. (ed.), *The First Sea Lords* (Westport, CT, 1995).

Murfett, M., *Fool Proof Relations: The Search for Anglo-American Naval Co-operation During the Chamberlain Years, 1937–1940* (Singapore, 1984).

Murray, W., *The Change in the European Balance of Power, 1938–1939: The Path to Ruin* (Princeton, NJ, 1984).

Murray, W. and Millett, A.R. (eds), *Military Innovation in the Interwar Period* (New York, 1996).

Neidpath, J., *The Singapore Naval Base and the Defence of Britain's Eastern Empire, 1919–1941* (Oxford, 1981).

Neilson, K., *Strategy and Supply: Anglo-Russian Relations, 1914–1917* (London, 1984).

Neilson, K., *Britain and the Last Tsar: Anglo-Russian Relations, 1894–1917* (Oxford, 1995).

Neilson, K. and Errington, J. (eds), *Navies and Global Defense: Theories and Strategy* (Westport, CT, 1995).

Neilson, K. and Kennedy, G. (eds), *Far Flung Lines: Essays in Honour of Donald Mackenzie Schurman* (London, 1997).

Neilson, K. and McKercher, B.J.C. (eds), *Go Spy the Land: Military Intelligence in History* (Westport, CT, 1992).

Nester, W.R., *Power Across the Pacific: A Diplomatic History of American Relations with Japan* (New York, 1996).

Nevins, A., *The New Deal in World Affairs, 1933–1945* (New Haven, CT, 1950).

Nicholas, H., *Britain and the USA* (Baltimore, MD, 1963).

Nicholas, H.G., *The United States and Britain* (Chicago, IL, 1975).

Nish, I.H., *Alliance in Decline: A Study in Anglo-Japanese Relations 1908–23* (London, 1972).

Nish, I.H., *Japanese Foreign Policy 1869–1942* (London, 1977).

Nish, I.H., *Anglo-Japanese Naval Relations* (London, 1985).

Nish, I.H., *Japan's Struggle with Internationalism: Japan, China, and the League of Nations, 1931–1933* (London, 1993).

Nish, I.H., *Britain and Japan: Biographical Portraits* (Folkestone, 1994).

Nish, I.H. (ed.), *Anglo-Japanese Alienation 1919–1952* (Cambridge, 1982).

Nish, I.H. (ed.), *Some Aspects of Soviet–Japanese Relations in the 1930s* (London, 1982).

Noel-Baker, P.J., *The Geneva Protocol for the Pacific Settlement of International Disputes* (Boston, MA, 1925).

Noel-Baker, P.J., *The League of Nations at Work* (Boston, MA, 1926).

Noel-Baker, P.J., *The First World Disarmament Conference 1932–33 and Why it Failed* (Oxford, 1979).

O'Connor, R.G., *Perilous Equilibrium. The United States and the London Naval Conference of 1930* (New York, 1962).

O'Connor, R.G., *Force and Diplomacy* (Coral Gables, FL, 1972).

Offner, A.A., *American Appeasement: United States Foreign Policy and Germany, 1933–1938* (Cambridge, 1969).

O'Halpin, E., *Head of the Civil Service. A Study of Sir Warren Fisher* (London, 1989).

Omissi, D.E., *Air Power and Colonial Control: The Royal Air Force 1919–1939* (Manchester, 1990).

Orde, A., *Great Britain and International Security, 1920–1926* (London, 1977).

Orde, A., *British Policy and European Reconstruction After the First World War* (London, 1990).

Osborn, G.C., *Woodrow Wilson in British Opinion and Thought* (Gainesville, FL, 1980).

Osgood, R., *Ideals and Self Interest in America's Foreign Relations: The Great Transformation* (Chicago, IL, 1953).

Ovendale, R., 'Appeasement' and the English Speaking World: Britain, the United States, the Dominions and the Policy of Appeasement, 1937–1939* (Cardiff, 1975).

Parker, R.A.C., *Chamberlain and Appeasement: British Policy and the Coming of the Second World War* (London, 1993).

Parrini, C.P., *Heir to Empire: United States Economic Diplomacy, 1916–1923* (Pittsburgh, PA, 1969).

Paterson, T.G., Clifford, J.G. and Hagan, K.J. (eds), *American Foreign Policy: A History Since 1900* (Toronto, 1991).

Peden, G., *British Rearmament and the Treasury, 1932–1939* (Edinburgh, 1979).

Pelcovits, N.A., *Old China Hands and the Foreign Office* (New York, 1969).

Pelz, S.E., *Race to Pearl Harbor: The Failure of the Second London Naval Conference and the Onset of World War II* (Cambridge, 1974).

Peters, A.R., *Anthony Eden at the Foreign Office, 1931–1938* (New York, 1986).

Pimlott, B., *Labour and the Left in the 1930s* (Cambridge, 1977).

Platt, D.C.M., *The Cinderella Service: British Consuls Since 1815* (London, 1971).

Plischke, E., *US Department of State: A Reference History* (Westport, CT, 1999).

Pollard, S., *The Development of the British Economy 1914–1950* (London, 1962).

Post Jr, Gaines, *Dilemmas of Appeasement: British Deterrence and Defense, 1934–1937* (Ithaca, NJ, 1993).

Potter, E.B. and Nimitz, C. (eds), *Sea Power: A Naval History* (New York, 1960).

Powaski, R., *Toward an Entangling Alliance: American Isolationism and Europe, 1901–1950* (New York, 1991).

Prados, J., *Combined Fleet Decoded: The Secret History of American Intelligence and the Japanese Navy in World War II* (New York, 1995).

Pratt, J.T., *China and Britain* (London, 1952).

Pratt, J.W., *Cordell Hull, 1933–1944*, 2 Vols (New York, 1964).

Pratt, J.W., *A History of United States Foreign Policy*, 3rd edn (New York, 1972).

Pratt, L.R., *East of Malta, West of Suez* (Cambridge, 1975).

Preston, A. (ed.), *General Staffs and Diplomacy Before the Second World War* (London, 1978).

Pritchard, R.J., *Far Eastern Influences upon British Strategy Towards the Great Powers, 1937–1939* (New York, 1987).

Quigley, H.S., *Far Eastern War 1937–1941* (Boston, MA, 1943).

Ramsden, J., *The Age of Balfour and Baldwin* (New York, 1978).

Rapson, R.L., *Britons View America: Travel Commentary, 1860–1935* (Seattle, WA, 1971).

Rauch, B., *Roosevelt from Munich to Pearl Harbor: A Study in the Creation of a Foreign Policy* (New York, 1951).

Reynolds, C.G., *Command of the Sea: The History and Strategy of Maritime Empires* (London, 1974).

Reynolds, D., *The Creation of the Anglo-American Alliance, 1937–1941* (London, 1981).

Reynolds, D., *Lord Lothian and Anglo-American Relations, 1939–1940* (Philadelphia, PA, 1983).

Reynolds, D., *Britannia Overruled: British Policy and World Power in the Twentieth Century* (London, 1991).

Reynolds, P.A., *British Foreign Policy in the Inter-War Years* (London, 1954).

Rhodes-James, R., *Anthony Eden* (London, 1986).

Rhodes-James, R., *The British Revolution: British Politics 1880–1939* (London, 1977).

Richardson, D., *The Evolution of British Disarmament Policy in the 1920s* (London, 1989).

Richmond, Admiral Sir Herbert, *Sea Power in the Modern World* (London, 1934).

Rimer, J. Thomas (ed.), *Culture and Identity: Japanese Intellectuals During the Interwar Years* (Princeton, NJ, 1990).

Robbins, K., *The Abolition of War: The 'Peace Movement' in Britain, 1914–1919* (Cardiff, 1976).

Roberts, A., *'The Holy Fox': A Biography of Lord Halifax* (London, 1991).

Roberts, P. (ed.), *Sino-American Relations Since 1900* (Hong Kong, 1991).

Robinson, E.E. and Bornet, V.D., *Herbert Hoover: President of the United States* (Stanford, CA, 1975).

Rock, W.R., *Appeasement on Trial: British Foreign Policy and Its Critics, 1938–1939* (Lincoln, NB, 1966).

Rock, W.R., *British Appeasement in the 1930s* (London, 1977).

Rock, W.R., *Chamberlain and Roosevelt: British Foreign Policy and the United States, 1937–1940* (Columbus, OH, 1988).

Roi, M., *Alternative to Appeasement: Sir Robert Vansittart and Alliance Diplomacy, 1934–1937* (Westport, CT, 1997).

Roosevelt, Elliott (ed.), *FDR: His Personal Letters*, 2 Vols (New York, 1950).

Rose, Norman, *Vansittart: Portrait of a Diplomat* (London, 1977).

Rosen, E.A., *Hoover, Roosevelt and the Brain Trust: From Depression to New Deal* (New York, 1977).

Roskill, S.W., *The Strategy of Sea Power: Its Development and Application* (London, 1962).

Roskill, S.W., *Hankey: Man of Secrets*, 3 Vols (London, 1970–74).

Roskill, S.W., *Naval Policy Between the Wars*, 2 Vols (London, 1968, 1976).

Ross, S.T. (ed.), *American War Plans 1919–1941: Plans for War Against the British Empire and Japan: The Red, Orange and Red Orange Plans, 1923–1938*, Vol. 2 (New York, 1992).

Rothwell, V.H., *Anthony Eden: A Political Biography* (Manchester, 1992).

Rowland, B.M., *Commercial Conflict and Foreign Policy: A Study in Anglo-American Relations, 1932–1938* (New York, 1987).

Sayers, R.S., *The Bank of England, 1891–1944* (Cambridge, 1986).

Schlesinger, A.M., *The Age of Roosevelt* (Boston, MA, 1957).

Schlesinger, A.M., *The Crisis of the Old Order, 1919–1933* (Boston, MA, 1957).

Schlesinger, A.M., *The Coming of the New Deal* (Boston, MA, 1958).

Schlesinger, A.M., *The Politics of Upheaval* (Boston, MA, 1960).

Schurman, D.M. *The Education of a Navy: The Development of British Naval Strategic Thought, 1867–1914* (London, 1965).

Schurman, D.M., *Julian S. Corbett, 1854–1922: History of British Maritime Policy From Drake to Jellicoe* (London, 1981).

Shai, A., *Origins of the War in the East: Britain, China and Japan, 1937–1939* (London, 1976).

Shay, R., *British Rearmament in the Thirties: Politics and Profits* (Princeton, NJ, 1977).

Shepherd, P.J., *Three Days to Pearl: Incredible Encounter on the Eve of War* (Annapolis, MD, 2000).

Shimizu, H., *Anglo-Japanese Trade Rivalry in the Middle East in the Inter-War Period* (London, 1986).

Silverman, D.P., *Reconstructing Europe After the Great War* (Cambridge, 1982).

Smith, D.M., *Mussolini* (New York, 1962).

Smith, Geoffrey, *To Save a Nation: American Countersubversives, the New Deal and the Coming of World War II* (New York, 1973).

Smith, Kevin, *Conflict Over Convoys: Anglo-American Logistics Diplomacy in the Second World War* (Cambridge, 1996).

Smith, M.S., *British Air Strategy Between the Wars* (Oxford, 1984).

Spector, R.H., *Eagle Against the Sun* (New York, 1985).

Sprout H. and Sprout, M., *The Rise of American Naval Power, 1776–1918* (Princeton, NJ, 1939).

Steiner, Z.S., *The Foreign Office and Foreign Policy, 1898–1914* (Cambridge, 1969).

Stimson, H.L., *The Far Eastern Crisis* (New York, 1936).

Stokesbury, J.L., *Navy and Empire* (New York, 1983).

Sturmey, S.G., *British Shipping and World Competition* (London, 1962).

Swartz, M., *The Union for Democratic Control in British Politics During the First World War* (Oxford, 1971).

Symonds, C.L., *New Aspects of Naval History* (Annapolis, MD, 1981).

Tarling, N., *Britain, Southeast Asia and the Onset of the Pacific War* (Cambridge, 1996).

Taylor, A.J.P., *The Struggle for the Mastery of Europe* (Oxford, 1954).

Taylor, A.J.P. (ed.), *Lloyd George: Twelve Essays* (Oxford, 1971).

Thorne, C., *The Limits of Foreign Policy: The West, the League and the Far Eastern Crisis of 1931–1933* (New York, 1972).

Thorne, C., *Allies of a Kind: The United States, Britain and the War Against Japan, 1941–45* (London, 1978).

Thorne, C., *Border Crossings: Studies in International History* (New York, 1988).

Thorpe, A., *Britain in the Era of the Two World Wars, 1914–45* (London, 1994).

Toland, J., *The Rising Sun: The Decline and Fall of the Japanese Empire, 1936–1945* (New York, 1970).

Tonsill, C.C., *Back Door to War: The Roosevelt Foreign Policy, 1933–1941* (Chicago, IL, 1952).

Towle, P. (ed.), *Estimating Foreign Military Power* (New York, 1982).

Trask, D.F., *Captains and Cabinets* (Columbia, MI, 1972).

Trotter, A., *Britain and East Asia, 1933–1937* (Cambridge, 1975).

Tuleja, T.V., *Statesmen and Admirals* (New York, 1963).

Utley, J.G., *Going to War with Japan, 1937–1941* (Knoxville, TN, 1985).

Van Deusen, G.G. and Wade, R.C. (eds), *Foreign Policy and the American Spirit* (New York, 1957).

Vlahos, M., *The Blue Sword: The Naval War College and the American Mission, 1919–1941* (Newport, RI, 1980).

Wark, W., *The Ultimate Enemy: British Intelligence and Nazi Germany, 1933–1939* (Ithaca, NY, 1985).

Watt, A., *The Evolution of Australian Foreign Policy 1938–1965* (Cambridge, 1967).

Watt, D.C., *Too Serious A Business: European Armed Forces and the Approach to the Second World War* (London, 1975).

Watt, D.C., *Succeeding John Bull: America in Britain's Place, 1900–1975* (Cambridge, 1984).

Watt, D.C., *How War Came* (London, 1989).

Watt, D.C. (ed.), *Personalities and Policies. Studies in the Formulation of British Foreign Policy in the Twentieth Century* (London, 1965).

Weir, G.E., *Building American Submarines 1914–1940* (Washington, DC, 1991).

Westerfield, H.B., *Foreign Policy and Party Politics: Pearl Harbor to Korea* (New Haven, CT, 1955).

Wheeler, G.E., *Admiral William Veazie Pratt, United States Navy: A Sailor's Life* (Washington, DC, 1974).

Wheeler-Bennett, J., *The Pipe Dream of Peace* (New York, 1971).

Wheeler-Bennett, J.W. and Latimer, H., *Information of the Reparation Settlement* (New York, 1930).

Wheelock, D.C., *The Strategy and Consistency of Federal Reserve Monetary Policy, 1924–1933* (New York, 1991).

Wigley, P., *Canada and the Transition to Commonwealth: British–Canadian Relations 1917–1926* (Cambridge, 1977).

Wildenberg, T., *Gray Steel and Black Oil: Fast Tankers and Replenishment at Sea in the US Navy, 1912–1992* (Annapolis, MD, 1995).

Williams, A.J., *Trading with the Bolsheviks: The Politics of East–West Trade, 1920–39* (Manchester, 1992).

Williams, W.A., *The Shaping of American Diplomacy* (Chicago, IL, 1956).

Williams, W.A., *The Tragedy of American Diplomacy* (Cleveland, OH, 1959).

Williams, W.A., *The Roots of the Modern American Empire: A Study of the Growth and Shaping of Social Consciousness in a Marketplace Society* (New York, 1969).

Williamson, P., *National Crisis and National Government: British Politics, the Economy, and Empire, 1926–1932* (Cambridge, 1992).

Willmot, H.P., *Empires in the Balance: Japanese and Allied Pacific Strategies to April 1942* (Annapolis, MD, 1982).

Willoughby, W.W., *The Sino-Japanese Controversy and the League of Nations* (Baltimore, MD, 1935 [1968 reprint]).

Wilson, J.F., *American Business and Foreign Policy, 1920–1933* (Lexington, KY, 1971).

Winton, J., *Ultra in the Pacific: How Breaking Japanese Codes and Ciphers Affected Naval Operations Against Japan* (Annapolis, MD, 1993).

Wohl, R., *The Generation of 1914* (Cambridge, MA, 1979).

Wright, P.Q. (ed.), *Gold and Monetary Stabilization* (Chicago, IL, 1932).

## Articles

Addington, L.H., 'The Nuclear Arms Race and Arms Control: An American Dilemma in Historical Perspective', *War and Society*, 1 (1983).

Agbi, S.O., 'The Foreign Office and Yoshida's bid for Rapprochment with Britain in 1936–37: A Critical Reconsideration of the Anglo-Japanese Conversations', *The Historical Journal*, 21 (1978).

Agbi, S.O., 'The Strategic Factor in British Far–Eastern Diplomacy 1937–41', *Nigerian Journal of International Studies*, 2 (1978).

Agbi, S.O., 'The Pacific War Controversy in Britain: Sir Robert Craigie Versus the Foreign Office', *Modern Asian Studies*, 17 (1983).

Aldrich, R.J., 'Imperial Rivalry: British and American Intelligence in Asia', *Intelligence and National Security*, 3 (1988).

Aldrich, R.J., 'Britain's Secret Intelligence Service in Asia During the Second World War', *Modern Asian Studies*, 32 (1998).

Allard, D.C., 'Anglo-American Naval Differences During World War I', *Military Affairs*, 44 (1980).

Anderson, D.G., 'British Rearmament and the "Merchants of Death": The 1935–36 Royal Commission on the Manufacture of and Trade in Armaments', *Journal of Contemporary History*, 29 (1994).

Andrew, C. and Aldrich, R.J., 'The Intelligence Services in the Second World War', *Contemporary British History*, 13 (1999).

Arnold-Forster, W.E., 'A Policy for the Disarmament Conference', *Political Quarterly*, 2 (1931).

Asada, S., 'The Revolt Against the Washington Treaty: The Imperial Japanese Navy and Naval Limitation, 1921–1927', *Naval War College Review*, 46 (1993).

Ashton-Gwatkin, F.T.A., 'Thoughts on the Foreign Office, 1918–1939', *Contemporary Review*, 188 (1955).

Babij, O.M., 'The Second Labour Government and British Maritime Security, 1929–1931', *Diplomacy & Statecraft*, 6 (1995).

Babij, O.M., 'The Advisory Committee on Trade Questions in Time of War', *The Northern Mariner*, 7 (1997).

Baer, G.W., 'US Naval Strategy 1890–1945', *Naval War College Review*, 44 (1991).

Balachandran, G., 'Towards a "Hindoo Marriage": Anglo-Indian Monetary Relations in Interwar India, 1917–35', *Modern Asian Studies*, 28 (1994).

Ball, D., 'Over and Out: Signals Intelligence (Sigint) in Hong Kong', *Intelligence and National Security*, 11 (1996).

Ball, S. 'The Conservative Party and the Formation of the National Government: August 1931', *The Historical Journal*, 29(1986).

Barnhart, M.A., 'The Origins of the Second World War in Asia and the Pacific: Synthesis Impossible?', *Diplomatic History*, 20 (1996).

Barua, P., 'Strategies and Doctrines of Imperial Defence: Britain and India, 1919–45', *Journal of Imperial and Commonwealth History*, 25 (1997).

Beck, P., 'Politicians versus Historians: Lord Avon's "Appeasement Battle" against "Lamentably, Appeasement-Minded" Historians', *Twentieth Century British History*, 9 (1998).

Beddie, B.D., 'The Australian Navy and Imperial Legislation', *War and Society*, 5 (1987).

Bell, C.M., '"Our Most Exposed Outpost": Hong Kong and British Far Eastern Strategy, 1921–1941', *Journal of Military History*, 60 (1996).

Bell, R., 'Australian–American Relations and Reciprocal Wartime Economic Assistance, 1941–6: An Ambivalent Association', *Australian Economic History Review*, 16 (1976).

Bennett, G., 'British Policy in the Far East 1933–1936: Treasury and Foreign Office', *Modern Asian Studies*, 26 (1992).

Best, A., 'Constructing an Image: British Intelligence and Whitehall's Perception of Japan, 1931–1939', *Intelligence and National Security*, 11 (1996).

Best, A., '"The Probably Over-Valued Military Power": British Intelligence and Whitehall's Perception of Japan, 1939–41', *Intelligence and National Security*, 12 (1997).

Best, A., '"That Loyal British Subject"?: Arthur Edwardes and Anglo-Japanese Relations, 1932–41', in J.E. Hoare (ed.), *Britain and Japan: Biographical Portraits*, Vol. III (Richmond, 1999).

Best, R.A., 'The Anglo-German Naval Agreement of 1935: An Aspect of Appeasement', *Naval War College Review*, 34 (1981).

Bialer, U., 'Elite Opinion and Defence Policy: Air Power Advocacy and British Rearmament During the 1930s', *British Journal of International Studies*, 6 (1980).

Boadle, D.G., 'The Formation of the Foreign Office Economic Relations Section, 1930–1937', *The Historical Journal*, 20 (1977).

Booth, A., 'Britain in the 1930s: A Managed Economy?', *Economic History Review*, 40 (1987).

Borg, D., 'Notes on Roosevelt's Quarantine Speech', *Presidential Studies Quarterly*, 72 (1957).

Bourette-Knowles, S., 'The Global Micawber: Sir Robert Vansittart, the Treasury and the Global Balance of Power, 1933–35', *Diplomacy & Statecraft*, 6 (1995).

Bowden, S. and Turner, P., 'The Demand for Consumer Durables in the United Kingdom in the Interwar Period', *Journal of Economic History*, 53 (1993).

Boyle, P., 'Reversion to Isolationism? The British Foreign Office View of American Attitudes to Isolationism and Internationalism During World War II', *Diplomacy & Statecraft*, 8 (1997).

Boyle, P.G., 'The Roots of Isolationism: A Case Study', *Journal of American Studies*, 6 (1972).

Bridges, B., 'Yoshizawa Kenkichi and the Soviet–Japanese Non-aggression Pact Proposal', *Modern Asian Studies*, 14 (1980).

Bridges, B., 'Britain and Japanese Espionage in Pre-War Malaya: The Shinozaki Case', *Journal of Contemporary History*, 21 (1986).

Broeze, F., 'Private Enterprise and Public Policy: Merchant Shipping in Australia and New Zealand, 1788–1992', *Australian Economic History Review*, 32 (1992).

Brown, K., 'Intelligence and the Decision to Collect it: Churchill's Wartime American Diplomatic Signals Intelligence', *Intelligence and National Security*, 10 (1995).

Buckley, J., 'Contradictions in British Defence Policy 1937–1939: The RAF and the Defence of Trade', *Twentieth Century British History*, 5 (1994).

Burke, C., 'Automating American Cryptanalysis 1930–45: Marvelous Machines, a Bit Too Late', *Intelligence and National Security*, 14 (1999).

Burks, D.D., 'The United States and the Geneva Protocol of 1924', *American Historical Review*, 64 (1959).

Burley, K.H., 'The Imperial Shipping Committee', *Journal of Imperial and Commonwealth History*, 2 (1974).

Cain, N. and Glynn, S., 'Imperial Relations Under Strain: The British–Australian Debt Contretemps of 1933', *Australian Economic History Review*, 25 (1985).

Callahan, C.M., McDonald, J.A. and O'Brien, A.P., 'Who Voted For Smoot-Hawley?', *Journal of Economic History*, 54 (1994).

Capie, F., 'Australian and New Zealand Competition in the British Market 1920–39', *Australian Economic History Review*, 18 (1978).

Carley, M.J., 'Down a Blind Alley: Anglo-Franco-Soviet Relations, 1920–1939', *Canadian Journal of History*, 29 (1994).

Carley, M.J., 'Generals, Statesmen, and International Politics in Europe, 1898–1945', *Canadian Journal of History*, 30 (1995).

Carley, M.J., '"A Fearful Concatenation of Circumstances": The Anglo-Soviet Rapprochement, 1934–36', *Journal of Contemporary European History*, 5 (1996).

Carlton, D., 'Great Britain and the Coolidge Naval Conference of 1927', *Political Science Quarterly*, 83 (1968).

Carroll, F.M., 'A Double-Edged Sword: Anglo-American "Special Relations", 1936–1981', *International History Review*, 6 (1984).

Cassese, S., 'The Long Life of the Financial Institutions Set Up in the Thirties', *Journal of European Economic History*, 13 (1984).

Cecil, R., 'Case for Disarmament', *Nation* (27 Apr. 1929).

Cecil, R., 'Facing the World Disarmament Conference', *Foreign Affairs*, 10 (1931).

Chapman, John W.M., 'Commander Ross RN and the Ending of Anglo-Japanese Friendship, 1933–1936', *International Studies*, 3 (1985).

Chapman, John W.M., 'A Dance on Eggs: Intelligence and the 'Anti-Comintern'', *Journal of Contemporary History*, 22 (1987).

Charles, D.M., 'Informing FDR: FBI Political Surveillance and the Isolationist–Interventionist Foreign Policy Debate, 1939–1945', *Diplomatic History*, 24 (2000).

Chatterji, B., 'Business and Politics in the 1930s: Lancashire and the Making of the Indo-British Trade Agreement, 1939', *Modern Asian Studies*, 15 (1981).

Clavin, P., 'The World Economic Conference 1933: The Failure of British Internationalism', *Journal of European Economic History*, 20 (1991).

Clavin, P., '"The Fetishes of So-Called International Bankers": Central Bank Co-operation for the World Economic Conference, 1932–3', *Contemporary European History*, 3 (1992).

Cockett, R.B., 'The Foreign Office News Department and the Struggle Against Appeasement', *Historical Research*, 63 (1990).

Cohen, W.I. (ed.), 'Responses to Charles S. Maier, "Marking Time: The Historiography of International Relations"', *Diplomatic History*, 4 (1981).

Costigliola, F.C., 'Anglo-American Financial Rivalry in the 1920s', *Journal of Economic History*, 37 (1977).

Cowman, I., 'Main Fleet to Singapore? Churchill, the Admiralty, and Force Z', *Journal of Strategic Studies*, 2 (1995).

Cowman, I., 'Defence of the Malay Barrier? The Place of the Philippines in Admiralty Naval War Planning, 1925–1941', *War in History*, 4 (1996).

Craft, S.G., 'The League of Nations and Sino-Japanese Conflict, 1931–39', *Diplomacy & Statecraft*, 11 (2000).

Cull, N.J., 'The Munich Crisis and British Propaganda Policy in the United States', *Diplomacy & Statecraft*, 10 (1999).

Cumings, B., 'Still the American Century', *British International Studies Association*, 25 (1999).

Current, R.N., 'The Stimson Doctrine and the Hoover Doctrine', *American Historical Review*, 59 (1954).

Darwin, J., 'Imperialism in Decline? Tendencies in British Imperial Policy Between the Wars', *The Historical Journal*, 23 (1980).

Davis, J.W., 'Anglo-American Relations and Sea Power', *Foreign Affairs*, 7 (1929).

Davis, J.W., 'The Permanent Bases of American Foreign Policy', *Foreign Affairs*, 10 (1931).

Davis, S., 'Keeping the Americans in Line? Britain, the United States and Saudi Arabia, 1939–45: Inter-Allied Rivalry in the Middle East Revisited', *Diplomacy & Statecraft*, 8 (1997).

Denniston, R., 'Diplomatic Eavesdropping, 1922–44: A New Source Discovered', *Intelligence and National Security*, 10 (1995).

DeWitt, H.A., 'Hiram Johnson and Early New Deal Diplomacy, 1933–1934', *California Historical Quarterly*, 53 (1974).

Dimuccio, R.B., 'The Study of Appeasement in International Relations: Polemics, Paradigms, and Problems', *Journal of Peace Research*, 35 (1998).

Dingman, R., 'Farewell to Friendship: The USS *Astoria*'s Visit to Japan, April 1939', *Diplomatic History*, 10 (1986).

Dixon, D.F., 'Competition in the Australian Petrol Market During the Inter-war Period', *Australian Economic History Review*, 16 (1976).

Dobson, A.P., 'Labour or Conservative: Does It Matter in Anglo-American Relations?', *Journal of Contemporary History*, 25 (1990).

Dockrill, M.L., 'The Foreign Office and the Proposed Institute of International Affairs', *International Journal*, 50 (1980).

Doerr, P.W., 'The Changkufeng/Lake Khasan Incident of 1938: British Intelligence on Soviet and Japanese Military Performance', *Intelligence and National Security*, 5 (1990).

Donnelly, J.B., 'Prentiss Gilbert's Mission to the League of Nations Council, October 1931', *Diplomatic History*, 2 (1978).

Dorling, T., 'Men of the Merchant Navy', *Brassey's Naval Annual*, 1938.

Drea, E.J., 'Reading Each Other's Mail: Japanese Communication Intelligence, 1920–1941', *Journal of Military History*, 55 (1991).

Drea, E.J., and Richard, J.E., 'New Evidence on Breaking the Japanese Army Codes', *Intelligence and National Security*, 14 (1999).

Dulles, A.W., 'The Threat of Anglo-American Naval Rivalry', *Foreign Affairs*, 7 (1929).

Dunbabin, J.P.D., 'British Rearmament in the 1930s: A Chronology and Review', *The Historical Journal*, 18 (1975).

Dutton, D., 'Anthony Eden and the Indian Viceroyalty, 1943', *Diplomacy & Statecraft*, 8 (1977).

Dutton, D., 'Simon and Eden at the Foreign Office, 1931–1935', *Review of International Studies*, 20 (1994).

Duus, P., 'Imperialism Without Colonies: The Vision of a Greater East Asia Co-Prosperity Sphere', *Diplomacy & Statecraft*, 7 (1996).

Edgerton, D.E.H. and Horrocks, S.M., 'British Industrial Research and Development Before 1945', *Economic History Review*, 67, 2 (1994).

Edmonds, L., 'Australia, Britain and the Empire Air Mail Scheme, 1934–38', *Journal of Transport History*, 20 (1999).

Enssle, M.J., 'Stresemann's Diplomacy Fifty Years after Locarno: Some Recent Perspectives', *The Historical Journal*, 20 (1977).

Erdmann, A.P.N., 'Mining for the Corporate Synthesis: Gold in American Foreign Economic Policy, 1931–1936', *Diplomatic History*, 17 (1993).

Felix, D., 'Reparations Reconsidered with a Vengeance', *Contemporary European History*, 4 (1971).

Ferguson, T., 'From Normalcy to the New Deal: Industrial Structure, Party Competition, and American Public Policy in the Great Depression', *International Organization*, 38 (1984).

Ferris, J.R., 'A British "Unofficial" Aviation Mission and Japanese Naval Developments, 1919–1929', *Journal of Strategic Studies*, 5 (1982).

Ferris, J.R., 'From Briadway House to Blechley Park: The Diary of Captain Malcolm Kennedy, 1934–46', *Intelligence and National Security*, 4 (1989).

Ferris, J.R., '"The Greatest Power on Earth": Great Britain in the 1920s', *International History Review*, 13 (1991).

Ferris, J.R., 'Worthy of Some Better Enemy?: The British Estimate of the Imperial Japanese Army, 1919–1941, and the Fall of Singapore', *Canadian Journal of History*, 28 (1993).

Ferris, J.R., 'Indulged in All Too Little?: Vansittart, Intelligence and Appeasement', *Diplomacy & Statecraft*, 6 (1995).

Ford, J., 'The Forlorn Ally – The Netherlands East Indies in 1942', *War and Society*, 11 (1993).

Fox, J.P., 'Britain and the Inter-Allied Military Commission of Control, 1925–26', *Journal of Contemporary History*, 4 (1969).

French, D., '"Perfidious Albion" Faces the Powers', *Canadian Journal of History*, 28 (1993).

French, D., 'Colonel Blimp and the British Army: British Divisional Commanders in the War Against Germany, 1939–1945', *English Historical Review*, 111 (1996).

Fry, M.G. 'The Imperial War Cabinet, the United States and the Freedom of the Seas', *Royal United Services Institute*, 110 (1965).

Fung, E.K.S., 'The Sino-British Rapprochement, 1927–1931', *Modern Asian Studies*, 17 (1983).

Gaddis, J.L., 'The Corporatist Synthesis: A Skeptical View', *Diplomatic History*, 10 (1986).

Gazeley, I. and Rice, P., 'Wages and Employment in Britain between the Wars: Quarterly Evidence from the Shipbuilding Industry', *Explorations in Economic History*, 33 (1996).

Gibbs, N., 'The Naval Conferences of the Interwar Years: A Study in Anglo-American Relations', *Naval War College Review*, 30 (1977).

Gladwin, L.A., 'Cautious Collaborators: The Struggle for Anglo-American Cryptanalytic Co-operation 1940–43', *Intelligence and National Security*, 14 (1999).

Goedeken, E.A., 'Doctoral Dissertations in US Foreign Affairs', *Diplomatic History*, 14 (1990).

Goldberg, M.D., 'Anglo-American Economic Competition 1920–1930', *Economy and History*, 16 (1973).

Goldman, A.L., 'Sir Robert Vansittart's Search for Italian Cooperation Against Hitler, 1933–1936', *Journal of Contemporary History*, 9 (1974).

Goldman, E.O., 'Arms Control: The Continuation of Politics by Other Means', *Diplomacy & Statecraft*, 4 (1993).

Goldstein, E., 'Neville Chamberlain, The British Official Mind and the Munich Crisis', *Diplomacy & Statecraft*, 10 (1999).

Goldstein, E. and Maurer J. (eds), 'Special Issue on the Washington Conference, 1921–22: Naval Rivalry, East Asian Stability and the Road to Pearl Harbor', *Diplomacy & Statecraft*, 4 (1993).

Gough, T.J., 'Origins of the Army Industrial College: Military–Business Tensions after World War I', *Armed Forces and Society*, 17 (1991).

Gough, T.J., 'Soldiers, Business Men and US Industrial Mobilisation Planning Between the World Wars', *War and Society*, 9 (1991).

Greenwood, S. '"Caligula's Horse" Revisited: Sir Thomas Inskip as Minister for the Co-ordination of Defence, 1936–1939', *Journal of Strategic Studies*, 17 (1994).

Greenwood, S., 'Sir Thomas Inskip as Minister for the Coordination of Defence, 1936–39', in Paul Smith (ed.), *Government and the Armed Forces in Britain, 1856–1990* (London, 1996).

Groth, A.J. and Froeliger, J.D., 'Unheeded Warnings: Some Intelligence Lessons of the 1930s and 1940s', *Comparative Strategy*, 10 (1991).

Grove, E.J., 'A War Fleet Built for Peace: British Naval Rearmament in the 1930s and the Dilemma of Deterrence Versus Defence', *Naval War College Review*, 44 (1991).

Hall, III, H.H., 'The Foreign Policy Decision-Making Process in Britain 1934–1935, and the Origins of the Anglo-German Naval Agreement', *Historical Review*, 19 (1976).

Hamilton, C.I., 'The Character and Organization of the Admiralty Operational Intelligence Centre during the Second World War', *War in History*, 7 (2000).

Harbutt, F., 'Churchill, Hopkins, and the "Other" Americans: An Alternative Perspective on Anglo-American Relations, 1941–1945', *International History Review*, 8 (1986).

Harris, H.W., 'Towards Disarmament', *Contemporary Review*, 139 (1931).

Harrison, R.A., 'A Presidential Demarche: Franklin D. Roosevelt's Personal Diplomacy and Great Britain, 1936–37', *Diplomatic History*, 5 (1981).

Harrison, R.A., 'The Runciman Visit to Washington in January 1937: Presidential Diplomacy and the Non-Commercial Implications of Anglo-American Trade Negotiations', *Canadian Journal of History*, 19 (1984).

Harrison, R.A., 'Testing the Waters: A Secret Probe Towards Anglo-American Military Co-operation in 1936', *International History Review*, 7 (1985).

Haslam, J., 'The Comintern and the Origins of the Popular Front 1934–1935', *The Historical Journal*, 3 (1979).

Haslam, J., 'Political Opposition to Stalin and the Origins of the Terror in Russia, 1932–1936', *The Historical Journal*, 29 (1986).

Hattendorf, J.B., 'The Anglo-American Way in Maritime Strategy', *Naval War College Review*, 63 (1990).

Hauner, M., 'The Soviet Threat to Afghanistan and India 1938–1940', *Modern Asian Studies*, 15 (1981).

Haycock, R.G., 'The "Myth" of Imperial Defence: Australian–Canadian Bilateral Military Co-operation, 1942', *War and Society*, 2 (1984).

Hecht, R.A., 'Great Britain and the Stimson Note of January 7, 1932', *Pacific Historical Review*, 38 (1969).

Hegmann, R., 'Reconsidering the Evolution of the US Maritime Strategy 1955–1965', *Journal of Strategic Studies*, 14 (1991).

Hein, L.E., 'Free-Floating Anxieties on the Pacific: Japan and the West Revisited', *Diplomatic History*, 20 (1996).

Henrikson, A.K., 'The Geographical "Mental Maps" of American Foreign Policy Makers', *International Political Science Review*, 1 (1980).

Herman, M., 'Diplomacy and Intelligence', *Diplomacy & Statecraft*, 9 (1998).

Hess, G.R., 'After the Tumult: The Wisconsin School's Tribute to William Appleman Williams', *Diplomatic History*, 12 (1988).

Hirama, Y., 'Japanese Naval Preparations for World War II', *Naval War College Review*, 44 (1991).

Hogan, M.J., 'Corporatism: A Positive Appraisal', *Diplomatic History*, 10 (1986).

Holland, R.F., 'The End of an Imperial Economy: Anglo-Canadian Disengagement in the 1930s', *Journal of Imperial and Commonwealth History*, 12 (1984).

Hone, T., 'Spending Patterns of the United States Navy, 1921–1941', *Armed Forces and Society*, 8 (1982).

Horowitz, D.A., 'Senator Borah's Crusade to Save Small Business from the New Deal', *The Historian*, 55 (1993).

Huff, W.G., 'The Development of the Rubber Market in Pre-World War II Singapore', *Journal of Southeast Asian Studies*, 24 (1993).

Hurd, A., 'The British Maritime Industries', *Brassey's Naval Annual*, 1939.

Immerman, R.H., 'In Search of History – and Relevancy: Breaking Through the "Encrustations of Interpretation"', *Diplomatic History*, 12 (1988).

Immerman, R.H., 'The History of US Foreign Policy: A Plea for Pluralism', *Diplomatic History*, 14 (1990).

Jones, G.G., 'The British Government and the Oil Companies 1912–1924: The Search For an Oil Policy', *The Historical Journal*, 20 (1977).

Kahn, G., 'Presidential Passivity on a Nonsalient Issue: President Franklin D. Roosevelt and the 1935 World Court Fight', *Diplomatic History*, 4 (1980).

Kavalio, J., 'Japan's Perception of Stalinist Foreign Policy in the Early 1930s', *Journal of Contemporary History*, 19 (1984).

Kellogg, F.B., 'The War Prevention Policy of the United States', *Foreign Affairs*, 6 (1928).

Kennedy, G.C., 'Great Britain's Maritime Strength and the British Merchant Marine, 1922–1935', *The Mariner's Mirror*, 80 (1994).

Kennedy, G.C., 'Depression and Security: Aspects Influencing the United States Navy During the Hoover Administration', *Diplomacy & Statecraft*, 6 (1995).

Kernek, S.J., 'The British Government's Reactions to President Wilson's "Peace Note" of December 1916', *The Historical Journal*, 13 (1970).

Kerr, P., 'Navies and Peace: A British View', *Foreign Affairs*, 7 (1929).

Kerr, P. and Howland, C.P., 'Navies and Peace: Two Views', *Foreign Affairs*, 8 (1929).

Kettenacker, L., 'Great Britain and the German Attack on the Soviet Union', in Bernd Wegner (ed.), *From Peace to War: Germany, Soviet Russia and the World, 1939–1941* (Oxford, 1997).

Kimball, W., '"They Don't Come Out Where You Expect" Roosevelt Reacts to the German–Soviet War', in Bernd Wegner (ed.), *From Peace to War: Germany, Soviet Russia and the World, 1939–1941* (Oxford, 1997).

Kimball, W.F. and Bartlett, B., 'Roosevelt and Prewar Commitments to Churchill: The Tyler Kent Affair', *Diplomatic History*, 5 (1981).

Kimura, M., 'The Economics of Japanese Imperialism in Korea, 1910–1939', *Economic History Review*, 48 (1995).

Kindleberger, C.P., 'Banking and Industry Between the Two Wars: An International Comparison', *Journal of European Economic History*, 13 (1984).

Kitaoka, S., 'The Army as a Bureaucracy: Japanese Militarism Revisited', *Journal of Military History*, 57 (1993).

Kleinfeld, G.R., 'Nazis and Germans in China 1933–37: The Consulate and the German Community in Tsingtao', *Canadian Journal of History*, 15 (1980).

Koistinen, Paul A.C., 'The Industrial-Military Complex', *Journal of American History*, 56 (1970).

Kovalio, J., 'Japan's Perception of Stalinist Foreign Policy in the Early 1930s', *Journal of Contemporary History*, 19 (1984).

Krebs, G., 'Japan and the German–Soviet War, 1941', in Bernd Wegner (ed.), *From Peace to War: Germany, Soviet Russia and the World, 1939–1941* (Oxford, 1997).

Kuehl, W.F., 'Webs of Common Interests Revisited: Nationalism, Internationalism, and Historians of American Foreign Relations', *Diplomatic History*, 10 (1986).

Kunz, D.B., 'When Money Counts and Doesn't: Economic Power and Diplomatic Objectives', *Diplomatic History*, 18 (1994).

Kuramatsu, T., 'The Geneva Naval Conference of 1927: The British Preparation for the Conference, December 1926 to June 1927', *Journal of Strategic Studies*, 19 (1996).

Kuznetsov, I.I., 'The Soviet Military Advisors in Mongolia, 1921–39', *Journal of Slavic Military Studies*, 12 (1999).

Lafeber, W., 'Fred Harvey Harrington', *Diplomatic History*, 9 (1985).

Lamont, T.W., 'The Final Reparations Settlement', *Foreign Affairs*, 8 (1930).

Larner, C., 'The Amalgamation of the Diplomatic Service with the Foreign Office', *Journal of Contemporary History*, 7 (1972).

Layton, W.T., 'The Forthcoming Economic Conference of the League of Nations and its Possibilities', *Journal of the Royal Institute of International Affairs*, 6 (1927).

Lee, J.M., 'The Dissolution of the Empire Marketing Board: 1933 – Reflections on a Diary', *Journal of Imperial and Commonwealth History*, 1 (1972).

Leopold, R.W., 'Historians and American Foreign Policy: A New Guide to the Field', *Diplomatic History*, 8 (1984).

Libby, J.K., 'The American–Russian Chamber of Commerce', *Diplomatic History*, 9 (1985).

Lilley, C.R., 'American–East Asian Relations in the Heroic and Whig Modes', *Diplomatic History*, 18 (1994).

Lippman, W., 'The London Naval Conference: An American View', *Foreign Affairs*, 8 (1930).

Lowe, P., 'The Dilemmas of an Ambassador: Sir Robert Craigie in Tokyo, 1937–1941', *Proceedings of the British Association for Japanese Studies*, 2 (1977).

Lowe, P., 'War and War Plans in the Far East', *International History Review*, 21 (1999).

Lynn, J.A., 'British Naval Operational Logistics, 1914–1918', *Journal of Military History*, 57 (1993).

MacFall, R.C. (ed.), 'Professional Notes – The Lapse of Our Merchant Marine', *US Naval Institute Proceedings*, 55 (1929).

MacFall, R.C. (ed.), 'Professional Notes – Strategic Naval Bases Throughout the World', *US Naval Institute Proceedings*, 55 (1929).

Mahnken, T.G., 'Gazing at the Sun: The Office of Naval Intelligence and Japanese Naval Innovation, 1918–1941', *Intelligence and National Security*, 11 (1996).

Maiolo, J.A., '"I Believe the Hun Is Cheating": British Admiralty Technical Intelligence and the German Navy, 1936–39', *Intelligence and National Security*, 11 (1996).

Maiolo, J.A., 'The Admiralty and the Anglo-German Naval Agreement of 18 June 1935' *Diplomacy & Statecraft*, 10 (1999).

Maiolo, J.A., 'Deception and Intelligence Failure: Anglo-German Preparations for U-boat Warfare in the 1930s', *Journal of Strategic Studies*, 22 (1999).

Mallett, R., 'The Anglo-Italian War Trade Negotiations, Contraband Control and the Failure to Appease Mussolini, 1939–40', *Diplomacy & Statecraft*, 8 (1997).

Mallett, R., 'Fascist Foreign Policy and Official Italian Views of Anthony Eden in the 1930s', *The Historical Journal*, 43 (2000).

Manne, R., 'The Foreign Office and the Failure of Anglo-Soviet Rapprochement', *Journal of Contemporary History*, 16 (1981).

Marder, A., 'The Royal Navy and the Ethiopian Crisis (July–October 1935)', *The Historical Journal*, 75 (1970).

Mark, E., 'October or Thermidor? Interpretations of Stalinism and the Perception of Soviet Foreign Policy in the United States, 1927–1947', *American History Review*, 94 (1989).

Martel, G., 'The Meaning of Power: Rethinking the Decline and Fall of Great Britain', *International History Review*, 13 (1991).

Martel, G., 'The Prehistory of Appeasement: Headlam-Morley, the Peace Settlement and Revisionism', *Diplomacy & Statecraft*, 9 (1998).

May, E.R., 'Writing Contemporary International History', *Diplomatic History*, 8 (1984).

McBride, W.M., 'Challenging a Strategic Paradigm: Aviation and the US Navy Special Policy Board of 1924', *Journal of Strategic Studies*, 14 (1991).

McCarthy, J.M., 'Austalia and Imperial Defence: Co-operation and Conflict 1918–1939', *Australian Journal of Politics and History*, 17 (1971).

McKale, D., 'The Nazi Party in the Far East, 1931–45', *Journal of Contemporary History*, 12 (1977).

McKercher, B.J.C., 'Austen Chamberlain's Control of British Foreign Policy, 1924–1929', *International History Review*, 6 (1984).

McKercher, B.J.C., 'A Sane and Sensible Diplomacy: Austen Chamberlain, Japan, and the Naval Balance of Power in the Pacific Ocean, 1924–29', *Canadian Journal of History*, 21 (1985).

McKercher, B.J.C., 'Belligerent Rights in 1927–1929: Foreign Policy Versus Naval Policy in the Second Baldwin Government', *The Historical Journal*, 29 (1986).

McKercher, B.J.C., 'Wealth, Power, and the New International Order: Britain and the American Challenge in the 1920s', *Diplomatic History*, 12 (1988).

McKercher, B.J.C., '"Our Most Dangerous Enemy": Great Britain Pre-eminent in the 1930s', *International History Review*, 13 (1991).

McKercher, B.J.C., 'Reaching for the Brass Ring: The Recent Historiography of Interwar American Foreign Relations', *Diplomatic History*, 15 (1991).

McKercher, B.J.C., 'From Enmity to Cooperation: The Second Baldwin Government and the Improvement of Anglo-American Relations, November 1928–June 1929', *Albion*, 24 (1992).

McKercher, B.J.C., '"No Eternal Friends or Enemies": British Defence Policy and the Problem of the United States, 1919–1939', *Canadian Journal of History*, 28 (1993).

McMahon, R.J., 'The Study of American Foreign Relations: National History or International History?', *Diplomatic History*, 14 (1990).

Meredith, D., 'British Trade Diversion Policy and the "Colonial Issue" in the 1930s', *Journal of European Economic History*, 25 (1996).

Millman, B., 'Toward War with Russia: British Naval and Air Planning for Conflict in the Near East, 1939–1940', *Journal of Contemporary History*, 29 (1994).

Mills, O.L. and Roosevelt, F.D., 'Our Foreign Policy: A Republican View and a Democratic View', *Foreign Affairs*, 6 (1928).

Moore, B., 'Anglo-American Security Policy and its Threats to Dutch Colonial Rule in the West Indies, 1940–42', *Journal of Imperial and Commonwealth History*, 23 (1995).

Moore, B., 'British Economic Warfare and Relations with the Neutral Netherlands During the "Phoney War", September 1939–May 1940', *War and Society*, 13 (1995).

Morrisey, C. and Ramsay, M.A., '"Giving the Lead in the Right Direction": Sir Robert Vansittart and the Defence Requirements Sub-Committee', *Diplomacy & Statecraft*, 6 (1995).

Mouré, K., 'The Limits to Central Bank Co-operation, 1916–36', *Contemporary European History*, 3 (1992).

Muir, M., 'American Warship Construction for Stalin's Navy Prior to World War II: A Study in Paralysis of Policy', *Diplomatic History*, 5 (1981).

Muir, M., 'Rearming in a Vacuum: United States Navy Intelligence and the Japanese Capital Ship Threat, 1936–1945', *Journal of Military History*, 54 (1990).

Munting, R., 'Becos' Traders and the Russian Market in the 1920s', *Journal of European Economic History*, 25 (1996).

Murfett, M.M., 'Living in the Past: A Critical Reexamination of the Singapore Naval Strategy, 1918–1941', *War and Society*, 11 (1993).

Neilson, K., '"Greatly Exaggerated": The Myth of the Decline of Great Britain Before 1914', *International History Review*, 13 (1991).

Neilson, K., '"Pursued By a Bear": British Estimates of Soviet Military Strength and Anglo-Soviet Relations, 1922–1939', *Canadian Journal of History*, 28 (1993).

Neville, P., 'Sir Alexander Cadogan, Lord Halifax and the Godesberg Terms 1938', *Diplomacy & Statecraft*, 11 (2000).

Nichols, J., 'Roosevelt's Monetary Policy in 1933', *American Historical Review*, 56 (1992).

Noel-Baker, P.J., 'Menace of Armaments', *Nation*, 35 (1924).

O'Connor, R.G., 'Thomas A. Bailey: His Impact', *Diplomatic History*, 9 (1985).

Offner, A.A., 'Appeasement Revisited: The United States, Great Britain and Germany, 1933–1940', *Journal of American History*, 64 (1977).

Ohlin, B., 'The Reparations Problem: A Discussion', *Economic Journal*, 39 (1929).

Owen, G.L., 'The Metro-Vickers Crisis: Anglo-Soviet Relations between Trade Agreements, 1932–1934', *Slavonic and East European Review*, 114 (1971).

Oye, K.A., 'The Sterling–Dollar–Franc Triangle: Monetary Diplomacy, 1929–1937', *World Politics*, 38 (1985).

Parker, R.A.C., 'Great Britain, France and the Ethiopian Crisis', *European History Review*, 89 (1974).

Parker, R.A.C., 'Economics, Rearmament and Foreign Policy: The United Kingdom Before 1939 – A Preliminary Study', *Journal of Contemporary History*, 10 (1975).

Patejak, S., 'Hector C. Bywater and the Great Pacific War', *Strategy and Tactics* (August 1992).

Paterson, 'Defining and Doing the History of American Foreign Relations: A Primer', *Diplomatic History*, 14 (1990).

Peden, G.C., 'The Burden of Imperial Defence and the Continental Commitment Reconsidered', *The Historical Journal*, 27 (1984).

Peden, G.C., 'A Matter of Timing: The Economic Background to British Foreign Policy, 1937–1939', *History*, 69 (1984).

Perras, G.R., '"Our Position in the Far East Would Be Stronger Without This Commitment": Britain and the Reinforcement of Hong Kong, 1941', *Canadian Journal of History*, 30 (1995).

Perras, G.R., 'Anglo-Canadian Imperial Relations: The Case of the Garrisoning of the Falkland Islands in 1942', *War and Society*, 14 (1996).

Peter, G., 'Central Bank Diplomacy: Montagu Norman and Central Europe's Monetary Reconstruction after World War I', *Contemporary European History*, 3 (1992).

Philpott, W.J., 'The Campaign for a Ministry of Defence, 1919–36', in Paul Smith (ed.), *Government and the Armed Forces in Britain, 1856–1990* (London, 1996).

Post Jr, G., 'Mad Dogs and Englishmen: British Rearmament, Deterrence, and Appeasement, 1934–35', *Armed Forces and Society*, 14 (1988).

Pratt, L., 'The Anglo-American Naval Conversations on the Far East', *International Affairs*, 47 (1971).

Purcell, W.R., 'The Development of Japan's Trading Company Network in Australia 1890–1941', *Australian Economic History Review*, 21 (1981).

Quartararo, R., 'Imperial Defence in the Mediterranean on the Eve of the Ethiopian Crisis (July–October 1935)', *The Historical Journal*, 20 (1977).

Ragsdale, H., 'Soviet Military Preparations and Policy in the Munich Crisis: New Evidence', *Jahrbücher für Geschichte Osteuropas*, 47 (1999).

Reynolds, C.G., 'The US Fleet-in-Being Strategy of 1942', *Journal of Military History*, 58 (1994).

Reynolds, D., 'Roosevelt, the British Left, and the Appointment of John G. Winant as United States Ambassador to Britain in 1941', *International History Review*, 4 (1982).

Reynolds, D., 'FDR's Foreign Policy and the British Royal Visit to the USA, 1939', *Historian*, 45 (1983).

Reynolds, D., 'Rethinking Anglo-American Relations', *International Affairs*, 65 (1988/89).

Rhodes, B.D., 'The British Royal Visit of 1939 and the "Psychological Approach" to the United States', *Diplomatic History*, 2 (1978).

Ritchie, S., 'A New Audit of War: The Productivity of Britain's Wartime Aircraft Industry Reconsidered', *War and Society*, 12 (1994).

Ritschel, D., 'A Corporatist Economy in Britain? Capitalist Planning For Industrial Self-Government in the 1930s', *English Historical Review*, 151 (1991).

Roberts, G., 'The Alliance that Failed: Moscow and the Triple Alliance Negotiations, 1939', *European History Quarterly*, 26 (1996).

Roberts, P., 'The First World War and the Emergence of American Atlanticism 1914–1920', *Diplomacy & Statecraft*, 5 (1994).

Roberts, P., 'The Anglo-American Theme: American Visions of an Atlantic Alliance, 1914–1933', *Diplomatic History*, 21 (1997).

Robertson, J.C., 'The Hoare–Laval Plan', *Journal of Contemporary History*, 10 (1975).

Rohwer, J., 'The Development of Strategic Concepts and Shipbuilding Programmes for the Soviet Navy, 1922–1953: Stalin's Battleships and Battlecruisers', *The Northern Mariner*, 7 (1997).

Rohwer, J. and Monakov, M., 'The Soviet Union's Ocean-Going Fleet, 1935–1956', *International History Review*, 18 (1996).

Roi, M., '"A Completely Immoral and Cowardly Attitude": The British Foreign Office, American Neutrality and the Hoare–Laval Plan', *Canadian Journal of History*, 29 (1994).

Roi, M.I., 'From the Stresa Front to the Triple Entente: Sir Robert Vansittart, the Abyssinian Crisis and the Containment of Germany', *Diplomatic History*, 6 (1995).

Rose, N., 'The Resignation of Anthony Eden', *The Historical Journal*, 25 (1982).

Rosen, E.A., 'Intranationalism Versus Internationalism: The Interregnum Struggle for the Sanctity of the New Deal', *Political Science Quarterly*, 81 (1966).

Rosenberg, E.S., 'Walking the Borders', *Diplomatic History*, 14 (1990).

Rothwell, V.H., 'The Mission of Sir Frederick Leith-Ross to the Far East, 1935–1936', *The Historical Journal*, 18 (1975).

Sabel, R., 'The Role of the Legal Advisor in Diplomacy', *Diplomacy & Statecraft*, 8 (1997).

Salerno, R.M., 'Multilateral Strategy and Diplomacy: The Anglo-German Naval Agreement and the Mediterranean Crisis, 1935–1936', *Journal of Strategic Studies*, 17 (1994).

Salerno, R.M., 'The French Navy and the Appeasement of Italy, 1937–9', *English Historical Review*, 112 (1997).

Salter, A., 'The Economic Conference: Prospects of Practical Results', *Journal of the Royal Institute of International Affairs*, 6 (1927).

Samuelson, L., 'Mikhail Tukhachevsky and War-Economic Planning: Reconsiderations on the Pre-war Soviet Military Build-Up', *Journal of Slavic Military Studies*, 9 (1996).

Sato, K., 'Japan's Position Before the Outbreak of the European War in September 1939', *Modern Asian Studies*, 14 (1980).

Schatz, A.W., 'The Anglo-American Trade Agreement and Cordell Hull's Search for Peace, 1936–1938', *Journal of American History*, 57 (1970).

Schedvin, C.B., 'Monetary Stability and the Demand for Money in Australia Between the Wars', *Australian Economic History Review*, 11 (1971).

Self, R., 'Treasury Control and the Empire Marketing Board: The Rise and Fall of Non-Tariff Preference in Britain, 1924–1933', *Twentieth Century British History*, 5 (1994).

Shalom, S.R., 'Ties That Bind: A Century of US–Philippine Relations', *Diplomatic History*, 21 (1997).

Sibley, K.S., 'Soviet Industrial Espionage against American Military Technology and the US Response, 1930–1945', *Intelligence and National Security*, 14 (1999).

Simpson, M., 'Force H and British Strategy in the Western Mediterranean 1939–42', *The Mariner's Mirror*, 83 (1997).

Singh, A.I., 'The Limits of "Super Power": The United States and South Asia', *International History Review*, 14 (1992).

Sissons, D.C.S., 'More on Pearl Harbor', *Intelligence and National Security*, 9 (1994).

Smith, Gaddis, 'The Two Worlds of Samuel Flagg Bemis', *Diplomatic History*, 9 (1985).

Spear, L.Y., 'Battleships or Submarines?', *Foreign Affairs*, 6 (1927).

Stafford, P., 'Political Autobiography and The Art of the Plausible: R.A. Butler at the Foreign Office, 1938–1939', *The Historical Journal*, 28 (1985).

Steele, R.W., 'Preparing the Public for War: Efforts to Establish a National Propaganda Agency, 1940–1941', *American Historical Review*, 75 (1970).

Steele, R.W., 'The Great Debate: Roosevelt, the Media, and the Coming of the War, 1940–1941', *Journal of American History*, 71 (1984).

Stimson, H.L., 'The United States and the Other American Republics', *Foreign Affairs*, 9 (1931).

Strang, B., 'Two Unequal Tempers: Sir George Ogilvie-Forbes, Sir Nevile Henderson and British Foreign Policy, 1938–39', *Diplomacy & Statecraft*, 5 (1994).

Strang, Lord, 'The Formulation and Control of Foreign Policy', *Durham University Journal*, 49 (1957).

Sugihara, K., 'The Economic Motivations Behind Japanese Aggression in the Late 1930s: Perspectives of Freda Utley and Nowa Toichi', *Journal of Contemporary History*, 32 (1977).

Swain, G., 'Bitten by the Russia Bug: Britons and Russia, 1894–1939', *Intelligence and National Security*, 13 (1998).

Tamchina, R., 'In Search of Common Causes: The Imperial Conference of 1937', *Journal of Imperial and Commonwealth History*, 1 (1972).

Tarling, N., 'Britain, Portugal and East Timor in 1941', *Journal of Southeast Asian Studies*, 27 (1996).

Thomas, M., 'Imperial Backwater or Strategic Outpost? The British Takeover of Vichy Madagascar, 1942', *The Historical Journal*, 39 (1996).

Thompson, J.A., 'The League of Nations Union and the Promotion of the League Idea in Great Britain', *American Journal of Political History*, 18 (1972).

Thorne, C., 'Diplomatic History: Some Further Reflections', *Diplomatic History*, 14 (1990).

Thorne, C., 'Viscount Cecil, the Government and the Far Eastern Crisis of 1931', *The Historical Journal*, 14 (1971).

Thorne, C., 'The Shanghai Crisis of 1932: The Basis of British Policy', *American Historical Review*, 75 (1970).

Thorpe, A., 'Stalinism and British Politics', *History*, 83 (1998).

Trimble, W.F., 'Admiral Hilary P. Jones and the 1927 Geneva Naval Conference', *Military Affairs* (Feb. 1979).

Trotter, A., 'The Dominions and Imperial Defence: Hankey's Tour in 1934', *Journal of Imperial and Commonwealth History*, 2 (1974).

Tsokhas, K., 'Anglo-American Economic Entente and Australian Financial Diplomacy', *Diplomacy & Statecraft*, 5 (1994).

Tsokhas, K., 'The Australian Role in Britain's Return to the Gold Standard', *Economic History Review*, 47 (1994).

Tsokhas, K., 'Anglo-Australian Relations and the Origins of the Pacific War', *History*, 80 (1995).

Turner, A., 'Anglo-French Financial Relations in the 1920s', *European History Quarterly*, 26 (1996).

Varg, P.A., 'Sino-American Relations Past and Present', *Diplomatic History*, 4 (1980).

Venn, F., 'A Futile Paper Chase: Anglo-American Relations and Middle East Oil, 1918–34', *Diplomacy & Statecraft*, 1 (1990).

Waldon, A., 'War and the Rise of Nationalism in Twentieth Century China', *Journal of Military History*, 57 (1993).

Wark, W.K., 'In Search of a Suitable Japan: British Naval Intelligence in the Pacific Before the Second World War', *Intelligence and National Security*, 1 (1986).

Wark, W.K., 'Appeasement Revisited', *International History Review*, 17 (1995).

Watt, D.C., 'The Anglo-German Naval Agreement of 1935: An Interim Judgment', *Journal of Modern History*, 28 (1956).

Watt, D.C., '1939 Revisited: On Theories of the Origins of Wars', *International Affairs*, 65 (1989).

Watt, D.C., 'Intelligence and the Historian: A Comment on John Gaddis's "Intelligence, Espionage, and Cold War Origins"', *Diplomatic History*, 14 (1990).

Watts, E.H., 'The Merchant Marine as a Factor in Imperial Defence', *Brassey's Naval Annual* (1937).

Weir, G.E., 'The Search for an American Submarine Strategy and Design, 1916–1936', *Naval War College Review*, 44 (1991).

Weir, G.E., 'Coming up to Speed in American Submarine Construction, 1938–1943', *War and Society*, 11 (1993).

Weland, J., 'Misguided Intelligence: Japanese Military Intelligence Officers in the Manchurian Incident, September 1931', *Journal of Military History* 58 (1994).

White, S. and Revell, S., 'Revolution and Integration in Soviet International Diplomacy, 1917–1991', *Review of International Studies*, 25 (1999).

Williams, W.A., 'The Age of Mercantilism: An Interpretation of the American Political Economy 1763–1828', *William and Mary Quarterly*, 15 (1958).

Williamson, P., 'Safety First: Baldwin, the Conservative Party, and the 1929 General Election', *The Historical Journal*, 25 (1982).

Wilson, J.R., 'The Quaker and the Sword: Herbert Hoover's Relations with the Military', *Military Affairs*, 38 (1974).

Wilson, S., 'The Manchurian Crisis and Moderate Japanese Intellectuals: The Japan Council of the Institute of Pacific Relations', *Modern Asian Studies*, 26 (1992).

Wilson, S., 'Containing the Crisis: Japan's Diplomatic Offensive in the West, 1931–1933', *Modern Asian Studies*, 29 (1995).

Wolcott, S., 'The Perils of Lifetime Employment Systems: Productivity Advance in the Indian and Japanese Textile Industries, 1920–1938', *Journal of Economic History*, 54 (1994).

Wolfe, R., 'Still Lying Abroad? On the Institution of the Resident Ambassador', *Diplomacy & Statecraft*, 9 (1998).

Yasuba, Y., 'Did Japan Ever Suffer from a Shortage of Natural Resources Before World War II?', *Journal of Economic History*, 56 (1996).

Young, R.J., 'Spokesmen for Economic Warfare: The Industrial Intelligence Centre in the 1930s', *European History Review*, 6 (1976).

Yu-Jose, L.N., 'World War II and the Japanese in the Prewar Philippines', *Journal of Southeast Asian Studies*, 27 (1996).

## Theses

Andrade, Ernest, Jr, 'United States Naval Policy in the Disarmament Era, 1921–1937', Ph.D. Dissertation, Michigan State University, 1966.

MacCarty, Kenneth G. Jr, 'Stanley Hornbeck and the Far East, 1931–1941', Ph.D. Dissertation, Duke University, 1970.

Ross, A.T., 'The Arming of Australia: The Politics and Administration of Australia's Self Containment Strategy for Munitions Supply 1901–1945', Ph.D. Dissertation, New South Wales, 1986.

Smith, K.E., 'The Causes and Consequence of Dependence: British Merchant Shipping and Anglo-American Relations, 1940–1943', Ph.D. Dissertation, Yale University, 1990.

Varey, D.K., 'Fraught with the Gravest Difficulties: Sir Robert Vansittart, the Foreign Office and the Global Balance of Power, 1931–1934', MA Dissertation, Royal Military College of Canada, 1995.

# Index